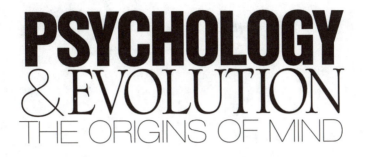

PSYCHOLOGY
& EVOLUTION
THE ORIGINS OF MIND

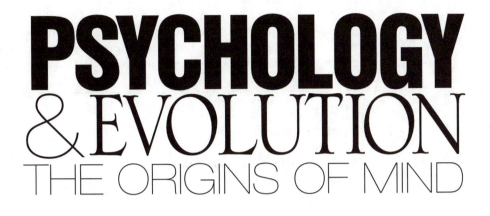

PSYCHOLOGY
& EVOLUTION
THE ORIGINS OF MIND

BRUCE BRIDGEMAN
University of California, Santa Cruz

SAGE Publications
International Educational and Professional Publisher
Thousand Oaks ■ London ■ New Delhi

For information:

Sage Publications, Inc.
2455 Teller Road
Thousand Oaks, California 91320
E-mail: order@sagepub.com

Sage Publications Ltd.
6 Bonhill Street
London EC2A 4PU
United Kingdom

Sage Publications India Pvt. Ltd.
B-42, Panchsheel Enclave
Post Box 4109
New Delhi 110 017 India

Printed in the United States of America

A catalog record for this book is available from the Library of Congress.

ISBN 0-7619-2479-5 (c.)

03   04   05   06   10   9   8   7   6   5   4   3   2   1

Acquiring Editor:	Jim Brace-Thompson
Editorial Assistant:	Karen Ehrmann
Production Editor:	Sanford Robinson
Indexer:	Molly Hall
Cover Designer:	Michelle Lee

CONTENTS

PREFACE

Psychology is a long-lost stepchild of the biological sciences, just beginning to take its place as the biological science of human behavior and experience. Biology is the study of living things. It's hard to deny that a human being is a living thing, and that human behavior and experience are aspects of being human. If these ideas ring true, it seems inescapable that psychology, the study of human behavior and experience, should be closely related to biology. Both academic psychologists and biologists study various aspects of life, how it functions and what makes it work. Psychology, then, cannot ignore the theoretical basis of biology—evolutionary theory, beginning with Darwin's insight of evolution by natural selection.

Not long ago the study of biology was mostly the description of living things and the chemistry that makes them work. Now, within a generation, biologists are exploiting enormously powerful techniques to peer into the machinery of the living cell. Genetics is the engine that drives both the biological sciences and the organism itself. Being able to see the genes themselves at work, ordering life practically atom by atom, has made it possible to look at life from the inside out.

The new understanding of genetics and molecular biology puts the most basic mechanisms of life at the forefront, with implications far beyond the level of single cells. Indeed, it allows us to understand the physical basis of evolution, practically molecule by molecule, for the first time. It is time to apply this new biology to the subject matter of psychology.

ORGANIZATION ●

Approaching psychology from the standpoint of evolution means more than adding new techniques and new types of evidence to the existing discipline. Evolution also invites, practically demands, a reorganization of the major branches of psychology itself. Evolutionary theory allows us to orient to different kinds of functions, integrated challenges that every human must address.

Traditional psychologists study particular abilities, previously called faculties, such as memory or perception or motivation. Those specializing in memory study working memory, long-term memory, and various other kinds of memory that people employ in widely diverse ecological situations. Each memory system, though, is bound up with motivations, perceptual systems, and emotions connected to particular functions. Courtship of the opposite sex, for instance, involves many faculties, bound together by evolution into a coherent set of needs, abilities, and attitudes that help to make interaction of the sexes successful. The evolutionary approach allows us to take a step back, to look at the faculties from the perspective of their functions in larger units of behavior, the natural units that correspond to important challenges of life.

A good place to start describing the new psychology is with reproduction, along with all the courtship and mating behaviors that make reproduction possible. These behaviors are influenced by culture, to be sure, but they are far older and more built into us than that—our genes guide us along the perilous journey to reproduction. Culture and genetics are intricately interwoven, with environment and tradition influencing how the guidance of the genes is felt.

The study of reproduction leads naturally to childhood and parenting, where again many of our motivations and behaviors are older than humanity, and the genetic mechanisms that smooth the way for these functions show both our similarity to other primates and our differences. From here the text branches out to interactions with the natural environment and the larger social world. These interactions constitute another category that can be studied at many levels, from the standpoint of evolved mechanisms that enable us to interact with the world.

Organizing this book required a decision about whether to organize around the life challenges to which we have adapted, or around traditional academic specialties such as perception, memory, and thought. The solution that I have arrived at is a compromise; after two chapters introducing the biological study of psychological questions, Chapters 3 through 6 are organized around life's major challenges and the adaptations that help us to confront them.

Reorganizing psychology around problems rather than levels is a recognition that evolution has adapted humans to survive in a world defined by persistent challenges that must be engaged if the organism is to succeed. Particular adapted systems enable us to deal with the enduring challenges of life: courtship, reproduction, child-rearing, family, and society.

Many of the capabilities that allow us to meet these challenges cut across several areas, however, and deserve to be investigated closely in their own right. Language and perception, memory and consciousness, are examples of capabilities that are essential for nearly all human activities. These are the subjects of Chapters 7 and 8. Finally, evolutionary ideas are applied to practical problems of aberrant behavior, where the evolutionary approach makes possible a new categorization and interpretation of mental illnesses.

My goal in this book is to approach psychology in a new way, guided by human evolution to identify what is at the core of being human, and to understand how humans engage these core challenges. Much of conventional psychology can be incorporated into this perspective, and much that is new to psychology can be integrated from related disciplines.

ORIGINS ●

This book grew out of a seminar that I have taught since the early 1980s on psychology and evolutionary theory. At the beginning, such a field did not exist, and my students helped me to feel my way to an understanding of how evolved mechanisms affect every aspect of human life. I found that the students were ready for an overarching theory in psychology, even hungry for it, and grew enthusiastic when they discovered what evolutionary theory could do for psychology. This book is largely a description of what we have discovered together, with many of the students' insights so ingrained in my own thinking that I can no longer identify them separately. Together we jacked up psychology to put a new foundation under it.

In the past few years, a pioneering group of scholars has emerged, calling themselves evolutionary psychologists. Their powerful insights have demonstrated the value of the evolutionary approach to psychological functions, asking questions that other psychologists might not ask and finding answers that everywhere challenge the conventional wisdom. At the beginning, the effort was somewhat speculative and was roundly criticized for reaching too far; perhaps it did. But now the field is rich with arresting new ideas that are backed up by solid empirical evidence. This book is enriched by the work of these psychologists, as well as the students in my seminar who were not afraid to turn psychology on its head. At the same time, biology offers far more to psychology than has been integrated so far; in these pages I attempt a broader mining of biological ideas and data to establish a more complete evolutionary psychology.

Many psychologists still deny the connection of psychology with evolutionary theory. Isn't it enough to analyze behavior, its mechanisms and components, to observe how humans interact with one another, how they develop? The answer is that these steps are useful, even essential, but they are no longer enough. We now know that evolved genetic mechanisms structure us to interact with the world and with each other in particular ways, so that we must engage both the gene and the environment if we are to truly understand the basis of human behavior and experience.

The genetic mechanisms are often unconscious, influencing our behavior by making certain paths natural, others difficult, without our knowing it. Much of our evolution is a co-evolution with our own culture and with our capacity for culture, a relationship so close that the study of genetic evolution cannot be separated from the study of human culture. The better we understand that we are part of nature, nothing more or less, the better we can take advantage of the new knowledge of our biological structure to understand ourselves.

In *Sociobiology,* the book that arguably founded the discipline of evolutionary psychology, E. O. Wilson (1975) predicted that psychology would wither away as a discipline, to be replaced by biologically based ideas about human behavior. Psychology has not withered yet, and is unlikely to do so in the future, because its core concerns revolve not around methods but around a unique subject matter, the understanding of human behavior and experience. Someone using biological tools to understand human behavior remains a psychologist. By sharing methods and insights, psychology and biology become allies rather than academic competitors. In *On the Origin of Species* (1859), Charles Darwin had predicted that "psychology will be based on a new foundation." The new foundation has been a long time coming—now, nearly a century and a half after Darwin revolutionized biology, it is time to take up his challenge and revolutionize psychology in the same way.

In writing I have attempted to be rigorous without being dry, scholarly without being pedantic. These ideals are not conflicting—indeed, they should be mutually reinforcing, as the endless fascination of a real understanding of human behavior and experience emerges.

● TO THE READER

A number of pedagogical devices are intended to make it easier to master the material presented here. New terms are introduced in **bold** type, with a definition or contextual explanation near the new term. These terms are also defined in a glossary at the end of the book. Each figure and table is mentioned in the text; at that point, read the caption and examine the figure or table. References are cited in the text by author and year of publication, with a complete citation in the references section at the end of the book. An index should help you find particular topics quickly.

TO THE INSTRUCTOR ●

Each chapter ends with a set of discussion questions and further readings. The questions do not necessarily have correct answers; rather, they are intended to encourage thinking about the issues raised in the chapter and to help in structuring discussions of the material.

To facilitate effective teaching, an instructor's manual is available on CD-ROM, provided by Sage Publications without cost to instructors who adopt this book as a course textbook. For each chapter the manual provides background material for the text's discussion questions, to facilitate discussion and further research. There are also 10 multiple-choice questions for each chapter, for those who find this format useful, and an expanded Further Readings section. The five largest chapters (1, 2, 3, 7 and 8) have a few more multiple-choice questions, and reading assignments from them can be split for instructors who wish to spread assignments from the text over a longer period. Chapter 1 has a natural break point at "How Evolution Works," Chapter 2 at "Human Prehistory," Chapter 3 at "Mate Selection," Chapter 7 at "The Anatomy of Language," and Chapter 8 at "Consciousness and Planning." This provides flexibility for a variety of academic schedules.

ACKNOWLEDGMENTS ●

Many people, and many intellectual influences, have contributed to this book. My first debt is to the students, graduate and undergraduate, in my seminar on psychology and evolutionary theory. At first, they volunteered for a course in a subject no one had ever heard of, and one that remains controversial within psychology. Every year for more than two decades, they have led me to new insights and new ways of thinking. Not being committed to the old ways, they were especially creative with the new. I also thank Robert Trivers, who in his many years at the University of California, Santa Cruz, contributed probably more than he knows to my biological education; M. Brewster Smith, UCSC's scholar among scholars, who helped integrate radical biology with mature psychology; Andy Neher, my well-read skeptic; numerous other friends and colleagues; and my editor at Sage Publications, Jim Brace-Thompson, whose wisdom, optimism, and patience have seen the publication process through from start to finish. Lara Foland did a wonderful job as permissions editor.

I am indebted most of all to my wife, Diane Bridgeman, and my daughters, Natalie and Tess, who provided counterpoint, references, deep discussion, and support. This book is for them.

CHAPTER 1

THE EVOLUTION REVOLUTION

"We can no more keep evolution out of psychology than we can keep psychology out of human evolution."

— Henry Plotkin (1998)

WHY EVOLUTION? ●

A revolution is occurring in psychology. It stems from the realization that psychology can be studied as a biological science, a science that takes a living thing as its subject matter. Because biology is the science of living things, psychology is by definition a part of the broad scope of biology. Even if university psychology departments are separate from biology departments, the discipline of psychology owes much of its intellectual base to its broader relationship with biological sciences, for biology provides a theoretical orientation that can unite all of psychology under a single framework.

If psychology recognizes its relationship to biology, it also recognizes the basic theory that underlies all of biology: Charles Darwin's theory of **evolution by natural selection**. In his book *On the Origin of Species* (1859), Darwin observed that most organisms produce far more offspring than will ever mature and reproduce. Most are lost to disease, predators, or competition with other members of their species. If those that survive and reproduce have a different genetic inheritance from those who do not, the genes of those survivors will become more frequent in the next generation. The insight that drives evolutionary psychology is that the adapted characteristics of the successful reproducers include not only features of the body, such as strong hearts and resistance to disease, but also behavioral capabilities, attitudes, and motivations.

The theory requires three conditions. First, there must be some *variation* in the members of a species, a variation that is at least partly due to differences in their **genes**. Second, the survival of members of the species must depend on the differences in their genetic inheritance, a *selection* of some individuals over others. Third, there must be a *retention* of the selected traits by the descendants of the selected individuals. Because almost all natural populations meet all three conditions, evolution by natural selection is nearly universal among living species. Humans are no exception.

Biologists recognize evolution as the basis of biological thought, with its accounts of what organisms are and how they come to be the way they are. Evolution is an epic tale, the constant selection of the most successful individuals for more than 3 billion years. The great stretch of evolutionary development means that it takes more than physics and chemistry to explain life—the history of life is important too, as random accidents of genetic mutation or lucky combinations of genes change the direction of life itself.

We are the products of millions of genetic accidents, some lucky, some less fortunate, and of environmental changes as sweeping as the changes in our genes. Any organism is a bundle of **adaptations**, specific bits of physical machinery originating in the genes, developing in a particular environment, and increasing the biological success of the organism. The adaptations of the most interest here are not the physical structures of the legs, the heart, or the eyes, but the brain structures that endow us with particular capabilities and motivations.

Psychologists who study perception, memory, or brain processes take for granted that evolutionary theory is indispensable to their work. No scientist would propose a theory of human vision, for instance, that was not consistent with what we know about vision in monkeys. After all, the visual pigments of the eye, the chemicals that start the whole process, are nearly identical not only in humans and monkeys, but also in animals as distant from us as fruit flies. So are the nerve cells that carry the signals from the eye. They evolved only once, and all animal life shares ancient evolutionary inventions like these. Because of our common origins, we can understand some aspects of human vision by examining the visual machinery of fruit flies.

This interpretation of psychology as a part of biology can be applied not just to physiological studies but to all of psychology: to social psychology as much as perception, and even to clinical practice. In each of these areas, the contribution of evolutionary theory will be different, depending on the roles of culture, history, social interactions, and biological structure in their makeup.

Evolutionary Psychology

The gathering revolution in psychology is based on the insight that evolution is critical for understanding not only the physiology of our bodies but also our perceptions, experiences, and behaviors. For the human is an animal like any other, a very successful one, but as much dependent on its biological inheritance as any monkey or fly. We come into the world with an enormous heritage of biological structure that affects everything about us, including how we pick up information from our environment and from our society.

Human behavior and experience cannot be understood without knowing what this biological equipment is and what possibilities and limitations it offers. For example, the human eye responds best to the range of wavelengths that is present in natural sunlight. Because most of the information that we can pick up from the visual environment is contained in this range of wavelengths, natural selection has given us biological mechanisms of vision that work where they are most effective. In a similar way, we are adapted to solve the cognitive and social challenges that our ancestors faced. To investigate these challenges, we must study both the environment and the adaptations, though—the genetics of color vision won't be interpretable without knowledge of the spectrum of sunlight.

Evolutionary psychology, then, is "psychology that is informed by the additional knowledge that evolutionary biology has to offer, in the expectation that understanding the process that designed the human mind will advance the discovery of its architecture" (Cosmides & Barkow, 1992). The new psychology is inclusive, sweeping both traditional psychological inquiry and insights from biology and other disciplines into its web. It applies the principles of biological evolution to the great questions of psychology: What are the bases of experience, behavior, mind, and memory, of development and social interaction? Where do they come from, and what are they for? The study of evolutionary psychology links all of these questions together by grounding them in a consistent theoretical orientation.

This does not mean that a psychology recognizing the key role of evolution in organizing human behaviors and attitudes should ignore culture, or assign it only secondary importance. The interaction of genes and culture is older than humanity itself. All the work of psychologists on the effects of culture on behavior is made no less valid by an evolutionary perspective, because culture profoundly affects every aspect of human life.

Psychology from the standpoint of evolutionary theory has reaffirmed, in fact, that culture affects human adaptations at every level, from social and linguistic adaptations all the way down to the structure of our teeth. (Teeth could evolve to become smaller only after cultural inventions such as fire and cooking changed our diet.) If this book emphasizes biological contributions to the human condition, it is partly to redress a historical imbalance in thinking about the sources of human behavior.

● SOCIAL SCIENCE VIEWS OF HUMANS

We humans sometimes like to think of ourselves as above nature or apart from it, as if our technology and culture have freed us from the biological limitations that chain other animals to particular ways of life. A squirrel, for instance, is trapped forever in woodlands, storing and eating nuts, whereas humans can live in woodlands, plains, jungles, deserts, arctic tundra, almost anywhere, can eat anything and can change lifestyles without genetic modification. Social science often embraces this conceit, with a conception of the human being traditionally influenced by philosopher John Locke's view of the mind as a **tabula rasa**, a blank slate on which the content of one's culture is written. According to this view, we have some structure, to be sure, but it is only a physical framework that we share with animals. The content and even the organization of the mind are free to vary as its culture demands.

Evidence for the centrality of this interpretation of the social sciences comes directly from the founders of the modern social sciences. Working about a century ago, they were quite explicit about the dominant role that culture and environment would play in their new disciplines. Emile Durkheim, perhaps the founder of modern sociology, wrote, "Individual natures are merely the indeterminate material that the social factor molds and transforms" (Durkheim, 1895/1962, p. 106). With such a beginning, it is no surprise that even today sociology pays little heed to the biological structure of the people who make up societies.

Psychology has had a similar history. It developed from several sources, one of them as an outgrowth of a European philosophy that was linked only indirectly to the natural sciences. In the United States, this philosophical tradition led many early psychologists to reject any significant influence of biological structure on the fates of individual humans. John Watson founded the **behaviorist** school, which dominated psychology in the United States from the 1920s until the 1960s and still influences psychological thought. In a famous boast he wrote:

> Give me a dozen healthy infants, well-formed, and my own specified world to bring them up in and I'll guarantee to take any one at random and train him to become any type of specialist I might select—doctor, lawyer, artist, merchant-chief, and yes, even beggar-man and thief, regardless of his talents, penchants, tendencies, abilities, vocations, and race of his ancestors. (Watson, 1925, p. 82)

At least we can give him credit for not being racist. Watson went on to insist that psychology could be built from presenting stimuli and measuring behavioral responses, correlating the two without regard to the internal structure of the organism. As it turned out, this stimulus-response approach proved to be too simple to account for even the behavior of laboratory rats, let alone humans. In the words of psychologist Don Symons (quoted in Allman, 1994), "There is no such thing as a 'general problem solver' because there is no such thing as a general problem."

In a highly structured learning situation, for example, behaviorists predicted that a rat would respond only to the stimuli that will result in a reward. The rat, however, has other ideas. It explores its training cage, sniffs everything, marks its tiny territory, and generally spends a lot of time engaged in behaviors that the behaviorist cannot explain. Although in its time behaviorism represented a great step forward in demanding scientific and methodological rigor, it is no longer seen as a viable psychology.

The Standard Social Science Model

These and similar founding ideas have led to an attitude of the social sciences to the role of biological structure, termed the **Standard Social Science Model (SSSM)** (Tooby & Cosmides, 1992). In this model, the human tabula rasa is a general-purpose brain, into which not only the technologies and conventions of a culture but also the most basic hopes and fears, needs and attitudes, are added from the outside. The SSSM assumes that the mind is highly malleable, its structure depending on what it experiences during development. Genes and instincts are there, but their influence remains in the background, offering a wide range of possibilities. Just as a general-purpose computer can become a typewriter, a calculator, a mailbox, or a hundred other tools, depending on a program added from the outside, the SSSM's human can become doctor, lawyer, or thief, depending only on its environment.

Psychology began long before Watson as an effort to analyze the mind into its constituent parts, much as chemistry had already analyzed matter into its elements. The new science of the mind did not link itself intellectually to chemistry or to the other natural sciences, however. All of the natural sciences are tied together—facts of biology are explained in terms of chemistry, chemical processes are understood in terms of physics, and so on. Together they form a broad and consistent body of knowledge. E. O. Wilson (1998) calls this process **consilience**. The relationships among the natural sciences are not reductionistic, however—each adds something unique that cannot emerge from the previous level (Hass et al., 2000). Biology, for instance, includes a body of facts and theories that cannot be derived from chemistry, and not all chemical facts and theories can be derived from physics, but theories in each discipline must be consistent with established principles in all the others.

The social sciences in contrast talk to one another much less; each works independently of the others. Psychology does not use anthropology to explain the nature of humanity, and sociologists pay little heed to explanations from psychologists in understanding social behavior. Anthropologists study differences among human groups, whereas sociologists are more concerned with modern Western society. Economists often assume that people are rational and will optimize their economic behavior, without looking at a wealth of disconfirming evidence from psychology. Sigmund, Fehr, and Nowak (2002) caricature economists as studying a mythical Homo Economicus, making rational choices in complete isolation.

According to Hass et al. (2000), the various social sciences seem to be parallel rather than hierarchical, each explaining human behavior and experience in its own way. What they have in common is the SSSM, the idea that the critical variables for understanding human behavior, experience, and social structure are primarily environmental and cultural rather than biological. Human nature in this view is reduced to not much more than a capacity for culture. Because social scientists are trained to seek environmental explanations for all of their observations, they often tend to avoid alternative explanations. Consilience is not an issue. Of course every discipline has its scholars who do pay attention to other disciplines and to their biological base, and the SSSM is one end of a continuum from environmental determinism to biological determinism, but its influence remains significant.

Though there is value in the SSSM insight that environment and development are critically important in understanding the human situation, this book will examine whether the SSSM conception of the mind as unstructured and culture as apart from nature is consistent with what we know about how human beings are put together.

The SSSM's mind is like a trellis upon which a culture grows—and it can grow in any direction that its history takes it. The biological trellis, though, channels that vine in some directions and prevents development in others. Research has begun to reveal more structure in that trellis than anyone had dared imagine. The social sciences are at last beginning to become broader and more interdisciplinary, linked more closely with the natural sciences and with one another. This book is a part of the movement in that direction.

Several forces have led to the current efforts to establish a more broadly based psychology, with roots in both biological and social science. One influence has been the limitations that have emerged in the SSSM, with the social sciences making little progress in understanding the human condition. According to some psychologists,

> The social sciences are still adrift, with an enormous mass of half-digested observations, a not inconsiderable body of empirical generalizations, and a contradictory stew of ungrounded middle-level theories expressed in a babel of incommensurate technical lexicons. (Tooby and Cosmides, 1992, p. 23)

By this assessment, it is surprising that we know anything at all about people and their societies. The situation is beginning to improve, with efforts to integrate social sciences and evolutionary theory (Gandolfi, Gandolfi, & Barash, 2002).

Another impetus for the evolutionary approach is the enormous power of new biological tools that we can apply to psychological problems, tools that include our new ability to study, sequence, and define the genes themselves, and a theoretical reorientation that allows us to ask new questions and progress in unexpected directions. A century and a half of progress in biology, understanding what Darwin's (1859) evolution by natural selection means and how it works, can now be applied to the problems of psychology. Let's get started.

● NATURE VERSUS NURTURE?

Questions about biological and environmental influences on a human trait are often phrased in the SSSM as "nature versus nurture," a framework that pits one cause in competition against the other. It is as though both heredity and environment can fill the bucket of the human mind, and the question becomes how much water enters the bucket from each source. As a result, interactions between the two causes are viewed as competitions among equals, as though these two giants are struggling with one another for control of the human mind.

But the competitive framework misinterprets the way in which human traits come to be. It is not a matter of nature and nurture competing for influence. Rather, every trait begins with genes that direct the construction of every part of the body and the brain. The trait of running speed of an individual human is a good example for understanding this process in the context of psychology, because it is defined by a behavior rather than by a physical characteristic. For running speed, genes largely set the length of the legs, the rate of metabolism, and other body properties that will influence speed.

Without an organism, though, the genes are just bits of deoxyribonucleic acid, **DNA**, microscopic wisps of organic molecules that seem unrelated to running speed or any other trait. They acquire their power over traits only in the right environment, in an organism that develops according to the genes' instructions. The environment also allows the genes to do their work either more effectively or less effectively, and in the end running speed is tested in an environment. Good nutrition, for instance, allows the genes to develop strong muscles in the good runner. Without that nutrition, the good genes won't matter, because the raw materials they need to do their work are not at hand.

So the organization of genes and environment is not parallel but sequential: every trait begins with genes. They work through an environment to create an organism with certain traits (Figure 1.1). All the genes together constitute a **genotype**, the set of genes that an organism starts with, and the genes and environment together in turn direct the development of a **phenotype**, the actual properties of the physical organism. Eventually, the success of a phenotype influences the structure of the genotype, by survival of the individuals with the most successful phenotypes. These individuals then contribute their genotypes to the next generation.

Seen in this way, it doesn't make sense to ask whether nature or nurture has the stronger influence: all traits are determined by genes working through an environment to create an organism with traits.

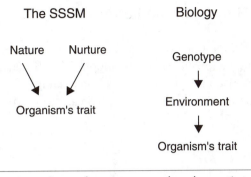

Figure 1.1   Alternative conceptions of environmental and genetic contributions to an organism's traits.

Heritability

There is one restricted instance in which one can distinguish what heredity and environment contribute, and this is in the distribution of a trait in a population. The range of running speeds of all the students in a classroom, for instance, will be determined both by their genetic diversity and by the diversity of their environments, including both their current condition and their circumstances during development. If all the people in the class had the same genes, for example (admittedly an unlikely situation), there would be less variability of running speed, and all of it would be contributed by the environment. If instead all the students had identical environments (even more unlikely), there would again be less variability of running speed, but all of it would come from genetic differences.

These extreme examples show that the proportion of the variability contributed to a group by genes and by environment is not fixed, but is affected by the variability of the genes and of the environments themselves. In the real world, each influence, heredity, and environment contributes something to the diversity of capabilities in the group. **Heritability**, the proportion of a population's variance on a trait that can be accounted for by differences in genes among its members, depends on the variability of the group as well as the genetic origins of the trait.

The nature of that influence from genetics, which changes only between generations, will be fundamentally different from the effects of the environment, which changes individuals within a generation but cannot influence succeeding generations. And in the end we will have to stage a race to determine how fast each member of our population can run, introducing another source of error into our estimate of heritability.

The Lizard and the Retriever

We often think of physical traits as being given by the genes, and behavioral characteristics as being supplied by the environment. Indeed, this is the SSSM conception. Some counterexamples from nature show that the division of labor between the physical and the behavioral is not so simple, however.

The Lizard

In California's Mojave Desert, black lava flows are the habitat of an inconspicuous lizard, no bigger than the span of the hand. The lizard is as black as the surrounding lava. A few kilometers away, in the light-colored desert sand, similar lizards of lighter color and more textured pattern thrive. In between, where fingers of lava stretch into the sand, other lizards display an intermediate coloring. These "side-blotched lizards" appear to be a perfect example of animals finely adapted to their environments by evolution, with selective pressures caused by predators that eat lizards of the wrong color, leaving only the appropriately camouflaged ones to reproduce.

On closer inspection, though, some facts don't fit the theory. First, the hatchling lizards in all of these areas look identical. Over a period of months, the lava-dwelling lizards grow darker while those in the lighter environment grow lighter. Second, any animal that evolves into separate, genetically distinct populations should have variability in several features. The side-blotched lizards, though, show variation only in pigment density between groups. Third, a genetically distinct population should be large enough to sustain itself, but isolated croppings of black lava not much larger than the territory of a single lizard can be found in the Mojave, with lizards that show a definite color-matching tendency. The lightest lizards of all, in fact, live in the snow-white dust downwind of a desert cement plant!

These observations lead to an unexpected conclusion: the side-blotched lizard is genetically equipped not to develop a specific coloration but to adjust its color during development to match the surroundings in which it is hatched (Norris, 1967). All of those desert lizards are of the same species— eggs moved from the lava-dwelling group will develop into perfectly normal sand-dwelling lizards, and vice versa. The humble lizard has not merely adapted to its environment but has achieved something much more powerful—it has adapted to adapt to its environment. Not only the inheritance of its genes but also the conditions of its nurture determine the color of the side-blotched lizard.

The Retriever

An example of animal adaptation closer to home is the retriever. When a hunter shoots a bird, the faithful dog scrambles through the underbrush and unerringly brings the prey back in its teeth. To a psychologist who has spent a career training rats, this seems to be a good example of an intelligent animal, the dog, learning to perform a useful function for its master.

But look more closely. Though the hunter knows little of the psychology of animal training, the dog retrieves nonetheless. Retriever puppies start fetching things as soon as they can walk—a stick, a ball, your missing slipper. A retriever raised by humans without ever seeing another dog will retrieve for hours without obvious reward. Though some work is needed to coordinate the dog-human team, their teamwork is built on a behavioral pattern bred into the animal by generations of artificial selection. The dog is born to fetch.

The lizard and the retriever seem distant from issues of the evolution of human behavior, but they yield the insight that most characteristics of animals and humans, whether physical or behavioral, result from intricate interactions of environment and heredity. The gene-environment path is sequential—it's never just one or the other.

The Human as a Biological Organism

How can we determine whether the SSSM is incomplete, whether biological structure is as critical as culture for understanding human nature? One way to approach this question is to put people in perspective, to compare humans with other animals. We can especially compare humans to other primates, most appropriately to chimpanzees, our closest living relatives. We share about 98% of our genes with chimpanzees (Kim & Takenaka, 1996), making humans and chimpanzees about as closely related to one another as horses and donkeys. In fact, chimpanzees are more closely related to humans than to gorillas, our next nearest primate relative. Biologically, we are not a unique end point in an unerring progression from worms to philosophers, but just another animal in another ecological niche. The rules of inheritance are the same for us as for every other creature.

One way to test the SSSM directly is to find out whether genetic inheritance can indeed affect what seem to be social conventions such as mate preference, aesthetic preferences, language, a sense of duty, and many other psychological characteristics of humans. The chapters of this book show that all these things include strong genetic as well as cultural influences. We see similarities in these characteristics in all cultures, and we can find good biological reasons why we have evolved to handle these human challenges in particular ways. In some cases, we can even trace the history of the genes that nudge us along certain paths. And it is usually a nudge that the genes give us, through motivations, attitudes, and aptitudes, not a reflex-like command (Ehrlich, 2000).

In mate preference, for example, we are finely tuned to find the partners who are most likely to provide the resources necessary to raise offspring successfully. Each sex has its own preferences for the opposite sex; the preferences are partly overlapping, partly distinct, and mostly cross-cultural. They can be shown to optimize reproductive success. Most people are unaware that these genetically influenced traits exist, even while their genes profoundly affect their own behavior in this most personal and most important aspect of our lives. The genetic nudges, however, push us in directions that would have been appropriate in the Stone Age, and may or may not lead to wise choices today. Later chapters give the details.

● THE PLACE OF EVOLUTIONARY PSYCHOLOGY

What's different about evolutionary psychology? First, taking evolution into account vastly increases the scientific base on which psychology can build. We can investigate not only who we are but also where we have been, and we can look to the structure of minds and genes to provide insight about human behavior and experience. Genetics, ethology, and a half dozen other disciplines become fodder for the psychological theorist. Furthermore, we have begun to see past the **proximate causes** of much current psychological theorizing to the **ultimate causes**, describing not only how things are but also understanding how they came to be that way.

From language to mate selection, from visual perception to reasoning, evolutionary theory has given us a context, linked us to other traditions, and helped us to ask new questions. Evolutionary theory is not the only tool of the psychologist, though: it is only one of many ways of organizing psychological data and better understanding how the mind works.

● HISTORY OF EVOLUTION IN THE BEHAVIORAL SCIENCES

The idea of evolution by natural selection was developed by two men at about the same time, Charles Darwin and Alfred Russel Wallace. Darwin had been sitting on his explosive insights for nearly 2 decades when he heard that Wallace had developed a similar theory to his own and had independently collected evidence supporting it. Darwin generously offered to cointroduce the idea with Wallace to the Royal Society, but history has given the credit to Darwin and left Wallace as a footnote in Victorian science.

Darwin

One reason for this disparity is that Darwin was a gifted writer as well as a great scientist—his book *On the Origin of Species* (1859) is still worth reading today. Within both the social and biological sciences, perhaps the most significant reason why Darwin is remembered, whereas Wallace is not, is that Wallace didn't go all the way with his theory. He admitted to natural selection for animals and for human physical characteristics, but like Descartes two centuries before, he reserved a special place for human sentience, linking it to a gift from God. Darwin did not stop at the physical, but courageously followed his ideas through to the heart of the human condition, to the mind and its origins.

Objection and Response

One of the reasons why Darwin procrastinated so long in publishing on evolution by natural selection is that he correctly anticipated the firestorm of criticism that it aroused. He also feared that it would offend his wife, Emma, whom he loved dearly and who was very religious. Less visible from the current perspective, though, is the immediate and enthusiastic reception of the idea by most of natural science and medicine of the time. For example, Ewald Hering, a giant of 19th-century German physiology, was incorporating evolutionary ideas in his explanation of the structure of the visual system less than a decade after the appearance of *On the Origin of Species* (Hering, 1868).

The objections came more from the general public, and specifically from religious leaders. A clear differentiation of the domains of science and of religion could have ameliorated this conflict, for there is a principled division between the two domains in the distinction between structure and content. Science explicates the rules by which the natural world works, but it is largely silent on the actual contents of culture—the rich historical and contemporary content of events, ideas, and human interactions. If you want to know the rules in the football game of life, you should ask a scientist. But if you want to know the score, you should inquire of a poet or a writer, a historian or a journalist. Religions had developed their own cosmologies and biologies in the vacuum of the incomplete science of previous centuries, and unfortunately some religious leaders were reluctant to let go of them. Some, especially in more conservative religious circles, still are.

Late in his life, Darwin published two additional books, again both well worth reading even today, that would have earned him an honored place in the history of psychological biology even without his *Origin of Species*. One dealt with the descent of humans (Darwin, 1871), pointing out many similarities between the human and the chimpanzee, and introducing the idea of sexual selection, and the other (Darwin, 1872) began the comparative study of emotional expression in animals and humans. Both contributed to the founding of the science of **ethology**.

Ethology

Twentieth-century field biology, centered in Europe, gave rise to the discipline of ethology, the explication of behavior by biological principles. Ethologists such as Niko Tinbergen (1951) were able to understand reproductive behavior in birds, for example, by analyzing the characteristics of the species. If it takes two parents to feed the chicks until they reach maturity, a stable pair bond will form between the parents. It may last just for a breeding season, or for a lifetime. The mating rituals that establish the bond evolve from already-established patterns of social interaction in the species, usually from either dominance/submission displays or nurturance behaviors. As is typical in evolution, new capabilities arise from old parts.

Konrad Lorenz discovered imprinting in young birds, a specialized form of learning that induces chicks to follow their mothers as soon as they hatch. He showed in a dramatic way that the behavior is learned, by imprinting chicks to follow him, in the process demonstrating that imprinting can occur to a very wide variety of possible objects. At the right time in life, the chicks will follow any large thing that moves, and will remain imprinted on it. It is an example of a simple genetic program that usually produces the desired result without a detailed plan of the mother's characteristics.

Ethologists studied social behavior in a wide variety of animals, but rarely investigated humans. That job fell to a new discipline.

Sociobiology

In 1975, E. O. Wilson published *Sociobiology: The New Synthesis*, a book that founded a field and ignited a storm of controversy. Wilson predicted that psychology would eventually be subsumed within biology. Most of the book was a masterful analysis of social behavior in animals, but in his last chapter, Wilson speculated on the possibility of applying his genetic analysis to human social behavior. Though the applications were mostly speculations about how human behavior might be driven by evolved mechanisms, Wilson was criticized because his speculations were not backed up by empirical evidence. Sociobiologists were accused of telling *just so stories*, after the stories of that name published by Victorian author Rudyard Kipling. The stories describe not how things are, but how things might have happened.

Many psychologists were offended by the idea that evolved adaptations as well as cultural conventions could be regulating human social behavior, whereas other psychologists extended the speculations further. The data weren't yet there to establish the role of biological structure in social behavior— before it really got started, the new discipline fell into disrepute.

Evolutionary Psychology

In the 1980s, a new group of psychologists began to appear, calling them- selves evolutionary psychologists and building much of their theoretical stance on Wilson's ideas and on the pioneering work of Robert Trivers. They have done most of their research in social interaction, broadly interpreted, because the theoretical base of psychology seems weakest there. The new field is broader than sociobiology, however, encompassing fields such as thinking, problem-solving, perception, and memory as well as social behavior, putting more emphasis on humans, and engaging life challenges at every level.

While the debates about sociobiology continued to rage, this group began quietly gathering the empirical base on which much of the content of this book rests. Pursuing their goal of putting a new theoretical foundation under psychology, they found at the base of the existing body of psychology a welter of small theories, each plausible in itself but unrelated to the others, and compact descriptions of phenomena disguised as theories. As the empir- ical base broadens, it has become possible to base psychology more firmly on theory that applies both within and outside psychology, to make psychologi- cal theories more consistent with one another, and also to address new prob- lems from the perspective of the new orientation. Most workers in this field are not dedicated to evolutionary psychology as much as to the goal of build- ing evolutionary ideas into all of psychology.

Evolutionary psychology has attracted its own set of critics, though. Their concern is motivated partly by the unhappy record of past attempts to apply evolutionary theory to public life.

● USES AND MISUSES OF EVOLUTION

There is a general rule that all powerful things are dangerous, be they chain saws, televisions, or scientific ideas. Evolution, being a very powerful idea, also proved very dangerous in the wrong hands.

Social Darwinism

As the idea of evolution filtered through Victorian society, it became diluted and distorted. If the more fit are more successful, Herbert Spencer and some others reasoned, then the people at the top of the social heap must be more fit than the others. It was Spencer, not Darwin, who coined the term *survival of the fittest*. The famous saying distorts Darwin's insight that it is not mere survival but reproduction that defines biological fitness, and it implies that the fittest have the right to suppress the less fit.

Nonetheless, the socially powerful seized on the idea to justify their dominant positions and their exploitation of others as a "natural" condition. German philosopher Friedrich Nietzsche extended this to the idea of the *Übermensch*, often mistranslated as "superman" but meaning "dominant person." You can guess who got to be the *Übermensch*.

Since the socially dominant and their apologists spent a lot of effort broadcasting their ideas while scientists quietly went about their empirical studies, only one side was heard, and segments of the public began to associate Darwinism with social exploitation. Part of the reason why the social sciences at their birth rejected biological ideas was in reaction to social Darwinism. Another movement, though, was about to make social Darwinism look benign by comparison.

Eugenics

Throughout history, people have observed that some of their fellow human beings are more capable than others. The human race could be improved, they argued, if only the most capable were allowed to reproduce. We could develop superior humans in the same way that we develop superior dogs or roses, by artificial selection. The idea is formalized in **eugenics**, the effort to produce superior humans by selective breeding. One of its first champions was Charles Darwin's cousin, Francis Galton.

Assumptions of Eugenics

Although the goal of making humanity better through eugenics seemed admirable at first, and was advocated by many idealistic reformers, it is based on fundamental misunderstandings of evolutionary theory. First and most important, it assumes that the genes of one group are by some measure superior to the genes of another. However, everyone in the population stands at the pinnacle of an equally long series of successful reproductions. Traits that we value at the moment are mixed with other less-valued traits in each of us, and sexual recombination will reshuffle them again in the next generation. What is valuable will itself vary from one environment to another, like the lizards' skin pigment example earlier.

What about traits that nearly everyone values, such as high intelligence? If a higher intelligence would have been good for humans, providing superior fitness, the average intelligence level of the population would have drifted up to that level a long time ago, by mechanisms to be described below. There are reasons, that we often don't understand, why average intelligence has settled where it has. Manipulating such traits assumes that we can successfully second-guess millions of years of hominid evolution.

More fundamentally, eugenics has built into it the assumption that some have the right to reproduce more than others, or even the right to prevent others from reproducing. It's social Darwinism writ large. Who has the authority to decide, on what criteria, and with what justification?

Eugenic Experiments

Examples of past efforts at eugenics have thrown these objections into relief, especially the last one. One of the most widespread eugenic experiments was an effort to sterilize the "feeble-minded," which victimized thousands of people in the United States and other countries in the early 20th century.

Other experiments have attempted to increase the fertility of those judged most desirable. Among the largest was a movement called Lebensborn in Nazi Germany, intended to produce babies by unwed mothers. The mothers were not particularly selected, but the fathers were Nazi SS officers—arguably the most aggressive and vicious members of that society. Another experiment, in the United States, encouraged and subsidized families of a group of men also judged to be particularly worthy—in this case, military test pilots. Again, inexplicably, there was no effort to select the mothers. Fortunately, both of these efforts were too small and too short-lived to have had a significant impact on the population.

In the idyllic village of Irsee, Germany, stands another reminder of eugenic efforts. Behind the elegant baroque cloister in the center of the town, a small plaque commemorates about 4,000 occupants of the building, which had been converted into a psychiatric hospital. All of them had been killed by the Nazis and buried in mass graves behind the church. The mounds of earth are still visible.

Genetic Determinism

One of the persistent objections to evolutionary explanations in psychology, and to biological explanations generally, is that if something is found to be genetic, it can't be changed, and therefore it is dangerous to investigate the genetic basis of intelligence, personality, mental illness, and so on. The objection argues that some aspects of the human condition are better left uninvestigated, lest we find something uncomfortable. A gene for alcoholism, for instance, would tell us that some people are doomed to become alcoholics, so we may as well forget about treating them.

Treatment of Genetic Conditions

The history of actual discoveries about genetic contributions to human behavior has revealed the flaw in such arguments. An example is **phenylketonuria** (PKU), a degenerative form of mental retardation. A PKU baby seems normal at birth, but after a few months begins to decline while normal babies are progressing. The parents watch helplessly as the disease progresses, until the child inevitably dies.

The discovery that PKU is caused by a single recessive gene did not cause physicians to abandon efforts to treat the disease, though. Instead, the function of the gene could be found. It turned out to direct the manufacture of the enzyme phenylalanine hydroxylase, needed for the metabolism of the essential amino acid phenylalanine. Without the gene, toxic byproducts of phenylalanine build up in the blood, sometimes to 100 times normal levels, and metabolic derivatives such as phenylpyruvic acid accumulate, slowly poisoning the child (Gardner, 1983).

The discovery of the metabolic defect and its genetic basis led directly to a treatment for the disease. If PKU is diagnosed early in infancy, the progressive mental retardation can be prevented by carefully controlling the amount of phenylalanine in the diet, enough to allow synthesis of body proteins but not enough to allow toxic byproducts to accumulate. Discovery of a genetic basis for PKU led not to hopelessness but to effective treatment.

A more common example is early-onset diabetes, which is also inherited. Discovery of a genetic basis for the disease meant that physicians could stop looking for a virus or bacterium, and get down to the business of compensating for the missing sugar-digesting enzyme. Because its genetic and biochemical basis is understood, diabetes has changed from a sentence of a slow, drawn-out death to an inconvenience.

It is the same with many of the serious mental illnesses reviewed in Chapter 9—knowing the genetic bases of the diseases helps in efforts to control them. The objection to genetically based studies implicitly assumes the SSSM competition model of genes versus environment. But since genes work only through an environment (Figure 1.1), manipulating the environment can modify the effects of the genes.

Defending the Status Quo

A similar objection to evolutionary analyses of the human condition is that they seem to legitimize the status quo. If the genes have determined some aspect of human thinking or human interaction, the argument goes, there is no sense in trying to change it. Better to deemphasize the genetic contribution, lest an unjust social situation become legitimized and perpetuated. Because current social and economic conditions have resulted from an interaction of human environments and the permanent inheritance of our genes, the evolutionary argument must conclude that conditions are what will always be.

In a way, this objection is a leftover reaction to the failed movement of social Darwinism. The fallacy in this stance is similar to that of genetic determinism in dealing with diseases or disabilities, because genes work in environments, and only by understanding the genes can we change our environments in such a way that our genes work for us rather than against us. By knowing how we are made, we can improve our quality of life. The organism that is capable of understanding itself and its place in nature is finally beginning to do so.

Male-Female Differences

The status quo arguments become particularly important, and particularly contentious, when applied to gender differences. Evolutionary analysis tackles the problem of disentangling natural and cultural differences between the sexes by using evolutionary theory to generate hypotheses about natural differences. Darwin recognized that emotions and intelligence would be as relevant to the evolutionary fate of their possessors as would any other traits. When the sexes are considered from this viewpoint, it becomes clear that we expect males and females to have significantly different temperaments because their reproductive needs are so different.

A human female, reproducing flat out, can produce only about one child a year, a limit that does not apply to the male. Thus different psychological characteristics were needed for success in the evolutionary arena. The problem is that many familiar differences between men and women, often interpreted as culturally induced, are turning out to be the very ones that natural selection might be expected to have planted deep in our natures.

Evolutionary reasoning suggests, for instance, that women should be strongly devoted to the care of their children, and should prefer impressive, high-status males from whom they seek undivided commitment. Men should be competitive, adventurous, and motivated to possess women and control their sexuality. They should prefer youth and beauty, but also grasp whatever sexual opportunities present themselves. The specifics are in Chapter 3.

It seems that, after its early promise as an ally of liberation, evolutionary psychology leads back to traditional views. This is why some people object to evolutionary psychology as politically motivated pseudoscience, rife with genetic determinism, gross oversimplification, insensitivity to variation and overlap, categorizing, stereotyping, and rampant sexism.

But the new claims about sex differences, although they may sound like the old ones, are quite different. Some of the traditional ideas are contradicted: nothing in evolutionary psychology suggests, for instance, that women are less intelligent than men. There is also a more fundamental and more subtle point. Even when evolutionary psychology's claims about male and female differences sound like traditional ones, they are not because of the radical change in the idea of nature (Richards, 2000).

Traditional claims about the natures of men and women were made in the context of a long-established view of the world as a naturally ordered whole, harmonious as long as everything stayed in its ordained place. If things went wrong, that was due to interference in the natural order of things. The most familiar version of this approach is the religious view that sees order and complexity as underlain by divine plan. In such traditions, to understand the nature of something is to identify its place in the scheme of things, so that to understand the nature of men and women is to know how they should live harmoniously together.

But evolution by natural selection, which shows in principle how complexity can arise without any design or intention, revealed a very different world without any underlying moral order or natural harmony. In this modern, scientific world, describing the nature of something says nothing about its natural place or what it is good for. It gives only a neutral account of what something is like and how it interacts with other things.

The trouble is that prescientific, pre-Darwinian ideas about nature are so deeply ingrained in our culture that they persist even among otherwise scientifically oriented people. This leads to systematic misinterpretation of the worldview of evolutionary psychology.

In a Darwinian world, for instance, claims about the way evolution has shaped male and female emotions do not imply psychological homogeneity within each sex, or firm boundaries between them. Variation is to be expected, because it is the raw material of evolution. Ideas of fixed essences and clear distinctions between natural kinds belong to earlier interpretations of an ordered universe.

Similarly, claims about sex differences cannot imply genetic determinism. To say that men and women are different by nature does not say that their development and actions are fixed in their genes; it implies only that they are likely to react in different ways to similar environments. Recall that the genes offer nudges, not commands. The idea that natures are immutable also belongs to the pre-Darwinian world and is irrelevant to evolutionary psychology.

Most important, discoveries in a Darwinian world about the natures of the sexes have no direct implications whatever for how they should live and relate to one another. There is no reason to expect their interests—either evolutionary or personal—to coincide. Natural selection produces harmony only to the extent that harmony promotes reproduction, for evolutionarily speaking, the sexes are rivals.

Paradoxically, the same mistake shows even in the apparently opposed idea that Darwinism justifies constant struggle. But interpretations of evolution as all-purpose progress also depend on the idea of a natural order through which evolution progresses. Darwinian evolution has no such onward-and-upward path. The only hope for progress lies in deciding within our culture what counts as progress, and then trying to bring it about.

By whatever standard, we cannot progress without understanding what we are up against. If science indicates that men and women are different, that is something we need to know. We do not need resistance that comes from encumbering Darwinian insights into human nature with relics of a pre-Darwinian world (Richards, 2000).

These are the claims and counterclaims. To evaluate them scientifically requires a look at the nuts and bolts of evolution.

● HOW EVOLUTION WORKS

The process of evolution is built into the most fundamental machinery of life itself—the genetic material and its inheritance. Once the basic mechanisms are described, the workings of evolution will be obvious. All the chemical reactions that make up living things are based on directions from the genes, the molecular instruction codes in the nucleus of each cell. To understand evolution, we will begin by zooming down from the level of organisms to the level of the macromolecules that direct the processes of life.

Genes

Genes themselves are made up from strings of DNA, a molecule that can form into pairs of long chains with a double helix structure (Figure 1.2). Each chain consists of a series of organic molecules bonded together one after another. Because each molecular chain has a long "backbone" of identical units, they are called **polymers** (poly = many). There are four types of molecules that bridge between the two chains: they are the organic bases adenine (A), thymine (T), guanine (G), and cytosine (C). It happens that A and T have complementary shapes, so that they bond to each other across the gap between the two helical backbones of DNA. Each base has two electrically charged regions that match charged regions in the other, so that a pair of hydrogen bonds (relatively weak chemical bonds) links the two molecules together. G and C have a similar compatibility, but with three hydrogen bonds linking them.

In a genetic DNA molecule, these four bases string together like a four-letter alphabet, encoding the information that a living cell eventually uses to direct the production of proteins. When the information is read, the DNA is uncoiled, breaking the hydrogen bonds between **base pairs**, so that the order of the pair in the DNA double helix (A-T or T-A, for example) makes a difference in what information is represented.

Because there are only four letters in the genetic alphabet, it is possible to measure the amount of information that genes can carry. The smallest unit of information is the **bit**, a two-alternative choice where each choice is equally likely. Each base pair contains exactly two bits of information, because I would have to ask you two yes/no questions to find out which of the four bases occupies a given location. First I would ask whether the location in question contained an A-T pair or a C-G pair. Then I would ask whether the

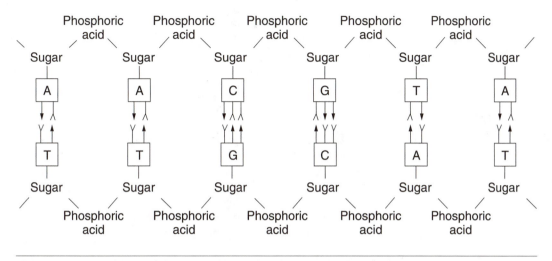

Figure 1.2 Structure of the DNA molecule, showing the four bases that line up to create base pairs.

base was A in one case or C in the other (Figure 1.3). The two questions define two bits of information. So the number of bits of information in the genes is twice the number of base pairs.

How many base pairs are there in the human genome? The number is known, and here is one way it can be determined. Because we know the molecular structure of DNA down to the last atom, we know the molecular weight of a section of DNA that contains one base pair. We take a sample of cells, strip away all the membranes and other structures in the sample, and purify the DNA, removing all the proteins that normally coat its surface. Then we simply weigh the sample and divide by the molecular weight of a base pair and the number of cells that went into the sample. The result is that human genes contain about 3 billion base pairs. At two bits per base pair, this works out to 6 billion bits of information.

Six billion seems like a large number, but the bit is a very small unit. Computer scientists usually measure information in bytes, consisting of eight bits. For large numbers the bytes are combined, a million at a time, into megabytes. So the 6 billion bits in the human genome work out to about 750 megabytes. The hard drive in my desktop computer can hold many times this amount of information. And compared to the trillion or so cells in your body, the number is very small indeed. Later we shall see some tricks that nature uses to squeeze a large amount of structure from a small amount of genetic information.

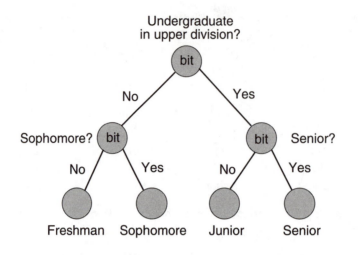

Figure 1.3   Deciding a multialternative problem with a series of binary choices. Each choice requires one bit of information. Extending this logic, one can decide among 2^n choices with n bits.

From Genes to Bodies

How do these wisps of DNA construct a body? This is the domain of embryology, encompassing some of the enduring mysteries of biology.

Individual genes have no body plan built into them, because each gene can do only one thing—to direct the construction of a specific protein molecule. In short, we don't know the details of how bodies are constructed from genetic instructions. But we do know the first steps in the process. The base pairs of the DNA polymer chain are grouped into threes: each triplet codes for a particular **amino acid** (amino acids are strung together to make up proteins). There are $4^3 = 64$ possible triplets of A, T, C, and G, but only 20 different amino acids, so the code is redundant. Both TTT and TTC, for instance, code for the amino acid lysine. And there are three different codes that mark the end of a gene.

Normally, the DNA is covered with specialized proteins that prevent the genetic material from being read out. When these proteins are removed, a segment of DNA can uncoil and pair up with a strand of **RNA** (ribonucleic acid), a molecule similar to DNA but with a different sugar in its backbone. This RNA carries a copy of the genetic instructions out of the nucleus, where the DNA resides, into the cell body, where a **ribosome** transcribes the RNA into a protein. The ribosome is like a complex biological zipper—it reads the

RNA, triplet by triplet, and constructs the corresponding protein according to the three-letter codes for amino acids. The protein is just a string of amino acids chained together, echoing the corresponding chain of RNA. The structure of the protein chain allows it to twist and fold in complex ways, giving it the properties that make it biologically useful.

Reproduction in Cells

When a cell divides, its DNA separates along the line of hydrogen bonds that joins the base pairs. Each base picks up a new complementary base, and a new DNA backbone, to make up two new strands of DNA (Figure 1.4). Each is a replica of the original, and each migrates to one of the new daughter cells. In the process of sexual reproduction, though, there is a different sort of replication. The two coils of the double helix divide into single helices, without picking up new base pairs. Each part is a single strand of unmatched base pairs. These single DNA strands become the genetic material of an egg or sperm cell. When egg and sperm unite to form a new organism by sexual recombination, the DNA from the two parent cells comes together. New double-strand DNA is made, some of it duplicating from the egg's single strands, and some from the sperm's single strands. Once the DNA from the two parents is recombined, it directs the construction of a new organism, complete with all the brain structures that will influence emotions, motivations, instincts and capabilities.

The recombining of genes in a new organism is not quite random, for human genes are aligned on 23 pairs of **chromosomes**, continuous chains of DNA containing sequences of genes, and also including DNA that does not code for production of proteins. If two genes are on different chromosomes, their inheritance will be independent—knowing the identity of the parent who contributed one gene will not help in predicting which parent contributed the other gene. But if two genes are close together on the same chromosome, it is likely that both came from the same parent.

Once the human genome had been sequenced, identifying in order all the base pairs of human DNA, one would think that it would be a simple matter to count the number of genes. It isn't. One can't simply count the number of start sequences in the genome, for instance, because some start sequences are followed immediately by end sequences. Other regions repeat the start sequence over and over. Still other sequences are perfectly good genes that are never expressed in the organism. What had seemed an elegant, clean system turned out to be a mess. As a first estimate, the human genome project revealed that the number of human genes is smaller than the 100,000 or so that had been expected (The Genome International Sequencing Consortium, 2001). Early estimates maintained that the entire

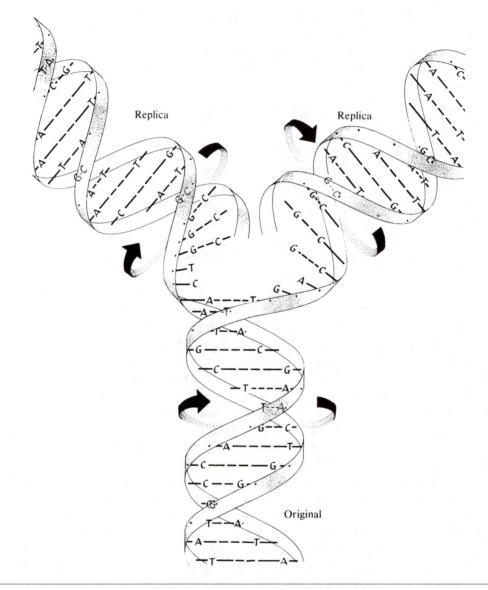

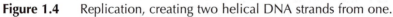

Figure 1.4   Replication, creating two helical DNA strands from one.

human body and brain are based on only about 30,000 genes, and most of the 3 billion base pairs are "junk" DNA that does not code for the production of proteins. Later revisions estimate two to three times as many genes. It will take a lot of careful work to identify the sequences that actually represent working genes.

Reproduction in a Population

Most of the genes that make up a human are the same for every member of the species. Some, including those that direct such basic design features as our bilateral symmetry and our repeating patterns of ribs and vertebrae, are common to nearly all multicellular animals. Others code for such features as the structure of the eye, the enzymes of the liver, and the lobes of the brain. But of our 3 billion base pairs, about 2.5 million differ from one individual to the next, reflecting one difference for every 1,200 base pairs (Cann, 2001). Because these base pairs make up genes that produce characteristics of the organism, they affect the success of that organism in its life in the natural world. It is these differing base pairs that constitute the raw material of evolution.

In a particular environment, one variety or **allele** of a gene may make its carrier more successful than other alleles of that gene that are carried in other individuals. The person who is the carrier of that gene will tend to do better in life and to produce more surviving offspring than people without the superior allele. For example, a gene that provides resistance to a disease will tend to make the carriers of that gene more successful. In Darwin's term, these carriers will have greater biological **fitness** than other people.

Over many generations, the genes of those with the greatest fitness will come to dominate the population, and the genes of the less fit will tend to disappear. This is the basic mechanism of Darwinian evolution by **natural selection**. It is an inevitable result of the facts that genes vary, genes make proteins, proteins influence the traits of an organism, and different traits mean that individuals have differing fitness. Natural selection is the increase in numbers of the individuals with greatest fitness, due to their ability to survive in the natural world.

People often speak about the evolution of a culture, or the evolution of the automobile, and so on. In this book, for the sake of clarity, the word *evolution* will be restricted to its Darwinian sense of evolution by natural selection. It is a change in genes or gene frequencies across generations, through the influence of the environment.

The effectiveness of an allele depends both on what the gene does and on the environment in which it acts. For instance, the genetic mutation that produced the lightness of Europeans' skin has been traced back to a single individual somewhere in northern Europe about 30,000 years ago. Before humans invaded Europe, their dark skin pigmentation was a vital defense against damage from the sun's ultraviolet radiation (Robins, 1991). But as anyone who has spent any time in northern Europe can attest, getting too much sun is the least of one's worries in the northern climate. Rather, people with darker skin cannot produce enough vitamin D from reactions in their skin to avoid rickets, a vitamin-D deficiency disease (Branda & Eaton, 1978). Rickets distorts the skeletons of growing children and reduces their biological fitness.

As a result of this mutation, light-skinned mutated individuals and their descendants had greater fitness; they could have more successful children. The mutation that would spell disaster in the tropics spelled survival in the north. Now, after millennia of cultural adaptation and a few fortuitous mutations, the descendants of those lightly pigmented Europeans have turned around and colonized California, where they tend to get skin cancer.

Biological fitness does not depend on one's physical fitness, as in well-toned muscles, and it is not measured by how much one possesses of such virtues as intelligence, social skills, trustworthiness, kindness, or other valued traits. It is based on one thing, and one thing only—the number of offspring one has. A person with a rich array of valued traits, but who has no children, has no biological fitness by this definition. If someone has high fitness, with many surviving offspring, then the genes of that person will be more strongly represented in the next generation.

Inclusive Fitness. There is another way for one's genes to get into the next generation, and that is through one's relatives. My brother shares half of my variable genes, so that each of his children carries half as much of my genetic inheritance as one of my own children. Because genetic fitness must include these relatives, the idea of **inclusive fitness** (Hamilton, 1964) means that the success of my relatives increases the fitness of my own genes in proportion to the closeness of the relation. Inclusive fitness explains an otherwise incomprehensible statement, "I'd lay down my life for five cousins and a brother." In genetic terms, each cousin shares one eighth of your genes, and the brother one half, so together this group of relatives possesses more of your genes than you do.

This applies only to the 2.5 million variable base pairs, of course—for the rest of the 3 billion base pairs, it doesn't matter how many children one has, for everyone in the next generation will have the same alleles of those genes in any case. Alternatively, some genes are represented by several alleles that are equally effective in doing their job, so that there is no advantage of having one allele over another.

Mutation Versus Recombination. There are two ways that DNA can change to produce individuals of particularly high fitness. One is by **mutation**—a cosmic ray, a poison from the environment, or a mistake in DNA replication can change a base pair at random, thus modifying the protein that is eventually produced. Usually, the mistake makes things worse, because it took billions of years to get it right in the first place, and the unfortunate possessor of the mutated gene has a lower fitness. We have molecular DNA repair mechanisms to keep these changes to a minimum.

Once in a great while, however, a lucky accident occurs, and the mutation creates a protein that does its job better, increasing the fitness of its possessor. The mutation that reduced the skin pigment melanin in our northern European is an example. Then the altered gene can spread through the population because of the greater fitness of its possessors. Statistically, each of us has a small number of mutations, usually affecting less than 20 out of our thousands of genes, and most of them don't have dire consequences one way or the other.

The second way that fitness can be changed is by **recombination** of existing genes. In sexual recombination, it is possible for two or more genes from the two parents to cooperate, working together in new ways. And the genes get reshuffled in every generation. Because most human traits are influenced by more than one gene, this mechanism allows for a healthier or more capable individual of greater fitness. The process is much faster than mutations at changing fitnesses, for nature does not have to wait for the right mutations to come along. As soon as the right gene combination appears, the inheritor of that combination can have increased fitness (more children) right away, and the children who inherit that combination of genes will also be more successful. Again, the combination will tend to spread through the population, and evolution will take place.

The process of gene change in a population, driven by natural selection, takes a very long time, because the change in fitness that a particular gene or gene combination imparts is usually very small. There might be only a tiny chance of raising an extra child because of a beneficial gene combination, or a small chance of raising one child fewer because of an unlucky combination or mutation. The small influence of the gene or genes might take many generations to make its influence felt in the population as a whole. The influence will be felt more quickly if the population is small, because the genes do not have to diffuse through very many people to alter the population. As we shall see, this was the case through most of the period of human existence.

The process of change cannot work miracles, though. Each change is very small, compared to the vast number of unchanged genes and gene combinations in each of us. And nature cannot make investments, putting together elaborate combinations of genes to eventually produce a genetic superman or superwoman. The recombinations and mutations have to succeed in every generation, or at least not get in the way, to contribute to the next. If it turned out that a totally different body plan would serve us better (for instance, four legs and two arms), we would simply be out of luck, for that radical a change is too much for evolution to manage. We shall see in later chapters that many human traits are clumsy constructions that are more or less functional, but could have been done better. In the words of Richard Dawkins (1986), evolution is a "blind watchmaker" putting things together at random and keeping what works.

All of these ideas—influence of genes on human traits, variable fitness resulting from those traits, resulting changes in gene frequency, and the biological mechanisms that drive these changes—sum into a set of concepts called **evolutionary theory**, the application of evolutionary ideas to understanding the design of organisms. Because according to evolutionary principles most of our traits are adaptations that best fit us to our environments, evolutionary theory tells the story of the acquisition and modification of those traits during the course of human evolution. The design of the human organism is based on thousands of adapted traits, some affecting the body and others affecting behavior, each tuned by thousands of generations of natural selection.

● GENETIC MECHANISMS OF EVOLUTION

The processes that we have examined so far belong to "classical" mechanisms of genetic change, those described by Gregor Johann Mendel in the 19th century (he knew about the combinatory processes, but not about the molecular mechanisms). Geneticists have identified several other mechanisms and properties of gene change, however, that can alter the rules in ways that are sometimes surprising.

Genetic Drift

Normally, it is small differences in biological fitness that drive changes in the gene frequencies of a population. But luck is involved as well. Suppose, for instance, that one of your relatives inherits a supereffective combination of genes that makes them likely to have a large and prosperous family. From there, the superior genes should spread rapidly through the population. Just before reaching adulthood, though, your superperson relative is hit by a truck in a tragic but random accident. The gene combination, and its high fitness potential, is lost to the population.

In a small population, the process can also work the other way. Some random trait that doesn't affect fitness, such as long earlobes or a particular shape of nose, might spread through a population by a series of lucky reproductive accidents. The process can even work for slightly disadvantageous genes. Humans may have lost their capacity to synthesize vitamin C in this way, for instance. The phenomenon, **genetic drift,** does not depend on Darwinian fitness but only on chance. It turns out that genetic drift can work only in very small, reproductively isolated groups; if a group grows from a few dozen to even a few hundred reproducing individuals, the mathematics quickly become hopeless, and drift no longer has much effect. The likelihood of any trait spreading at random becomes vanishingly small.

Linking of Traits

A quirk of genetics generates another exception to the rule that nature tends to select genes that confer increased fitness on their owners. Ideally, genes are reassorted randomly in each new individual, so that each gene is favored by natural selection to the degree that it increases overall fitness. But we already saw that those genes that happen to be located close together on the same chromosome are more likely to be inherited from the same strand of DNA, contributed by one parent. This means that if a gene is particularly useful, endowing its owner with increased fitness, the genes near it on its chromosome will tend to be selected as well. These hitchhiking genes may be neutral, or even slightly harmful, but they will continue to spread in a population if the **linking** is strong and if the benefits of the "good" gene outweigh the costs of the "bad" ones. They come along for the ride in a kind of genetic coattail effect.

Fixation

Sometimes a gene becomes so common due to either natural selection superiority or genetic drift that it replaces all the other alleles of the gene that formerly existed in a population. Now that gene no longer shares any of the 2.5 million variable base pairs, but is made up from the 3 billion that are immune from selection pressures. It is no longer a quirk of some people that is not shared by others, but becomes one of the design features of the human species. The now-frozen trait is **fixated**; the species is committed to it, and the only way to change it is through mutation. To know the number of eyes a person has, for instance, I don't have to know their talents, penchants, tendencies, abilities, vocations, or the race of their ancestors. Because this is a fixated trait, all of those things are irrelevant. The person will have exactly two eyes, no more and no less, no matter what.

Most human traits are fixated in this way: only a relatively small number of traits, and the genes behind them, are free to vary. Whether a trait seems fixated or not can depend on the reference group; if you are Chinese, for example, black hair is a universal and fixated trait. At the beginning of human evolution, when there were probably only a few hundred of us, many traits might have become fixated by chance.

It is possible that the turned-down nose of humans, for instance, became fixated from the many variations presumably present in the common ancestor of chimps and humans. A few modern chimp noses look rather like human noses, whereas most look quite different. The range of variation in human noses, like the variation in human genes, is much smaller than that in chimpanzees.

Other traits began as fixated but later acquired variability. It is the variable traits that give humanity its diversity. Hair color, earlobes, eye color, curliness of hair, and shape of the nose are some of the obvious traits that can vary. Perhaps more important are variations in hidden properties, such as capabilities of the immune system or of the brain that give us different mixtures of health, temperament, intelligence, and personality.

There are actually two ways that a trait can be fixated. It can either be controlled by genes for which there is only one allele in all humans, or the trait can be controlled by one of a family of genes that all produce the same result, a phenomenon called **canalization**. Several genetic paths all produce the same phenotype. Particularly important traits are sometimes coded redundantly in the genome, so that if you don't get the trait from one gene, you will get it from another. If the environment varies, one group of these genes or another will guarantee that you express the trait. The strict definition of canalization requires that different genotypes all lead to the same phenotype on the canalized trait. As evolution makes sure that everyone gets the vital traits, they become canalized along with a host of incidental traits.

Punctuated Equilibrium

Darwin thought of evolution as a long, continuous process, with populations constantly evolving into new forms in response to new challenges. Because fossil remains of extinct species are few and far between, it seemed in Darwin's day that every fossil that was found represented a unique stage in a continuous evolutionary process. Now that the fossil record is much better known, some exceptional locations have been discovered where we have an almost continuous record of fossils reaching back for millions of years.

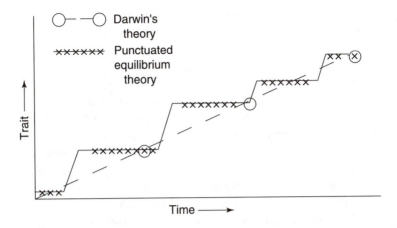

Figure 1.5   Comparison of Darwin's conception and punctuated equilibrium theory. The trait on the vertical axis might be the size of an animal, the complexity of its brain, or some other feature.

An example of such a record is in several African lakes, where small aquatic snails leave their shells on the lake bottom when they die. Some lakes have layers of shells many meters thick, so that biologists can study the forms and colorations of the shells over thousands of successive generations. Not surprisingly, the shells changed as the snails evolved over millions of years. But the change was not continuous. Instead, the snails remained identical from one generation to the next over many generations. Then, abruptly, a new form would replace the old one, and it too would go unchanged for a long period (Figure 1.5). Most of the time the species was not changing. Then for some reason—random genetic events, a new predator, climate change, or some other challenge from the environment—the species quickly evolved into a new form.

During the periods of stability, the snails were in equilibrium with their environment. The most successful alleles of every gene were the most common ones, and any deviation was selected against. The exceptional periods, when evolution was changing the characteristics of the snails, were short compared to the periods of equilibrium, so the periods of rapid evolution were colorfully termed **punctuated equilibrium** (Eldredge, 1985). Even the punctuations, though, might last hundreds or thousands of generations, and are still very gradual when one looks from one generation to the next. The punctuations seem abrupt only in relation to the millions of years that the snails have existed unchanged. During equilibrium, which is most of the time, natural selection does not cease. It continues as vigorously as ever, but now it serves only to maintain the existing form, weeding out deviants.

Punctuation and the Tyranny of the Average

What does all this have to do with the human situation? It means that most human traits are in a state of equilibrium, where the mean of the population also reflects the greatest biological fitness. One can argue about whether humans are evolving at present; but even during a period of punctuation, only a few of an organism's traits change while the rest remain stable. So this means that most, perhaps all, of our traits are at an equilibrium where the average trait is also the best adapted one.

Here, evolutionary theory leads to a startling and counterintuitive conclusion: it is not the exceptional person who is the most fit, but the most average. Though this conclusion violates many peoples' intuition, it is easy to prove. Suppose for a moment that people who are exceptional in a certain trait, say high intelligence, are more biologically fit than people of average intelligence. Intelligent people would leave more offspring in each succeeding generation, until the intelligent people dominated and they became the new average of the population. After that, it would be people of average intelligence (intelligent children of their successful intelligent parents) who would have the greatest fitness. Now the tables are turned—people more intelligent than the new average will have so many problems that their extra intelligence will reduce their fitness relative to those of the new average intelligence. So it is with all traits: the population evolves until the traits that yield the greatest fitness are also the average of the population. When the population reaches equilibrium, the average confers the best fitness.

Empirical Tests of Punctuation in Humans

Because the predictions of this theory seem so peculiar, it is important to investigate it empirically. A theory is useful if it predicts things we otherwise wouldn't have thought to look for, or explains things that otherwise seem mysterious. In this case, a demonstration of the consequences of equilibrium theory comes from studies of physical attractiveness. People are quite consistent in rating the physical attractiveness of others, even from photographs, a capability that is culturally universal (Richardson, Goodman, Nastorf, & Dornbusch, 1961). We might expect some exceptional people to be judged as particularly beautiful, people far from average. This idea can be tested.

In one study, a group of college students judged the attractiveness of a group of women, on a scale of 1 to 10, from photographs in their college yearbook. Then the psychologists running the study used a program to combine faces together, a process called *morphing* in computer graphics. They morphed 2, 4, 8, and more faces together. When they got up to a composite of 32 faces, they presented the resulting image to the original judges and had them judge that face also. The result was that the composite face was judged to be more attractive than any of the faces that were morphed into it (Cunningham, 1986). As you can imagine, the experiment caused an uproar when it first appeared, but the result has been replicated (Langlois & Roggman, 1990) and appears to be solid.

How can this be? According to punctuated equilibrium theory, the average traits should be the most desirable because they confer the highest fitness, and we would expect humans to be most attracted to partners with the highest potential fitness. Thus the theory predicts that people with the highest attractiveness should not be the unusual, but the most average. And when you look at the morphed composite (Figure 1.6), you may find her to be quite attractive, just as the subjects in the study did. Alas, you will never meet her. She exists only in a computer, a concatenated ideal who is average on more traits than any real person.

This does not mean that the average of any group of people will always be perceived as the most attractive, however. The group from which the sample was taken may have included many people who were not at the peak of their own attractiveness. The average of a group of people in their eighties, for instance, will produce a particularly attractive eighty-year-old. The average appearance can be enhanced by adding features that normally are considered attractive, such as those that signal youth or fertility.

Preferences are one thing, but actual behavior is quite another. Throughout this book, it is important to look beyond perceptions and preferences to see how adapted traits affect human actions. Because punctuated equilibrium predicts that average people should be the most successful reproductively, the theory can be tested by looking at reproductive behavior.

A survey that probed both the number of children a woman had and her socioeconomic status (SES) showed that the highest-status women were not the most successful reproductively (Hewlett, 2002). In the United States in the 1990s, one third of high-salary career women were still childless at age 40. The lowest-SES women were also less successful, because of higher mortality in the poorest groups. The women with the largest proportion of surviving children were those who did not go to college, but who married working-class men and started their families early. It was not the highest- or the lowest-SES women, but a group somewhere in the middle that was most successful reproductively, just as punctuated equilibrium theory predicts.

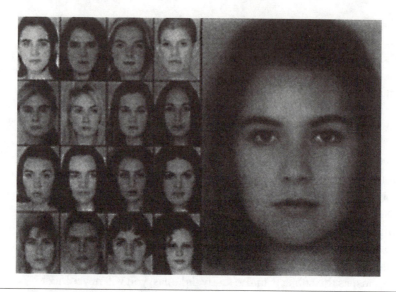

Figure 1.6   Effect of morphing many female faces together. The large photo is a computer-generated composite of all the faces in the small photos.

Exceptional success in education or careers does not necessarily translate into Darwinian fitness.

The average-is-best property, of course, applies only during periods of equilibrium. A population in a period of punctuation is a population in crisis, when the dominant traits are not the best ones, and exceptional individuals are being selected. For modern humans, such a crisis occurred over a period of probably tens of thousands of years, ending about 100,000 years ago.

Sexual Selection

Evolution normally selects traits that enhance an organism's ability to cope with its environment. Adaptations such as good visual acuity, fine motor coordination, and ability to work with a group can clearly evolve by natural selection, because people who are strong in those traits are more likely to survive and prosper than those who are weaker in the traits. In order to pass the genes supporting these traits along to the next generation, however, an organism must jump one more hurdle—it must find a mate and reproduce. Mating becomes the final common path through which all the other traits, good or bad, are funneled. Without a mate and a successful reproduction, all the other traits count for nothing.

Charles Darwin recognized the need for **sexual selection**, the selection of animals that successfully reproduce. It generates an exception to the rule that adapted traits should enhance the ability of an animal to survive, because sexual adaptations are directed toward the preferences of potential mates rather than toward the challenges of the environment.

We chuckle at the male peacock, with its absurd overdevelopment of tail feathers that evolved to attract the peahen. Because the peahen is attracted to the male with the biggest and most colorful display, the males with the most elaborate displays are the most successful in mating. The destabilizing factor is that, given the choice, the hen prefers not the average display but the biggest and gaudiest (Houle & Kondrashov, 2002).

The biggest display signals the best genes. Eventually, nature sets a limit on the size of the display when the male can no longer fly and is easily caught by predators before it can transfer its genes to the next generation. So the peacock's display becomes as large as nature can contrive, driven by the female's preference for large displays.

Ridiculous though the peacock example may seem, humans have some similar characteristics. When asked to pick which female profile is most attractive, for example, men generally pick a profile with larger-than-average breasts, violating the rule from punctuated equilibrium theory that the average should be preferred. We don't know how much this is a product of current fashion, or whether the same preference would have appeared 1,000 or 10,000 years ago, but we have no reason to suppose that a survey of our distant ancestors would have turned out very differently.

This brings up two questions. First, why do men prefer larger breasts? One answer is that large breasts are a sign of sexual maturity, and it is better to be sure about that than to rely on subtle signs. Second, given that large breasts are preferred, why don't women evolve larger breasts? Again there is a compensating factor, for it is impractical to carry them around, especially for a Paleolithic nomad, so the benefit of large breasts in sexual attraction is balanced against their cost in energy and agility. Nature finds a compromise, of course with individual variation as well.

In the spirit of equality, consider a similar example that goes the other way. Women prefer men who are taller than average. We can explore this preference not only through surveys but even by analysis of personal advertisements in newspapers (women seeking men). When a preferred height is mentioned, a woman almost always requests a taller-than-average partner (Pawlowski, Dunbar, & Lipowicz, 2000). Furthermore, height is correlated somewhat with status in men.

Does all this make a difference in reproductive success? There is now evidence that it does. A survey of Polish and British men revealed that on average, the taller men in both cultures had more children than shorter ones. Furthermore, childless men averaged 3 cm (1.2 in.) shorter than men with at least one child, and bachelors averaged about 2.5 cm (1 in.) shorter than married men. Pawlowski, Dunbar, and Lipowicz (2000), who did the research, undertook the study after they noticed that men in personal ads (men seeking women) advertised their height only if they were tall.

If this is so, why doesn't natural selection make men taller and taller, until the tall men are average? The answer again is a compromise, this time between the desirability of height and the practicality of balancing on two legs, which limits the height of men. Almost all of the tallest men have trouble with their knees before retirement age, and there are circulatory problems as well. So again, a sexual preference that deviates from the average keeps a trait pushed against a ceiling, in this case almost literally.

This doesn't necessarily mean that humans are evolving to be taller, though. To be exceptionally tall means that everything during development has to have gone right, including inheriting reasonably appropriate genes, an unproblematic pregnancy, optimal nutrition as a child, and so on. A tall phenotype isn't dependent entirely on a tall genotype.

Though some cross-cultural work has been done on these questions, most of the studies investigate European populations. A broader sample of cultures would strengthen and generalize the conclusions.

Sexual selection, like other kinds of selection, has always been a part of human life. The beginning of humanity ushered in the **Paleolithic** era, or *old stone age* (Greek *paleo* = old, Greek *lithic* = stone), a world so different from today's human environments that it is difficult even to imagine what life must have been like then. But because it is the world to which humans are adapted, we will have to examine it closely to understand what we are like. This is the subject of the next chapter.

● DISCUSSION QUESTIONS

1. Why do you think some scholars resist the idea that biological structure and evolution are important in understanding human life?
2. Is the present human population evolving? If so, how?
3. If natural selection tends to optimize traits, why do we have strange characteristics such as sweat glands that let us drip with sweat (wasting water) and excrete salt (wasting salt)?

FURTHER READING ●

Alcock, J. (2001). *The triumph of sociobiology.* Oxford, UK: Oxford University Press.

John Alcock, a leading expert in Darwinism and animal behavior, explains why there was so much objection to E. O. Wilson's book *Sociobiology.* Many rejected Wilson's ideas not because they were demonstrably wrong, but because the moral implications were uncomfortable. Alcock dissects moral from scientific knowledge, asserting that those who would improve moral behavior should first understand its basis.

Darwin, C. (1859). *On the origin of species.* London: Murray.

The founding book of evolution by natural selection is still in print, still readable, and still fascinating in the power of its insights and the wealth of the evidence that Darwin assembles in defense of his theory.

Tooby, J., & Cosmides, L. (1992). The psychological foundations of culture. In J. Barkow, L. Cosmides, & J. Tooby (Eds.), *The Adapted Mind*. New York: Oxford University Press.

Two leaders of evolutionary psychology lay out the SSSM, its shortcomings, and the alternative that evolutionary theory offers. The article appears in a volume that has become the bible of evolutionary psychology.

Wilson, E. O. (1975) *Sociobiology: The new synthesis.* Cambridge, MA: Harvard University Press.

Edward O. Wilson's masterful synthesis of material on the biological basis of social behavior founded a new discipline and is still worth reading. It links psychology with animal ethology, enriching both disciplines.

CHAPTER 2

THE PAST

95% of Human History

"The secrets of evolution are death and time."

— Carl Sagan (1980)

Like other creatures, humans are adapted to the environment in which they evolved. Unlike other creatures, though, we do not live in that environment. In fact, contemporary humans live in environments so different from our Paleolithic beginnings that it is a difficult intellectual and archeological challenge to reconstruct that world and the pressures that made us what we are. To understand what life was like for the founders of our species, we must look back farther yet, to the split between the evolutionary line that led to humans and the line that led to chimpanzees.

● PHYLOGENETIC ORIGINS

Humans have been on a distinct evolutionary track for about 6 million years, the time when the last common ancestors of both modern humans and modern chimpanzees flourished (Corballis, 1999). Differences between ourselves and the chimpanzee can provide insight to what must have happened after the two species split. First, humans prefer environments that are different from those in which chimpanzees live; the chimpanzee dwells in dense tropical rain forest, whereas humans generally prefer a dryer, cooler, more open habitat.

This difference reflects changes in the African climate about 6 million years ago. While a series of ice sheets was advancing in Eurasia and North America, the ice ages brought cooler and dryer weather to tropical Africa. Rain forests gave way to grassy savannas on much of the continent, and the ancestors of humans began to venture from the forest onto the plains. Or, more likely, the forest gradually became dryer and sparser, and the animals there adapted without venturing anywhere. A part of the ancestral species stayed in the forest and evolved into our nearest living relatives, while another part went through a series of stages, perhaps evolutionary punctuations, on the way to becoming modern humans.

Because evolution cannot think ahead, it is a mistake to think of these intermediate species as steps along a pathway, or experiments that didn't come out quite right until we arrived. It just happened that our species became a product of a series of evolutionary events, just as other species can look back on long evolutionary histories of their own. The structure of **hominid** (human-like ape) evolution is more like a bush than a ladder, with many extinct species on the branches. And all the various species of hominids that preceded us existed for much longer stretches of time than modern humans have so far. So if you want to know whether modern humans are a more successful species than their now-extinct hominid predecessors, ask me again in a million years.

Our knowledge of hominid evolution in the distant past is fragmentary, and probably will always remain so. Fossil finds are few and far between, for it is a vanishingly rare event that preserves the bones of a primate for millions of years. We don't get a random sample, or even a very large sample, and we are still at a stage where a single fossil find can reorganize our ideas about prehuman evolution. Think of a future anthropologist trying to reconstruct our own society a million years from now, with only a pelvis and perhaps a couple of Christmas tree ornaments to go on. We would become the "glass-bulb people," and the anthropologist wouldn't have much chance of reconstructing what our lives were like. So all the theories about prehuman evolution and lifestyle are somewhat uncertain, open to contradiction and controversy. All the numbers in this chapter are approximate, and many are in dispute.

Australopithecus

The first hominid species that we know about, called **Australopithecus** (southern ape), emerged from the forests more than 4 million years ago.

Bipedality

Ever since Darwin's time, paleontologists have puzzled over which of the unique human adaptations came first—was it the large brain, the upright stance, the reliance on tools? Now we have the answer, for the brain of *Australopithecus* wasn't much bigger than that of a chimpanzee. But the creature stood upright (Jablonski & Chaplin, 1993). Otherwise, it was very like the modern pigmy chimpanzee (bonobo) in size and proportions (Figure 2.1).

Australopithecus was a slight creature, about 1.1 meters tall, two thirds the height of modern humans, and it walked with its knees slightly bent, not quite like us. It was a fairly successful species in its time, though, ranging widely through tropical and subtropical Africa, radiating into several varieties, and enduring for more than a million years.

The early **bipedal** (Latin *bi* = two, *ped* = foot) apes paid a big price for their two-legged gait. Walking on two legs is not as efficient as walking on four; bipedal locomotion is among the slowest ways for vertebrates to get around. It wasn't until humans took to bicycles that they became more efficient at locomotion than their **quadruped** (Latin *quad* = four) ancestors. Even standing is a major feat, for both human and *Australopithecus* are unstable in any two-legged posture. Their brains must compensate for their inherent postural instability.

These simple facts of physiology had complex implications for lifestyle and technology. For one thing, because a two-legged creature cannot outrun other animals of similar size, either predators or prey, even quadrupeds smaller than *Australopithecus* would have been able to catch it.

Technology and Culture

To survive in its open woodland and savanna environment, then, the puny *Australopithecus* must have relied on technology, and on the brains and creativity necessary to support it. The technology was nearly nonexistent by modern standards, perhaps nothing more than thrown rocks and sharpened sticks, but it was enough to make bipedalism worthwhile. This modest human-ape attacked and escaped not only with its legs but also with its tools. Because both chimpanzees and humans hunt when they can, it is likely that *Australopithecus* hunted too, developing the necessary technology along the way.

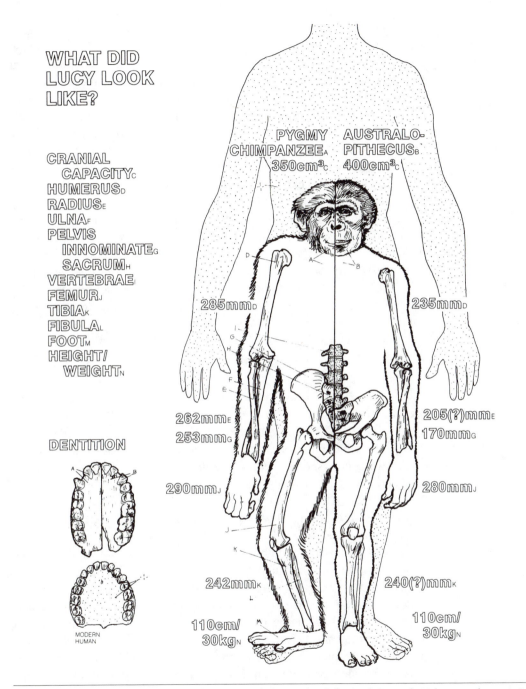

WHAT DID LUCY LOOK LIKE?

CRANIAL
    CAPACITY_C
HUMERUS_D
RADIUS_E
ULNA_F
PELVIS
    INNOMINATE_G
    SACRUM_H
VERTEBRAE_I
FEMUR_J
TIBIA_K
FIBULA_L
FOOT_M
HEIGHT/
    WEIGHT_N

DENTITION

PYGMY CHIMPANZEE_A
350cm³_C

AUSTRALO-PITHECUS_B
400cm³_C

285mm_D
235mm_D

262mm_E
253mm_G
205(?)mm_E
170mm_G

290mm_J
280mm_J

242mm_K
240(?)mm_K

110cm/ 30kg_N
110cm/ 30kg_N

MODERN HUMAN

Figure 2.1   The modern pigmy chimpanzee is on the left, *and Australopithecus afarensis* is on the right. Arrows show modifications in the skeleton of *Australopithecus*: a flattened pelvis that held the viscera and anchored the upper leg muscles, a turned-in knee, and a turned-out toe. Human proportions are represented in the background (from A. Zihlman et al.).

If *Australopithecus* gave up so much for bipedalism, what did it gain? There are some minor advantages in heat budgets, for an upright animal casts a smaller shadow than a quadruped in the tropical midday sun. But all the other successful mammals of the African savanna are four-legged walkers, so this advantage does not appear to be decisive. A more important benefit is that bipedalism frees the hands for other things—carrying tools, food, babies. These new capabilities benefited *Australopithecus* more than the loss of the forelimbs for locomotion. From that time to this, evolution has pressed the advantage of technology, guided by the brain and expressed through the hands, over brute force. Once this step was taken, the evolutionary pressure for bigger brains became tremendous.

The first variety of *Australopithecus* to appear in the fossil record, *Australopithecus afarensis*, had a brain of about 400 cc, only slightly larger than that of a chimpanzee. Later, a larger and heavier form appeared, *Australopithecus robustus*. Probably specialized as a tuber-eating vegetarian, with huge grinding teeth and a heavy jaw, it became extinct without leaving any successors, at least none that have been discovered. Another more lightly built omnivorous variety, *Australopithecus Africanus*, was probably the ancestor of the next hominids. In *Africanus* the brain grew to 460 cc while the body remained about the same size.

Homo Habilis

The next big jump, or at least the next big jump that we know about, came with a new species, **Homo habilis** (handy man). These creatures appeared about 2.2 million years ago in Africa (Hill, Ward, Deino, Curtis, & Drake, 1992). Their brains were nearly twice as large as those of *Australopithecus*, around 700-750 cc, about half as large as the brains of modern humans (McHenry, 1994). But the hands were like modern human hands, with opposable thumbs and modern proportions. Essentially, today we walk around with the hands (and feet) of *Homo habilis*.

The teeth of *Homo habilis* were less massive than those of their predecessors, but more massive than those of modern humans. The fact that teeth were evolving to become smaller means that these creatures were beginning to prepare their food with hands and tools as well as teeth. How could smaller teeth confer an advantage to a creature living in the harsh African savanna? Smaller teeth would require less energy to grow, and less calcium from a pregnant mother, but they would be a death warrant if *Homo habilis* had not already begun to use tools to prepare food. The food preparation, which we cannot see in the fossil record, had to come before the reduction in tooth size, which we can see. From this point, behavioral adaptations for using tools and physical adaptations of the teeth could evolve together, an example of **co-evolution**. In co-evolution, change in one characteristic creates adaptive pressure to change another, which in turn allows more change in the first, in a cycle of adaptation.

Here it is humbling to recall that about 2% of our genes differentiate us from chimpanzees. So the differences between us and the extinct ape-people would have been even smaller. It is tantalizing, but forever out of reach, to understand how we would relate to such beings—as animals, as people, as something else? Perhaps it is significant that none of the major monotheistic religions arose in areas where apes are common. The similarity of the humans with souls and the apes without would have seemed too great, the dividing line too arbitrary.

Technology and Culture

Homo habilis had more than brains. They also had tools and the first recognizable style of stone tool manufacture (Semaw et al., 1997). Our impression of the technology of early prehumans is distorted because we see only what was durable, but surely they were no more concerned with their fossil record than we are. *Homo habilis* probably had an array of wood, bark, and grass tools and possessions, but we know nothing of them. Stone tools are permanent by accident, used because of their hardness but valued by us for the glimpse they allow into the minds of our distant ancestors.

The stone tools of *Homo habilis* come mostly from Olduvai in east Africa. They are little more than pebbles with a few flakes chipped off, just enough to make a sharp edge (Figure 2.2). The resulting tool was the right size to hold in the hand. The tools seem improvised, without characteristic shapes, and with little in common except a technique of flaking away bits of rock until a sharp edge emerged where two flaked surfaces met. And the technology did not change for a million years.

Homo Erectus

The next punctuation in our evolutionary history appears not just in Africa but throughout the old world. The remains of ***Homo erectus*** were first discovered in Java; then earlier fossils were found in Europe, Africa, and Asia. *Homo erectus* was the first of the hominids to expand out of Africa. The *erectus* brain was about 1,000 cc, two thirds as large as that of modern humans. They had tall, lean builds with long legs, much like our own (Rightmire, 1990).

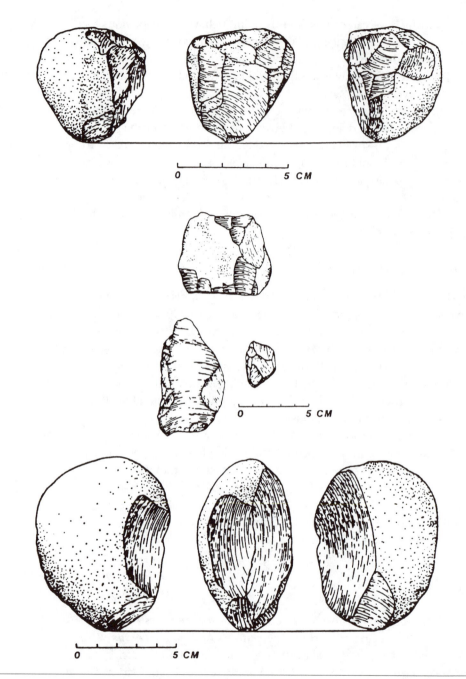

Figure 2.2 Stone tools made and used by *Homo habilis*. There is little standardization of style or function.

Homo erectus first appeared in Africa about 1.9 million years ago, on the savannas where other early species of *Homo* have been found. Their mastery of a more complex tool technology, and perhaps social innovations, enabled them to spread where other early hominids could not. It is probably technology that enabled *Homo erectus* to escape the tropics as well as to leave Africa. Remains found in Europe and in northern China mean that shelter had become an essential part of the *erectus* lifestyle, and some sites are associated with fire. For *erectus* is decidedly a tropical animal, as we are, biologically adapted for a hot climate. Tropical animals tend to be thin, gangly, and long-legged, whereas animals biologically adapted to colder climates are more compact and efficiently insulated. The fact that *Homo erectus* was able to invade cold climates with a tropical body meant that they had to bring the tropics with them, in the form of clothing, shelter, and fire. I like to think of *erectus* as almost-human, closer to humans than to apes in every way.

What was the mind of *Homo erectus* like? Were they small-brained humans, or was there something more apelike about them? Some answers to these questions about the hominid mind have come not from study of their brains but from their teeth. It has recently become possible to examine the ages of teeth by examining thin sections of the teeth under an electron microscope. Daily incremental markings within the enamel, each only a few molecules thick, allow researchers to determine the age of fossil teeth in the same way that botanists can count tree rings to find the ages of trees. The age of the teeth can then be compared with the maturity of the rest of the skeleton. Of 13 fossil tooth fragments studied, ranging from the earliest *Australopithecus* that lived roughly 4 million years ago to early members of the *Homo* genus that lived about 1.5 million years ago, none showed the slower pattern of modern human enamel growth (Dean et al., 2001). *Homo erectus,* like ape species, including chimpanzees and gorillas, matured in just 11 or 12 years.

The stone tools of *Homo erectus* are more elaborate and better made than those of *Homo habilis* (Figure 2.3). They are carefully constructed, with long sharp edges on both sides, and they are symmetrical, as though made from a detailed mental plan (Tattersall, 1995). These tools do not appear until hundreds of thousands of years after the first appearance of *erectus* in the fossil record. But again, once established, the stone tool style remained frozen until *Homo erectus* was replaced by *Homo sapiens*. The nonhuman hominids appear to have had the intelligence to make and use tools, but possessed limited aptitude for innovation. Compared to ours, their worlds must have seemed static and unchanging.

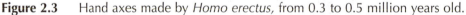

100 millimeters

Figure 2.3   Hand axes made by *Homo erectus,* from 0.3 to 0.5 million years old.

Out of Africa

The migrations of *Homo erectus* might lead us to characterize these beings as wanderers, driven to explore new territory and to settle unoccupied land. The reality would have been much less exciting. The migrations out of Africa might have occurred in as little as 0.1 million years, just a blip in the 6-million year sweep of prehuman evolution. But that 0.1 million is 100,000 years, a very long time compared to the distances traveled. The 10,000 km treks to distant China and Java might have averaged about 0.1 km, or 100 meters, per year. At this rate, in each 15-year generation *erectus* might have established themselves another 1-1/2 km down the trail, about a 15-minute walk. (*erectus* would have walked about as well as we do.) To the individuals involved, it would not have been perceived as a migration at all. The same applies to many of the vast "migrations" of early humans.

Why did *Homo erectus* move for such vast distances? Though we will never be certain, one possibility is that population pressure forced these hominids to expand their range. Even favorable land in the tropics cannot support a high density of large hominids, and their simple technology meant that some food sources that are available to us would not be available to them. Thus a small population could fill the limited space of the tropical savannas, forcing migrations to other regions.

About 950,000 years ago, disaster struck the *Homo erectus* population. The onset of an ice age split the dispersed population into three isolated groups, one in Africa, one in Europe, and one in east Asia. The African group eventually evolved into modern humans, and the European group into Neanderthals, while the Asian group became extinct (Asfaw et al., 2002). *Homo erectus* endured in Java until sometime between 27,000 and 53,000 years ago (the uncertainty comes from archaeological dating methods), certainly over-lapping with modern humans (Swisher, Curtis, Jacob, Getty, & Widiasmoro, 1994). Whether the two species ever met face-to-face, we do not know.

Neanderthal

Over a century ago, shortly after Darwin's book *On the Origin of Species* was published, a German schoolteacher found some human-looking bones while on an outing. He alerted the authorities, and eventually a local paleon-tologist found the bones to be human-like but not quite human. The bones were much heavier than those of modern humans, and there were other dif-ferences as well—projecting brow ridges, a long thick skull, and massive pro-truding jaws. The species was named after the valley of the Neander River, where the bones were found. **Homo Neanderthalensis** (German *Thal* or *Tal* = valley) is the best known of the extinct hominids, and perhaps the greatest mystery. This is not an ape-human or a primitive form, but a dis-tinctly human line with a brain of about 1,500 cc, as large as ours, perhaps slightly larger. The slow maturation of its teeth, a pattern that it shares only with modern humans, shows an 18–20 year growth to maturation (Dean et al., 2001).

The ancestry of the species is somewhat murky. The Neanderthal is the only hominid species that appears not to have evolved in Africa; most of the remains have been found in Europe and the Middle East. The range of the species extended in a broad belt from what is now France and Spain in the West to central Asia in the East. The earliest remains are about 230,000 years old, though earlier finds that have some Neanderthal characteristics have been found in southern Europe and dated at 300,000 to 400,000 years ago.

Anatomical Specializations

Most of the history of hominid evolution has been a movement away from specialization toward more generalized forms, creatures able to specialize with technology rather than with biology. The Neanderthals seem to be an exception to this rule, clearly specialized for cold climates. Modern humans breathe through their mouths when exercising heavily, a good strategy for a small-nosed creature breathing warm air. But Neanderthals, with larger noses, could always breathe cold air with the protection of their larger nasal passages (Schwartz & Tattersall, 1996). Their limbs were short, like those of other cold-adapted animals, and their muscles strong and heavily used. Many Neanderthal skeletons show signs of wear and injury, indicating that they led hard lives. Some of the remains show bone fractures that healed during life, suggesting an energetic but risky way of life, as well as some care for the injured.

There are other unique Neanderthal adaptations. Because their birth canal is wider than the human's, Neanderthals may have had a longer gestational period than **Homo sapiens** (modern humans), perhaps a year in duration. This specialization would have made the infants more capable at birth and might have improved survival in severe climates, but it also would have lowered the reproductive capacity of the species.

Culture

The lifestyle of *Homo Neanderthalensis* was adapted to ice age conditions. They hunted large animals, and often lived in cold areas that offered few or no edible plants. Recent investigations suggest that they ate mostly meat, a conclusion drawn from analysis of isotope ratios in 28,000-year-old Neanderthal bones from a cave in Croatia (Richards et al., 2000). Animals and plants absorb carbon and nitrogen in different ways, each leaving a characteristic ratio of their isotopes in the bones of the animals that eat them. The ratios show that Neanderthals obtained more than 90% of their protein from meat. Modern humans, in contrast, are more omnivorous and have more varied diets; modern Europeans eat about 12% meat. The only exceptions occur in extreme northern tundra and ice sheet environments, where Eskimos (Inuit), Lapps, and other far northern groups ate mostly meat well into historical times. Some still do.

The Neanderthal diet, higher on the food chain, meant that most environments could support a density of *Homo Neanderthalensis* only a fraction as large as that of *Homo sapiens*. Neanderthal bands as a result had to be smaller than *Homo sapiens* bands, usually fewer than 25 individuals.

The Neanderthal tool kit, called Mousterian after the place where the first finds were described, consisted of finer stone tools than other hominids possessed, including tools adapted for wooden handles. But again there was practically no change in the technology through the life of the species, except for the use of human-like tools (possibly traded) toward the end of the Neanderthal era. There is a little evidence of what appears to be jewelry, animal teeth with holes drilled in them, and shells with grooves for attaching to a necklace (Figure 2.4). Some Neanderthals buried their dead, preferentially in an east-west orientation (Bradshaw, 1997).

Like other protohuman and early human groups, the Neanderthals were nomads; their shelters appear to be simple windbreaks with brush or hide coverings, sometimes supplemented with stone or bone. Though we sometimes think of these groups as "cavemen," they probably used caves only rarely. Caves are dark and damp, and there simply aren't enough of them to go around, in any case. They are more likely than other sites to offer conditions in which remains are preserved, though, so a lot of what we know of Neanderthals and other early hominids comes from cave sites. Sometimes Neanderthals improved their caves by paving wet areas, and they also built stone walls, rock circles, and hearths (Hayden, 1993).

Very close relatives of ourselves, the Neanderthals seem to show all the human characteristics in some degree. We don't even know whether they possessed language, though there are strong arguments on both sides of the issue. If they did have language, their anatomy limited them to fewer sounds than *Homo sapiens* can produce. There is some evidence of planning, abstraction, art, and human compassion, but the Neanderthal life was everywhere nasty, brutish, and short. Few individuals survived beyond their forties, with high mortality at every age. About half the skeletons that have been found at archaeological sites are of children younger than 12. Everything about them seems heavy, rough, and primitive.

The Fate of the Neanderthals

Did modern humans ever come into contact with Neanderthals? The answer is almost certainly yes. In Europe they overlapped by more than 1,000 years, and in some regions of Southwest Asia they appear to have coexisted for about 40,000 years. During the ice ages the Neanderthals and modern humans may have migrated repeatedly north and south from Europe

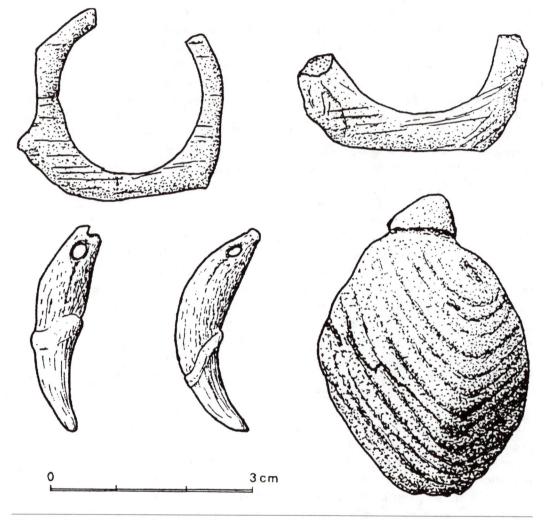

Figure 2.4 Decorative items found together with Neanderthal skeletons. The upper shapes are remains of an ivory ring. The shell has been grooved for attachment.

through the Middle East to Africa, retreating before the glaciers, with the Neanderthals occupying the harsher more northerly climates at any given time (Bunney, 1994). How the two species reacted to one another is a matter for speculation.

The last Neanderthal remains are dated to less than 28,000 years ago in Europe (Straus, 1995). Until recently, there was a controversy about whether they ever did, or could have, interbred with modern humans. We now have the answer, from analysis of Neanderthal and modern human DNA: Gradually accumulating mutations have led to a divergence of the genes of the two species, a divergence that points to a last common ancestor about 600,000 years ago (Ingman, Kaessmann, Pääbo, & Gyllensten, 2000). A date this old means that Neanderthals probably evolved from *Homo erectus*. Modern humans and Neanderthals never interbred, or if they did, the resulting hybrids did not contribute to the present human population.

In their last strongholds, in southern Europe and western Asia, Neanderthals clearly were replaced by modern humans. Organized battles between the two groups were unlikely, however—even 1,000 years of contact requires a measure of peaceful coexistence. It is more probable that *Homo sapiens* simply outcompeted and outbred the Neanderthals. Mathematically, it takes only a tiny reproductive advantage, about 1%, for one population to completely replace the other in the time that the fossil record allows (Lewin, 1993). By 30,000 B.C., bands of *Homo sapiens,* migrating out of Africa with superior tools and social organization, were better equipped for survival even on the Neanderthal's home ground.

We should not condemn the Neanderthal as an unsuccessful species, though, for they ranged widely in challenging climates and persisted twice as long as *Homo sapiens* have so far. Even at its height, their population probably never exceeded 100,000, though, and the low population density enforced by their hunting-oriented lifestyle may have prevented them from achieving the cultural takeoff that modern humans experienced. Language and social interaction may have been less useful simply because there were fewer individuals to interact with.

Despite their large brains and a quarter-million years of endurance, Neanderthals never escaped a Paleolithic lifestyle. They never developed metals, permanent settlements, or specialized crafts. One would think that herding would be a natural step for the Neanderthals, but there is no evidence that they ever made this critical advance. Another species did.

Homo Sapiens

The best estimate for the age of the modern human species is about 100,000 years, give or take 50%. It isn't a very exact figure, but it tells us several things. First, we are a very young species, as species go, born just yesterday in geologic time. Second, the figure tells us that even with our geologically tender age, the era of recorded history is only the very end of the human story. We have written records only for the most recent 5% or so of our history as a species, about the last 5,000 years, and for most of that time the records are fragmentary. Most of the expanse of human life is a prehistoric history that we must infer from the remains of people without written records.

Like the other hominids, with the exception of Neanderthal, modern humans evolved in Africa, probably somewhere in south or east Africa. The punctuation event or events that led to modern humans probably occupied several hundred thousand years, a history known only from a handful of bones and teeth from creatures that were very like us but retained some identifiable "primitive" features. The population was probably tiny, a few thousand or perhaps only a few hundred individuals, for most of that period. At first humans were only slightly different from their hominid ancestors in their tools and ways of life, but there was never a static tool kit or a stereotyped human style of stone implements. The tools were varied and finely made from the start.

There are three sources of information about what life was like for the earliest humans. The first is the archeological record of artifacts that our ancestors unintentionally left, both the remains of their settlements and the evidence of their own skeletons. The second source is comparisons with contemporary groups who live somewhat like our early ancestors, though anthropologists have found important differences between ancestral populations and any living groups. The third and most unexpected source of information about our origins comes from examinations of our own bodies and brains, the debris that evolution has left behind in all of us.

Genetic Origins

How do we know who our direct human ancestors were, and where they lived? Many of the answers come from genetic material, the DNA of living humans. Our origin as a species in Africa left behind artifacts in the diversity of human DNA. Genetic mutations gradually build up in an interbreeding population; the longer the population has existed, the more genetic variability accumulates. A population that has existed for a shorter time will have less variability. Thus by measuring the variability in the DNA of human groups, we can estimate the age of the population they came from. The group with the most accumulated variability would be the oldest, and would represent the ancestral population.

If humans originated in Africa, we would expect the rest of the world to have been colonized by originally African groups. The people who migrated out of Africa would have lived in small bands that became reproductively isolated as they moved away from the larger groups that remained behind. Because the migrating bands were small, they would have had less genetic variability than the parent population. Figure 2.5 shows the situation. The

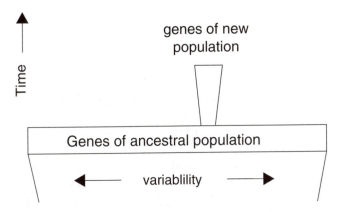

Figure 2.5   The horizontal axis is a measure of the variability, the number of different base pair sequences that individual humans have at selected locations in the genome. The number gradually increases with time, because many mutations are neutral, neither helping nor hindering the mutated individual. The mutations themselves are random events. When a new population divides off from the ancestral population and establishes itself in a new territory, it carries with it only a fraction of the diversity of the original population.

ancestral population has great variability. From that population a small group emerges to colonize a new area. The new group arises from a small segment of the original population, with a correspondingly small variability. Eventually, the descendants of the small group populate the rest of the world. There may have been several successive waves of migration, but each founding band would be more homogeneous genetically than the original African population.

In fact, the genetic structure of the present human population fits this picture. Several studies have found the world's greatest genetic variability in sub-Saharan Africa. Asians, Europeans, and Native American groups all have relatively less variability. The pattern of this variability suggests that small groups of *Homo sapiens* migrating out of Africa as little as 50,000 years ago replaced the other hominids that they found in the rest of the world, without interbreeding with them.

Compared to other species, though, humans remain a remarkably uniform lot. We have much less genetic variability than chimpanzees, for instance. Two randomly selected chimpanzees from neighboring bands are likely to be less genetically like one another than a pair of humans from opposite corners of the earth (Kaessmann, Wiebe, & Pääbo, 1999). Even today, we are a species of more than 6 billion with the genetic diversity of a population of a few thousand.

Eve

To learn more about the ancestral population requires a diversion into the genetic history of cells. The analysis that leads to the African-origin scenario comes both from nuclear DNA, the genetic material found in each cell's nucleus, and from another source of DNA in each cell's **mitochondria**. The mitochondria are organelles within each cell, molecular machines that handle conversion of sugars and oxygen into energy. They are vital to every living cell in every animal and plant. But they began their evolutionary history as free-living, bacteria-like organisms. Perhaps a billion years ago, one of the ancestors of our cells consumed one of the ancestral mitochondria. Instead of being digested, the mitochondrion began a **symbiosis**, or cooperation, with the host cell. The mitochondrion became the metabolic factory for a new, more complex organism.

Eventually, the symbiosis became so complete and so effective that it was difficult for biologists to detect the mitochondrion as a separate organism. But mitochondria retain some of their own ancestral DNA, and they replicate within a cell whenever that cell divides. And this is what makes them important for interpreting human evolution.

The mitochondria that colonize a new organism do not come from both parents—they divide within the mother so that each egg is inhabited by the mother's mitochondria. The sperm contain no mitochondria. So unlike the genes controlling the rest of the organism, the mitochondrial genes come only from the mother, passed down asexually from daughter to daughter. Each mitochondrion is a clone of its ancestors, not a sexually reproducing entity. There is not very much genetic material in the mitochondria, only 37 genes or 16,500 base pairs of DNA as compared to more than 3 billion base pairs in the nuclear DNA, but it is enough to trace the ancestry of the mitochondria as they gradually mutate from generation to generation.

Because the mitochondrial genes change only by mutation, and not by recombination, we can tell how closely two living women are related by analyzing their **mitochondrial DNA** (mtDNA) and determining how much the two samples differ. The more differences we find, the longer the two gene samples have been mutating independently, and the less closely related the two individuals are. The same principle can be applied to whole populations; this is the source of the finding that sub-Saharan Africans are the most diverse lot on earth. By the logic of Figure 2.5, they have been mutating and diverging from one another the longest.

Another result is more surprising—the diversity that exists in the mitochondria of all living women required less than 10,000 generations of mutation. Thus there emerges a time when all the mtDNA was identical (Ingman et al., 2000). It existed in a single woman, who was immediately dubbed "Eve." She lived about 170,000 years ago, and we are all descended from her.

We do not know what Eve looked like, or even whether she would have been identified with *Homo erectus* or with an archaic line of modern humans. She would have been a part of a small, distinct group. The Eve concept does not mean that some founding couple struck out on their own and established the human species, or even that she was the only woman who contributed genes to future humanity. She could have been part of an interbreeding group as large as several hundred, and it was just by chance that daughters in other lines died out as hers multiplied. Other women could have contributed nuclear DNA to future humans through their sons. The event was a dramatic example of genetic drift.

The ancestors of humanity have passed through other bottlenecks as well, when the population apparently had some close scrapes with extinction and diversity was lost. Using evidence from genetic variability, Bergström, Josefsson, Erlich, and Gyllensten (1998) estimate that sometime during the last million years, the population of ancestral hominids underwent a near-extinction, numbering about 10 individuals. But by 50,000 years ago, the species was firmly established.

Ingman et al. (2000) approached the problem of human origins by sequencing mtDNA from living individuals around the world. Previous efforts considered only the mtDNA control region (around 7% of the total sequence), and consequently had weak statistical significance. Ingman and his team overcame these difficulties by sequencing the entire mtDNA genome from their sample of 53 individuals, and excluded from the analysis parts of the sequence shown not to have a constant mutation rate. They found that the most recent common ancestor to the test group lived 171,500 ± 50,000 years ago. They also noted a distinct division in the human phylogenetic tree between Africans and non-Africans at 52,000 ± 27,500 years ago. Thus the age of the species, measured from the last common ancestor, might be as little as 120,000 years, and this common ancestor might not have been a fully modern human.

Adam

There is also evidence for an "Adam," traced back through the Y chromosome. This chromosome is nuclear DNA, but is passed down only through men, who have an XY genotype, and not through women, who have an XX genotype. Thus the Y chromosome cannot change by crossing over during sexual reproduction, because there is no Y chromosome in the female's genome. The genetic evidence points to a male common ancestor who lived as little as 50,000 years ago. At that time, the human population, or more precisely that part of the human population that was ancestral to all present humans, probably numbered about 2,000 people.

For as much as 70,000 years, and certainly more than 50,000 years, three different hominids were wandering the earth: *Homo erectus*, Neanderthal, and *Homo sapiens*. Now only one is left. What happened? The answer will always be uncertain, but we can gather some clues from the lifestyle and biological adaptations of modern humans in their original habitat, the east African savanna, and the epic story of how humans migrated from there to dominate nearly every ecosystem on earth.

● HUMAN PREHISTORY

About 100,000 years ago, individuals indistinguishable from ourselves (at least by their skeletons) began expanding rapidly through Africa and eventually throughout the world. The migrations first reached beyond the Middle East about 50,000 years ago, into southern Asia, and later into Europe.

Remnants of these epic migrations remain in the genetic structure of humanity today. Hints about the structure of these migrations come not only from the mtDNA of living populations but also from the vastly larger number of nuclear genes. When the variation in a sample of 120 genes is analyzed for populations dispersed throughout the world, the largest proportion of the variability (statistically, the first principal component) shows an origin in Africa and a progressive differentiation of populations as one moves farther from Africa (Cavalli-Svorza, Menozzi, & Piazza, 1993). The genes most different from Africa are found in Australia. It is possible to read the genetic map the other way, with an origin in Australia, but the archaeological record firmly shows that the oldest human remains are in Africa. So the record that still exists in our genes reveals a west-to-east migration (Figure 2.6), filling all the world except for Antarctica and a few isolated islands by the end of the Paleolithic era, the old stone age, about 10,000 years ago.

A closer look at human genetic variability in some regions of the world reveals a history of successive migrations. Figure 2.7A shows the pattern accounting for the greatest amount of statistical variation in populations of Europe and the Middle East. The ring-like progression from the edge of Africa to the farthest reaches of Europe is clear, representing the initial push of humans into the region. The second component takes into account sources

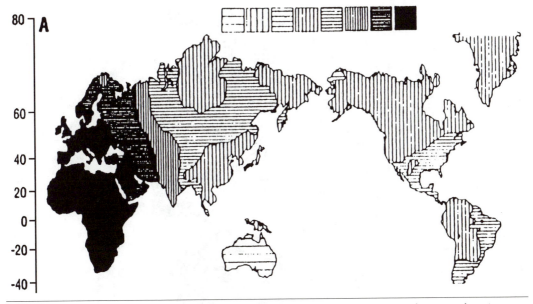

Figure 2.6   A map of genetic similarities of contemporary human populations, showing evidence of a past migration out of Africa.

of variability that are weaker, but are independent of the first component (Figure 2.7B). Because this map shows a north-to-south gradient that follows climate, it may represent natural selection among the populations after they arrived in their present locations. The Lapps occupy the farthest northern regions (solid black in Figure 2.7B), and are the most distinct European group.

The third component (Figure 2.7C) is weaker yet, but reveals a gradient radiating out from southern Russia (Cavalli-Svorza et al., 1993). This region is the original location of people speaking Indo-European, people who radiated out from their homeland after the **Neolithic** farming revolution, partly replacing and partly intermixing with the original nomadic populations. For this migration, evidence from linguistic patterns supplements the genetic record. The only group that was not absorbed in this migration was the Basques, who still maintain their distinct non-Indo-European language, culture, and genetics in northern Spain and southwestern France.

Because the human creature remained adapted to its original habitat and its original technology, examining that habitat and the Paleolithic human's original ecological niche within it can tell us a lot about what humans are. We can examine the human ecological niche in much the same way that

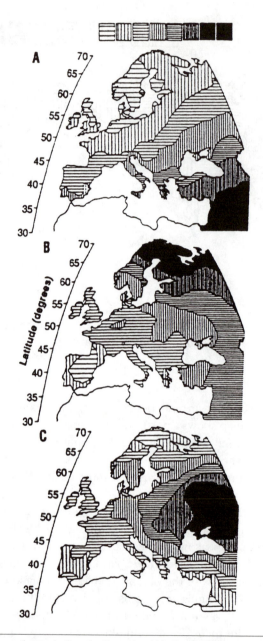

Figure 2.7   Human genetic variation in Eurasia: (A) Genetic remnants of human radiation from the Middle East into Europe; (B) climatic adaptation with a north-south gradient; (C) migration of an Indo-European-speaking population from central Asia.

biologists would examine the ecological niche of any other creature—its diet, its predators, its social structure, everything that characterizes its way of life. Throughout, we will be looking for evolved mechanisms, adaptations that help humans to cope with particular kinds of challenges.

Life on the Savanna

Because we are descended so recently from our Paleolithic ancestors, our current biological adaptations remain essentially the same as theirs. From the dawn of the species until about 10,000 years ago, their way of life changed very little.

From the start, the lifestyle of humans was more complex than that of other creatures. For most of their history, humans have been nomads, hunting and gathering but not producing their own food. They kept no animals, worked no metals, and built no permanent structures.

Humans are a grassland species, adapted to an opportunistic economy of hunting and gathering. We know that we evolved in Africa, but what is the evidence that the species evolved in the grassland and not in one of a wide variety of other African habitats? In addition to the fossil record, there is another source of evidence that humans evolved in a savanna environment, cognitive evidence from our own evolved preferences for certain kinds of landscapes. As Orians & Heerwagen (1992) interviewed a large number of people of many ages and from many cultures about their environmental ideals, they discovered a marked preference for a certain very specific type of landscape. The environment should have short grass with a few trees and shrubs, gently rolling hills, and some standing water.

How do we know that these preferences are not learned adaptations to the world as it is? One answer is that for most of the world's people, this landscape does not describe the world as it is. Another is that if these were learned preferences, we would expect to see them strengthen with age and experience. But exactly the reverse occurs—the savanna preference is strongest in young children, whereas older people develop two parallel sets of preferences, one for the savanna and another for their current environment.

The savanna preference extends not only to opinions but to behavior also. If we are not in an ideal environment, we emphasize the savanna-like aspects of wherever we are. On a broad plain, we orient toward the clump of trees; in a dense forest, we head for the clearing. Even landscape art shows such tendencies (Figure 2.8), though most of it was produced long before the savanna hypothesis appeared in science.

Figure 2.8   The photograph shows a formal garden, its elements designed centuries ago, that contains all the elements of the ancestral savanna—short grass, trees, shrubs, and water. Landscape art from the 20th century also shows savanna-like features.

Why is this particular environment favored? Orians and Heerwagen (1992) hypothesize that the preferences reflect landscapes in which humans were historically (or prehistorically) the most successful. Those who preferred these landscapes were more biologically fit than those who happened to prefer less advantageous locations, so the preference could become fixated in our genes. Short grass, for example, indicates the presence of grazing animals that are potential prey. Tall grass means few animals and hiding places for predators. Water is a necessity for a water-wasting species such as ours. It may also mean fish and an opportunity to clean the body. Trees provide shade, firewood, and perhaps a chance to escape from ground predators. There is even a preference for certain types of tree shapes: those with dividing trunks and foliage of intermediate density (Figure 2.9). An environment of rolling hills offers more opportunity to see for long distances than does a flat, treeless plain.

Modern preferences for savanna-like environments are more than just academic (using that word to mean "irrelevant"). Indeed, they shape contemporary ways of life to a surprising extent. All over the world, people create savanna-like environments when they can. The traditional yard in the United States is dominated by short grass—try letting it grow and see how long it takes before the neighbors start to complain. There are a few trees, but not too many, and some shrubs. This sort of landscape is created artificially all over the world,

Figure 2.9   Forms of Acacia tree in Africa. Left: Growth in wet soil. Center: Growth in ideal soil. Right: Growth in dry soil.

sometimes at huge expense, in ecosystems ranging from the forests of northern Europe to the deserts of the U.S. Southwest. When a new housing development is carved from wild land, the developer will often put in a golf course if there is enough space—exactly re-creating the prescribed savanna, complete with trees, short grass, shrubs, and rolling hills. If there is an artificial lake, the houses fronting on the lake are the most desired and the most expensive. Throughout the world, lakes become the centers of recreational areas.

Sadly, humans all over the world also show a strong preference for natural environments over the artificial ones that we ourselves have created (Kaplan, 1992; Kaplan & Kaplan, 1982). The ancient human desire to live in a savanna-like environment results in urban sprawl and all the problems that accompany it.

Perhaps the most significant aspect of the savanna hypothesis is not that we prefer certain landscapes, but that the preferences seem to be built into our genetic heritage without our awareness of them. Evolutionary psychologists find in this case that our behavior is steered by what we interpret as aesthetic preferences. It is an example of genetic influences on human behavior being often felt as attitudes or motivations, not as fixed action patterns like reflexes.

For a time a few years ago, I felt lethargic, and avoided exercise. I found certain foods aversive, especially fatty foods, and ate little. Fortunately, the worst was over by the time I was diagnosed with hepatitis type A, and no treatment was necessary because inborn preferences and attitudes, working without my knowing why they were triggered, were the only remedies that I needed.

Humans do not gravitate to just anyplace on the savanna. Particularly attractive are lakes and river valleys, and indeed most of the earliest human artifacts are found in these environments. Indeed, humans require water on a scale that no savanna animal does.

The Aquatic Ape

There is even a theory that the group that eventually evolved into modern humans went through an era of semiaquatic life (Hardy, 1960; Morgan, 1997). No direct archaeological evidence supports this idea, but there is some circumstantial evidence in our own bodies. Modern humans share several characteristics with marine mammals and with no other creatures. These characteristics include subcutaneous (attached to the skin) body fat, chubby babies, near-hairlessness (shared only with marine mammals and a few semiaquatic tropical animals such as hippos and elephants), voluntary control over breathing (a possible preadaptation for language), and a second set of protective labia covering a woman's vagina. Coincidences? Perhaps. Hominid bipedality in this scenario arose to aid in wading, with the body partly supported by water.

Our aquatic adaptations can be reconciled with our savanna preferences in a two-stage model: A compromise between the aquatic and the savanna hypotheses holds that at an early stage of hominid evolution, perhaps as early as the *Australopithecus* era, our ancestors lived in coastal wetlands and river valleys, eating shellfish as well as soft wetland plants (Verhaegen, Puech, & Munro, 2002). The fats found in shellfish are more similar to those in the human brain than are any other known food source. Like marine mammals, which have larger bodies and larger brains than their nearest terrestrial relatives, we developed similar adaptations in this environment. Dietary evidence from tooth structure and tooth wear patterns is consistent with this idea.

The large-brained, bipedal ape that evolved in coastal wetlands was able to develop a technology sufficient to enable it to invade the much larger but less friendly savannas. It would have been just luck, then, that freed our hands for carrying things, denuded our bodies for clothing that was more flexible in varying environments than fur, and gave us control over breathing to get us started in language.

The Noble Savage

We sometimes look back nostalgically at the era of Jean-Jacques Rousseau's "noble savage," people so well attuned by evolution to their environment that every instinct is appropriate and every situation anticipated by unerring biological imperatives. Perfectly adapted to the environment in which they find themselves, these people experience none of the conflicts and frustrations of modern life, lived as it is in an environment so different from the ancestral world. Theorists have termed this Garden of Eden the "environment of evolutionary adaptedness" (Foley, 1996; Symons, 1979), the environment that evolution has tuned us to occupy.

No one has ever lived in such an environment. Evolution adapts us to an average environment, one that is just as inaccessible as is the average partner from the morphing experiments described in Chapter 1. No environment is average in all respects, just as no person can be average in all respects, with 2.1 children and 1.8 bathrooms. There have always been and will always be challenges for which a person is not prepared, and properties of the environment that deviate from the ideal. Our flexibility, our ability to learn and to create tools and other artifacts that interface between us and the environment, is the key to our success.

Furthermore, evolution may have tuned us specifically to expect the unexpected. The environment in Africa between 6 million years ago and 10,000 years ago became more variable than the environment before that time, with large, abrupt swings in both rainfall and temperature that led to frequent changes in vegetation and fauna (Potts, 1998). These changes accompanied the ice ages, but frequent and irregular oscillations of climate were superimposed on the slower ebb and flow of the great ice sheets. In such an unpredictable environment, many animals that were specialized for particular climatic niches became extinct or migrated to areas that were suitable for them. Some animals adapted over and over with each climatic crisis.

Hominids responded differently. From the standpoint of our genes, climatic changes were far more rapid for us than for other animals because of our long generation time. If the climate were modified and significant changes in available foods occurred in 1,000 years, a mouse species might have 2,000 generations or more to evolve adaptations to the new conditions. But humans or prehumans in the same time span would experience only about 40 generations, far too few to manage the major evolution necessary to adapt genetically to the new modes of living that the new climate would demand. With only 40 chances to reshuffle the genes, adaptation to a whole new way of life is not feasible. And migration was not practical, because the particular valley or hillside that might still have suited us would be too small to support a population of large primates.

Animals that function as specialists, their adaptations finely tuned to a particular ecosystem, can usually outcompete generalists who blunder about and forage less efficiently than their more specialized neighbors. Hominids struggling to survive rapid changes in climate, though, would have had too little time to specialize before the next wave of change swept over them. Those who evolved specializations for particular ecosystems would do well until the next climatic catastrophe, when they would be wiped out while their generalist fellows survived. At least two extinct hominid lines, the early *Australopithecus robustus* and the later Neanderthal, specialized and perished.

To succeed, humans would have to be equipped to handle highly variable environments without highly variable genes. The most useful adaptations would not be teeth adapted to chew particular foods, or visual systems tuned to find particular plants, but teeth and eyes and brains that could perform a wide variety of tasks. Selection would be not for special-purpose devices, but for variability itself (Potts, 1998). Variability selection would have favored widespread plasticity and strong sensitivity to environmental input. The cognitive mechanisms unique to humans, according to this theory, emerged in a complex series of highly diverse selection regimes. These mechanisms thus include analytical devices that alter behavior in the light of complex contextual information, mediators of novel response to adaptive problems. Mechanisms of learning and memory would loom large. Because such mechanisms permit analysis of factors not immediately present or visible, they require complex internal representations, including language. In a word, the human is specialized to generalize. The adaptations that made this possible were tools and strategies, modifiable without genetic change, that allowed us to compete in almost any environment.

Technology

Even the earliest humans possessed what to other hominids and other animals must have seemed a formidable technology, though it would have looked pitiful by today's standards. Nomadic life, moreover, prevented our ancestors from accumulating more goods than they could carry. Even the earliest archeological sites, though, show that humans have always planned ahead in producing artifacts. A tool might have elements collected by trade from sites distant from one another, and tools varied according to the ecology of the region and the requirements of the time. Human remains are usually associated with bits of clothing, buttons, decorative objects, and a great variety of household items.

Making stone tools required skill, instruction, and practice. Several modern anthropologists have taught themselves to make stone tools, redis-covering in the process the ancient tricks of the trade. They have found that it takes many hours of practice to master the art, but that with the right mate-rials, a proficient technician can produce a useful arrowhead or ax head in a few minutes (Marzke, 1997). Other apes have been taught to make and use simple stone tools (Toth, Schick, Savage-Rumbaugh, Sevcik, & Rumbaugh, 1993), so the reasons why they do not do this in the wild must relate not to their physical capabilities or coordination but to their brains.

Even with the simplest technology, though, most nomads could provide for their basic needs with a few hours of work per day. Reports on contem-porary hunters and gatherers—specifically on those in marginal environ-ments—suggest a mean of 3 to 5 hours per adult worker per day in food production (Sahlins, 1974). In better areas, less work is needed. Of course, the life of nomads had to be arranged so that survival was possible in the toughest of times. Most of the time, though, there was time for gossip, games, and religion. Life changed little from one generation to the next.

The Upper Paleolithic Revolution

About 50,000 years ago, something important happened to humanity. We will never know quite what it was, but we do know that it changed every-thing. Though there was no evolution in human skeletal remains, there seems to have been a revolution in human capabilities. The era after this rev-olution is called the **Upper Paleolithic** (UP) period. Mass migrations roughly coincide in time with the origins of art, more complex societies, and a greatly expanded and more flexible technology. The variability selection that had allowed us to survive in an unstable environment over time in Africa also allowed us to invade new environments outside Africa. Stone tools sud-denly become more varied and sophisticated (Ambrose, 2001). Of greater significance are ground, polished, drilled, and perforated bone, ivory, antler, shell, and stone, shaped into projectiles, harpoons, buttons, awls, needles, and ornaments. Such artifacts are extraordinarily rare before 50,000 years ago but are a consistent feature of UP and later stone age sites after 40,000 years ago. The "revolution" may have taken as long as 10,000 years, equal to all the time from the Neolithic revolution of around 8000 B.C. to the present—it is only from our distant vantage point that the change seems abrupt.

Recent finds in South Africa may answer a key question in the human ori-gins debate by providing proof that not only did early *Homo sapiens* come "out of Africa," but that they came out with fully developed modern behaviors that had evolved much earlier than previously thought. The new evidence includes the discovery in a South African cave of a large set of specialized bone tools, all dated at more than 70,000 years old. The artifacts suggest that behavioral modernity originated in Africa earlier than it appeared in Europe. Delicately worked bone tools, decorations, finely crafted stone implements, and ochre like that used by contemporary hunter-gatherers for body decoration are all found at this ancient site (Henshilwood et al., 2001).

The upper Paleolithic may have begun a good 20,000 years earlier than had been thought previously, spreading until it came to dominate the world about 50,000 years ago.

Until this time, change was very slow in both human and other hominid societies. A million years passed between the appearance of the first stone tools and the first improvements in stone tools. There was plenty of time for biological evolution to keep up with cultural advances. After the UP revolution, though, the rules changed. From that day to the present, cultural advances came more rapidly than biological evolution, and the world in which we live diverged more and more from the range of environments to which we are adapted. The Neolithic farming revolution accelerated the cultural changes, until technological culture, with its tens of thousands of years of invention and progress, now dominates our lives.

Origins of the Revolution. Though the details of what triggered the UP revolution will never be known with certainty, we can make some good guesses. First, the change would have had to be cultural, because a biological innovation would have required a wholesale replacement of hominid populations throughout the old world in a very short time. There is no evidence for such an event. Ian Tattersall (2000) feels that the invention of language was the critical innovation. All the anatomical specializations for language (Figure 2.10) have been present since long before the UP revolution, however, possibly as far back as half a million years ago and certainly for a quarter million (Corballis, 1999). A compromise between these two positions might be that spoken language replaced a highly developed gestural language around this time. The gestural language might have been accompanied by oral components, being replaced by speech over a period of several millennia (Corballis, 2002).

Another possibility is that the change was humans' ability, for the first time, to take full advantage of the intellectual power of language. Though the capacity for language is inborn, the actual content of the language must of course come from a culture, which in turn must make a long series of linguistic inventions, both words and the grammatical forms in which they are combined. Each new word or new grammatical subtlety must go through a period of cultural development. Literal language, with a name for each object

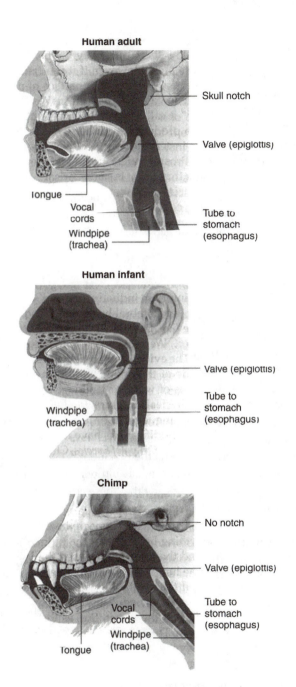

Figure 2.10 Mouth and throat structure in modern human adults (top), human infants (center), and chimpanzees (bottom). The descended larynx, allowing a greater variety of sounds and better control of them, is characteristic of modern adults only.

and each action, must have developed over tens of thousands of years, perhaps much more, to reach its full potential.

The UP revolution might have originated in a further development; the invention of abstract terms, indirect reference, and metaphor. The ability to talk about ideas as well as things would have produced a revolution in human symbolic thinking abilities, multiplying the ancient hominid planning capability by making minds more accessible to one another. Such an invention could spread from one group to another, without direct genetic inheritance, though a critical population density would have been necessary to provide opportunities to exploit any newfound linguistic inventions. With the development of nonliteral language, the stage would be set for further rapid advances in technology and symbolic thought.

Religion

An important change in human life at the time of the UP revolution is a much greater incidence of signs of religious belief. There are a few signs of religious or spiritual practices in Neanderthal sites, but the signs are far stronger in *Homo sapiens*, especially after the UP revolution. Indeed, some of the earliest human artifacts we have are religious or magical in nature. The human fascination with magic and religion begs for an explanation in evolutionary terms, for by definition the practices have no practical basis. Appealing to magic, or to a god or goddess, cannot help in a hunt or a migration, except to increase (perhaps falsely) the confidence of the participants. Yet we see religious symbols and artifacts in all cultures and over the whole span of human existence, strongly suggesting that there is something built into us that can be satisfied only with magic, ritual, religion.

This example illustrates a methodological rule of thumb—if some human trait is both universal and has always been with us, we have a good indication that there is some biological structure in the brain to help it along (Wenegrat, 1984). Any genetic change that can facilitate a universal and permanent aspect of human behavior is likely to be selected for. The permanent-and-universal requirement doesn't prove that a trait has a biological component, but it indicates a promising place to look for an evolved mechanism.

Cosmology and Order

A possible explanation for the emergence of magic and religion is people's insatiable curiosity. The child's insistent question "Why?" must have been with us always. We as a species exaggerate the playful curiosity and exploration that all young mammals share, carrying it into adulthood. But a Paleolithic human requiring an explanation for everything would soon encounter obstacles and seemingly intractable mysteries. It's an example of the old philosophical conundrum: What happens when an irresistible force meets an immovable object? When the irresistible force of human curiosity meets the immovable object of nature's mechanisms, magic and ritual might result from the collision.

Because Paleolithic bands knew nothing of the laws of physics, thunder could only be explained as being produced by a god, and hunting was good if the gods were happy. It doesn't seem like a very good answer to us, but we must remember that these Paleolithic hunter-gatherers were as smart as we are, and for them it was the best answer available. The human motivation to know everything and to explain everything is clearly beneficial when it comes to mastering the physical and social environment, but this motivation applied to the unanswerable questions resulted in arbitrary answers.

Even today, we hear references to religion when people try to explain the inexplicable, to find order and reason from "God's plan" in events that at base are random, such as a child's death in an automobile accident. In the extreme of this view,

> Our brain functions in such a way that it tries to find the cause of all of the things it experiences. If this is the case, then it is a biological necessity for us to seek out causality. Furthermore, there is evidence that our drive to determine causality may be present even as early as infancy. The causal operator has often led to the development of myth formation and in particular, religious beliefs. Religions, in general, offer an answer as to what ultimately causes things to happen in this universe. (Newberg, D'Aquili, & Rause, 2001)

Death

A second possible justification for religion originates in the increasing intelligence and awareness of evolving humans, who eventually came to realize the inevitability of their own deaths. This potentially debilitating realization could be neutralized by a belief in eternal life. When we ask what happens to people when they die, most of us would rather hear about heaven than decomposition.

Because all the sensory evidence points to a permanence of death, though, the promise of eternal life must be guaranteed by a supernatural being or beings (Alper, 2001). Even if the whole religious enterprise is just a giant exercise in wishful thinking, it serves the function of allowing self-consciousness and its cognitive advantages to exist in an ultimately meaningless world, according to this view.

If this idea is offensive to those who adhere to a modern religion, try to think of the attitudes of those who profess another religion. If you are a believer in the god of Abraham, that is, a Christian, Muslim, or Jew, imagine the function of the beliefs of Buddhists. If you are a Buddhist, imagine the position of a believer in the god of Abraham. Each is convinced that the religious beliefs of the other are in error, but both sets of beliefs have similar functions in the cognitive and emotional life of the believers, creating a feeling of order and justice in a disorderly and unjust world. Cultural traditions clearly dominate in deciding the form of belief, for almost all members of a given society come to believe in the religion of their culture and reject the religions of other cultures.

Social Cohesion

A third function of ritual and religion may have been to hold societies together. Common rituals bond people to one another, give them a permanent place in the group, and differentiate them from other groups. Worship of supernatural deities requires a degree of subordination; when all the members of a group are subordinate to a god or gods, they are more willing to cooperate with one another and less likely to become involved in debilitating disputes. It doesn't matter that the gods are imaginary.

Though Wenegrat's (1984) principle makes us suspect that the propensity of people to adopt religious beliefs has a genetic component, direct evidence for the idea is thin. There is indirect evidence, however, from two sources. The first is based on the observation that psychoactive drugs normally do not create new psychological capabilities. Rather, they are limited to facilitating or inhibiting existing capabilities. The fact that several types of drugs can induce religious experiences, then, indicates that the religious tendencies dwelt within the user before the drugs were taken. The drugs merely facilitated an existing potential. The second source of evidence comes from clinical neurology, where several neurological syndromes share a symptom of "hyperreligiosity." In extreme cases, the patient claims direct access to God, or even to be God himself. Again, the tendencies must have preexisted in the patient's brain (Alper, 2001).

The evolutionary bottom line for religion, like any other human activity, must be biological fitness. In contemporary societies, indexes of religious practice or spirituality correlate positively with a wide variety of healthful outcomes, including lower rates of heart disease, stroke, and high blood pressure; greater longevity; and advantages in a number of other measures of health (Seybold & Hill, 2001). It doesn't seem to matter which religion is practiced; benefits are similar for Protestants, Catholics, Jews, Buddhists, and Muslims. Nor is the region of the world important. Reasons for the benefits may include social support systems, stress reduction, and better health-related behaviors. Indeed, religious groups with particularly strict behavioral requirements (such as Mormons, Old Order Amish, and Orthodox Jews) tend to be healthier than the population as a whole (Pargament, 1997). The only systematically negative outcomes relate to religious fatalism ("leave it to God") or to beliefs in direct communication with a deity ("God told me . . . ").

Social Structure

Hunting large animals was always a cooperative enterprise because a human hunter had little chance of bringing down a much faster animal by himself. Hunting requires organization, teamwork, and planning, all capacities that benefit from large brains.

The evolution of a language capability was a key to the human style of cooperative life. Humans depend upon one another far more than groups of unrelated individuals in any other primate species, and language is one of the unique adaptations that makes cooperation work. Our brains are more capable than those of chimpanzees, to be sure, but not so much as to explain the vast differences between our lifestyle and theirs. One of our most critical advantages is as much social as neurological: All chimpanzees must learn chimp ways for themselves, imitating from time to time but hardly ever being instructed, and never having things explained. A modern human, with linguistic access to the minds of others, can tap the brains of billions of other humans past and present, multiplying enormously the reach of perception and of action. This advantage is so decisive that it dominated the evolution of other human traits.

Paleolithic bands had to remain small because the land could not support many large hominids in one place. Society was organized in bands of a few dozen to a few hundred people, usually on the smaller side of that range, each band normally situated several kilometers from its nearest neighbors. A member of a Paleolithic band lived in a small group of people, many of them relatives, and would see neighboring groups only sporadically. Later chapters review the consequences of this structure for such social imperatives as incest avoidance and tribalistic emotions.

Regional Differences

The human species is divided into a number of distinct subgroups, or races, and until the Europeans initiated great intercontinental migrations in the 16th century, each race could be identified with a particular region and often with a particular range of climatic or ecological conditions. The races must have differentiated relatively recently in human history, because they differ in only a few genes (Olson, 2002)—all human groups share the vast majority of genes, both the fixated and the variable ones. And it is the gene frequency that varies, there being no marker genes that uniquely identify a person as a member of one or another race.

In the modern world, so many people have ancestry in several of the prehistoric races that assigning everyone to a distinct race is a biological fiction. (Almost all blacks in the United States, for example, have both African and European ancestry, and many Latinos have both Native American and Spanish or Portuguese ancestry.) Many traits in addition to those that are physically obvious vary around the world, so that a "racial" map based on blood type or immune system genes would look very different from the conventional one.

Some of the differences between races are probably the results of genetic drift and of "founder effects," in which a small group of our ancestors migrated to a new region and eventually became a new race. Any random characteristics that those founders had, or lacked, would become part of the new racial pattern. This is particularly true of isolated populations founded by small groups of colonizers, such as Native Americans.

Other differences between races may be related to the environments in which they differentiated. The darker protective coloring of people from tropical regions is a well-known example that has already been discussed. Other differences are less obvious. Many northern Europeans, for example, retain into adulthood the ability to synthesize lactase, a digestive enzyme that helps to metabolize milk sugar. In most other human groups, lactase levels drop in early childhood at about the time that a child is weaned.

We can surmise that maintaining lactase production was beneficial for people living in northern Europe because of the extreme seasonality of their food supply. In winter, the Europeans could survive by consuming milk and cheese, preserved by cold rather than by fermentation, from their cattle. Europeans also digest alcohol more easily than some other races, suggesting that food preservation by alcohol may have been important to them for some time. These are examples of the co-evolution of biological inheritance and cultural practices.

Although there is no direct historical evidence for these ideas, they are consistent with the adaptations that we find in contemporary groups. Physiological changes such as these affect the range of cultural adaptations that is possible or necessary for a group, and in that way they affect psychology indirectly. Interaction of evolved characteristics with culture is a theme that recurs throughout the following chapters.

DISCUSSION QUESTIONS ●

1. When humans migrated from their original habitat to other ecosystems, what enabled them to compete successfully with the animals that were already adapted to those ecosystems?
2. If humans are best adapted to a tropical savanna environment, why did they migrate to other less desirable environments?
3. What roles might religion have in an era when science handles the great natural and cosmological questions?

FURTHER READING ●

Bradshaw, J. L. (1997). *Human evolution*. Hove, UK: Psychology Press.

All the stages and species of hominid evolution are discussed here, from the Pleistocene to the present, along with a view of 100,000 years of human existence through archaeological as well as genetic evidence.

Cavalli-Svorza, L., Menozzi, P., & Piazza, A. (1994). *The history and geography of human genes*. Princeton, NJ: Princeton University Press.

In an intellectual and technical tour de force, Cavalli-Svorza and his colleagues trace human prehistory through numerous expansions and migrations, using only the genetic and linguistic structures of present human populations as their raw material.

Olson, S. (2002). *Mapping human history: Discovering the past through our genes*. New York: Houghton Mifflin.

Reviewing the sweep of human prehistory that affects who we are, how we look, and how differences among human groups pertain to our lives today, Olson concludes that the group differences so often attributed to genetics could not have biological origins.

Tattersall, I. (2000). "Once we were not alone." *Scientific American, 282*(1), 56-62.

Archaeologist Ian Tattersall examines the now-extinct hominids and asks why they became extinct while only our species survived.

CHAPTER 3

COURTSHIP AND REPRODUCTIVE ADAPTATIONS

"Put simply, in our evolutionary history, it seems likely that a woman's value was usually her reproductive value, and a man's value was his resource value."

— Bobbi S. Low (2000, p. 83)

There is a good chance that you turned to this chapter before reading the ones that precede it in the book. If you did, there is a sound biological reason why: Reproduction is the "final common path" through which all other traits, good and bad, are passed into the next generation. Everything else depends on it (Darwin, 1871). Therefore, the motivations and emotions connected with reproduction are particularly intense: not strong enough to drive us completely crazy, but nearly so in most people.

● SEXUAL REPRODUCTION

Sexual reproduction is so much a part of our way of life that we seldom question it. But from a biological standpoint, it seems a disastrous way to handle such a vital function as reproduction. After all, the males are half of the population and bear no offspring. So sexual reproduction cuts the **reproductive capacity** of a species in half immediately. Because reproductive capacity tells us how many offspring a group of a given size can produce in a given time, it is critical to the survival of a species, and any reduction in reproductive capacity is a serious matter. Evolutionary theory tells us to look for a correspondingly huge benefit somewhere else.

The benefit comes in the reassortment of genes in every generation. By continually trying out new gene combinations, variability of the individuals in a sexually reproducing species is increased and evolution can proceed faster, as detailed in Chapter 1.

To see how this works, consider a population that encounters a new environmental challenge, for instance a new, potentially fatal disease. Imagine that the population that encounters the disease is genetically uniform. Because those who survive are genetically identical to those who succumb, the population cannot evolve an improved resistance to the disease. The individuals in the population will be either uniformly vulnerable or uniformly capable of meeting the challenge, and in either case any genes that might help to meet the challenge will not be selected. In a genetically varied population, though, some individuals will handle the disease better than others, so that their genes will be concentrated in successive generations by sexual recombinations.

There is circumstantial evidence that many northern Europeans became less susceptible to the HIV virus, for example, because of selective events that occurred during medieval European plagues, when a third of the population perished in one generation. Eight centuries later, the selective change of gene frequencies in the remaining population is still with us. This example, by the way, is also a counterexample to the general rule of slow evolutionary change. If the selection pressure is strong enough, and the successful alleles or combinations are already present in the population, evolution can be quite rapid. Most of the selection for disease resistance in this case occurred in a few decades in the 1300s.

Sexual reproduction addresses an important challenge that comes from the continual fight against parasites. Most parasites have shorter reproductive cycles than their hosts, so that the parasites (a daunting array of microbes, worms, and other disgusting creatures) can evolve to their benefit, but to the disadvantage of their hosts. If human reproduction were **asexual**, human parasites could go on evolving in one genetically identical generation of humans after another. As the parasites became more capable, the humans would be unable to fight back, because mutation alone could not change their genome quickly enough to counter the threat. Evolution in the parasites would continue until they finally brought down the cloned line of humans. But sexual reproduction produces new and unique combinations of genes in every generation. The parasites can never get the upper hand, because they must start over with every generation of hosts (Hamilton, 1980; Tooby, 1982).

Combine the antiparasite advantages of sex with the average-is-best rule from punctuated equilibrium theory (Chapter 1), and you have a new way to approach the opposite sex. When you feel particularly attracted to a member of the opposite sex, you should be thinking, 'Wow! You're really average. I'd like to stay one step ahead of the parasites with you!"

REPRODUCTIVE ADAPTATIONS ●

Any physical or behavioral characteristics that facilitate reproduction are counted as reproductive adaptations, most of which concern not copulation itself but a myriad of behaviors from mate choice to parental care. In humans, both sexes make particularly large investments in offspring. This **parental investment** (Trivers, 1972) drives many of the behaviors and attitudes that make reproductive systems what they are.

Parental Investment

The relative investment by the two parents of a new organism varies widely in the animal world. In species where the strategy is to produce a lot of offspring but to invest minimally in each, the physiological cost of each reproduction is so low that neither sex profits from being particularly discriminating about who the sexual partner is. The strategy is called **r-selection** in biology. In many animals, including most insects and fish, the female investment is limited to the physiological strain of producing eggs, and the male to producing sperm.

The unerring rule of reproduction selects those animals that are discriminating about sexual partners to the degree that they must invest heavily in the resulting offspring. In most mammals, this means that the female, who does essentially all the raising of foals, cubs, kittens, and so on, will be more careful about selecting a mate than the male, who will mate with just about any female. Choosiness in selecting mates goes the other way in the seahorse (actually a fish), where the male chooses his mate carefully from among the promiscuous females because he will spend a lot of time and effort guarding the eggs.

Humans, at the other end of the biological spectrum of parental invest-ment, have very low reproductive rates compared to most animals along with a huge investment in each child. This is a **K-selection** strategy, and because both parents make considerable investments in their children, we can expect natural selection to make both parents choosy about a mate. Naturally, this makes the process of finding and winning an appropriate mate all the more difficult. In a physiological sense, every male follows an r-selected strategy, producing billions of sperm at little cost, whereas every female is closer to the K-selection strategy, producing relatively few eggs and investing at least a month of her reproductive life in each one (Mealy, 2000). Actual selection pressures reflect the total parental investment, however, not just the production of gametes.

Asserting that human reproduction is sexual is one thing—making the system work is quite another. Like every other species, humans have evolved an array of biological adaptations that work to pair each member of the species with the most promising partner available and to facilitate the long sequence of actions that is necessary to raise successful offspring. Because human children are dependent longer than the young of any other species, these adaptations are particularly complex in us. In addition, we have acquired social adaptations to family life and child-rearing.

For most people throughout the world and throughout history, marriage or something like it has been the norm as a reproductive unit. Most societies allow some form of **polygyny**, where a man can take more than one wife, or more rarely **polyandry,** where a woman can take more than one husband. But even in those societies, many young adults find a single partner and stay with that person for life (Wilson & Daly, 1992). An exception is childless unions that often dissolve after a few years. Usually, one man and one woman cooperate to raise children, with more or less help from other relatives. And there is always a public ceremony to recognize the union, from the huge spectacle of a European royal wedding to the five-minute Las Vegas gesture.

The reproductive pattern in most apes, with the exception of the monogamous gibbons, is strikingly different.

Reproduction in Chimpanzees

The chimpanzee may share 98% of our genes, but its sex life is very different from ours. When a female chimpanzee comes into **estrus**, the period of fertility, a bright pink swelling on the rump and a distinct odor advertise her fertility to all the males in the female's band. Sex occurs frequently, with many partners but predominantly with the most dominant males, for a few days until the swelling (and the fertility) subside. Intercourse is quick, lasting about seven seconds, and foreplay is nil (Pusey, 2001).

Though the female is motivated to have intercourse during estrus, at other times she is indifferent or hostile to the idea and there is little sexual activity or interest from either sex. Occasionally, a single male manages to escort an estrous female away from the band and mate with her until the time when she is no longer fertile.

Males apparently do not know who the father of any chimpanzee is, and though they are solicitous of infants, they take no part in child-rearing. Why should they? More likely than not, they would be raising someone else's baby.

Male investment in child-rearing is a huge resource that is wasted in most mammals. In effect, chimpanzee mothers are single moms raising children of unknown paternity, with no help from the father. Their fertility is limited because it takes a long time for a single parent to raise a child.

Monogamy

With the difference between the child-rearing pattern of humans and that of most other primates, we identify one of the critical advantages that makes humans such a successful species (so far, at least). In this sense, the reproductive unit of two pair-bonded parents is as important as our much vaunted brains in forging the human lifestyle. **Paternal investment** (Trivers, 1972) doubles the economic resources available to raise offspring, making possible the long period of immaturity that humans require to learn their language, technology, and culture.

Monogamy, or at least a social convention of monogamy, functions to reduce male-male competition in complex societies, where it seems to be the most common. The reason why this is the case is as simple as counting—because the number of men and women is the same, everyone (or nearly everyone) gets a mate if they are paired one to one. The limiting factor is the number of women, because they control the limiting resource of reproductive capacity. Only if each man gets only one woman will there be enough women to go around, and the desperation of mateless men is not such a problem for society. The resulting stability may benefit everyone in situations that require extensive social cohesion, such as managing large modern societies.

Adaptations for Monogamy

The bonobo chimpanzee, perhaps our closest living relative (Zihlman, Cronin, Cramer, & Sarich, 1978), shares with us important social functions of sex beyond reproduction, though those functions have little in common with ours. In several traits related to reproduction, the bonobo seems to sit between us and the common chimpanzee. The female bonobo's genital swelling lasts nearly from one estrous period to another, so that sexual receptivity is nearly continuous, and females not in a fertile phase remain sexually attractive. Bonobo pairs also share with us the face-to-face copulation position.

For bonobos, sex functions to reduce conflict and increase social cohesion. Periods of excitement, such as reuniting of a group or discovery of a particularly rich food source, are accompanied by intense sexual activity in all possible social combinations (DeWaal, 2001). Because sex serves important group functions, bonobos are anything but monogamous.

Humans show an important difference from the bonobo in sexual behavior—in all human groups, sex is usually conducted in private when possible. Sequestering sexual activity then has the result of transferring its function, from facilitating social cohesion within a band to facilitating marital cohesion in a bonded couple.

This is an example of a simple behavioral change causing extensive realignment of a social structure. When the sexual context transfers from the group to the couple, cohesion within the band must be achieved by another mechanism, in our case by language.

There are not many physiological differences between chimpanzee and human reproductive physiology, but those that we know about point humans in the direction of monogamy. First, estrus is better hidden in human females than in chimpanzees; it is difficult to tell when a woman is fertile and when she is not (this is why couples who rely solely on the rhythm method of birth control are called "parents"). A second unique feature of human reproductive physiology is behavioral, the continuous sexual receptivity of the female. This can aid in maintaining the bond between spouses; sexual activity helps to hold a couple together over the long period of time that is needed to raise children.

Hormonal Mechanisms. The fundamental differences between humans and all other primates raise an evolutionary mystery: How could these differences, requiring the coordinated actions of many genes, have arisen so quickly in the course of hominid evolution? Hints to the genetic solution of this problem come from a closer examination of the differences between humans and other primates in hormonal control of sexuality. In most primates, male sexuality is regulated by testosterone and related androgens, whereas female sexuality depends on estrogens. For humans, in contrast, androgens regulate sexual arousal in both sexes. Sexual receptivity is continuous because there is always some concentration of androgens in a woman's bloodstream.

This simpler pattern of regulation is not new. In fact, it has been found to be similar to the pattern of sexual regulation in the musk shrew, one of the most primitive surviving mammals (Rissman, 1995). These tiny creatures, very like the mammals that scampered around the feet of the dinosaurs, are believed to retain an ancestral pattern of hormonal regulation. Female musk shrews have continuous sexual receptivity, controlled by testosterone acting directly on the medial preoptic area of the hypothalamus, the same brain center that regulates sexual response in males.

The musk shrew's primitive pattern of sexuality was replaced over the course of mammalian evolution by the estrous cycles that govern sexual response in most female mammals. As a reproductive strategy, estrus concentrates investment in sexual activity to a limited period, freeing animals for other pursuits most of the time. Estrus not only uses different hormones, the estrogens, but relies on a brain mechanism based in a different area, the ventromedial hypothalamus. One can hypothesize that the genes controlling the more primitive pattern did not disappear, though. They were retained, but not expressed, through millions of years of mammalian existence, reactivated at the dawn of hominid evolution to resume control of sexual responses. According to this idea, then, the human pattern is not an innovation but a throwback to the most primitive mammalian pattern, pressed into service for new applications in pair bonding and social cooperation.

Swelling of the breasts is a sign of estrus in chimpanzees. Human females' breasts are always swollen, at least compared with those of other primates. The tissue that actually produces milk is just a thin layer near the surface of the breast. The rest is a fatty deposit that has one function, and one function only: to serve as a sexual attractant, a sign of fertility (usually a false sign, because the female is fertile for only a few days each month).

Unconscious Signaling of Fertility

There is some evidence that sexual behavior increases around the time of ovulation due to subtle cues that men receive from women. The signs are both physical and behavioral; although they are not as obvious as the signs of estrus in the chimpanzee, and are expressed unconsciously, they are there. They change the frequency of sexual activity rather than preventing it altogether for most of a cycle.

Physiological changes. The first indication of fertility is that blood vessels in the skin enlarge, leading to a healthy "glow" in ovulating women. The glow is reminiscent of the flushed red skin that appears during sexual excitation.

More apparent in younger women, with their smoother skin, it enhances the attractiveness of youth.

The second sign is that the skin becomes slightly lighter, perhaps to make the glow more obvious. Apparently, men take advantage of this cue, for lighter-skinned women are judged to be more attractive in 47 out of 51 societies surveyed (van den Berghe & Frost, 1986), though the average lightness of people in these societies varies widely, and often it is not the very lightest who are preferred. (In one of the four exception cases, women paint their faces black, but only during menstruation.)

Whether the increased attraction is an adapted capability or is somehow learned by each man is not known, but the fact that most men respond to it even though hardly anyone knows about its relation to fertility makes one suspect a genetic adaptation. Lightening of the skin around the time of ovulation is probably hormonally influenced; throughout the menstrual cycle, women are lighter than men in most human groups throughout the world, a phenomenon first documented by Hulse (1967) for Japan, and later recorded in many cultures. Testosterone tends to darken the skin, explaining the middle term of the woman's desire for "tall, dark, and handsome."

Women's skin darkens during pregnancy, again a period of infertility, and in some women it darkens when they take birth control pills with chemical formulas that simulate the hormonal state of early pregnancy (Resnik, 1967). Cultural practices and preferences grow up around these differences, an example of co-evolution, the simultaneous evolution of several traits that work in concert (van den Berghe & Frost, 1986). The skin also lightens at puberty and darkens again at menopause (Jones, 2000), marking the period of fertility in a woman's life separately from the briefer intervals of ovulation. This longer-term lightening signals long-term suitability of a potential mate rather than short-term fluctuations in actual fertility.

Because emotions run high in this area, it is important to separate the science from cultural racism originating with European domination of many other groups during the last five centuries. Preference for lightness predates European colonialism, however, being recorded for the pre-Columbian Aztecs (Soustelle, 1970) and in ancient Egyptian paintings (Mekhitarian, 1978). It is found in societies that were never colonized by the West, such as Japan, and even where the ruling class was darker than the general population (Moorish Spain from about 700 to 1492). Preference for lighter complexion in women coexists with rejection of other European characteristics: According to Burling (1963), for the Garo of Assam, "the light eyes of the Europeans look like those of a goat, but they admire a light skin."

A third indication of fertility is the hips filling out, leading to a decrease in the waist-to-hip ratio (Figure 3.1). This is another feature that is universally

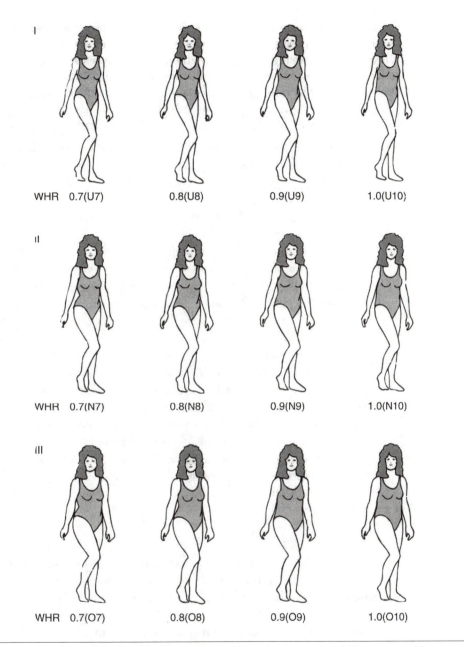

Figure 3.1 Profiles of thin women (top row), normal women (middle row), and heavy women (bottom row), and waist/hip ratios of 0.7 to 1.0 from left to right. Men consistently prefer the left figure in the middle row, with a normal weight and a low waist/hip ratio (Singh, 1993).

attractive to men, again because it signals fertility and sexual maturity (Singh, 1993). In this trait and in skin coloration, secondary sexual characteristics that originate at puberty are accentuated around the time of ovulation.

Behavioral changes. Women change their behavior even when they do not realize that they are ovulating. They become more active as their metabolic rate increases, and they wear clothing that shows more skin (if cultural customs allow it). Some of the research that established these behavioral biases was done not in a laboratory but in a setting where one might expect spontaneous displays of sexual attractiveness—singles bars (Grammer, 1996). The study omitted the behaviors of women on the pill, who do not ovulate. Men touched ovulating women more than other women, and the ovulating women wore shorter and tighter skirts.

One might object that the women don't show more skin to be sexy but only because their higher metabolic rate makes them warmer. To nature, though, the important thing is that the women become more attractive; the mechanisms by which this comes about are secondary. For the same reason, the woman's intentions in displaying these cues are equally irrelevant. What counts is the result.

Sexual desire also increases in women around the time of ovulation, though. This was the finding of a diary study (Stanislaw & Rice, 1988), in which married women reported an increase of sexual desire before ovulation and a decrease afterward (Figure 3.2). Their poor husbands probably remained clueless, not knowing why their wives were sometimes more amorous and sometimes less. Or could they tell, in some subtle way? In humans, there is of course another layer superimposed on the older physiological mechanisms, intentional strategies that make things even more complicated.

Exceptions to Monogamy

Despite its advantages for stable child-rearing, monogamy is not the universal strategy in human reproduction. The adapted human reproductive pattern seems to be monogamy with a certain amount of infidelity, a recipe for conflict (Trivers, 1985). Even the difference in relative size of human males and females, **sexual dimorphism**, tells us that.

Among mammals, a larger-sized male is a giveaway that male-male competition has been important in the evolution of the species. In all the polygynous great apes, the males are larger and heavier than the females, and for good reason. Males must compete with one another to gain access to resources and to females. The advantage of being larger than your adversary

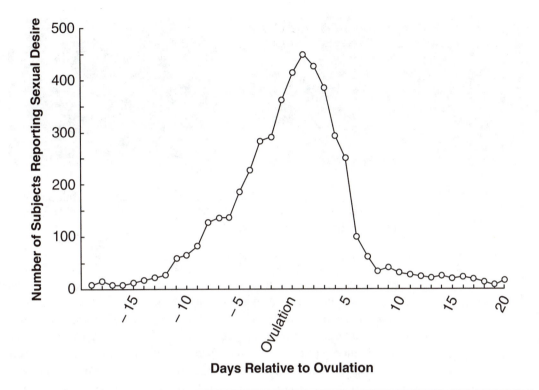

Figure 3.2 Reported sexual desire of fertile women as a function of day in the ovulation cycle (Stanislaw & Rice, 1988). The desire is close to the level of fertility throughout the cycle.

in these confrontations creates a selective pressure for males to evolve large sizes so that they can compete successfully with other males. The pressure does not exist for females, who must conserve their energy for reproduction. Humans have a distinct sexual dimorphism, though not as extreme as in great apes. In more closely monogamous animals, such as gibbons and many birds, male-male competition is not as much an issue, and the two sexes are equal in size (Figure 3.3).

The relative size of the male genitals gives a more precise indication of the intensity of male-male competition. In the gorilla, where a single male dominates a band and has exclusive mating rights, the testes are 0.02% of body weight. Humans, with a not-quite-monogamous lifestyle, weigh in at 0.08%, whereas the sexually promiscuous chimpanzee's testes grow to 0.27% of body weight (Smith, 1984). The greater the male-male mating

Figure 3.3   A high degree of sexual dimorphism in the promiscuous common chimpanzee (left) contrasts with little dimorphism in the monogamous gibbon (right). Both are African great apes.

competition, the larger the testes, another example of co-evolution. In this case, behavioral and physical characteristics evolve together.

If male-male competition is critical in reproductive success, one would have to predict that healthier males are more likely to be reproductively successful. Evidence on this issue comes from surveys of more than 5,000 men in two samples, one born at Helsinki Central Hospital in 1924-33, and another born in Hertfordshire, England, in 1920-30. Because these two regions experienced little immigration or emigration in those periods, it was possible to track down statistics on almost the entire male population in each case. The proportion of unmarried males was much larger among those men who had had a low birth weight more than 65 years before; nearly one fifth of those with the lowest birth weights, less than 2.25 kg, had never married (Phillips, Handelaman, Eriksson, Osmond, & Barker, 2001). The precarious status of these men at birth had already put them at risk for lower reproductive potential throughout life (Figure 3.4).

Sexual Jealousy

A consequence of male-male competition is sexual jealousy, one of the chief sources of murder and mayhem in all human groups, from the Yanomamo of Brazil's rain forest to modern industrial societies. It is summarized in John Lennon's shocking but all-too-accurate lyric with Paul McCartney in the song "Run For Your Life," that he would rather see his girl dead than see her with another man.

In keeping a spouse away from contact with other men, a husband ensures that her children are indeed his, and his reproductive investment is

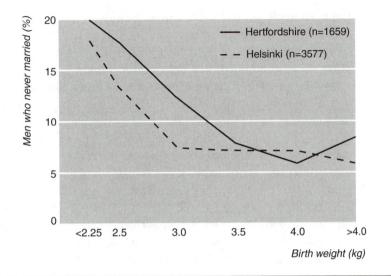

Figure 3.4 Proportion of men who had never married among those born at Helsinki Central Hospital, 1924-33, and in Hertfordshire, England, 1920-30. Men of low birth weight were less likely to marry decades later, with indistinguishable differences between British and Finnish samples (Phillips et al., 2001).

protected. The widespread male tendency to treat women as property, responsible for so much violence and oppression, may have originated with this reproductive motivation (Wilson & Daly, 1992).

Evolutionary psychological theories predict pronounced and universal male-female differences in sexual jealousy, originating from the differing needs of males and females in reproduction. Buss, Larsen, Westen, and Semmelroth (1992) predict that men will give more weight to cues for sexual infidelity, whereas women will be more concerned about emotional infidelity. The reason for this asymmetry is that men require assured paternity from their mates, based on sexual exclusivity, and women require resources that might be more closely connected to emotional attachment. Indeed, cross-cultural research has been done asking whether sexual or emotional infidelity would be more distressing.

Such studies have repeatedly found a large sex differential on these self-report measures: men significantly more often than women choose their mate's imagined sexual infidelity to be more distressing or upsetting to them than an imagined emotional infidelity (Buss et al., 1992). For women, it is the other way around.

However, this body of evidence is solely based on undergraduate samples and does not take into account demographics. Do undergraduates live in an institutional bubble where the rules are different? Another study examined male-female differences in sexual jealousy in a community sample ($N = 335$, Eastern Austria), with other variables controlled for, the effect of sex differential was only modest (Voracek, 2001). These findings stress the pitfalls of generalizing evidence from undergraduate samples to the general population and the need for representative population samples.

An even stronger critique came from a study that surveyed not only paper-and-pencil opinions about what people feel would be most threatening but also asked participants about actual instances of infidelity in their own partners (Harris, 2002). Both men and women, regardless of their sexual orientation, on average focused more on a mate's emotional infidelity than on a mate's sexual infidelity. The study found that the same participants gave responses to hypothetical infidelity that were uncorrelated with their reactions to actual infidelity. This result reminds us that adaptations frequently work by mechanisms distinct from conscious motivation, and that actual behavior rather than opinions about hypothetical situations are the real stuff of adapted psychological mechanisms.

Women and men also have similar physiological reactions in circumstances of imagining the two forms of infidelity (Harris, 2000). The physiological reactions are useful supplements to opinion surveys because they are less likely than verbal reports to be filtered by cultural expectations. The further one moves away from asking college students forced-choice questions about hypothetical infidelity, the less support one finds for the hypothesis of different effects in the two sexes.

In sum, recent studies fail to find differences in the triggers for male and female jealousy, contradicting the original prediction based on evolutionary reasoning. It appears that in the real world, both partners are most concerned with a single question: What is the likelihood that this relationship will survive? The functioning sexual relationship is the key to reproduction for both sexes.

Harris and Christenfeld (1996) suggest that the sex differences seen so far are based on how people interpret infidelity: men think that women can have sex only when in love, whereas women think that men can have sex without love. Further research will be required to explore actual behaviors in men and women—asking about opinions and memories can go only so far. This example also shows that evolutionary theory does not always offer a single prediction about the structure of adapted mechanisms. The actual adapted system, when it is understood, tells us more about the human condition than the theoretical predictions.

One would think that marital dissension would interfere with smoothly functioning reproduction and the economic activities that support it. That is indeed the case, but both humans and other animals seem to be trapped in situations that lead to dissension. The ultimate cause of the dissension is the different interests and resources that different individuals bring to the reproductive situation. Each individual is adapted to spread his or her own genes, if necessary at the expense of others.

MATE SELECTION ●

In a heavily K-selected species like the human, where a long-lasting relationship is so important for successful reproduction, the challenge of finding a mate becomes particularly important. Mate choice is a tricky business, one of the most difficult cognitive tasks that humans face, because it involves a large element of prediction. Each partner must judge the suitability of the other not only in the present but for decades to come. The wrong choice can mean reproductive disaster, the biological equivalent of death.

Because both partners will make a substantial investment in the family, parental investment theory tells us that both will be choosy about whom their partner will be. Adaptations for mate choice must have evolved completely within the hominid line, because our chimpanzee relatives, both bonobos and common chimpanzees, form relationships that endure for periods varying from a week to about three minutes.

If the SSSM is an accurate description of the human condition, each culture should develop its own definitions of beauty and desirability in mates. It should be impossible to predict what the definitions would be in a newly discovered culture. The evolutionary approach, in contrast, predicts great regularity in standards of beauty, because evolved mechanisms will define the biological fitness of the partners. Standards of mate choice, then, constitute a point of empirically testable divergence between SSSM and evolutionary predictions.

Of course, there is variation in what is seen as attractive, but the evidence now favors a universality of criteria for attractiveness in mates (Symons, 1992) and even for attractiveness in general (Richardson et al., 1961). All over the world, people look for the same characteristics in mates, with the result that in surveys, a group of members of the opposite sex will be ranked in desirability in the same way by people in their own culture and by people half a world away (Etcoff, 2000).

An exception to the universality of standards for beauty is the ideal weight of a female partner. In European and especially North American societies, it is desirable to be thin, whereas in much of sub-Saharan Africa, heavier women are judged to be the most beautiful. The ideal in most other regions falls somewhere in between. These standards are somewhat ephemeral, though— a century or two ago the European and American standard favored a heavier partner than is the case today. The preferences may be related to the reliability of the food supply: If the supply is precarious, it is better to carry a little insurance along, but if food is plentiful and reliable, the extra weight is not necessary. Apparently, though, cultural traditions have outlasted the realities of nutrition in this case.

Beyond the enduring criteria of beauty, there are fashions that change from one year to the next, driven largely by commercial interests. Fashions generally concern only the most surface appearances of dress and decoration, though, and do not affect the judged desirability of the characteristics of the person underneath. Some preferences may simply be aberrations, such as the standard for female fashion models in the late 20th century, women too thin to be either healthy or fertile. The models' appearance, though, may be intended more to shock and to attract the attention of women than to attract mates. In the same culture at the same time, men found women of somewhat more average weight to be most attractive (see Figure 3.1) (Singh, 1993).

Arranged Marriages

How did humans historically find the right partners? One alternative in traditional societies is an arranged marriage. Two families would come to an agreement, and the bride and groom would not meet until their wedding day. If love eventually developed, fine; if not, so be it. The arranged marriage is a good way to ensure that property distribution and social standing are optimized for both partners. The custom was described in the musical play *Fiddler on the Roof*, depicting traditional Jewish villages in czarist Russia where arranged marriage was the social norm. The play is the story of this system's breakdown and the collapse of the whole Yiddish society at about the same time.

The arranged marriage was definitely not how most of our ancestors found partners. We have no historical records of this, for the adaptations governing mate selection evolved long before written history began. Rather, the evidence of evolved courtship mechanisms exists in all of us. If courtship had been handled by parents or others, rather than by the partners themselves, the finely tuned behavioral and motivational mechanisms of courtship would never have evolved—they would have only gotten in the way, with no selective pressure to create and maintain them.

Patterns of Courtship

The delicate dance of courtship and mutual commitment is played out in basically the same way by women and men all over the world. Because mate choice is much more complex in the huge societies of the modern world than it was in smaller Paleolithic groups, modern societies construct a complex set of institutions, standards, and customs around this important human activity. In all groups, though, layers of cultural convention cover a primeval, largely unconscious interplay of actions and reactions. It begins with a glance that, if returned, can lengthen into the "lovers' stare" as each partner gazes into the other's eyes. Both partners may flush red, a literal embodiment of the "heat of passion." With this involuntary gesture of the autonomic nervous system, each partner signals interest to the other. And the interest of a partner is one of the most important criteria for attraction in both sexes—unrequited love, though popular in tragic romance novels, is an evolutionary dead end.

Behavioral Cues

Interest in the opposite sex is communicated by several signs, generated by one sex and appreciated by the other. Naturalistic observation has shown that women use some of the following behaviors (Grammer, Kruck, Juette, & Fink, 2000):

• Primp: This is a positive signal in which the woman straightens and orders her clothing, even if it's not necessary.

• Head Toss: The head is moved down, followed by a fast circular upward motion.

• Hair Flip: Same as the head toss, but using the hand to "throw" the hair backward.

• Head Tilt: This signal involves simply tilting one's head sideways. This is a means of neck presentation, which can be seen as a signal of invitation or submission reminiscent of the surrender gesture in some animals.

• Head Down: The head is tilted forward slightly and a gaze is directed slightly upward. Again, this signal may have evolved from submission gestures in animals.

• Coy Smile: A quick, small smile is directed at the man, followed by looking away.

● Look Through: In this subtle positive signal, the woman looks at the man, but does not fixate on him, then looks away. It as though the women noticed but didn't notice the man.

● Short Glance: This gazes lasts less than three seconds, and is used under the same circumstances as looking through.

These are just a few of the signals that women express. The signals that show the highest correlation with female interest are the Primp, Coy Smile, Short Glance, and Look Through.

Negative signals have been investigated less than positive signals, but there are some female negative signals:

● Head Akimbo: The hands are laced together and placed behind the back of the head; then the elbows are pulled back. Initially, this was seen as a positive female signal with a purpose of showing off the body, but research showed a negative correlation between frequency of use of this signal and female interest.

● Slow Head Toss: This motion is much like the hair flip, in which the head is lowered, followed by an upward circular motion. This signal too was initially seen as a positive signal due to its similarity to the hair flip, but like the Head Akimbo, there was a negative correlation between use of this signal and female interest. In some eastern European and Middle Eastern cultures, a head toss much like this one means "no."

Men do not use nonverbal communication in courtship as much as women, and what signals they do use are simple and small in number. Two commonly used signals for positive interest are the following:

● Fixed Gaze: The male focuses his sustained gaze on the female. Gaze is used as a sign of interest in her and a lack of interest in anything else at the moment. Duration of the gaze is longer than the female's short glance.

● Arm Flex: This is the motion of gripping the hands together and flexing the arms in front of the body. It is used to show off the arms, and hence the man's physical strength.

Males too have negative signals, but the only well-established one is looking around. When a male is not interested in a female, he will look around rather than fix his gaze on her. This communicates an interest in other things, and a lack of interest in her (Grammer et al., 2000).

Most of these behaviors are triggered without each partner's awareness of either producing or receiving them. If the signals are positive, these and other behaviors lead the couple through many further steps, first a touch and later erection in the male and vaginal moistening in the female (again controlled by the autonomic nervous system), as the bodies of both partners prepare for eventual intercourse.

But the autonomic reactions are more often than not premature, for now follows an elaborate array of checks and counterchecks under increasing cultural influence. Failure of the partner to respond at any stage can break off the courtship ritual. Each partner evaluates the other, judging the potential mate's suitability, in a process that can stretch over months or years. Some of the results of these decision processes are also communicated in largely unconscious gestures.

Chemical Cues

An important but only recently discovered source of variability in attraction concerns the potential genetic compatibility of the partners. But how does each partner evaluate the other's genes, especially the genes that don't code for visible features? The mechanism appears to be a set of unconscious olfactory cues. Fragrances have been used in courtship for at least 5,000 years, with all traditional scents represented in modern perfumes. Although perfumes are obviously involved in sexual communication, the significance of great individual differences in preference for fragrances is an evolutionary puzzle—or it was until recently.

The source of the variability may be related to the genes that control the immune system; some of these genes are highly **polymorphic** (each gene having many alleles) to give each individual a unique genetic signature. Having immune system genes different from anyone else's is an advantage in maintaining resistance to parasites that have evolved in other individuals. The **major histocompatibility complex** (MHC) is a highly polymorphic and conserved set of genes that plays an important role in immune function in vertebrates. Both mice and humans have been shown to prefer the body odor of potential partners that have a dissimilar MHC genotype, which would result in **heterozygous** offspring for MHC genes.

Milinski and Wedekind (2001) tested whether individual preferences for perfume ingredients correlate with MHC genotype. A total of 137 male and female students who had been typed for their MHC scored 36 scents in a first test for use on themselves ("Would you like to smell like that yourself?") and a subset of 18 scents 2 years later—genetic researchers are very patient—either for use on oneself or for a potential partner ("Would you like your partner to smell like that?").

Statistical analysis showed a significant correlation between the MHC and the scorings of the scents "for self" in both tests. That is, people with similar MHC genotypes tended to identify themselves with the same scents. A more detailed analysis found a significant interaction of the two most common MHC variants with the rating of the 36 scents in the first study as well as with the 18 scents in the second study when evaluated for self. People who share a given MHC have a similar preference for many of the perfume ingredients. The significant repeatability of these preferences in the two tests showed that the volunteers were consistent in their preferences for the perfume ingredients.

As the heterozygosity theory predicts, hardly any significant correlations were found between MHC genotype and ratings of the scents "for partner," in agreement with the hypothesis that perfumes are selected "for self" to amplify in some way body odors that reveal a person's immunogenetics.

Of course, if you wear a perfume or cologne because your partner bought it for you, even though you hate it, the whole mechanism breaks down.

In many animals, **pheromones** are important sexual signals. Sexual pheromones are chemicals, usually related to hormones, that are released by one sex to influence the behavior of the other. Most mammals have a **vomeronasal organ** that is specialized for detecting pheromones. The organ is located in the nasal cavity near the olfactory system but is distinct from it, with its own receptors and brain centers.

The human vomeronasal organ develops in the fetus but regresses before birth, like the tail and gill slits, leaving only a small patch of receptors. Nonetheless, both men and women seem to respond to chemical signals released by the opposite sex (Savic, Berglund, Gulyas, & Roland, 2001). A candidate male pheromone is 4,16-androstadien-3-one (mercifully abbreviated AND), a derivative of testosterone produced in human axillary (armpit) glands. It is secreted in concentrations up to 20 times higher in men than in women. When exposed to this compound, women show increased activity in the anterior hypothalamus, a region that regulates sexual response, though they show no response in the olfactory regions (amygdala, piriform, orbitofrontal, and insular cortex). Men, in contrast, show hypothalamic activation to oestra-1,3,5(10),16-tetraen-3-ol (EST), a substance resembling naturally occurring estrogens. Again, there was no response to this substance in the olfactory regions. Thus each sex responds more to the hormone (pheromone?) secreted by the other, women reacting to AND but men reacting to EST.

There are also differences in the brain regions activated by putative pheromones in the two sexes. Women smelling an androgen-like compound activate the hypothalamus, with the strongest response in two regions linked to emotional regulation, the preoptic and ventromedial nuclei. Men, in contrast, activate the hypothalamus with the strongest response in paraventricular and dorsomedial nuclei when smelling an estrogen-like substance. This sex-dissociated hypothalamic activation suggests a physiological substrate for sex-differentiated behavioral responses.

In another study of the same pheromone candidates (Jacob, Hayreh, & McClintock, 2001), both steroids produced sustained changes in digit skin temperature and palmar skin conductance (an indicator of sympathetic nervous system tone). The subjects could not smell the chemicals consciously, especially when they were masked by strongly odorous carriers—clove oil and propylene glycol (antifreeze)—and they were also unaware of the physiological changes in themselves, which were recorded while they were completing psychological questionnaires or reading. In both studies, the responses to these chemicals were measured only as physiological changes, though. It is still unknown what behavioral changes might result from stimulation in the right contexts.

Although many people in Western cultures strive to conceal or eliminate natural body odor, there is evidence that it plays a role in mate choice, or could if it were given a chance. Several investigations of human body odor have revealed a role for olfactory communication in human sexual behavior (reviewed by Schaal & Porter, 1991). One study has focused on the question of whether olfactory cues could signal general mate quality, like other cues in sexual selection (Rikowski & Grammer, 1999). The mate choice criteria that the researchers measured were rated physical attractiveness and body symmetry. Both symmetry and physical attractiveness are presumed to signal individual developmental stability, that is, heritable mate qualities (Gangestad, Thornhill, & Yeo, 1994; Grammer & Thornhill, 1994).

Instead of elaborate olfactory stimulation instruments, Rikowski and Grammer used a simple technology—T-shirts. The investigators compared ratings of attractiveness and measurements of body symmetry with the evaluated quality of body odor from both male and female subjects. Their mean age was 23.5 years, near the optimum age for female reproduction. Each subject wore a T-shirt on three consecutive nights, without using deodorants or perfumes (hopefully their roommates were willing to make sacrifices for science). Immediately after use, the T-shirts were deep frozen to preserve any odorants and then heated up to 37 degrees Celsius (body temperature) to release the odorants just before the evaluation of odor. Fifteen nonsmoking subjects of the opposite sex rated the smell of each T-shirt on intensity, pleasantness, and sexiness on a 7-point scale. Another 22 men and women evaluated portraits of the same subjects on attractiveness. Body symmetry was calculated as the mean of the relative differences between left and right side on three traits.

The results showed significant positive correlations between facial attractiveness and sexiness of body odor for female subjects. For males there was a positive correlation between the attractiveness of the T-shirt smell and bodily symmetry, but only if the female odor raters had been in the most fertile phase of their menstrual cycles (days 5 to 16). In other words, women tend to prefer the odor of physically attractive and symmetric men only when they are fertile. This study supports the hypothesis that human body odor reveals information about general mate quality. Odor signals seem to have a different significance for the two sexes, however, probably depending on different reproductive strategies.

Personality Criteria

What traits do lovers value in their potential spouses? All over the world, both partners value personality characteristics the most (Buss, 1989). The spouse should be kind, understanding, intelligent, loving, and caring. Also high on the wish list are an exciting personality, good health and looks, and adaptability. In this light, the quotation at the start of this chapter is an overstatement.

The adolescent who gushes, "We have so much in common!" about her new boyfriend is performing an unconscious calculation of mate fitness. One way to increase the proportion of your own genes in your offspring beyond the mathematical 50% is to find a partner who shares many of your genes. The criterion for such a search is a person whose phenotype is similar to yours, including similar interests and preferences. So finding a similar partner is a way to cheat nature, at least a little bit, without running into the problems that incest produces (reviewed at the end of the chapter).

Beyond these first and most important criteria, though, the interests of the two sexes diverge. Men value different characteristics in a spouse than women do (Low, 2000). The reason for the divergence is that both partners are striving for a relationship that will maximize their biological fitness, but their different needs require that their partners bring different resources to the match. Because the woman historically will spend most of her adult life gestating and caring for children, she needs a steady supply of economic resources from her partner. The man, because he can have no offspring of his own, needs the fertility of his partner.

The criteria for choosing a partner are different for short-term liaisons than for long-term partnerships. We will consider the characteristics of long-term relationships first.

Women's Strategies

Today, women in developed countries devote relatively little of their lives to child-bearing. To bring two children to maturity usually requires two births and several months of nursing for each infant. The most intense part of the process is over in a decade or so, depending on societal norms, as society takes on part of the job of schooling and preparing the children for life. In 20 years, the children are mature enough to leave the home. Much of a woman's 80-year life is free for other pursuits.

Reproductive strategies, though, do not match the current reality. They continue to reflect the conditions that applied during the period of human evolution, the tough and hazardous life of nomads roaming the savanna, and young people still choose partners as though they were preparing for those conditions. Our genes tell us what is appropriate for the Paleolithic nomad.

Because infant and child mortality were high, a Paleolithic woman might have to endure six or more births to ensure that two children would survive to adulthood, each birth carrying a significant risk of her own death. Each baby would nurse for perhaps 3 or 4 years (baby food hadn't been invented yet). If she was lucky, she would live to be 50, so that pregnancy, lactation, and child-rearing would occupy most of her adult life. And that was if the family was fortunate. Even as late as the 18th century, about half of all 18-year-olds had already lost at least one parent.

Resources

Because she will be committed to physiological reproduction for such a large proportion of her adult life, an important criterion that a woman investigates in choosing a husband is the resources he can bring to the partnership. Does he have the material wealth, or the prospect of acquiring it, that is necessary to raise children? The man's social standing can tell part of the story—the higher the better. Demonstrated skill in hunting (sometimes formalized in games or rituals) is also important, and resources already acquired are a good predictor of future success. In the modern world, sports can be an important indicator of physical prowess, taking the place of hunting in demonstrating skill and strength.

It takes time for a man to acquire status and resources, and this is one reason that women tend to prefer slightly older males, other things being equal. All over the world, the actual behavior of couples shows this. The actual age at marriage averages about 3 to 4 years older for men than for women, regardless of the average age of marriage in a society, the actual accumulation of

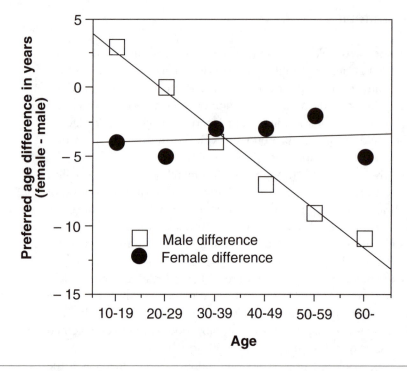

Figure 3.5   Preferences for age of a marriage partner. Each curve shows the female's age minus the male's age, so that negative numbers indicate preference for the female being younger than the male.

wealth, or the economic system. Being strong and handsome is nice, and women value it, but possessing resources is essential, as David Buss (1989) shows in his review of data from 37 cultures. In all 37 cultures surveyed, men desired a mate who was younger than themselves and physically attractive (Buss, 1989).

There are also age differences in the preferences of men and women for marriage partners. As men age, they seek progressively younger partners. Women, in contrast, consistently prefer husbands who are 3 to 4 years older than they are (Figure 3.5). The women's and the men's preference ranges cross in their 20s and 30s, when most marriages occur (Kenrick & Keefe, 1992). The age preference might be nature's way of reducing the number of marriages in people who are too young or too old to begin married life. Teenage boys, for instance, prefer older girls who won't look at them (Kenrick, Keefe, Gabrielidis, & Cornelius, 1996), on the left of

Figure 3.5. Actual age at marriage closely parallels the preferences shown in the figure.

Loyalty and Other Traits

Another valued trait in a husband is loyalty, the willingness to stick with a partner "in good times and bad, in sickness and in health, 'till death do us part." This perhaps is where love comes in, the emotional bond that ties two people together. Rationally, it is clear that many men would make suitable partners for a given woman, and vice versa. If there were only one Mister Right in the world, the chances of a woman ever meeting him would be negligible. At some point, though, each partner decides that the other will become a lifetime commitment. The formation of a loving bond, though irrational in a logical sense, is a necessary part of forming a reproductive unit, a statement that two people are moving from the courtship phase into a reproductive phase of life.

Ideally, finding a stable partner and raising children with his resources would seem to be the best reproductive strategy for a woman. Some women, though, find themselves in situations where stable partners are not available. As they grow up, girls are sensitive to features of their environment that provide cues to the quality of male-female relationships and whether males can be counted on to invest in their offspring.

Compared to girls with active, supportive, and affectionate fathers, girls whose family experiences are characterized by discordant male-female adult relationships and relatively low or unreliable paternal investment (such as father absence or harsh, rejecting, inconsistent parenting and caregiving, especially from their father) develop more precocious sexual interest in boys and more promiscuous sexual behavior, as well as earlier onset of puberty (Belsky, Steinberg, & Draper, 1991; Ellis, McFadyan-Ketchum, Dodge, Pettit, & Bates, 1999). Somehow the girls sense the instability of their social environment, and unconsciously adjust their reproductive strategy accordingly. Earlier onset of sexual activity might be a learned behavior or the norm of a subculture, but early puberty is driven by hormonal changes. Apparently, girls are adapted to adapt their behavior to reproductive opportunities and circumstances.

Postmarriage Strategies

Once the pair bond is sealed, a woman faces other challenges. Given the compulsory parental investment that nature imposes on mothers, it may seem peculiar that a woman would be willing to engage in extramarital affairs.

One reason why a woman would find reproductive advantage in a short-term fling is that other males may have better genes, or at least different genes, than her husband (usually, of course, only one male would possess those champion genes). If she can get away with it, her best strategy may be to mate with the strongest male while she and her husband raise the resulting children. Again, this is a recipe for dissension.

Indeed, about 50% of men and 30-50% of women admit to extramarital affairs in the nominally monogamous U.S. society, and a significant fraction of children are not fathered by a woman's husband (Barash & Lipton, 2001). Recently developed tools of genetic analysis have shown, social conventions notwithstanding, that children of men to whom the wife is not married are more common than was previously thought (Gangestad, Thornhill, & Garver, 2002), ranging from about 1% to 30%, depending on the culture. As you might guess, though, obtaining accurate data about human infidelity is difficult because people lie about it, according to Lipton.

A further advantage accruing to a woman who has children by several men is that the genetic variability of her children is greater (Smith, 1984). She spreads the risk that her husband's genes may be disadvantageous to her off-spring. Variability also increases the chances that some children will survive if the family is unlucky enough to encounter an environmental challenge that is difficult for the genes of the married pair to meet. Examples of such challenges include new diseases, new foods, or climate changes.

Several human adaptations point in the direction of facilitating extra-pair reproduction. Around the time of ovulation, a woman's fantasies about sex with someone other than her long-term partner increase while fantasies about the partner remain stable throughout the cycle. Consciously or unconsciously, her mate responds with enhanced attention within the same period, such as vigilance (e.g., unexpected phone calls), monopolization (e.g., spending more free time with her), or spoiling (e.g., unexpected gifts, etc.). Flowers become a weapon in the continuing sexual contest.

Data also show that women's attitudes about short-term liaisons translate into actual behaviors that result in higher fertility. First, extra-pair copulations are more frequent around the time that a woman is ovulating, and therefore is most fertile. The conclusion comes from a survey of 2,000 women who reported that they had a steady relationship (Baker & Bellis, 1995). A second behavior is an increased frequency of female orgasm, which when it occurs soon after male ejaculation, increases the retention of sperm (Gangestad & Simpson, 2000). The contractions of a woman's orgasm effectively pump sperm toward her reproductive tract. If a woman has intercourse with several men in a short period, the one with whom she experiences an orgasm is far more likely to fertilize her egg.

Attractiveness

Any feature of attraction that changes with the stage of the menstrual cycle is likely to affect short-term mating strategies because the long-term mate is available throughout many cycles in any case. Inasmuch as body symmetry is a good indicator of health and good genes (Figure 3.6), evolution should favor women who seek out symmetrical men when they are most fertile. Indeed, the body scent of men who have greater body bilateral symmetry was rated as more attractive by normally ovulating women during the period of highest fertility, based on the day within the menstrual cycle (Thornhill & Gangestad, 1999). Women in low-fertility phases of the cycle did not show this pattern. Eighty men (aged 17-33 yrs) and 82 women (aged 17-53 yrs) participated in the study, which also examined women's scent attractiveness to men.

Finding no evidence that men prefer the scent of symmetric women, the authors proposed that the scent of symmetry is an honest signal of phenotypic and genetic quality only in the human male. Symmetry of the partner may be of less concern to men because their investment in short-term relationships is negligible—after all, someone else will be raising the children.

In both sexes, facial attractiveness as judged from photos appears to predict body scent attractiveness to the opposite sex. Like the symmetry preference, women's preference for the scent associated with men's facial attractiveness was greatest when their fertility was highest across the menstrual cycle, as we saw above. The results overall confirm that women have an evolved reproductive preference for men with good genes.

A disturbing finding of the study was that women using hormone-based contraceptives did not show the pattern. Because these contraceptives simulate early pregnancy, they cause a woman to prefer scents of relatives, presumably an adapted mechanism to keep her close to the family when she needs its aid the most. The implications for single women who are in the courtship phase of life, but taking contraceptives, remain to be worked out. Are they attracted to the wrong men, and would they have to stop taking contraceptives to find out?

All these strategies are unconscious, of course, driven directly by adapted motivations that may have little to do with their end results—a bit of lust here, an inexplicable longing there, but no explicit calculation of the odds of genetic advantage or even a realization that a genetic optimization process is taking place.

In summary, the evolved strategy for a female is to mate with the most resource-rich male she can find who also has desirable personality characteristics, and to have children fathered by the most successful males she can find.

Men's Strategies

Though the need to raise successful children is a goal that both partners share, the male partner also has a unique set of needs. Because he will contribute economic resources that amount to most of the fruits of his labor for the rest of his life, he must make sure that there is a return on that effort. His wife's resources are relatively unimportant (recall that it is the Paleolithic lifestyle that is relevant here), but her childbearing capacity is critical. The male is also making a difficult decision, estimating the reproductive capacity of his potential wife for the next two decades, but nature provides cues that help to inform his decision.

Beauty and Fertility

Despite these serious considerations, most men go after beauty in a spouse. Though it seems like a frivolous, and reproductively risky, way to go about choosing a life partner, evolutionary psychologists have found that beauty and reproductive potential are closely linked, and in fact the concept of beauty may be nothing more or less than a series of cues that enable men to assess a woman's reproductive potential. As a result, beauty became beautiful because it predicted reproductive fitness (Etcoff, 2000). Those of our male ancestors who were attracted to healthy, fertile women became the most successful.

One key to beauty is youth. All over the world, men prefer to marry women in their early to mid 20s, regardless of their own ages or other economic and social considerations. As it happens, the age at which women can bear children with the fewest complications, the age of peak fertility, is 23. Features that are universally considered beautiful, such as smooth skin, lustrous hair, and clear eyes, are indicators of youth and health. Smooth skin is also a sign of freedom from parasites.

Other indicators of reproductive potential are less obvious but equally important in determining actual mate-selection behavior. One is the bilateral symmetry of the spouse, with greater symmetry being more valued (Figure 3.6). Research investigating men's judgments of attractiveness of photographs of women shows that symmetrical faces and bodies are judged to be more beautiful, other things being equal. The same is true for women's judgments of men. Although symmetry is an indication of normal genetic development, it is also an indication of health, as many disfiguring diseases leave one side more affected than the other. Furthermore, symmetry might indicate some of the same features that make averageness attractive, as was shown in the studies of averaged faces reviewed in Chapter 1. Indeed, symmetrical faces

Figure 3.6   Symmetrical and asymmetrical faces. The face on the left of the figure is
asymmetrical: the right side of the subject's face (left in the figure) is larger than
his left side. The woman's face is more symmetrical.

are more attractive than normal individual faces, though the averaged faces are
judged more attractive even after symmetry is taken into account (Rhodes,
Sumich, & Byatt, 1999).

Another feature of women that indicates fertility and that we have
already encountered is an optimal waist-to-hip ratio. Women with a ratio near
the optimum of about 0.7 are more likely to be fertile than women with larger
ratios (i.e., the obese, the pathologically thin, and the sexually immature).
The studies that established the ideal ratio gave men a series of outline
figures of women, varying in waist-to-hip ratio, and asked them to pick the
most attractive (Singh, 1993). Unfortunately, the preferred ratio of 0.7 was
also the lowest choice available in Singh's outline figures (Figure 3.1), so
the ideal ratio may be even lower. The classic 36-24-36 ideal for a woman's
figure suggests that a slightly lower ratio may be the optimum, though the
research has not yet been done to investigate this question. Historically,
women have sought to reduce the ratio artificially, sometimes to very low
values, by binding the waist or extending the hips.

The biological mechanism that regulates waist/hip ratio is the female sex hormone estrogen, which inhibits fat deposition in the abdominal region and facilitates it in the hips, thighs, and buttocks. Thus a hormone that maintains fertility also maintains an important social signal for that fertility.

Few men are consciously aware that waist-to-hip ratio is an indicator of fertility, or even that they are attracted to an ideal ratio, but that does not matter. The important thing is that men are attracted to the right women, not what (or whether) they think about their choices.

Virginity and Disease

There is a good deal more variability among cultures in the value males place on some other female characteristics, such as virginity. In many societies, such as the Chinese, virginity is highly valued, so that both men and women should be virgins going into a marriage. In others, such as the Swedish, hardly anyone is a virgin by the time of marriage, and anybody who has had no sexual experience by then is looked upon as a bit odd. Most societies fall somewhere in between, but for these societies, there is an invariant pattern (Figure 3.7). In nearly all of them, virginity is valued more in women than in men (Buss & Schmitt, 1993).

If valuing virginity is an adapted trait, why would it apply more strongly to men evaluating women? Freedom from sexually transmitted diseases may be one reason why virginity is more valued in women, as these diseases are more likely to cause sterility in women than in men. Another reason for valuing virginity is that, as an indication of chastity, it means that the woman has not had sexual relations with any other man (at least not yet), so that future faithfulness is more likely. Furthermore, in a Paleolithic environment, virginity was the male's only guarantee that a woman had not recently become pregnant. A woman with too much sex drive is more likely to be unfaithful, whereas one with too little is likely to be less fertile and in any case less satisfying to the husband, so selective pressures favor a compromise, a strong but more discriminating sexual motivation in women.

Investment in Children

A man takes a risk in investing in his wife's children because, before the introduction of DNA testing, he could never be quite sure of their paternity. There was always the possibility that things were not as they seemed. Nature has ways of reducing this risk, the risk of being cuckolded. A child that looks like his or her father, especially at a young age, is more likely to be accepted by the father as his own, and in turn is more likely to benefit from the father's

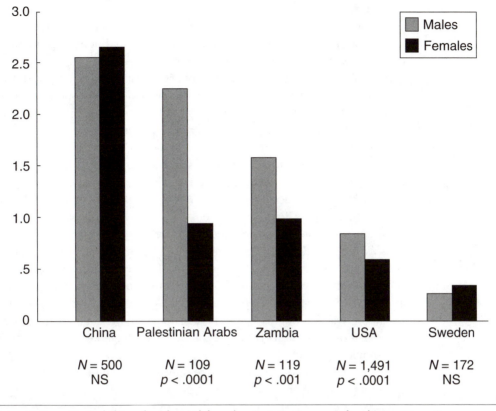

Figure 3.7   Desirability of male and female virginity in several cultures (Buss & Schmitt, 1993).

investment. Thus a selective pressure exists for young children to look more like their fathers than like their mothers. Is the prediction borne out in the real world?

One way to study perceived likeness is to ask what the parents of newborns think. Daly and Wilson (1982), recording remarks made by parents at actual births, found that when the new mother made a remark about the baby's resemblance to a parent, 80% of the time she said something like "He looks like you." Only 20% of the time would she assert that the baby looked like herself. The result has been replicated cross-culturally at least once, in the Yucatan region of Mexico (Regalski & Gualin, 1993).

Another way to study likeness is to examine the actual physical resemblance of children and their fathers. Subjects who didn't know the families involved saw photographs of a child at the ages of 1, 10, and 20, along with photos of three possible mothers and fathers. Their assignment was to match the parents with their children. The matches were no better than random, except in one case—the 1-year-olds were matched with the correct father about half the time. The sex of the child didn't matter, but the matches of the children with their biological mothers were no better than chance (Christenfeld & Hill, 1995). The true biological relationship might be stronger than this study indicates, because paternity tests were not conducted on the fathers, and some of the husbands may not have been the biological fathers of the children depicted in the photographs. The area remains controversial, with one failure to replicate this result (Brédart & French, 1999).

Men have other, more deliberate strategies to ensure paternity as well. Guarding of mates is widespread in human cultures, in some reaching extreme requirements for the seclusion of wives. Wilson and Daly's chapter "The Man Who Mistook His Wife for a Chattel" (1992) explains many of the factors involved. The guarding strategy requires a degree of control over the wife's choices, the attitudes that accompany control being ancient. Some of our earliest written records, in the Old Testament of the Bible, list wives along with other property. The 10th commandment of Moses in the Book of Exodus reads in part, "Thou shalt not covet thy neighbor's house, thou shalt not covet thy neighbor's wife, . . . nor his ox, nor his ass, nor anything that is thy neighbor's." The wife is only one item in a long list of the (male) neighbor's possessions that one should not covet.

Mate guarding appears to be more prevalent, and more accepted, in cultures that allow a man to acquire multiple wives. A consequence of polygyny is an excess of unmarried men in polygynous cultures, men who are desperate for any mating opportunity but find only women who are already married. The presence of these men increases the pressure for extramarital copulation among wives, necessitating stringent mate guarding.

In contemporary China and India, the ratio of males born to females is significantly greater than 1, for different reasons in the two cultures but both resulting in many couples' desire to have sons. Evolutionary theory predicts that mate guarding will become more emphasized in these cultures in future decades, driven by the presence of large numbers of unmarried men. Eventually, the shortage of women should lead to an increase in their value in these societies, because women will have a higher average fertility than men. This will in turn create a pressure to return the ratio of male to female births closer to parity.

Postmarriage Strategies

Most human reproduction takes place in the context of stable marriages, whether monogamous, polygynous, or polyandrous. The evolved reproductive strategy of males is not entirely monogamous, however, because the rewards in terms of biological fitness overwhelmingly favor a more complex approach. The cost of an extra fling is negligible, a few minutes of effort and a few milliliters of fluid, but the potential reproductive payoff is enormous. Under these conditions, the motivation is strong to make the most of any opportunities.

Human male physiology is also adapted to opportunistic mating. Normally, a man must recover for some time after copulation, but if a new partner becomes available, he experiences a resurgence of sexual ability. This phenomenon, known in reproductive biology as the **Coolidge effect,** has a clear advantage for the evolutionary fitness of the male animal.

The effect is said to have been named after an incident that occurred when President Calvin Coolidge was visiting a farm with his wife. Mrs. Coolidge asked whether the unceasing sexual activity in a flock of hens was due to a single rooster; the farmer replied that it was. She remarked, "You might point that out to Mr. Coolidge." The president then asked whether the rooster approached a different hen each time, and when told that he did, replied, "You might point that out to Mrs. Coolidge."

In opportunistic mating, the male usually takes less note of the woman's qualities, whether she has a good share of intelligence, personality, and beauty, than he would for a long-term partner (Buss & Schmitt, 1993). Nor is he usually concerned with how she will raise any resulting children. As a result, the value of a child from an opportunistic copulation is less than the value of a child in a stable relationship, because the father will make no contribution to the child's welfare. The chances of the child surviving, and being psychologically healthy enough to compete in his or her own turn, are reduced. The biological father also forgoes the benefits as well as the costs of parenthood, such as alliances with a grown child and support in old age.

Rape. What does a loser in the courtship battles do, a man who has no prospect of attracting a mate? The harsh answer, sometimes, is rape. By forcing a woman to have sex, a man can get his genes into the next generation without courtship, provisioning, and all the investment that successful parenting normally requires. Evolutionary theory, then, predicts that men who are relatively unsuccessful in competition for resources and status may resort to forced sex (Thornhill, Thornhill, & Dizinno, 1986), an explanation based on possible reproductive benefits to the person showing the behavior. As in all applications of evolutionary theory, though, empirical evidence is essential to test the theory.

The behavior is risky for several reasons. First, the woman may abort the fetus or abandon the resulting infant, or her spouse may do it for her. Today, an early abortion is far safer than a normal pregnancy. In the Paleolithic world of our evolution, however, safe abortion was not an option.

Second, both women and their spouses strenuously resist the idea, and it is punished in at least certain instances in all cultures (Thornhill & Palmer, 2000). Male protection is fairly effective in preventing rape, according to a survey conducted by the U.S. Department of Justice National Crime and Victimization Department, for women who have never been married or who are divorced/separated show higher rates of rape than women who are married or widowed (Mesnick, 1997).

Despite these risks, rapes still occur. There are two theories about the nature of the act: one that rape is not about sex or reproduction, but about exerting power, and the other that rape is an adapted human behavior that expresses itself in certain extreme circumstances. To decide between these two theories, we can look at the predictions that each one makes, and test those predictions empirically.

The power theory predicts that rape should occur whenever a man has physical power over a woman and is not likely to be caught. It should not matter whether the victim is likely to become pregnant. The adapted trait theory, in contrast, predicts that most rape victims should be of reproductive age. Statistics show that most rape victims are women of reproductive age (Thornhill & Palmer, 2000). The much less frequent rapes of children or post-menopausal women are thought to be rooted not in sexual strategy but in a debilitated capacity for self-control (Knudsen, 1991).

A close relationship of rape with forced reproduction can be found in the probability of pregnancy resulting from a single sex act. If the act is consensual, the rate of pregnancy is about 3.1% in the absence of contraception, but in rape the pregnancy rate climbs to about 8% in women not using contraception (data reviewed by Walker, 2001). Studies such as these are difficult to interpret, however, because the definition of rape is problematic; it depends on reports of past events filtered by social conventions, memory, and sometimes a sense of shame or desire for self-protection. A woman may be reluctant to report a rape, for instance, if no pregnancy resulted. In the case of a pregnancy, though, it may be to her advantage to admit to rape rather than face charges of promiscuity or voluntary infidelity.

These data suggest that rape is ultimately about reproduction, even if the proximate motivations of the rapist are different. What about the social status and personal motivations of rapists? Personality characteristics of rapists, and of men who engage in sexual aggression, tend to combine an insecure, hostile, and distrustful orientation with a pleasure in dominating and controlling women (Malamuth, 1996). In personality tests, such men tend to agree with opinions such as "I have been rejected by too many women in my life" and

"I am sure I get a raw deal from the women in my life." Not all rapists are powerless losers, but a disproportionate number are, according to this study.

Translating these attitudes into actual behavior has been more problematic. Men who admit to using sexual coercion rate themselves higher on mating success, measured by questions such as "Members of the opposite sex that I like tend to like me back" or "I receive sexual invitations from members of the opposite sex" (Lalumiere et al., 1996). They also anticipate a high future earning potential, and prefer a greater variety of partners along with more casual sex.

These results contradict the rapists-are-losers theory. Of course, this test too is indirect, measuring reports of behavior and attitudes rather than actual behavior. Men inclined toward sexual coercion may overestimate their attractiveness to women. Whether these coercive men actually were attractive to the opposite sex and had higher future earnings remains an open question—studies of actual coercive behavior, as opposed to attitudes toward it, are understandably difficult to conduct. And interviews with actual rapists often elicit denials that coercion was involved, again possibly a self-serving justification.

Sperm competition. Male-male competition does not stop in the singles bar or on the dance floor—it extends all the way to the female vaginal tract and beyond. In species where sperm from two or more males is likely to compete within the female for fertilization, it is vital to each male to produce more sperm, but it is also advantageous to minimize the potency of competitors' sperm. Recently, specialized human sperm cells have been discovered that have no role in reproduction. They are "killer sperm," whose only function is to destroy the sperm of other males in the female's reproductive tract. Sperm competition is widespread, occurring even in flies (Birkhead, 2000).

In the highly promiscuous chimpanzee, it turns out that as few as 1% of sperm cells are even capable of fertilizing an egg; the others have been labeled blockers, or more colorfully, kamikaze sperm. Their sole function is to prevent the sperm of others from doing its job. The Type A kamikaze specializes in killing sperm that enter the female after the kamikazes have been deposited in the vaginal tract, and Type B specialize in attacking sperm that they find on arrival in the tract (Baker, 1996).

Without knowing it, men adjust the amount and kind of sperm ejaculated depending on the social conditions. The volume of sperm depends on how much time has passed since a man and his partner have had sex, and not on the amount of time that has passed since the last ejaculation. And sperm volume depends not only on duration since their last intercourse but on how long the couple have been separated. If they have lived together continuously, the sperm volume is independent of time since last intercourse, but after they have been apart, the volume can rise threefold (Baker, 1996).

In summary, the evolved male strategy is to mate with as many women as possible, while investing in children who are likely to be his own.

Homosexuality

The existence of homosexuality in about 1-5% of the population in all known cultures (LeVay & Hamer, 1994), as well as its persistence despite sometimes vicious persecution, is a mystery in terms of evolution. Not all homosexuals are childless, but because the overall fertility of homosexuals is lower than that of heterosexuals, evolutionary theory predicts that the trait should be selected against, and should long since have disappeared from the human genome.

It is already clear that male homosexuality is not a result of events or experiences during childhood (Herdt & Boxer, 1993). Homosexuality does not correlate with any early experiences or living situations. The orientation is not learned, for many homosexuals grow up thinking they are the only boys in the world who feel sexual attraction to other males, and they have great difficulty dealing with such feelings. Thus the objections to homosexual teachers, scoutmasters, and so on are misguided, as though mere social contact with a homosexual man could reverse a boy's sexual orientation. Despite ambitious and sometimes horrific attempts at retraining, it has not been possible to change homosexuals into heterosexuals by training or experience, though behaviors can sometimes be changed for a while by sheer terror. We must seek a genetic explanation.

Two theories about the existence of homosexuality reflect two ways of thinking about evolution in general. One theory is that homosexuality is a genetic cost of evolution, analogous to the inadequate design of our lower backs or the inefficiency of our bipedal gait. The other theory holds that there is a compensating benefit somewhere for the appearance of the trait.

The Cost Theory

This theory starts from the fundamental observation that men and women are very different on a myriad of traits, yet their genes are very nearly identical. The male's Y chromosome, the only uniquely male genetic material, has only a handful of functional genes. Worse, some of them are expressed only before birth, becoming permanently suppressed even before a male infant is born. Nothing in the female's X chromosome is unique to females, for each male has a single copy of that chromosome. The genes are selected to be as similar as possible because males contribute genetically to female children and vice versa. Nature has a very difficult job in keeping things sorted out with so little to go on, in this theory, so that occasionally mistakes are made.

Backing up this theory at the physiological level are observations about hormonal links to homosexuality. Stress in the mother late in pregnancy is one possible precursor. After pregnant rats were exposed to stressful events, such as bright lights and physical restraint, their sons were tested for male- and female-typical behaviors. Following injections of estrogen and progesterone, the sons showed more female sexual behavior and less male sexual behavior than control rats (Ward, 1992; Ward & Ward, 1985). They also had lower testosterone levels. These results must be interpreted with caution, however, for rats grow throughout life and therefore have different physiological responses to many challenges than humans. Also, female human sexual behavior is more influenced than rat behavior by androgens and by cultural convention. Finally, display of some female-like behavior is very different from human male homosexuality. About the only female-like trait that all homosexuals share is an attraction to men. In short, closer examination leads to the conclusion that the feminized rat is not a very useful model of human homosexuality.

A variant of this theory posits that infants tend to grow up to be homosexual if they are either exposed to excess hormones specific to the opposite sex during gestation, or not exposed to the appropriate hormones at a critical period during development. Supporting this mechanism, at least for female homosexuals, are observations that female rats born in litters with a large number of male siblings tend to show more male-like characteristics than rats born in litters that are predominantly female (Clemens, 1971). The explanation for this effect is that androgens from the developing brothers masculinized the female fetus.

This mechanism does not work as an explanation for human homosexuality, of course, because most of us are born one at a time, and most homosexuals are not twins. Recent studies of humans, however, have uncovered a related mechanism that may predispose mothers to have homosexual sons. Homosexual orientation correlates with the number of a man's older brothers, each additional older brother increasing the odds of homosexuality by about 33% (Blanchard, 2001). The older brothers may progressively immunize the mother against Y-linked minor histocompatibility antigens (H-Y antigens), components of the immune system that appear on the Y chromosome and thus are linked to male body and brain structures. According to this hypothesis, anti-H-Y antibodies produced by the mother pass through the placenta to affect aspects of sexual differentiation in the fetal brain.

This explanation is consistent with a variety of evidence, including the apparent irrelevance of older sisters to the sexual orientation of later-born males and the probable involvement of H-Y antigen in the development of sex-typical traits. In effect, homosexuality in this theory becomes a by-product of a selective pressure for strong immune systems to fight disease. The theory predicts that a smaller proportion of homosexuals should be born in societies with smaller families, a hypothesis that should be tested.

The Benefits Theory

Because homosexuals in most societies have lower fertility than hetero-sexuals in comparable social strata, explanations in terms of evolved adapta-tions revolve around kin selection. The theory is supported indirectly by findings that contemporary homosexuals tend to have lower crime rates and higher incomes than their heterosexual neighbors (Hewitt, 1995). In many traditional societies, homosexuals take the roles of shamans or healers, increasing the social status of their families.

Benefits are difficult to justify in terms of natural selection, though, because kin selection theory requires that losses in homosexuals' fertility must be made up by corresponding gains in fertility of relatives, divided by their degree of relationship. Thus a sibling would have to have 4 additional children to make up for two that a homosexual man does not have, his cousins would have to have 16, and so on. In contemporary societies, there is no evidence of increased fertility of homosexuals' relatives on this scale. We don't know what the fertility balance was in Paleolithic societies, of course, but absence of con-tradictory evidence does not constitute supportive evidence.

The case for female homosexuals is not comparable to that of male homosexuals. A larger number of lesbians assume this role later in life, after a period of heterosexual relationships and child-rearing. And the incidence of homosexuality in the population is much lower for females than for males.

Incest

An infant boy, abandoned at birth, grows and thrives in the care of strangers. Reaching adulthood, he seeks his fortune in another country, where he falls in love with a beautiful woman, but she is already married. The desperate young man kills her husband in order to marry her. Only then does he discover that the woman is really his own mother, her husband his father. Horrified, he gouges out his eyes and wanders forever after, a blind beggar.

Already an ancient myth when Sophocles based his play *Oedipus Rex* on it more than 24 centuries ago, the story speaks to an ageless human fear, that of marrying a close relative, unable to discern the relationship until it is too late. Why is it so terrible to marry a relative, and what are the evolved mechanisms that normally prevent us from doing so?

The Genetics of Incest

Mating with close relatives puts the offspring of the match at a distinct disadvantage for purely genetic reasons. Each of us contains many **lethal recessives**, genes that are not expressed in our phenotype because they are paired with a normal gene from our other parent. A recessive gene is expressed only if it is **homozygous,** inherited in the same form from both parents, while a **dominant gene** will be expressed even if it is inherited from only one parent. A particular lethal recessive gene will not be selected against if it remains very uncommon in the population, because the chance of the same lethal recessive appearing in two unrelated people is remote. The chance is very small of two people mating who share the same lethal recessive alleles of these genes. A gene with a population frequency of 1 in 10,000 (10^4), for example, will appear in both of two unrelated people with a frequency of 1 in 100 million (10^8).

If your mate is a close relative, however, it is likely that both of you have inherited some of the same lethal recessive genes from your common ancestors, and your union will be less fertile because the lethal genes will be expressed in your offspring, causing a high miscarriage rate. Some other recessive genes are not lethal, but are defective and will cause birth defects, lowered intelligence, and other problems in children of incestuous unions.

This is more than just abstract genetic theory. In the 19th century, a wealthy and prominent biologist married his cousin, had 10 children, and lost 3 of them before maturity. His name was Charles Darwin.

Incest-Avoidance Mechanisms

Given this grim reality, it is no surprise that we have evolved mechanisms to prevent incest. In humans they are expressed as motivations, evolved emotions of disgust at marrying a close relative, and a lack of sexual attraction to those relatives. Given the disastrous consequences of its failure, it is critical that the mechanism be reliable. Most mammals have a well-developed system of olfactory cues for this purpose, and can literally smell their relatives.

Having lost this ancient safeguard, humans have developed another, less reliable mechanism. Because we cannot sense our relatives directly, but we invariably grow up in their presence, the incest-avoidance mechanism in humans is simply a genetically given imperative not to be sexually attracted to those with whom we grew up. The tendency even has a name, the **Westermarck effect,** after its early 20th-century discoverer (Westermarck, 1921). Most cultures have additional but widely varying arrays of customs and taboos to forbid marriage of close relatives.

The mechanism is simple, it doesn't require the direct recognition of genetic relationship, and it works most of the time. Unfortunately, it is not fail-safe, as the Oedipus tragedy makes clear. The danger of mistakes is perhaps the origin of our deep-seated terror of winding up like Oedipus.

How do we know that this mechanism exists and that others do not? Oedipus (and documented modern cases of a similar sort) gives us one piece of evidence, that in fact incest can occur between blood relatives if they are raised separately. There is also evidence from the opposite situation, sexual disinterest in wholly unrelated people with whom one was raised. Such disinterest is a stronger test of the familiarity theory of incest avoidance, because failure to avoid incest might result from the failure of some other incest avoidance mechanism as well. The strongest evidence comes from the kibbutz movement of self-contained agricultural communities in Israel, where the intent of the founders was to raise all the children communally in central housing and to perpetuate the community when the children matured, married one another, and raised a second generation of kibbutzniks.

It didn't work that way—out of 2,769 recorded marriages, there is not a single documented instance of two children of the opposite sex, raised together throughout childhood, who married one another, according to a study by anthropologist Joseph Shepher (reported in Wilson, 1998). Despite social encouragement to the contrary, the communally raised children invariably sought marriage partners outside their own kibbutz and were sexually uninterested in genetically unrelated partners from their own community. Following the evolved human pattern that we share with the chimpanzee, men usually sought mates in another community and brought them back to their own. The social mechanism that ordinarily prevents reproduction with relatives in this case prevented reproduction with unrelated members of their own community.

Another lesson from the kibbutz experiment was that even though the founders were imbued with a strong motivation to do everything communally, the practice of rearing all the children together in large groups did not last. In all of Israel's kibbutzim, children now live with their parents. The evolved mechanisms and motivations that facilitate the child-rearing process are the subject of the next chapter.

DISCUSSION QUESTIONS ●

1. Are there any aspects of the chimpanzee form of sexual activity in the motivations or behaviors of modern humans?
2. Why do we find parasites disgusting?
3. Why do we judge some evolved human mating strategies to be immoral?
4. Why do societies differ so greatly in their degree of control over the activities of fertile women?

FURTHER READING ●

Mealy, M. (2000). *Sex differences: Development and evolutionary strategies*. San Diego, CA: Academic Press.

A biologist describes differences in lifestyles and strategies of a variety of animals as well as humans.

Sapolski, R. M. (1997). *The trouble with testosterone*. New York: Simon & Schuster.

A superb writer, endocrinologist Robert Sapolski examines reproductive realities in a series of essays about baboons and humans, making each seem more like the other than either would like to admit.

Trivers, R. (1985). *Social evolution*. Menlo Park, CA: Benjamin/Cummings.

One of evolutionary biology's most creative minds examines the evolution of social life, emphasizing reproductive adaptations in a wide variety of animals as well as humans.

Barash, D. P., & Lipton, J. E. (2001). *Myth of monogamy: Fidelity and infidelity in animals and people*. New York: W. H. Freeman.

This book will change your ideas about relationships between bonded partners, human and nonhuman.

CHAPTER 4

CHILDREN AND CHILD-REARING

"A person's a person, no matter how small."

— Dr. Seuss, *Horton Hears a Who!*

Traditionally, psychology views children as helpless beings, utterly dependent upon their parents and others for everything. Despite this view, it is clear that children survive, like other organisms, in the same hostile world that their parents inhabit. They succeed not because they are good hunters or gatherers or farmers, but because they are virtuoso beggars—others, mainly parents, are happy to provide for their needs until they are old enough to create their own resources. The parents are motivated not by explicit calculations of inclusive fitness but by signals that the child produces.

Another traditional view of children in psychology is that they are intellectually incompetent, born into a world that they cannot understand because experience has not yet organized their perception of the environment. The world of the infant, according to William James (1893), is "a buzzing, blooming confusion." Is it? Developmental psychologists in recent decades have discovered more structure in the cognitive world of the infant and young child than we had dared imagine, structure that enables the infant not only to survive but to quickly make sense of the world and to learn the essentials of life as a human being.

These are just two of the ways that evolutionary theory, and the empirical work that supports it, have changed the way psychologists think about children and development. But it's best to begin at the beginning of life.

PREGNANCY AND CHILDBIRTH ●

Pregnancy begins a developmental process that progresses until birth without direct behavioral intervention; it would seem to have nothing to do with psychology. Behaviors and attitudes, however, regulate the process from start to finish.

Pregnancy: Parasitism or Symbiosis?

The fetus is genetically distinct from the mother, sharing only half of its genes with her, but it lives within her body. Because of this genetic difference, the fetus plays many of the physiological roles of a parasite. After it implants in the uterus, it begins absorbing the mother's resources while maintaining a separate blood supply. Of course the fetus ultimately is not a true parasite, because it is in the mother's interest to support it. From this perspective, pregnancy is a **symbiosis**, an interaction between two organisms that benefits both.

For the fetus, resources are all-important. The mother, though, has other interests, including past and future offspring, so that she must manage her resources in ways that are not always to the fetus's advantage. The fetus wants as much of the mother's blood sugar as possible, for example, pumping its hormones into her bloodstream to get it. The mother defends herself with her own hormones, neutralizing the fetus's biochemical attack. Thus begins a biological competition that will continue throughout the mother-child relationship. The hormonal balance is similar to the hormonal regulation of many functions within a single person, where two hormones with opposite effects are activated, the balance between them determining the action of the system.

Normally, the result is a standoff, with the fetus's sugar supply staying about where it would have been without the biochemical arms race. If the process gets out of balance, gestational diabetes can result for the mother. It seems a futile conflict, but neither side can give up; each is trapped by evolution, forced to continue the hormonal escalation. Changing the fetus's genes that request more sugar would lead to its starvation; changing the mother's genes that defend her sugar supply would lead to her exhaustion. And changing both at once is vanishingly unlikely, because two distinct sets of genes, one in the fetus and one in the mother, would have to change together.

Nature ensures that the developing fetus will get not only sugar but also the other nutrients and minerals it needs, even at the mother's expense. The calcium for its bones comes not from the mother's diet but mostly from her bones and teeth. If she doesn't convert enough dietary calcium into usable forms, the fetus will get it anyway, even though the mother might lose a tooth or two. And pregnancy continues even if the mother doesn't get enough to eat. Perhaps this is why menstruation and also fertility are interrupted when a woman's percentage of body fat drops too low. The fat reserves, and the other stored nutrients that accompany them, must be on hand before pregnancy begins.

"Morning Sickness" as an Adaptation

The first sign to a prospective mother that she is pregnant is often morning sickness, also called pregnancy sickness. Despite its name, the sickness can occur at any time of the day. Its principal symptoms are sustained nausea, sometimes vomiting, combined with distaste for certain foods, symptoms that most pregnant women experience at one time or another. The nausea isn't a brief episode, as you might feel when you've had too much to eat or drink, but can go on for weeks, usually during the first trimester of pregnancy. It occurs in all human groups, from hunter-gatherers to industrial societies.

Why should a woman feel sick just when her body is at its peak, doing what it was designed by nature to do? At first glance, the body seems poorly adapted to its role in pregnancy, for a normal function should not make one feel sick. But the first glance would deceive—there is a wealth of evidence that pregnancy "sickness" is an adaptation to increase the fitness of the unborn child. It is not an immune response to microorganisms, like most maladies, but is part of the normal functioning of an adapted behavioral system (Profet, 1992).

The biological function of pregnancy sickness is to prevent exposing the developing embryo to dietary toxins. The poisons are defenses of plants against being eaten; they prevent any halfway sensible predator from attacking the plants that manufacture them. Humans eat the plants anyway, but our talented digestive systems can usually neutralize the toxins before they do much damage.

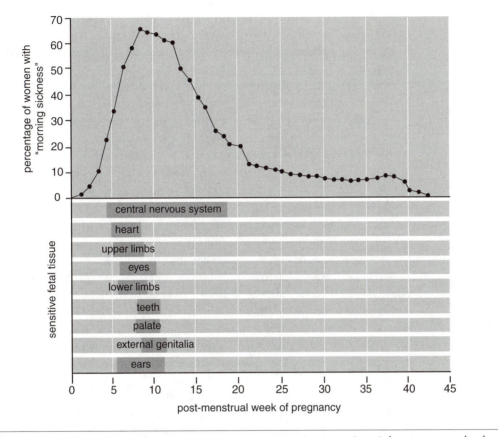

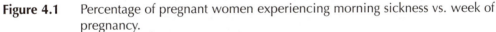

Figure 4.1   Percentage of pregnant women experiencing morning sickness vs. week of pregnancy.

Most of these chemicals are **mutagens**, agents that cause genetic mutations, or **carcinogens**, agents that induce cancer. They attack cells that are dividing, a characteristic that makes rapidly growing embryonic tissue especially vulnerable to their effects. A few plant toxins are **teratogens**, interfering specifically with the processes of embryonic development.

Not only vegetables, but also meats and even some fruits can contain such substances. These are foods that might have harbored harmful bacteria in the Paleolithic world, before refrigeration. Only a few bland foods, such as rice, are low in toxins and tend not to induce aversion. Mothers also show an aversion via olfaction to foods that are the least bit rotten.

Pregnancy sickness normally begins 2-4 weeks after conception, peaks at 6-8 weeks, and subsides by 14 weeks, coinciding closely with **organogenesis**, the period of organ formation in the embryo (Figure 4.1). Its function thus seems to be to prevent dietary toxins from interfering with the normal development of the embryo's organs. The symptoms, triggered by the hormones of pregnancy, subside at about the time that organ formation is complete.

Preventing the ingestion of toxins is a problem in the management of behavior, and here is where the psychology comes in. Like the genetic influence on many other behaviors, the effect is on attitudes and emotions—it is not a knee-jerk, reflex-like compulsion. Women with pregnancy sickness are particularly repelled by tastes and smells associated with toxicity in foods, including foods that they usually enjoy. Even cooking odors can trigger nausea, for toxins are often released during cooking. Thus the mother avoids toxins before they can be ingested.

The aversions are quite specific. Studies of a total of 5,432 pregnant women showed the strongest aversions to animal products, such as fish, poultry, and eggs, to nonalcoholic beverages (mostly containing caffeine), and to alcoholic beverages (Flaxman & Sherman, 2000). Meat and eggs are often infested with bacteria, because they are removed from their usual protection inside some animal's immune system, and many beverages have strong flavors. Because we can't detect toxins directly, the adapted mechanism works on flavors that historically have correlated with presence of the toxins. Aversion to vegetables is less severe, presumably because they contain lighter doses of toxins.

Pregnancy sickness is not completely effective in preventing damage to the fetus, because deformities originate from so many sources. Though many birth defects result from maternal drug exposures, vitamin deficiencies, or genetic syndromes, about two thirds have no known cause (Profet, 1992).

Ironically, there is a way of alleviating pregnancy sickness—smoking. Women who smoke tobacco during pregnancy are much less likely to suffer from pregnancy sickness than those who do not (52% vs. 79%; Little & Hook, 1979). The toxins that pregnancy sickness protects against are limited to the sorts that would have threatened Paleolithic mothers, and the toxins in tobacco smoke are not among them. Although tobacco smoke is full of carcinogens, cigarette smoking also interferes with olfactory and taste receptors. Other modern environmental stresses, such as air pollution, drugs, or radiation, also fail to trigger pregnancy sickness.

Another consequence of smoking is that it decreases maternal estrogen (estradiol) levels. High estrogen levels help to maintain pregnancy, and it is thought that they are part of the trigger mechanism for the symptoms of pregnancy sickness. The reason for the lowered estradiols might be that the mother produces enzymes to detoxify tobacco products, enzymes that also metabolize estradiol. As one could guess from this chain of biochemical disasters, miscarriage rates are much higher among smokers than among nonsmokers (Profet, 1992).

The conclusion from all of this is that pregnancy sickness is an ancient, evolved mechanism to protect the developing embryo. A study of 16 countries shows that it is universal, not restricted to specific cultures or circumstances (Sherman & Flaxman, 2001). It is to the mother's genetic advantage, because it reduces the chances of her embryo being damaged. Defects in an embryo often lead to miscarriage, and spontaneous miscarriage rates are much lower in pregnant women who suffer from pregnancy sickness (about 3.8%) than in those who do not (about 10.4%). Unfortunately the process is uncomfortable for the mother, but adaptations are driven only by their outcomes. The fact that the process is unpleasant does not reduce its biological usefulness.

There are also cravings during pregnancy, especially for foods that are rich in calories but are less likely to contain toxins (Sherman & Flaxman, 2001). These include dairy products, sweets, grains, and many fruits. Pickles and ice cream, anyone?

Life in the Womb

What is life like for the developing fetus? The nervous system is the last of the major organ systems to develop, so that experience in the womb is not an issue through most of prenatal development. There is simply not enough functioning brain to support cognitive processes: the cerebral cortex does not begin to come on line until several weeks after birth. During intrauterine development, the fetus is protected from sights and sounds in the outside world, and what does get through is blurred or muffled. Motor activity, of course, is also severely restricted, limited to spasms, kicks, and occasional thumb sucking.

As the brain develops toward the end of pregnancy, the placenta's limitations become more obvious; it cannot provide enough oxygen to support normal human brain function. The fetus survives on the difference between the oxygen affinities of maternal blood and fetal blood, the fetal blood having a higher level of binding so that it can take oxygen from the mother's circulation (Silverstein, 1980, p. 481). Not enough oxygen can cross the placenta to support the growing body and brain. This is why newborns look bluish before they take their first breaths, even if the placenta is still functioning and the umbilical cord is pulsating. The partial pressure of oxygen is only about a third as great in the full-term unborn infant as it is just after birth, a reduction in the level of oxygen that would render an adult unconscious. We will never know for sure because we can't ask the newborn baby, but low oxygen pressure might prevent the brain from functioning as it will just after birth. Whether a newborn is aware of its surroundings is a perplexing question, but awareness before birth is unlikely.

Control of body temperature is an example of a brain mechanism that must engage behavior immediately after birth, but should not be functional in the womb. If the baby's brain controlled its own temperature before birth, it would continually fight a losing battle with the mother, because the two biological thermostats would not be set to exactly the same level. The baby would exhaust its limited resources trying to slightly heat or cool itself, using mechanisms that generally are of little use in the womb in any case. Shortly after birth, the already mature thermostatic control system of the baby becomes functional. Similar switches trigger several other changes, including regulation of blood pressure, breathing, and of course crying.

● INFANCY AND EARLY CHILDHOOD

Newborns provide unique opportunities for psychologists interested in biological structure, because only in infancy is one guaranteed that a capability or a structure did not result from interaction with a person's culture or surroundings. Thus infancy provides a valuable testing ground for evolutionary psychology to uncover biological adaptations before cultural influence can make itself felt.

Social Capabilities of the Infant

Infants elicit caregiving from the adults around them with features that we consider "cute," such as large heads and pudgy limbs. Why might we consider these features to be adorable? The short answer is that we come from an unbroken line of ancestors who considered babies to be cute, and who had "cute" features as babies themselves. The two characteristics, cute features in the young and appreciation of them in their elders, underwent a co-evolution.

The proximate cause of our protecting and nurturing of infants is not to promote our genetic heritage but is rather a response to innate triggers that infants release to elicit caregiving behavior in others (Figure 4.2). The triggers are the same all over the world, and throughout history. Again the ultimate cause of the behavior, preservation of our own genes, is unrelated to the evolved proximate mechanisms. Even cartoons exploit the **sign stimuli** that

Figure 4.2 Popular characters often display infantile features. The eyes in this cartoon figure are larger than in the original bird, and face the front rather than the side. The head, like that of a human infant, is large in proportion to the body. Dolls often emphasize the same features.

make babies adorable—the pudgy cheeks, high voice, smooth skin, large forehead, and large eyes (Gould, 1980). Baby animals that share these features also share our indulgence of them.

Sign stimuli as social releasers came into evolutionary psychology from the European tradition of ethology (Tinbergen, 1951). Examples from etho-logical work on animals include a spot on a gull's beak that elicits pecking from chicks; the adult gull in turn regurgitates food for the chick. Gull chicks will peck just as enthusiastically at a pencil, if it has the right spot painted on it. Similarly, a red belly on the small stickleback fish is displayed only on males, and will elicit a challenge from another male. The stickleback will also display to a pencil with a red streak on the bottom, showing that it is the red marking and not some other releaser that triggers the behavior. Though we humans like to think that we are above being influenced by such simple releasers, the cute baby example shows that we're not.

Face Recognition

Being cute isn't enough by itself, though. Other, behavioral traits emerge that facilitate success in the social world. The baby's ability to recognize faces is particularly important in its earliest social interactions, because survival may depend on it. This ability appears without experience, as shown by studies using the technique of **preferential looking**: an observer watches a baby's eyes as the baby looks at two patterns, one a cartoon-like human face made of dark spots and the other made up of the same features turned upside down, so that the "eyes" are below and the "nose" is on top. Babies only a few hours old have been studied with this technique, and the results are clear: the baby looks more at the realistic face, showing both an ability to discriminate faces from nonfaces and a behavioral preference for looking at faces (Valenza, Simion, Cassia, & Umiltà, 1996).

A small brain area, about the size of a pea and located in the temporal lobe of the cortex just behind the ear, controls face recognition. Without this area, adults are unable to distinguish one face from another, though they can readily recognize friends and family members by their voices or mannerisms. Anatomical studies show this area to be active when people are perceiving faces (O'Craven & Kanwisher, 2000).

These studies use **functional magnetic resonance imaging** (fMRI) to look at brain activity of normal, conscious adults. The technique measures cerebral blood flow, which correlates with brain activity, by magnetic probes of the brain. An experimental subject is asked to look at random patterns for a minute or so while blood flow in the brain is measured. Then the subject looks at pictures of faces, again for a minute or so. Brain blood flow under the two conditions is subtracted to take away any activity that is not specific to face perception, and the result reveals an area of cortex devoted to face recognition that is built into all of us.

Neurological patients who lack this area are unable to recognize faces, whereas other perceptual abilities remain nearly unaffected. The deficit, called **prosopagnosia**, is sensory in nature—patients are unable to recognize either familiar faces, such as those of family members, or people they have met since the onset of the problem.

The patients are not totally without information about faces, though. They still have autonomic signs of orienting when shown photographs of familiar faces (Tranel & Damasio, 1985). Orienting was measured by changes in the galvanic skin response (GSR) of the hand, a change in the skin's electrical conductivity presumably caused by slight sweating (salt water is a conductor of electricity). Thus some processing of the faces is going on, enough for some brain areas to be informed about face identity. Yet the patient remains unable to use this processing to guide behavior, including verbal behavior.

The specialized area for processing faces is older than humanity—there is a similar area in monkey brains, and removing it interferes with the monkey's face recognition ability.

Here a mystery arises, for we know from studies of anatomical development that the newborn's cortex is not yet functional. How can the newborns recognize faces without a cortex? The evidence from infants points to subcortical mechanisms, in older parts of the brain, that orient the infant toward faces. At about 6 weeks of age, as the maturing cortex begins to function, new mechanisms take over the job of face recognition. The infant still looks longer at faces than at nonfaces, but the criteria for a face-like pattern change. The newborn, for example, shows no preference for positive (black-on-white) over negative (white-on-black) images of faces, but by 12 weeks of age, all of 12 babies tested preferred positive images (Mondloch et al., 1999). So the world of the newborn is in some ways like ours, but in other ways very different. The newborn's face processing system may be a relic of primate or even preprimate evolution.

Smiling and Imitation

At about 4 weeks of age, the first smile appears, at first directed at anything face-like, but eventually concentrating on the primary caregivers (Figure 4.3). Of course the parents are enchanted by the smile, because they have been programmed to be enchanted by it. As the baby matures into a toddler, a myriad of other interactions facilitates a tight bond between parents and child.

Imitation, another facilitator of social interaction, begins with the mouth. In general, embryological development proceeds from the top of an organism to the bottom, and from the centerline to the distal limbs, so the mouth is a reasonable place to look for the most developed capabilities of infants. Parents have endless patience for initiating the imitation of mouth-opening, sticking out the tongue, and so on, activities that the infant can reciprocate at least to some degree from the first day of life (Meltzoff & Moore, 1977, 1999).

It seems a simple game, but the game requires considerable understanding on the part of infants: they must recognize that the gesticulating form is another human being with a mouth like their own, perceive the specific gesture, and be able to use their own body to perform the seemingly useless movements, knowing which muscles to activate. Infants must also possess from the beginning the motivation to engage in such economically

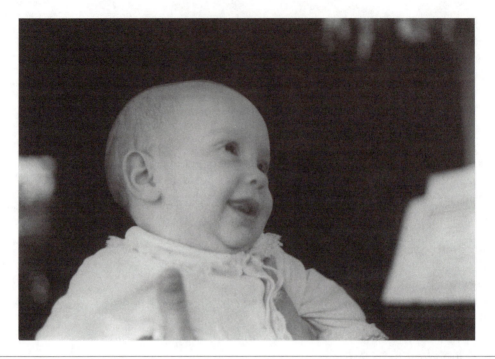

Figure 4.3   At 4 months of age, this baby is already a veteran smiler, aiming her charms at her caregivers. Head and eyes are coordinated in orienting.

useless activities. Altogether, it is an astonishing repertoire for newborn infants, but the empirical evidence for it is good, especially for the activity of sticking out the tongue.

One of the primary social adaptations of humans is language, the subject of a later chapter. Social communication has a long history in infants even before the first word appears at about 1 year of age, beginning with the smile and moving on to gestures and vocalizations.

Moral Development

The traditional socialization view holds that very young children are not initially social, and that only through later experience do they become social (D. L. Bridgeman, 1983). Infants in this view arrive in the world self-centered and egoistic; they must be socialized, taught to take cognizance of the needs and rights of others. Lest this be interpreted as an exaggeration, here is a statement from Professor Alberta Siegel of the Stanford University Medical Center:

A horde of untutored savages arrives in our midst annually; these are our infants, who come among us knowing nothing of our language, our culture, our values. . . . The child starts life totally ignorant of . . . decency, gentleness, compassion, sympathy, kindness. (Siegel, 1974, p. 23)

Careful studies of children from 1-1/2 years to 3-1/2 years of age in their own homes, rather than in unfamiliar laboratory settings, contradict the traditional view, with the youngest children showing as much prosocial behavior as older children. Although young children undeniably show generous amounts of shortsighted and selfish behavior, the activities of helping, sharing, and nurturing appeared even in the youngest children (D. L. Bridgeman, 1983). When my young daughter offered me her treasured pacifier after I became upset about something, I knew that such effects influence real social interactions.

As soon as they are old enough to interact with others, children are aware of rules that limit behavior, and concepts of fairness govern many social interactions. Furthermore, young children consider moral transgressions to be more significant than transgressions of social rules, even though social transgressions involve violations of specific rules but moral transgressions do not. Even for children, social conventions are evaluated relative to the social context, whereas moral values are seen as absolute (Smetana, Bridgeman, & Turiel, 1983).

Theory of Mind

All of us are continuously interpreting the moods, attitudes, and knowledge of others, an activity so routine that we seldom consider what a remarkable feat it is. Inferring the mental states of others requires that we have a model of the other person, a theory of mind, within our own brains that enables us to infer mental states from behavior. In engineering this is called backward modeling, constructing a model that describes a transition from cause to effect, and then running it the other way by observing the effect and inferring the cause. If I notice that I shout and throw things when angry, for instance, I can infer that another person has mental processes similar to my own, and when they shout and throw things (effect), I will conclude that they are angry (cause).

How does this ability originate? Is it based on inborn capabilities and sensitivities, or must we learn it like the vocabulary of a language? Studies of theory of mind require two steps of inference: first observing a subject making inferences about another person, and then making inferences about the subject's own mental activity. The studies are doubly difficult when studying infants, who cannot describe their own attitudes and opinions.

We have already seen that newborns orient selectively to human faces; by about 9 months they follow adults' gazes, looking not at the eyes of the adult but at the place where the adult's gaze is directed (Corkum & Moore, 1998). Do these abilities imply a theory of mind, or are the infants simply responding to releasing stimuli, like gull chicks pecking on their mothers' beaks? A way to address this question is to examine the goal-directed behavior of infants. If infants are shown a goal-directed behavior such as dropping beads into a cup, for instance, they will often imitate the act. By 18 months of age, though, the infant will drop the beads into a cup even when the human actor tried but failed to accomplish the goal. Thus both the goal and the activity were inferred by the infant, and were never directly observed (Meltzoff, 1995).

But perhaps such behavior represents only a familiarity with people and their actions, rather than with minds per se. To examine this question, 15-month-olds interacted with an orangutan-like puppet or with a faceless pile of cloth of about the same size and shape (Johnson, Boothe, and O'Hearn, 2001). With the cloth orangutan, the infants imitated in waving and in the game of dropping beads into a cup, even when the puppet failed at the task. Further work showed that the key requirements for the infant treating the puppet as having goals were contingent interaction with the infant and presence of a face, though a human-like face was not required. The pile of cloth did not elicit consistent attributions of goals in the infants. Thus the infants conditioned their willingness to infer a mind in an outside agent not on familiar human features, but on actions that implied goal-directed behavior.

Though a rudimentary theory of mind is already developed before infants can speak, 2 to 3 more years must pass before a child can master more stringent tests, such as inferring false beliefs in another person (or puppet) (Wimmer & Perner, 1983). Before about 4 years of age, children assume that everyone knows what they know and perceives what they perceive.

These experiments require a good deal of sensory as well as cognitive sophistication of the infant, an ability that is well developed quite early.

Sensory Capabilities of the Infant

The sense of vision develops rapidly in the first months. At birth the infant is sensitive only to gross forms and motions. **Acuity,** the ability to resolve fine detail, is low. Over the first few months, the acuity steadily improves, though it does not reach fully adult levels for several years. Binocular vision begins to appear at 3-4 months of age.

Much of this development is driven by interactions of the genetically competent organs of sight with the visual environment, an interaction that offers an example of how a relatively sparse genome can generate a precisely adapted organism in harmony with its environment. It would take a lot of genetic instruction to construct an eye with a precise enough geometry and optics to reliably establish high visual acuity, but the genes controlling eye development are not precise.

Instead, the infant is born with an eye that is too short to support high acuity. The eye simply grows longer until the image on the retina is sharp. Then it stops growing (Wallman & McFadden, 1995). So rather than a command to "grow to exactly the right preprogrammed length," an expensive and difficult task, the genes give only the command to "grow until the retinal image is sharp, then stop." Thus environmental information simplifies the job of the genes in creating a functioning organism, one of the ways of escaping the 6-billion-bit limit of the human genome. Collecting feedback from the environment allows nature to take advantage of information that is not present in the genome.

In concert with anatomical development, the infant's understanding of the world also improves rapidly. Using mostly the preferential-looking technique, developmental psychologists have found that by 3-4 months of age, the infant knows a good deal about the properties of the physical world: It is composed of physical objects that are solid (Gibson & Walk, 1960), continuous in time and space, and interact with one another by direct contact and force transmission (Figure 4.4). Infants at 3 months react with surprise when a rolling ball passes through a barrier rather than stopping (Spelke, Breinlinger, Macomber, & Jacobson, 1992), staring longer at the impossible event than at the possible event. At this age, infants are already tiny physicists, expecting a ball to remain stationary unless it is contacted by another object (Spelke, Katz, Purcell, Ehrlich, & Breinlinger, 1994). These characteristics of objects cannot be derived from infants' experience, for at this age they are not yet mobile and their ability to manipulate objects is limited. The interactions of biological beings, though, follow different rules.

Older infants can discern causality in a sequence of actions—an immediate result, such as one toy moving just after being hit by another, is perceived as causal, whereas the same action after a 2-second delay is interpreted as an unrelated event (Cohen, Rundell, Spellman, & Cashon, 1999). Preferential looking also reveals that the 4-month-old knows that all objects must be supported by other objects or surfaces, and will fall if support is withdrawn (Baillargeon, 1994). Thus just 18 weeks after birth the infant already possesses considerable knowledge about cause and effect in the sensory world.

It is still uncertain how infants know these things. Their nervous systems are probably tuned to pick up the key information from their environments, in a series of interactions analogous to the rules that govern lengthening of

Figure 4.4   A Visual Cliff in an infant's normal environment. Using depth perception, the infant perceives that the drop is small enough to negotiate before venturing further.

the eye. Because infants are never rewarded for knowing about causality in object interactions, the motivation to learn must come from within. The baby's developing brain is exquisitely sensitive to the critical aspects of the environment that can provide the information needed to construct perceptual and cognitive systems. When locomotion and more coordinated motor action become possible for the toddler, the cognitive systems are ready.

Motor Capabilities of the Infant

The principle that development proceeds from the top down and from the centerline to the extremities applies to motor systems as well as to sensory capabilities. Thus the mouth and eyes loom large in the infant's life. Just after birth, the eyes seem to roam about at random, without being coordinated. But even at this point, the two lines of sight remain in the same plane, restricted by the inborn organization of the **oculomotor** control system (Hering, 1868). Though search strategies are not yet established, their geometric basis is already present. Soon the infant is staring intently at objects of interest, for no one has yet admonished him or her that staring might be rude or aggressive. The preferential-looking technique exploits the fact that babies have good control over their eyes when they can't control much else, and aren't afraid to stare. The baby's primary job at this stage is to absorb information, quickly and in large quantities.

The mouth is the other well-developed organ. Infants put everything into their mouths, because for an infant that is the best way to sense what an object is like. By a few weeks of age, the mouth is already a skilled sense organ as well as a motor structure.

When visually guided reaching begins, the reach and grasp are stereotyped behaviors, triggered by visual or tactile stimulation. The baby produces an arm extension and hand closure, but they are not aimed at anything. If the reach happens to contact an object, it is grasped, but if not, the baby grasps the air (Figure 4.5) (von Hofsten, Vishton, Spelke, Feng, & Rosander, 1998). Reaching that is modified by the location of a goal object and the hand develops later. In general, the action comes first, the control later.

Parent-Infant Interactions

A rich array of behaviors and attitudes facilitates the social interactions of parents, especially mothers, and their infants. It begins with the simple act of holding the baby. Almost all mothers, whether left-handed or right-handed,

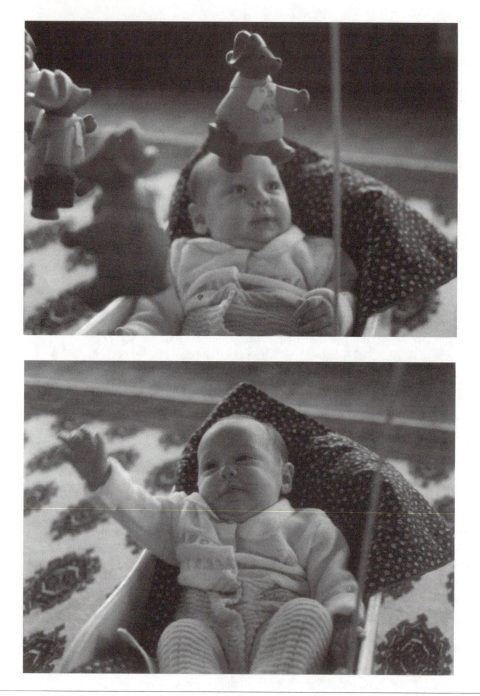

Figure 4.5   Reaching begins as a stereotyped gesture and develops into a skilled, feedback-controlled grasp.

spontaneously prefer to hold the baby on their left. Right-handed mothers explain that they do this because it frees their dominant hand for other tasks, whereas left-handers argue that it simply makes sense to hold this most precious being in their dominant hand. In this behavioral tendency, normal mothers are like split-brain patients who can't report what is going on in their nonlinguistic right hemispheres—instead, they attempt to justify their behavior after the fact. Mothers do the same thing, performing a behavior first and justifying it afterward.

Perhaps the decision about how to hold the baby is less voluntary than it seems. The preference has also been around for a long time, as attested by analyses of paintings of mothers with children through the ages and throughout the world. Historians tend not to note the side on which babies are held, but an analysis of 594 sculptures and 1,251 paintings, dating from the Egyptian Middle Kingdom to the present, found the baby to be depicted consistently on the left side about 80% of the time through a span of more than 4 millennia (Grüsser, 1983). The major exception was a period during the late middle ages when the Gothic aesthetic considered symmetry to be important in art. The function of this behavior is suggested in the observation that the sound of the mother's heartbeat tends to quiet an infant (Salk, 1973).

Parent-infant interactions include a variety of games played throughout the world, such as hide-and-seek or tickling. The games make contact fun for the parents, and they function to assure babies that someone is attending to their needs. Language interaction begins immediately, long before babies will attempt their first words. Speech of mothers to children is in a pattern dubbed **motherese**, a high-pitched singsong patter that sometimes makes little sense ("Aren't we a CUTIE today?"), but is very effective at capturing the infant's attention.

Studies of infants have shown that almost from birth they orient more strongly to motherese than to normal intonation (Brown, 1965). The vocabulary is small, the words simple, the phrases short, and the speed slow, just what infants need to begin language learning. Of course most mothers are unaware of the pedagogical functions of motherese—they simply can't resist using it. Males, for some reason, seldom engage in this form of communication.

EDUCATION ●

In early childhood, a set of capabilities seems to develop in a coordinated way. By about the age of 4, a typical child can speak well enough to make his or her wants and needs understood, is physically capable of keeping up with a traveling group most of the time, and can eat and take care of personal hygiene unaided. Nature's push at this age seems to be to provide the child with all the survival skills needed to achieve independence within the context of the band or village. Others will provide food, shelter, and protection for another decade, but the child no longer needs the constant supervision of his or her parents. Children at this age are ready to engage society as well as the family.

As they grow older and more capable, children begin learning the skills they will need to survive and prosper as adults. Throughout most of human history, and still today in some parts of the world, formal education did not exist. There were no schools, universities, or training programs, because education was part of family and village life, integrated with everyday economic and cultural activities. In this sense the "reluctant schoolboy" of Shakespeare is protesting an unnatural act: formal instruction that has no immediate application.

Technical Education

Education can be considered in large part as a giant exercise in technical communication, bringing a portion of the content of a culture to each new generation. The ability to communicate one's experiences to others multiplies the power of each person's experiences, combining them with the experiences of millions of others over thousands of years. In this light, the historical development of culture and technology is largely a development made possible by linguistic communication.

Once the process of cultural transmission began, at the very dawn of hominid evolution, the selective pressures would increase to favor individuals in whom the process works better. Thus a co-evolution could begin between culture and the biological equipment needed to make the best use of it; this process continued for millions of years in hominids and finally in modern humans (Blackmore, 1999), as our ancestors became more and more skilled at the activity.

There are two kinds of imitation, "copy-the-product" and "copy-the-instructions." To borrow Blackmore's (1999) example, suppose that I visit your house and taste some of your particularly delicious pumpkin soup. If I ask you for the recipe, I can copy the instructions for making the soup, with the result that my soup will come out more or less like yours. I can send the recipe to my granny, memorize it, or publish it. The recipe is not the soup, though; it is analogous to a genotype, instructing the production of a product (in this case, a pumpkin soup, not a baby) while remaining distinct from the product.

Now suppose that rather than asking for the recipe, I try to re-create the soup in my own kitchen based on what I had tasted at your house. My soup will not be quite the same as yours because I am guessing at the ingredients (except for pumpkin) and their amounts. I am copying the product, with inevitable distortions, and someone tasting my soup and reconstructing it in their own kitchen will produce yet a different soup. Now the copy is analogous to a phenotype, and copying the phenotype is possible only in cultural transmission. The fact that I imitated Blackmore's soup example betrays the ubiquity of the whole process.

Cultural transmissions of this sort can occur even if they reduce the biological fitness of those who transmit them. Many religions, for example, expect harmful activities such as self-flagellation, fasting, or time-consuming, sleep-depriving rituals, but they spread because part of the cultural package of the religion includes urging others to adopt it, and persecuting or killing them if they do not.

The process of formal education usually involves copy-the-instructions learning, and the imitative learning that occurs in a village or band setting more often reflects copy-the-product. Children imitate what their elders do.

Contemporary hunter-gatherer cultures, and presumably all of our ancestors before the Neolithic revolution, exploit little specialization of labor except by gender and to some extent by age. Exceptions might be made for a shaman, healer, or chief; or someone particularly skilled in making weapons might for instance concentrate on that activity in exchange for food or other favors. But in general it was expected that each adult would acquire all the skills necessary for living. Often the requisite skills are learned at first not from adults but by imitating the activities of older children. Even after the development of farming, each adult was expected to possess all the skills necessary for adult life—specialized trades developed slowly.

Under these conditions, children's technical skills normally would be the same as those of their parents, so that Paleolithic nomads learned the skills necessary for life largely by imitating their parents and older same-sex children.

These facts of Paleolithic life point to some of the reasons for the difficulty we have in organizing effective education, and indeed in handling large-scale political and economic activities in general. Nature has not equipped us with skills in these realms—we are on our own. The way we deal with a very complex social and technical world is to master almost none of it, each of us relying on others to be competent in some small domain. Specialization is one of the tricks that allow our Paleolithic brains to handle modern society.

According to Merlin Donald (1991), prehuman and human cultures went through a series of revolutions in which cultural information was reorganized. The final revolution brought in symbolic culture and eventually reading and writing, making it possible to hold most of a culture's wealth of knowledge and experience in external records that reach beyond the capacity of the human mind. In this way, human cultures could become more complex without extending the biological capacities of human brains. Still, acquiring what is essential is a long process.

Adolescence

Children in modern societies become sexually mature at about age 12, but do not marry until their early to mid-20s. This leaves a decade-long span of physical and sexual maturity combined with an extension of childhood's social dependency on parents and family—the confusing and chaotic teenage period. In the Paleolithic conditions of our evolution, though, this period hardly existed. There are two reasons for this—later maturation and earlier economic independence. In both boys and girls, sexual maturation is strongly influenced by one's nutritional status and weight, the maturation process beginning only when the body has accumulated the critical mass and nutrients needed to go through puberty. Nomads even today tend to undergo puberty late because children do not reach the required physical status until their mid-teens.

In historic times, the situation was similar. Because historians seldom note such details as when sexual maturity occurs, preferring to record who won what battles, we have to look to indirect evidence to discover maturation patterns and their changes over time. One such source is the meticulous records of the Vienna Boy's Choir, extending from the present back through 400 years. For most of that period, boys retained their soprano voices until age 16-18, following the prehistoric pattern. Only in the last century did puberty, and the loss of the boy soprano voice, begin to occur earlier.

At about age 16-18, a Paleolithic nomad was old enough to become economically independent and to marry. Thus sexual maturation marked the time of achieving economic and social independence and starting a family. There was little time to enjoy, or suffer through, the teenage phase of sexual maturity combined with economic dependency.

The teenage period, then, has little or no parallel in the conditions of human evolution. As a result, both teenagers and society are poorly equipped to deal with this phase of life. Nature is telling teenagers on one hand to be sexually active, while culture must tell them on the other hand not to reproduce until their education is complete and they are socially ready. The social solutions to this situation must take the evolutionarily paradoxical situation of teenagers into account in order to arrive at appropriate institutional and behavioral expectations.

RELATIONS WITH CARETAKERS ●

Our cultural ideal is that all members of a family should live and work together harmoniously, as "one big happy family." As everyone with a family knows, that is not always the case. According to Robert Trivers (1974), who worked out many of the social implications of genetic relationships in families, the family is an inevitable source of conflict. All over the world, when people are asked what bothers them most, family conflicts rank high on the list, whether the interviewees are wealthy Western teenagers or nomadic Bushmen in the harsh Namibian desert.

The ultimate cause of intrafamily conflict is that family members, while socially related to one another, are not always genetically related, and of course no two people (except identical twins) share the same genes. Evolutionary theory predicts that conflict among any two family members should be inversely related to their degree of genetic similarity. In helping a closely related person, one is also helping one's own genes to reach the next generation, and the closer the relationship, the stronger the benefit. The motivation to aid one's close relatives, even at great personal cost, is called **kin-directed altruism**. It is a consequence of inclusive fitness, the idea that your own genes benefit from the increased fitness of relatives who share some of those genes (Dawkins, 1976). There is more on kin-directed altruism in Chapter 5.

Sibling rivalry, in this context, arises because the siblings compete with one another for the family's resources. As children, brothers and sisters seem always to be fighting with one another. It doesn't happen in every family, but it's common enough. In modern Western societies, the conflict seems pointless. But when resources are scarce, getting more than your share might mean survival, even at your siblings' expense. The only person who shares 100% of your genes, after all, is yourself (or, to be completely accurate, you and your identical twin).

Later, as children become more able to provide for themselves, the rivalry diminishes. At some point, sibling rivalry begins to seem childish, and the siblings reconcile. This is near the point when each young adult becomes economically independent of the family. Now the siblings become allies in a world full of strangers, and kin-directed altruism can dominate. The pattern of rivalry in youth, and reconciliation in adolescence or young adulthood, matches the pattern of genetic advantage.

Genetic Relatives Versus Social Relatives

Evolutionary theory makes the disturbing prediction that those who are related only by convention, and not by blood, should not share the benefits of kin-directed altruism. How can researchers penetrate the privacy of families to test this prediction? One method is to investigate crimes that one family member commits against another, the extreme case of a failure of altruism. Daly and Wilson (1988) reasoned that the best strategy for studying this question was to investigate murders—homicides are an easy-to-measure, all-or-none quantity, and they are difficult to hide. Would murders, traditionally explained as acts of unthinking, violent passion, follow genetic rules? The investigators studied records from Canada, which has particularly good statistics about family relationships.

The result was that almost all murders of one family member by another, over 90%, involved nonblood relatives—husbands killing wives, stepparents killing stepchildren, and so on. There seems to be an unwritten but strictly enforced rule built into us: "Thou shalt not kill blood relatives." This despite the fact that most of the people in any family are genetically related. In a typical nuclear family, for example, only the husband and wife are not genetically related to each other. The children of course are related to both parents.

Sometimes, however, children do die at the hands of their parents; these cases are particularly shocking because they violate the primary imperative of kin-directed altruism. In 1994, a mother named Susan Smith gained notoriety by letting her car roll into a lake, with her two children in it. Before reading beyond the headlines, one could predict that two conditions were likely to apply to this case: first, the children would be young, and second, Ms. Smith would be involved with a man who was not their father. Both predictions turned out to be correct.

The event caused a sensation not only because such cases are unusual but also because the mother initially blamed another man, of another race, for the crime. How can evolutionary theory offer predictions about the structure of such rare and tragic events? The predictions are based on parental investment theory. Consider first the age of the children. At the beginning, the investment of parents in a child is minor, but as the child ages the investment becomes greater and greater. As the child matures and the parents age, the child's value to the parents increases as he or she nears reproductive age and gradually becomes irreplaceable. We would predict that killing of offspring should become less frequent as children age. Indeed, that is the case—most parental murders of their children occur in the first few years of life (Figure 4.6). This is why it was possible to predict that the children in the Smith murder case would be young.

The other part of the case, involvement with another man, is part of the brutal calculus of reproductive success. Something in Ms. Smith saw a benefit in getting rid of her existing children to start over with this new man, of higher status than her original husband. In today's culture, the effort of

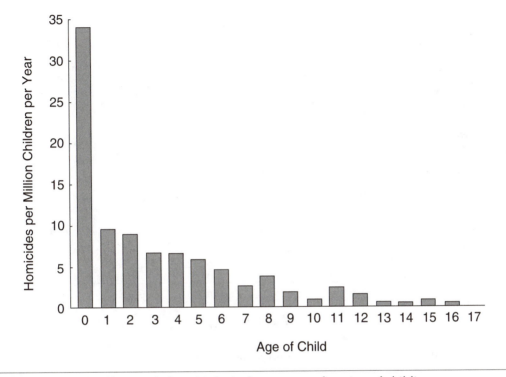

Figure 4.6   Risk of homicide by a biological parent as a function of child's age.

course was tragically unsuccessful, and Ms. Smith is serving a life sentence in prison. Her defense was a kind of insanity that would drive a person to do such a thing, but in light of evolutionary theory that diagnosis is not so certain. Such behavior is more common in animal groups such as lions, where a group of males that takes over a pride will kill the existing cubs, bringing the females into estrus and multiplying the genes of the new males.

Other cases of parental **infanticide** (killing one's very young children), though infrequent in Western cultures, also follow rules derived from the theory of inclusive fitness. Killing one's own child is always an act of desperation, and we expect to see it only under extreme circumstances. Age of the mother is one important variable. We can predict that older mothers would be less willing to kill their offspring than younger ones, because older women will have fewer future chances at reproduction. Indeed, there is a strong relationship between maternal age and frequency of infanticide (Figure 4.7), with the frequency far higher in teenage mothers than in older mothers (Daly & Wilson, 1988). Furthermore, the rate is several times higher in unmarried mothers than in married mothers at every age, reflecting the

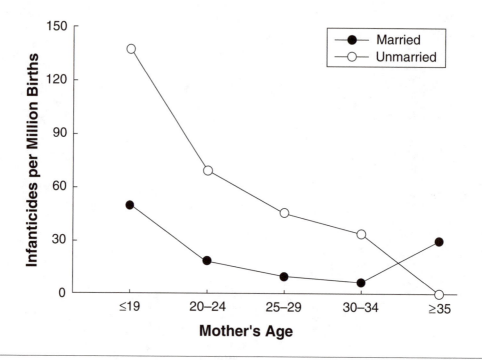

Figure 4.7 Risk of homicide as a function of mother's age.

more precarious social situation of the unwed mothers, the difficulty of raising a child alone, and the reduced prospects of attracting a husband who is
willing to raise someone else's child.

Another situation where infanticide is practiced is in the case of twins,
especially in nomadic groups where a mother cannot care for two infants at
the same time. In this situation, many families conclude that it is better to let
one infant survive than to see both die.

Mothers Versus Fathers

In most cultures, both parents invest heavily in their children, though
men's investment of time in direct child care is generally less than that of
women, an evolved strategy that reflects specialization of labor between the
sexes. The man provides protection and resources, whether Paleolithic meat
or modern salary, while the woman does most of the direct care.

Investment by the human father in his children is unique among the
great apes, its mechanism working indirectly through emotions of warmth

and attachment. MacDonald (1992) interprets warmth as a reward system that evolved to facilitate cohesive family relationships and paternal investment in children. Fathers indulge their children because it makes them feel good. On the other side of the relationship, warmth plays an important motivational role in children by facilitating compliance and the acceptance of adult values. The variable of warmth appears consistently in factor analyses of personality.

Though mothers and fathers each contribute 50% of a child's genes, their interest in the child is not identical, for several reasons based on the biology of reproduction. The differences in parental behavior are extensions of the differing goals of courtship in the two sexes, ultimately based on the irreducible biological asymmetry between male and female parents.

Because parental uncertainty is possible only for fathers, they are less sure than their wives that their children are biologically theirs. By investing in his wife's children, a husband is gambling that the children are his own. Husbands spend less time than wives rearing children, a characteristic that is seen to varying degrees in all cultures.

What is the evidence that greater maternal involvement in child-rearing is an evolved strategy rather than a cultural convention? One type of evidence is the cross-cultural generality of the asymmetry. A study of traditional societies in Mexico, Java, Peru, Nepal, the Philippines, and several other regions showed that mothers spend far more time than fathers with their children in every society surveyed. Fathers averaged about 8% of their waking hours in child care, and mothers averaged 85% (Barash & Lipton, 1997). The mothers, in other words, did more than nine tenths of the child care.

Are there any exceptions to this rule? In an isolated group of central African pygmies, known for very close family relations, a lot of time is spent in child care and interactions with children. The father traditionally cleans and grooms the infant. Even there, though both sexes spend more time than average with their children, mothers spend more than eight times more of their day holding their infants than fathers.

We might also look for exceptions in modern Western cultures, where technology has made it possible for fathers to raise infants, and families are smaller than was traditionally the case. Fathers can specialize in child care, if they so choose, and mothers can contribute to the family by earning income outside the home. But the asymmetry remains, with men doing less than one fifth of the child care (Barash & Lipton, 1997).

Western societies have also made it possible (though not easy) for one parent to raise a child or several children alone, by providing income subsidies, health care, education, and other benefits at public expense. In some groups within Western societies, a majority of children are born to unmarried mothers. But again, when only one parent raises a child, it is the mother in nine tenths of the cases. The Paleolithic adaptation persists in the modern world.

The asymmetry in parental investment extends even to grandparents, as maternal grandparents typically invest more in their grandchildren, and see them more often, than paternal grandparents. This is true even after controlling for distance between the grandparents' and the children's homes.

The human situation is less extreme than that in other primate species, however, where generally the mother does all the work of child-rearing and the father does none. Chapter 3 reviews the differences between humans and the great apes in courtship and relations between the sexes that seem to point in the direction of greater paternal certainty and greater male investment in children for humans. Hidden estrous, stable marriages, and continuous sexual receptivity all seem to be part of this recipe. The advantage for humans is enormous, because most males dedicate considerable resources to their offspring, even if they don't offer much time. Human evolution seems to have pushed us toward two-parent families. This doesn't mean that they always function harmoniously, however.

Parent-Child Conflict

Kin-directed altruism predicts that conflict should be least among those who are the most closely related genetically—parents and children, or siblings with one another. Indeed, parents expend enormous time and effort raising their children, but within the parent-child bond, subtle conflicts appear that can be explained only by a combination of genetic relatedness and social circumstance.

First, the parents are more important to the child than the child is to the parents. For the child, the parents mean survival, and everything depends on a close relationship with them. The parents, however, see things differently. They have or hope to have other children, who will compete with one another for the family's resources. Under these circumstances, it is in each child's interest to monopolize as much of the family's limited resources as possible, while the parents attempt to provide less, optimally dividing their resources among their children, thus enabling them to raise a maximal number of children. Even parental love has its limits, according to this application of evolutionary theory.

Weaning is an experience where the evolutionary interests of parent and child come into particularly sharp focus. The initiation of weaning is almost invariably the mother's idea, not the child's, and most children protest throughout the process, no matter how old they are when it happens. The mother's interest is in accumulating resources for the next pregnancy, whereas the child sees only withdrawal of a life-giving resource. Again, though, the evolutionary calculus is not done consciously, but rather in terms of emotional responses that neither party can explain very well. The same pattern repeats in other mammals, the offspring attempting to suckle while the mother pushes them away.

Parental Investment in Sons and Daughters

We strive to be egalitarian, not favoring one gender or group over another. Yet all over the world there is a sex difference in the investments made in children, the males receiving more resources and attention than females. Why should this be? Are cultures all over the world dominated by sexist men and women, or is something else at work?

The advantage of males in parental investment stems in part from a quirk in patterns of mammalian reproduction. The average reproductive success of the sexes must be equal, of course, because every child is the offspring of exactly one male and one female. But in most mammalian species, the variability of reproductive success is greater in males than in females. This simple fact has a host of unexpected consequences.

Deer

The calculus of sex differences in reproductive variability in the wild was first worked out quantitatively in a population of deer that inhabit a small island off the coast of England. Biologists tagged every animal in the population and kept records of reproductive success (Clutton-Brock, Albon, & Guiness, 1988). Although most of the does had a calf every year, a few bucks dominated the male side of reproduction by defending harems of several does. Thus the reproductive success of the bucks was more variable than that of the does. Furthermore, the does would allow male offspring to suckle longer than females, would wean them later, and would stay with them longer (Clutton-Brock et al., 1989).

In some other closely studied mammals, such as a population of elephant seals near Santa Cruz, California, that do all of their reproduction and mating on a single easy-to-study beach, the sex difference in reproductive variability is even greater. A few dominant males push the other males off the beach, reserving all the females for themselves. Only a handful of males sires all of the pups.

Humans

Birth records for humans show a similar pattern, though the extent of the difference is not as extreme as it is in such highly polygynous animals as deer or elephant seals. Some men have several families and many children, and others have none, a characteristic of human societies that is formalized in the polygynous marriages that most societies allow. In other societies, such as our own, a man may have several families sequentially rather than simultaneously.

These asymmetries arise because the male's capacity to father children is practically unlimited. For a male, the stakes in the mating game are higher, because he can win again and again. The reasons for greater variability in male reproductive success, then, have more to do with basic mammalian biology than with quirks of culture (Mealy, 2000). And because the mathematics of biological fitness is the same for humans as it is for deer, some of the same biological adaptations and some of the same sorts of behaviors are evident.

In response to the greater male variability of reproduction, males themselves show greater variation in a wide variety of traits than do females. One of the most consistent findings from a meta-analysis of a number of cognitive tests in educational settings is that boys show greater variability than girls (Di Lisi & McGillicuddy-Di Lisi, 2002). Because the variability of males is greater, we see more males than females at the extremes of distributions on many traits, including intelligence, with the result that classes for slow learners and accelerated classes for the gifted both have more boys than girls. Men should be overrepresented both in the numbers of the homeless and of top corporate executives or Nobel Prize winners, not because of discrimination against men at the bottom and against women at the top but because of the structure of the population. (This is not to say, of course, that discrimination should not be eliminated wherever it is found.)

Under these conditions, suppose that you are a mother of a son and a daughter. In which do you invest more of your resources? The daughter is likely to reproduce even with minimal attention, but the son is a biological gamble. If he succeeds, he might hit the reproductive jackpot, attracting a lot of women and fathering their children. Perhaps he'll be a legendary basketball star. If he fails in competition with other men, though, all will be for naught.

It is in the mother's interest to ensure that her son will be in the category of winners rather than losers, and this takes a big investment. To optimize her own fitness, the mother should invest more in her son than in her daughter—having sons is a crapshoot.

Every mother of both sons and daughters knows that sons demand more attention, and mothers usually are willing to give it. In circumstances where differences in parental or caregiver investment can be measured, the pattern is the same. Teachers, even those who are struggling mightily to be fair, call on boys in class more often than girls, even if the girls raise their hands more. Parents are willing to spend more money on a son's education than a daughter's, on average. And the list goes on.

The reason why many people behave in this way is not that they want to unfairly restrict the rights of women, but rather that they come from a long line of ancestors who increased their biological fitness by putting more resources into their sons. Even if the variability of reproductive success evens out in some cultures, the motivations and adapted psychological structures that favor investment in males will remain.

This is not to assert that the differing social investment in boys and girls is morally right, only that it exists. Any attempts to change the situation are more likely to meet with success if they start from knowledge of what the situation is, and why it is that way.

DISCUSSION QUESTIONS ●

1. What skills, besides those noted in the text, might be useful for a young child in camp or village life?
2. What would you predict about the rates of parental infanticide for disabled children relative to the rates for healthy children?
3. Why might fathers spend less time with their children than mothers, even when they are certain of paternity?

FURTHER READING ●

Blackmore, S. (1999). *The meme machine*. Oxford, UK: Oxford University Press.

Susan Blackmore finds a similarity between genes and cultural ideas, such as words, tunes, or bits of technical knowledge. Once invented, they are copied or imitated by others, becoming replicators that can spread through a population if they appeal to enough people. The book is so well written that you won't be able to put it down. The foreword by Richard Dawkins is also an entertaining read.

Bridgeman, D. L. (Ed.). (1983) *The nature of prosocial development: Interdisciplinary theories and strategies.* New York: Academic Press.

I must admit being partial to this one because I am married to its editor. The book offers a wide range of approaches to the development of prosocial behavior, however, and includes a chapter by Robert Trivers on the evolution of cooperation.

Bartsch, K., & Wellman, H. M. (1995). *Children talk about the mind*. New York: Oxford University Press.

Refining techniques pioneered by Swiss psychologist Jean Piaget, Bartsch and Wellman reveal children's thinking in their own words.

CHAPTER 5

FAMILY AND SOCIETY

"Sex is a divisive force in society."

— Robert Trivers (1971)

We think of sex as a force that unites people in marriage and reproduction, and we consider the close-knit family to be the basis of society. Yet divisiveness comes from the same source as the closeness—unrelated individuals, and related individuals with different genetic makeups, live and work together, sharing resources and opportunities. From the standpoint of evolution, each member of the family is a genetically distinct individual adapted to bring his or her genes into the next generation, at the expense of other family members if necessary.

FAMILY STRUCTURE ●

At its base, the family is a reproduction machine, generating children, protecting them, and preparing them for independent life. Humans must possess all the social skills, aptitudes, and motivations that make the family work.

Chapter 4 reviews the functioning of the family in the context of reproduction, as well as some of the adaptations that characterize the reproductive unit. This chapter concerns the family's function as the primary social unit of societies, facing outward to the social and economic challenges of the larger world.

Nuclear and Extended Families

In a Paleolithic world, with low population densities, a nuclear family was the rule (Nimkoff & Middleton, 1968), with close alliances among families, especially families of relatives. The extended family tends to appear in more advanced societies, as social stratification increases. In these societies, an extended family, consisting of the nuclear families of a group of brothers, sisters, or even cousins, lives together and cooperates as an economic, social, and child-rearing unit. Grandparents are often part of the group as well.

The arrangement carries with it a risk of dissension, though, because many of those in the extended family are genetically unrelated to most of its members. Someone marrying into an extended family is related only to his or her eventual children, and is linked to the others only by social alliances and conventions. One such set of conventions surrounds kinship terms, which in European/North American cultures, and in many other cultures around the world, do not differentiate between relatives by genetic relationship and relatives by marriage.

The English language uses the term *uncle,* for instance, to refer both to a parent's brother and to a parent's sister's husband. The first of these relatives shares a genetic relationship, and the second is genetically unrelated, yet use of the kinship term *uncle* for both relationships implies a similar set of obligations and privileges in both cases. We can speculate that the use of kinship terms for people related only by marriage is a way of conferring some of the benefits of kin-directed altruism to genetically unrelated individuals who are socially members of the same family and who are committed to its success.

Evolutionary theory predicts that the nuclear family should be more stable than the extended family, because of both its smaller size and its higher proportion of genetically related individuals. Indeed, historically in Western societies the extended family began to disperse at about the time when the economic situation made dispersal possible. In many traditional societies, economic factors reinforce kin-directed motivations in holding extended families together.

COOPERATION ●

Human social interactions are unique in the animal world. The only animals with a comparable range and degree of dependency on social interaction are the social insects, which include ants, bees, and wasps. In their case, though, cooperation is strictly among closely related individuals. Due to a quirk in the genetics of these insects, daughters in a colony are even more closely related to one another than are members of a human nuclear family. Other social insects such as termites, and highly social mammals such as naked mole rats, have a more conventional genetic structure but are highly inbred.

Cooperation in all these species is extensive but stereotyped, controlled mostly by an elaborate system of chemical signals (Wilson, 1975). Interactions of social insects with individuals in other colonies, who are not genetically related, are exclusively competitive—establishing territorial boundaries, raiding, and even destroying one another. A colony of social insects may be a very large family, but it is still a family, the offspring of a single individual.

Modern humans, in contrast, depend on vast networks of unrelated strangers for every aspect of their existence. Our degree of dependency on one another has increased greatly in the past few centuries, with farming and industrial economies growing to hundreds of millions of individuals. This idea is developed further in Chapter 7, in the context of communication. The uniqueness of human social organization is that it extends far beyond the limitations of kinship.

Even more remarkable is that the relations of humans with other unrelated humans are generally relations of support and mutual economic dependency. Traditional societies as well as modern ones have elaborate systems of taboos, social expectations, and, well, traditions that regulate behavior toward others.

In modern societies, additional systems of formal laws, law enforcement, and punishment back up social expectations. The intensity of human social interdependency increased without a change in our genetic relatedness to one another—our genes follow the same rules of relatedness as those of all other mammals. Applying evolutionary theory, we should expect direct benefits in exchange for our extensive interactions with nonrelatives.

It is our relatively elaborate brains that make large-scale cooperation possible, for we must do a lot of mental bookkeeping to build networks of dependency. As we shall see, human societies have also developed social tools to make the networks more effective, facilitating communication, combating cheating, and fostering productive interactions. The building blocks of these networks are reciprocal relationships among nonrelated individuals.

Reciprocal Altruism

On a frigid winter day in Washington, D.C., an ice-encrusted airliner strug-gled into the air only to crash into the frozen Potomac River a few minutes later, in the middle of the city. Immediately, witnesses to the disaster ventured out onto the ice and into the freezing water to aid the survivors. Several rescuers died or were injured in the rescue attempt, but the lives of many passengers were saved.

The people who went to the rescue, at great risk to themselves, were not out of the ordinary. What motivated them to perform such heroic acts? These were instances of **altruism**, performing a service without expectation of a reward. A first glance at evolutionary theory suggests that people should not do such a thing—the altruistic helpers reduce their own fitness, without a corresponding reward somewhere else.

Group Selection

One explanation of such behavior is that altruistic motivations might be built into all of us. Early groups of people who cooperated, who acted altruis-tically toward one another, might have been more successful than groups that did not cooperate (Eibl-Eibesfeldt, 1998). These altruistically interacting groups would come to dominate the species, in a process described as **group selection,** the selection of genes in a group of individuals for some charac-teristic that aids the group.

Although it sounds plausible on the surface, the group selection explan-ation is not consistent with what we know about the laws of heredity. Genes are passed on by individuals, not by groups, and the success of a gene in getting into the next generation depends on the reproductive success of the individual who possesses it. If a person reproduces, his or her genes endure—if he or she fails to reproduce, they do not.

Applied to altruism, the problem with the group selection idea is that altruism within a group is not an evolutionarily stable strategy. It is vulnera-ble to cheaters, people who are not altruistic themselves but who live among altruists, benefiting from their generosity without reciprocating. These peo-ple should be even more successful than their altruistic neighbors, because they consume more resources from their neighbors than they produce for them. Being able to sustain a higher reproductive rate, the cheaters would gradually replace the altruists in the population.

This does not mean that group selection for altruists is impossible, however. Mathematical modeling has defined social situations in which group selection can work (Sober & Wilson, 1998). If a Group A containing mostly altruists is isolated from another Group B containing mostly selfish nonaltruists, Group A might grow and prosper, but Group B is so full of destructive conflict that it languishes. Under these conditions, the total number of altruists can increase even though the nonaltruists are more successful in each group. It sounds impossible, but an example will show how it works.

Suppose that two groups start with 100 individuals each. Group A has 90 altruists and 10 selfish cheaters. Group B starts with 10 altruists and 90 cheaters, so that across the two groups the total number of altruists and the total number of cheaters is the same, 100 of each. Over time, Group A prospers and grows to 1,000 individuals, but because the cheaters are relatively more successful, the group might now have 800 altruists and 200 cheaters. The altruists are selected against, their numbers as a proportion of the population declining from 90% to 80%. Group B, not growing at all, winds up with 8 altruists and 92 cheaters. When the groups are considered together, the original 100 altruists have grown to 808 while the cheaters have grown only to 292. What started out as an even split between the two types of people has ended up with a clear advantage for the altruists.

It is not likely, however, that the conditions presented in the example ever existed over a significant stretch of human evolution. The first problem is that the two groups must remain isolated. A group small enough to have intensive social interactions among most of its individuals would have to remain stable, and genetically isolated, for centuries if group selection were to be effective. In human groups, though, there is a continual flow of people, and therefore genes, among neighboring groups in every society. Given the opportunity, people prefer to find mates outside their group (Chapter 3), preventing group selection from gaining a toehold. Other problems are that altruists must appear somehow in the original groups, and that their proportions must be different in the two groups. For humans, group selection remains mostly a mathematical exercise.

There are examples of group selection in nature, but the conditions under which it occurs seem restricted mostly to groups of parasites that infect different hosts, thus isolating themselves from one another, then recombine after a period of reproduction in the hosts (Sober & Wilson, 1998). The "altruists" in these groups are altruistic toward the other parasites, of course, not toward their unfortunate hosts.

Individual Selection for Altruists

If group selection cannot explain the behavior of the Washington rescuers, and kin-directed altruism does not apply because the rescues clearly did not involve relatives, what is left? A disaster in the Paleolithic world might have carried with it a different calculus of costs and benefits than the Washington plane crash. The sorts of disasters that our ancestors faced would have been very likely to involve members of their own band, people who had close reciprocal relationships with one another over many years. Helping a person in the band, even if not a relative, would establish a debt of obligation that might benefit the helper in the future.

If the costs of the rescue are less than the benefits of being rescued, such **reciprocal altruism** can benefit the biological fitness of both parties, and can be evolutionarily stable. If you are drowning, it costs me almost nothing to extend a pole to you from the shore, but the act benefits you infinitely because your life is saved. Your gratitude becomes a kind of social insurance policy for me. If later the tables are turned, I can reap a large reward from you. In the end, both sides gain.

Other examples of reciprocal altruism that affected our Paleolithic ancestors involve activities such as hunting, where one hunter might be successful and have more meat than his family can eat. It costs him nothing to give some of his meat to another hunter whose family would otherwise starve. On another day, the debt might be repaid, benefiting both parties. This pattern of cooperation is common among modern hunter-gatherers, often enforced by elaborate rules about who gets what. Among chimpanzees, some of the few examples of food sharing involve gifts of meat.

How can we be assured that reciprocal altruism is an evolutionarily stable strategy, that some scheme of cheating cannot render it useless for increasing biological fitness? To answer this question, psychologists have quantified and formalized the reciprocal relationship into situations that can be analyzed mathematically and can be simulated with experiments on human subjects. The resulting discipline, called **game theory**, is anything but a game—it can shed light on some of the most basic mechanisms of social interaction.

The Prisoner's Dilemma. Reciprocal altruism has been simulated in a game called the Prisoner's Dilemma. In the game's scenario, you and a partner are imprisoned in separate cells, without being allowed to communicate with one another. You know that you are guilty of a crime, and that your partner is too. Now the police offer you a deal:

1. If you confess and betray your partner by agreeing to testify against him, but he keeps quiet, you will be freed and he will serve 10 years in prison. Prisoner's Dilemma theorists call this option "defecting."

2. If both you and your partner keep quiet, you both get a 6-month sentence. This option is called "cooperating." But:

3. If each of you betrays the other, you will both get 5 years. Of course,

4. If your partner defects and you don't, you get 10 years and he goes free.

What should you do? We can look at the possibilities one by one. In Scenario 1, you are better off to defect, because you serve no time. In Scenario 2, you get a short sentence, but you'll be better off if you defect and turn the scenario into Scenario 1. In Scenario 3, you are already betraying your partner, but things could be worse. You want to avoid Scenario 4 at all costs, because then you serve the longest prison term. Only by defecting in Scenario 3 can you can be sure of not getting into Scenario 4.

So under each of the four circumstances, you are better off to defect. But paradoxically, you risk a long prison term (Scenario 3) if you defect, and will get only a light term (Scenario 2) if both of you cooperate. This is the crux of the dilemma—your fate depends on trusting your partner.

This game, and the calculations behind it, are interesting only if the game can relate in some significant way to social situations that people encounter in real life. And in real life, something like the Prisoner's Dilemma plays out many times between people interacting in traditional cultures. Every act of generosity toward a nonrelative is also an act of faith, the hope that the favor will be reciprocated later. The delay of a returned favor is analogous to the noncommunication of the partners in the Prisoner's Dilemma—I cannot know what my partner will do in the future. The simulation shows that the best strategy is to defect, but only if the game is played just once. If it is played many times, simulating what often happens in real life, the best strategy is different.

The strategies for playing a repeated Prisoner's Dilemma were worked out by Axelrod and Hamilton (1981), who programmed the rules into a computer and pitted computer-simulated players against one another. Using total jail time as the criterion of success, the best of 63 strategies turned out to be a simple one called **tit-for-tat**. You cooperate on the first move, and then do what your partner does, cooperating as long as he or she cooperates. But if your partner defects, you defect on the next move. Tit-for-tat extends the ancient morality of the Old Testament of the Bible, "An eye for an eye, a tooth for a tooth." Robert Trivers summarizes the strategy in an extension of the golden rule: "First, do unto others as you wish them to do unto you, but then do unto them as they have just done to you" (Trivers, 1985, p. 392).

Keeping Track

Examples of reciprocal altruism are rare in nonhuman species, but there is a good example in vampire bats (ironic, isn't it, that humans and vampire bats share this behavioral trait?). Vampire bats feed only on the blood of large animals, but their nocturnal hunts are not always successful. A bat cannot always find a large enough animal and stay with it long enough to lick from the wound it inflicts without being chased away. The younger bats are generally less often successful than more experienced ones. An unrelated bat will often feed the unsuccessful hunter, but a hungry bat that has refused to share in the past is less likely to get a free meal (Wilkinson, 1984). The reciprocity also works the other way—a bat that has been fed, staving off starvation, is more likely to regurgitate blood for the bat that has fed it in the past. It's tit-for-tat in nature.

Modern hunter-gatherers engage in similar but more complex reciprocal relationships. People keep track of different kinds and degrees of favors owed to or owed by dozens of other individuals, keeping a detailed and usually accurate mental record of who owes what to whom. If you think about your own possessions, you will probably be able to identify those you acquired as gifts, from whom, and when, even if you are a bit vague about where you got all of your purchased stuff.

The record extends to relationships among third parties—a large fraction of "gossip" involves keeping track of such debts (Barkow, 1992), in the process establishing not only a public record of debts and credits but also reputations of who is a reliable reciprocator and who is not. In a modern hunter-gatherer group, or presumably in any Paleolithic group, this mental calculus is highly effective in maintaining mutually beneficial reciprocations and in excluding cheaters. Gossip, discussion of the activities of others, was serious business, because it was necessary to hold the group together and allow it to function efficiently.

In fact, a lot of ordinary, everyday conversation even today is gossip. Empirical studies have shown that we remember gossip better than data (Dunbar, 1996; Sugiyama, 2001). An economy based on reciprocal altruism can function better in this sort of social environment, with language supplementing individual memory.

Punishing Cheaters

Even these mechanisms of enforcing cooperation may not be enough, though. Humans have evolved at least one other strategy—we punish cheaters, even at some cost to ourselves. The behavior has been demonstrated in another game, designed as a simulation of social interactions that involve cooperation with the possibility of cheating. In the game, each person starts out with a small cache of money. A group of four people is formed, in which each person can contribute to a common pool that is enriched by the experimenters, so that everyone gains if everyone contributes. Someone who fails to contribute, or contributes very little, however, still splits the gains evenly with the rest of the group. Such people are termed free riders.

As you might expect, subjects used a variety of strategies. Some contributed a lot in hopes of giving the group (including themselves) a big bonus, but others held back and hoped that others would enrich them without them having to invest much. Up to this point, it's a standard altruists-versus-cheaters dilemma. Now comes the twist that makes the game interesting and tells us something about human social behavior: In a second round of interactions, members of the group could purchase the right to take money away from other players.

Eighty-four percent of the players punished another player at least once, even though punishing always meant a cost to the punisher and never a benefit. Furthermore, in three fourths of the punishment episodes, someone who had contributed more money than the group's average punished someone who had contributed less than average. This despite the fact that the players did not know the other players and the groups were remixed at random after each game so that no subject met another subject again (Fehr & Gächter, 2002).

The authors of the study attributed their subjects' behavior to negative emotions aroused by the free riders, and in a second experiment showed that negative emotions were indeed present. Unanswered, however, was the question of ultimate causes: Why did the emotions driving the punitive behavior arise in the first place, and is there some selective advantage to having such emotions?

Two other evolved strategies help to stabilize such behavior and make it worthwhile. The first is payoff-biased transmission, a tendency to copy the most successful individual; and second is conformist transmission, a tendency to copy the most frequent behavior in the population. Simulations show that these strategies are effective in establishing punishment of free riders, but only if the cost of doing the punishing is small (Henrich & Boyd, 2001).

In the real world, unlike the world of simulations, though, punishing is often accomplished at little cost, and sometimes with a gain. When working in a factory, I once saw a worker literally kick a lazy worker in the butt, an act that elicited the admiration of the other workers even though all were paid by the hour and saw no direct benefit from the act of aggression. The increase in the attacker's prestige would have more than compensated for the minimal cost of the kick. A tendency to express admiration for those who punish free riders would also be positively selected, because the punisher benefits the admirer at no cost to the admirer.

In other situations, a similar calculus would apply—for instance, punishing a free rider in group hunting activities by not inviting the slacker on the next expedition. The cost of the punishment is minimal, and the punishers would gain by not having their efforts diluted on the next hunt. Willingness to contribute to a public good can be evolutionarily stable as long as free riders are punished, along with those who refuse to punish free riders (Price, Cosmides, & Tooby, 2002).

As in all other such interactions, strategic success depends on keeping track of complex social situations and relationships, a talent that can require a lot of cognitive ability and logical analysis of situations. How much cognitive ability does it take to handle such problems, and how specialized is that ability?

Logic: Abstract Machine or Adapted Mechanism?

All of us have the feeling that we possess a logical engine somewhere in our brains, a mental machine that allows us to put together several pieces of evidence to arrive at a correct conclusion. For instance, if A is larger than B, and B is larger than C, most of us have little difficulty concluding that A is larger than C. With only slightly more complex logical situations, however, most people's abilities begin to falter.

The adapted mental machinery that underlies these abilities seems somewhat underwhelming, for the logic that is available to us tends to be situation-specific. Human subjects in experiments have difficulty keeping track of the logical structures of many relationships unless the situation is couched in terms of social debts and obligations, such as those that support reciprocal altruism. There is a considerable body of evidence that people are better at reasoning about social situations than about other domains, paradoxical as it may seem (Cosmides & Tooby, 1992). More specific yet, the improvement in performance applies only to situations where it is possible to cheat.

A classic tool for testing such human logical abilities is the Wason Selection Task (Wason, 1966), a test of conditional rules. Wason wanted to test philosopher Karl Popper's assertion that the structure of science is hypothetico-deductive, that is, that we extract logical rules from structured events in the world. His test is shown in Figure 5.1. You are confronted with four cards, each with a letter on one side and a number on the other, and you are asked to assess the truth of the statement that if a card has a *D* on one side, then it must have a 3 on the other. In this example of the task, the four cards are marked *D*, *F*, 3, and 7. Which card(s) must you turn over to test the statement? Try part *a*, and then go on to the next paragraph.

a. Abstract Problem

Part of your new clerical job at the local high school is to make sure that student documents have been processed correctly. Your job is to make sure the documents conform to the following alphanumeric rule:

"If a person has a 'D' rating, then his documents must be marked code '3'."
(if   P   then   Q   )

You suspect the secretary you replaced did not categorize the students' documents correctly. The cards below have information about the documents of four people who are enrolled at this high school. Each card represents one person. One side of a card tells a person's letter rating and the other side of the card tells that person's number code.

Indicate only those card(s) you definitely need to turn over to see if the documents of any of these people violate this rule.

D	F	3	7
(P)	*(not - P)*	*(Q)*	*(not-Q)*

b. Drinking Age Problem (adapted from Griggs & Cox, 1982)

In its crackdown against drunk drivers, Massachusetts law enforcement officials are revoking liquor licenses left and right. You are a bouncer in a Boston bar, and you'll lose your job unless you enforce the following law:

"If a person is drinking beer, then he must be over 20 years old."
(if   P   then   Q   )

The cards below have information about four people sitting at a table in your bar. Each card represents one person. Once side of a card tells what a person is drinking and the other side of the card tells that person's age. Indicate only those card(s) you definitely need to turn over to see if any of these people are breaking this law.

drinking beer	drinking Coke	25 years old	16 years old
(P)	*(not - P)*	*(Q)*	*(not-Q)*

c. Structure of Social Contract Problems

It is your job to enforce the following law:

Rule 1- Standard Social Contract: "If you take the benefit, then you pay the cost."
(If   P   then   Q   )
Rule 2 - Switched Social Contract: "If you pay the cost, then you take the benefit."
(If   P   then   Q   )

The cards below have information about four people. Each card represents one person. One side of a card tells whether a person accepted the benefit and the other side of the card tells whether that person paid the cost.

Indicate only those card(s) you definitely need to turn over to see if any of these people are breaking this law.

	benefit accepted	benefit *not* accepted	cost paid	cost *not* paid
Rule 1	*(P)*	*(not - P)*	*(Q)*	*(not - Q)*
Rule 2	*(Q)*	*(not - Q)*	*(P)*	*(not - P)*

*The logical categories (*Ps* and *Qs*) marked on the rules and cards are here only for the reader's benefit; they never appear on problems given to subjects.

Figure 5.1   The Wason card-sorting task. Though all three tasks have the identical logical structure, most people find Task B easier than Task A.

The logically valid solution is to turn over the *D* and the 7. In the language of logic, the rule is described as "if P then Q"; it is clear that P here corresponds to the *D,* the subject of the test, so one must turn over the *D* card. If any number other than 3 is on the back, the rule is violated. The *F* never enters into the rule, so it's not-P and is irrelevant. It is not necessary to turn over the 3 card either (Case Q), because if there is a *D* on it, the rule is true, and because we started with "if *D,*" any other letter on the card means that the rule does not apply. But a *D* on the other side of the 7 card (not-Q) would violate the rule, so this card must be turned over. In general, the correct solution of the if-P-then-Q puzzle is to examine both Case P and Case not-Q, in the example cards *D* and 7. In numerous tests of logic puzzles like this one, less than 25% of subjects get the right answer, even in samples of college students. The most common mistake is to turn over the 3 card, Case Q.

Familiarity

Why are people so inept at solving such a seemingly simple logic puzzle? One hypothesis is that the categories are unfamiliar, so that a logically identical test using more familiar materials should result in more people solving the problem correctly.

Alas, substituting familiar categories for abstract ones does not help much. If the if-P-then-Q contingency is expressed as "If a person goes to Boston, then he takes the subway," performance is not much better than in the abstract case, even among people who live in Boston and ride (or don't ride) the subway. The majority of subjects still get the answer wrong. And the Boston subway is the contingency problem example that showed higher scores than any of a group of other similar variants (Cosmides, 1989).

Domain Specificity

Another hypothesis about such logical rules is that they are domain-specific; the ability to solve problems like these evolved in response to the needs of people living in complex social environments, so that the capability for logical analyses solved specific social problems. To test this, researchers couched the same if-P-then-Q logic as a social contract, such as "If you drink beer, you must be more than 20 years old." Suddenly the number of people successfully solving the problem tripled, to about 75% (Griggs & Cox, 1982).

A look at the alternatives shows the feel of the problem (Figure 5.1*b*). Our four cards translate to "drinks beer," "drinks water," "is 23 years old," and "is 18 years old." Who must the bartender keep an eye on? Clearly, the beer drinker and the 18-year-old. The P-and-not-Q solution now seems intuitively obvious, despite an added logical complication—the relevant ages have a more-than/less-than structure, rather than being simple numbers.

The difference in the apparent difficulty of these problems is so great that it is important to examine alternative explanations carefully. The familiarity theory might still apply, because people arguably have a lot more experience working with social problems than they do with figuring out who is riding the subway.

A powerful way to test the social-reasoning hypothesis is to stack the deck against the hypothesis, comparing an unfamiliar social contract with a familiar nonsocial contingency. When Cosmides (1989) tested unfamiliar social contract rules, such as "If a man eats cassava root, then he must have a tattoo on his face," she found that people did as well as they did on familiar social contract problems, about 75% correct, and much better than they did on familiar problems that were merely descriptive (such as the Boston subway problem). The results were consistent with the social contract hypothesis and inconsistent with the familiarity hypothesis. It is the content of the problem, not its logic or familiarity, that most influences how many people can solve it.

Social Facilitation. Still another hypothesis to explain these results is that social contracts somehow facilitate logical reasoning, making our general-purpose logic engine run better when social interaction and detection of cheaters in those interactions is at stake. The rules that people use to solve social contract problems, though, are not the same as the P-and-not-Q contingency under all conditions. There is a hidden set of contingencies in social contracts that depends on your role in the contract.

The contract "If an employee gets a pension, then that employee must have worked for the firm for at least 10 years," for instance, has the basic if-P-then-Q structure. But the definition of cheating depends on whether you are the employer or the employee. For the employer, cheating is getting a pension without having worked 10 years, so that the logical structure becomes "if and only if P, then Q." For the employee, because cheating means not getting a pension, the logic changes to "if P, then necessarily Q." The formal logic of the card task, though, remains the same for these variants. The difference is not stated in the problem, but one can test whether it is relevant to the adapted social reasoning strategy.

In a test of these ideas, Gigerenzer and Hug (1992) gave the pension problem to two groups of people, using exactly the same words to describe the problem. The only difference between the groups was that one was told, "You are the employer," and the other was told, "You are the employee." The results were strikingly different in a card-turning task based on these two

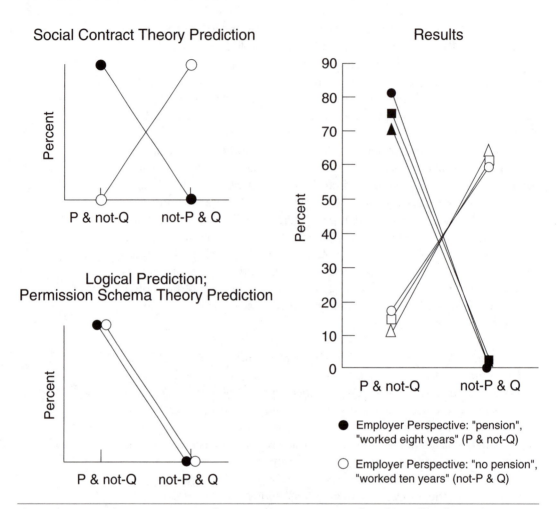

Social Contract Theory Prediction

Results

**Logical Prediction;
Permission Schema Theory Prediction**

● Employer Perspective: "pension",
"worked eight years" (P & not-Q)

○ Employer Perspective: "no pension",
"worked ten years" (not-P & Q)

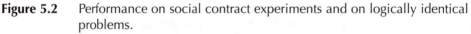

Figure 5.2 Performance on social contract experiments and on logically identical problems.

perspectives (Figure 5.2). To detect cheaters, most "employers" chose "pension" and "worked 8 years" (P and not-Q), whereas "employees" tended to choose "no pension" and "worked 10 years" (not-P and Q). When formal logic and detection of cheating were compared head-to-head, people tended to offer solutions that maximize the detection of cheating.

Other studies have asked whether the relative ease of solving logical problems extends to all social contracts, or only to those that involve the possibility of someone benefiting at someone else's expense. A test of this question, involving a story about a secretary assigning students to one of two equivalent high schools on the basis of residency requirements, showed no superiority in finding solutions—almost all the subjects in the experiment got the wrong answer when the scenario offered no possibility of cheating (Cosmides, 1989). In this case, where neither the secretary nor the students stood to gain from violating the rules, it was difficult for people to detect violations. The possibility of cheating seems to be a necessary component of effective reasoning even in social contract situations.

The Modern World

All these mechanisms are effective only on a person-to-person level, however. In the small societies of the Paleolithic world, the adapted mechanisms work well, but as societies become larger and more complex, the extent of the relationships that must be remembered becomes too large for human brain capacities. Keeping track of who owes what to whom, and who has cheated whom in the past, becomes impossible.

Furthermore, a trader may have trading relationships with people whom he or she sees rarely or only once, increasing the danger of encountering the one-shot Prisoner's Dilemma situation, where defecting is always the best strategy. The trading partner may sell us defective merchandise, or the banker might run off with our money. The strategies of reciprocal altruism and detection of cheating are no longer adequate in such situations. What is the alternative?

The solution of modern societies is to avoid such relationships almost entirely. Instead of relying on your gratitude and a possible future reciprocation, I might demand something else of value before I bestow that buffalo leg on you and your family. Barter becomes a way of obtaining benefits by immediate exchange rather than delayed obligation, making it possible to engage in an unlimited number of transactions without having to keep mental track of who owes what to whom.

Later, the invention of money established a way of keeping track of social debts with a common medium of exchange. A dollar in my pocket says that I have done someone a favor worth a dollar, and I can ask for a dollar's worth of favor from you in exchange for it. Instead of trying to detect and deter social cheaters, we detect and ,deter theft. Modern currency has almost no intrinsic value; its use is in keeping track of social favors and making them more flexible by substituting immediate symbolic wealth for social debts.

Though money is much more effective than reciprocal altruism in managing complex economic relationships with nonrelatives, our brains are still designed around the reciprocal relationship as a mainstay of social and economic interaction. We act as though we still lived in Paleolithic bands, where the imperative is to help those around us because they may help us someday. In the tit-for-tat game of social reciprocation, it pays to cooperate on the first move. And in the simple calculus of the genes, there is no room for elaborate conditional rules about who we are likely to encounter again, and under what circumstances. The rule is blunt and simple, but effective—help everybody. In the limited scope of the Paleolithic world, we are likely to see everyone again.

Here perhaps is the explanation of why the altruistic helpers in the Washington air crash did what they did, following this simple imperative. They did not engage in elaborate calculations of who was helping whom for what reason, but rather helped simply because help was needed.

Unfortunately, though, what seems like an imperative doesn't always operate that way. Society seems permeated by indifference, road rage, and petty crime, exemplified by notorious cases such as that of Kitty Genovese, a New Yorker who was brutally murdered on the balcony of her apartment while dozens of her neighbors witnessed the events and did nothing (Aronson, 1976). Apparently, diffusion of responsibility (let somebody else do it) and uncertainty about the costs of helping (I don't want to get involved with the police) are factors in differentiating situations where altruism occurs and where it does not, but the full story of the necessary conditions for helping remains obscure.

One principle that has been established seems at first paradoxical—the more people there are who could help, the less likely it is that one will do so. In the Paleolithic mind, there is almost always a benefit to helping, for the person in need is likely to be a member of the band on which you depend. Therefore, in terms of the unconscious adapted calculation of a payoff matrix, if you are the only person to witness an incident that requires altruistic help, you are likely to volunteer. If dozens or hundreds of other people are also witnesses, though, the possibility of an eventual payback is diluted by the presence of the others. You are more likely to hang back and let someone else do it. If someone else helps, after all, you get some of the benefit of the rescue while avoiding the cost of rescuing. Perhaps Kitty Genovese suffered from an excess of witnesses.

A more positive side of the helping equation is an ice-breaker phenomenon: If one person helps, then others are more likely to help as well (Aronson, 1976). In the Washington air crash, this applied almost literally. When several people pitch in, the risk and cost to each is reduced, but the benefit to the person helped remains the same.

Other adaptations help to make reciprocal altruism function smoothly among humans. First, one is more altruistic toward those one likes, and one tends to like those who are the most altruistic (Trivers, 1971, 1983). Again, the evolved calculation is realized through an emotional reaction. Yet people tend to show more moralistic aggression against friends, even for small infractions. Trivers (1983) explains that selection may favor a strong show of aggression because friends engage in extensive reciprocal behavior over many years, and small inequities repeated many times would exact a heavy toll in inclusive fitness. If you consistently take a little more than your fair share of meat every time I bring some home, I might not notice the deficit in each case. But over many years of reciprocal gift-giving, my family and I will lose a lot of meat.

Gratitude and sympathy are also emotions that might be selected to motivate altruistic behavior (Trivers, 1971), letting the provider of favors know that the favors are perceived and appreciated. In a sense, communication of these emotions establishes the nonmonetary debt owed to the objects of the gratitude and sympathy. This mechanism applies to both reciprocal and kin-directed altruistic interactions.

Kin-Directed Altruism

The existence of reciprocal altruism and of extensive cooperation among nonrelatives in human societies does not diminish the importance of kin-directed altruism in human social behavior. We see it everywhere, from the strength of family structures to the inheritance of political power.

Kin-directed altruism depends on genes that you have in common with your relatives. Genetic relation does not tell the whole story, though, because some relatives have a greater reproductive potential than others. You may favor your child over a parent, for instance, even though their closeness in genetic relationship to you is the same, because the child might perpetuate your genes, whereas the parent will not.

Behaviorally, the critical difference between reciprocal altruism and kin-directed altruism is that no payback is expected from kin. The reciprocal situation requires that I, and my eventual biological fitness, receive more benefit than cost from the exchange. If I help one of my children, however, the genetic payback comes from their success, not from mine. There is always a payback, but it comes to the genes, not necessarily to the individual. Evolutionary theory predicts no reduction in kin-directed altruism with age, or even an increase in it, because after reproductive age, all enhancements in fitness flow through relatives.

● SOCIAL ORGANIZATION

Family Versus Society

Inevitably, kin-directed altruism, directed toward the family, comes in conflict with the social world of unrelated strangers. One would think that people would interact with these strangers only when they recognize a benefit. The need for social interaction, however, clearly goes deeper than mere economic benefit. We seem to crave social interaction for its own sake, even when no obvious benefit is at stake.

Behaviorist psychologists had assumed that actions are driven only by rewards, punishments, or probabilities of future rewards or punishments. Applied to social interactions, this assumption resulted in the theory that societies are held together by dense networks of reciprocal debts and obligations. As we have seen above, however, modern societies have been able to grow only by minimizing such networks.

The reality of a deeper and more fundamental sort of social bonding was brought home to me when I participated in a course in California ecologies at the University of California, Santa Cruz. The course consisted of five extended weekend field trips, always with the same group of 20-some people, led by the universally admired professor of natural history Ken Norris. On these trips, the group members had close, constant contact with one another, but little contact with others, as we studied ecologies in wilderness environments. In an orientation session, we learned each other's names, and as the field trips went on we developed a deep loyalty and attachment to one another.

Even today, years later, members of that group seem qualitatively different from others when I encounter them on campus. The group had no economic life, everyone bringing their own resources to it, and no permanence. A strong feeling of group cohesion developed nonetheless, despite the lack of a network of reciprocal debts and obligations linking the participants. All that it took was close contact with one another, together with lack of contact with others, for a surprisingly short time.

Social psychologists have known about the cohesion of groups since the classic studies of Sherif (1956; Sherif, Harvey, White, Hood, & Sherif, 1961), who manipulated the loyalties of boys at a summer camp. In arbitrarily assigned groups, the boys quickly developed feelings of loyalty to their own group and animosity toward another (Figure 5.3).

Like the students in Professor Norris's course, the boys in these groups did not depend on each other economically. The group-cohesion emotions

Figure 5.3   What began as friendly competitions developed into serious hostility between arbitrarily assigned groups.

of attachment and animosity arose out of a feeling of belonging more than a recognition of economic or other benefit. Members of each group unanimously felt that their group was better than any of the other groups, so that any victories by the other groups must be due to luck or cheating. The groups were reconciled only when forced to cooperate during artificial emergencies manipulated by the experimenters.

The same thing happens to larger groups after disasters—they are brought together, forgetting their differences for a while as they cope with the emergency. The emotion can extend even to a nation of more than a quarter-billion people, as it did after the September 2001 terrorist attacks in the United States.

Group Membership and Sports

Modern sports fans show patterns of loyalty and animosity similar to those of Sherif's boys (Figure 5.4). Sports, in fact, are a good example of the

Figure 5.4   Sports fans can become very involved in their team's success, even though they have no direct stake in the corporate structure of the team.

intersection of Paleolithic motivations with contemporary social environments (B. Bridgeman & Azmitia, 1993).

Mental Practice

The relevant adapted motivations relate to acquisition of skills useful in activities such as hunting or starting a fire. Merely observing the performance of a skilled activity can improve one's ability to perform that activity at a later time, a human adaptation called **mental practice** that has clear advantages when one must perform dangerous activities such as spearing large animals. It is important to get it right the first time.

Once this mental practice ability is in place, the selective pressure is clear to establish a motivation to take advantage of it. Those who are motivated to observe skilled performances will be better able to take advantage of the phenomenon of mental practice. To be most effective, this motivation should be biased to observing the best skilled performances available—watching someone perform a skill poorly would provide less benefit, and might even degrade one's skills if the performance were really terrible. In a Paleolithic band, this motivation would usually involve nothing more than identifying the best hunter in the band and observing his activities carefully. The adapted tendency to copy the most successful individual, already discussed in the context of establishing punishment of free riders, applies in this case as well (Henrich & Boyd, 2001).

Contemporary Behavior

In the modern world, mental practice and the motivations that facilitate it become applied to spectator sports. People can satisfy their urge to observe superior physical performances by watching the best available athletes. Sports teams exploit a combination of mental practice motivations with ancient group cohesion motivations to create powerful incentives for sports fans. The group of fans is established on an astonishingly thin basis, merely the repeated observation of one group competing physically with another. Identification with the team can come from dwelling in the same large city as the team, even though one has never encountered any of the players personally.

Another source of identification is with a college team, even if the fan attended the college decades ago and doesn't know anyone who is presently there. And many people become fans of a particular team despite having no obvious social connection with it at all. Without such a group identification, sporting events are curiously unexciting—the game usually is judged to be not worth watching if one doesn't care which team wins, even if all the events that normally elicit cheers and groans are observed and understood.

It doesn't matter that the players are professionals who play for the highest bidder and usually don't come from the local hometown, or that the team is a private business that could pick up and move to another city. Only the appearance is important (B. Bridgeman & Azmitia, 1993). The team exploits for profit the adapted mechanisms that maintain motor skills and group cohesion.

Biological Design of Social Institutions

Having no alternative, humans apply their adapted mechanisms of social interaction even in institutional contexts, sometimes with surprising or unintended results. One particularly disturbing example emerged in a study of the social relationships in prisons, conducted at Stanford University by Philip Zimbardo (1971). Student volunteers were divided arbitrarily into groups of "guards" and "prisoners," with guards being given fixed shifts of duty and prisoners obligated to obey the guards, maintaining a prison-like schedule of exercise, meals, and lockdown. Everyone involved knew that the study was only a simulation, that both guards and prisoners could quit at any time, and that the prisoners had committed no crimes. Stanford students are among the brightest and most capable in the United States.

Nonetheless, after a short time, the guards began to denigrate the prisoners and the prisoners to resent the guards. Some of the guards became tyrannical and dictatorial, issuing arbitrary commands and expecting obedience. After only 6 days, things became ugly, violence threatened, and the appalled experimenters had to call off the study. In Zimbardo's (1971) words,

> In less than a week, the experience of imprisonment undid (temporarily) a lifetime of learning; human values were suspended, self-concepts were challenged, and the ugliest, most base, pathological side of human nature surfaced. We were horrified because we saw some boys ("guards") treat other boys as if they were despicable animals, taking pleasure in cruelty, while other boys ("prisoners") became servile, dehumanized robots who thought only of escape, of their own individual survival, and of their mounting hatred of the guards.

Urban street gangs acquire a similar life of their own, even without the functions and obligations of conventional social groups. Although gangs assert that they "own turf," theirs is neither ownership nor turf. To own it would require becoming responsible for it, maintaining and developing it. The real ownership and responsibility falls to legal property owners and governments. The turf is of course mostly a paved urban environment. It's just a game, a pretend ownership of pretend turf, but to the gang members it's all very real—they fight and die over it. In terms of evolutionary adaptations, the appearance trumps the reality, and people behave as the appearance dictates. Gang fights are not really over turf, but over social dominance.

At present, social institutions are designed by people without knowledge of adapted human social mechanisms, so that institutions must go through a sort of trial-and-error selection process. Some institutional experiments succeed, whereas others fail.

A particularly spectacular failure was the 1991 collapse of the Soviet Union, a huge empire dedicated to the concept that human nature could be molded to fit the interests of the state. Propaganda, education, and terror were the tools. The "new Soviet man" never emerged; instead, government policy festered at the official level while real life continued at a lower, person-to-person level with practices contradictory to official policy. At the end of the Soviet period, Soviet President Boris Yeltsin wistfully remarked that communism should have been tried first in some smaller place, such as Switzerland.

An institution that often succeeds in influencing economic and social behavior, despite all the complaints about it, is the income tax system in the United States and many other developed countries. The tax does more than raise money; it also shapes economic behavior with a combination of economic penalties and incentives. A family will find it in its best interest to own a house, so that people will almost feel that they are cheating the system when they take a large tax deduction for their mortgage. In fact, they are doing just what the government wants them to do.

Similar income tax regulations influence behavior in many other economic domains, from charitable contributions to business investments. The system works because of a perception that most people do not cheat, or at least do not cheat very much, on their income taxes. It is effective because it engages existing human motivations to maximize personal advantage, rather than appealing to a vague common good.

Psychology and Law

Society attempts to deal with the excesses of behavior through a legal system that at its base is an exercise in applied psychology. The behaviorist psychologist B. F. Skinner defined psychology, perhaps too narrowly, as the prediction and control of human behavior. Law can be characterized as the prediction and control of human behavior without science. Legal training is very different from scientific training, being based on the learning of conventions, sources of authority, and precedents of past litigation. Nonetheless, the legal system attempts to manage the behaviors of human beings who have evolved exquisitely sensitive adaptations for evaluating fairness, morality, and the appropriateness of punishment (Cosmides & Tooby, 1992).

Laws are necessary when the evolved mechanisms of human behavior prove inadequate to manage a society. They supplement or substitute for evolved mechanisms involving cooperation, prosocial behavior, and detection of cheating, mechanisms that fail when one no longer knows all the people and events personally. Legal institutions come into use when societies become too large for our evolved mechanisms to cope with misbehavior.

Figure 5.5   Details of auto accidents or other important events are often distorted in memory, and can be affected by subsequent events.

Court trials, with their traditions of eyewitness testimony, a 12-person jury, and rules of evidence, draw their institutional forms from a medieval epoch when issues of justice had to be decided by groups of illiterate citizens with weak educations. The prohibition against jurors taking notes, for instance, levels the playing field between literate and illiterate jurors. Insisting on personal testimony more than written protocols similarly engages older oral communication systems.

Evidence and Memory. The fairness and effectiveness of some of these traditions has been questioned by modern psychology. Eyewitness identifications and testimony about events surrounding a crime, for example, have proved to be less reliable than they seemed (Loftus, 1992). In one experiment, volunteers watched a videotape of a traffic accident in which one vehicle crashed into another (Figure 5.5). Later, some of the "eyewitnesses" were asked how fast the cars had been going when they "smashed" into one another, and the others were asked how fast the cars had been going when they "hit" one another.

As you might predict, the "smashed" group estimated higher speeds than the "hit" group. Both groups' experience was the same, but their memories were distinctly different. The eyewitnesses had incorporated the questions with their original memories of the events, rather than discounting them as interpretations of the events (Zaragoza & Mitchell, 1996). Other experiments have induced similar distortions in the circumstances of the accident (stop sign vs. yield sign) and even in the identities of suspects in lineups. These distortions of memory were measured under ideal conditions—the eyewitnesses were well rested, not under stress, and had a clear view of the events. In real life, of course, none of these advantages may apply. Eyewitnesses may see only a fleeting glimpse of the events surrounding the accident, they may not realize until after the fact that their testimony will be important, and often they are directly or indirectly involved in the events leading up to the crash. All of these factors would lead us to expect eyewitness testimony in applied settings to be even less reliable than it is in the experiments.

Why human memory should be so unreliable is a matter of debate. One school of thought holds that memory is fallible and prone to suggestions because biological memory simply isn't very good, and nature is doing the best it can with limited physiological materials. This does not explain, though, why memory should be phenomenally accurate and permanent in other domains, such as motor learning or word memory. Another school suggests that the function of memory is not to record past events, but to guide future action. The record of autobiographical memory that we experience is only a side effect, and we are misusing human memory when we expect a perfect re-creation of past events. Memory is explored more thoroughly in Chapter 8.

The other side of this coin is selective forgetfulness. Judges can admonish juries to disregard evidence that has been presented or statements that have been made, even though all present should know that experiences and the attitudes that they support cannot be erased at will. Jury deliberations often reveal how different the perceptions of different people were about the same events, even though all are striving to achieve a just outcome.

Juries and Justice. The discrepancy between legal conventions and psychological reality has attracted a wealth of jury studies. Psychologists usually impanel a simulated jury of undergraduate volunteers, and either stage a trial or show them a video of a trial. Then the subjects deliberate while the proceedings are recorded, they return a verdict, and they answer questions about what influenced their reasoning and their decisions. The evidence in the case is not the only factor that influences the simulated jury decisions. A host of variables, from the race of the defendant to the color of the lawyer's necktie, turn out to be important as well (Gerbasi, Zuckerman, & Reis, 1977).

But the procedures in these mock jury experiments have the same problem that plagues pencil-and-paper tests of reproductive behavior—what people say on a questionnaire and what they do in the real world are often two different things. A study of actual jurors from 10 felony trials produced a very different result: Real jurors were more cognizant of the law and of the evidence, and less swayed by circumstantial distractions, than simulated jurors (D. Bridgeman & Marlowe, 1979). Evolved mechanisms that foster a moral sense, a desire for fairness, and a sense of duty work better in real social interactions than in pretend ones.

The case of legal practices and traditions raises the issue of whether and how other social institutions, from legislatures to schools and prisons, are effective in engaging adapted human mechanisms of social interaction. At least, it is now possible to examine these institutions in the context of the intersection of adapted mechanisms and cultural conventions, perhaps making them both more humane and more effective.

● DISCUSSION QUESTIONS

1. If kinship is critical to inclusive fitness, why do people adopt unrelated children?
2. Can huge societies be stable even though they consist of people adapted to life in small societies?
3. In addition to the material in the text, what other aspects of legal practice assume psychological characteristics of humans that might be questioned?

● FURTHER READING

Gigerenzer, G., Todd, P. M., & The ABC Research Group. (1999). *Simple heuristics that make us smart*. Oxford, UK: Oxford University Press.

Gerd Gigerenzer and his large research team review a number of astonishingly simple ways of solving what seem to be complex problems. In the real world of context and experience, the methods often work quite well, revolutionizing our ideas about what is necessary for effective human reasoning.

Trivers, R. (1985). *Social evolution*. Menlo Park, CA: Benjamin/Cummings.

One of the most creative and original thinkers in biology, Robert Trivers works out the incentives and disincentives in various types of social interaction and how they shape evolved behaviors and attitudes.

CHAPTER 6

ECONOMIC AND PUBLIC LIFE

"The only course open to social theory is to stare biology square in the face and start again from the beginning."

— Peter Reynolds (1981)

LARGE-SCALE COOPERATION ●

The prehistory and history of humanity have seen a progression from small Paleolithic bands to gigantic industrial societies that coordinate billions of people in social and economic interdependence. There is archeological evidence that even small Paleolithic bands of nomads traded extensively with neighboring bands, in trade networks that could move goods from one group to another over hundreds of miles.

Our economic productivity has now become so specialized that today each of us relies on thousands, perhaps millions, of strangers to produce the goods and services that we require. As individuals, each of us contributes only a tiny and very specialized fragment to this network. One person does nothing but fix brakes, another teaches the subtleties of 19th-century German philosophy to the next generation, and so on. Language makes organization and specialization on this scale possible, but it does not explain why we attempt large-scale social institutions in the first place.

If our adapted capabilities for interacting with each other were honed during the era of small bands, how do we handle such large-scale societies and the interactions that go with them? Like other human capabilities, the ability to organize large-scale societies had simple beginnings. These beginnings constitute the building blocks from which larger organizations emerge.

Hunter-Gatherers: Dozens

As detailed in Chapter 2, humans evolved in bands of a few dozen to a few hundred individuals, so that our adapted social capabilities are attuned to groups of this size. Even at the small scale of the band, though, several uniquely human adaptations make possible social cooperation to a degree not seen in other primates.

In Paleolithic societies, the band was small enough that everyone would know everyone else by name. In interacting with anyone in the group, each party would bring a history of past interactions, gossip from third parties, and detailed knowledge of the other person's personality and circumstances. Governance was largely by consensus, as is common in contemporary hunter-gatherer groups, perhaps with a leader or a group of elders guiding the community. No formal governance structure was necessary because adapted mechanisms guided each person's actions. This does not mean that interactions were inflexible or stereotyped, but rather that a cluster of adapted mechanisms such as capacity for altruism, detection of cheaters, cooperation, and even language itself were usually adequate to manage social interactions.

Early Farmers: Thousands

After the **Neolithic** revolution, the spread of farming about 10,000 years ago, there were at first no great changes in the structures of societies. The revolution occurred so gradually that in many parts of the world the participants would hardly have realized that their way of life was changing. Hunting, gathering, and farming coexisted in many locations for millennia. As the band became a settled village, it remained small enough at first that the adapted social mechanisms could continue to structure social interactions. At first people were not very good at farming, with the result that early settled farming populations were not as healthy as their nomadic brothers. Farming for some was an act of desperation, a way to gather enough food to survive on a small amount of land. Eventually, though, farming profoundly changed every aspect of human life, the changes occurring gradually over centuries. Settling led to increases in population, however (Festinger, 1983), increases that had consequences far beyond the farmers' villages.

Population growth and technological development eventually forced the emergence of more formal political structures. If land was farmed, for example, there had to be a system of land tenure to decide who had the rights to farm each patch of land, and if cooperative irrigation was practiced, there would be a need to regulate water rights. Storage, transportation, and allocation of grain surpluses added further challenges. Thus most of the political structures of the modern world had their gradual beginnings in the Neolithic era. Organizations beyond the village level led to the first empires and all the political and military apparatus of the nation/state. Though some of these empires had populations in the millions, economic and social life continued to revolve largely around local regions, with perhaps a tribute or tax sent to the central government.

Industrial Society: Millions

By the late 18th century, at the dawn of the industrial revolution, there had been enormous technical and cultural progress, but for most people life had not changed fundamentally since the start of the iron age, about 1,000 B.C. About nine tenths of the world's people still made their livings as subsistence farmers, with some of their surplus supporting relatively small cities and their elites. The population of the world numbered less than a billion (it is more than 6 billion now).

Until the industrial revolution, most people lived and died within 50 km (30 mi.) of their birthplaces. They used no fossil fuels and had no medicine in the modern sense. Most of the food they ate was produced and stored locally; all manufactured goods were handmade and therefore were very expensive in terms of the hours of labor required. All of this changed radically within a few decades in the early 19th century.

As the industrial revolution changed ways of life, the scale of change that required centuries during the Neolithic agricultural revolution was compressed into decades. At first, again, the changes seemed modest—coal replaced the increasingly scarce firewood, iron and steel suddenly became less expensive, and textile and other manufacturing opportunities opened up in towns. Quickly, however, the revolution turned full circle, transforming the age-old agricultural life with mechanization, larger markets, and better transportation. Rural areas became depopulated as people moved to the cities, a trend that continues today. The challenges to human political organization, and its Paleolithic-adapted mechanisms, were enormous and fundamental.

Groups as Social Adaptations

Because there was no time for evolution to change human characteristics through these revolutions, the new ways of life had to be mastered with old minds. How does a creature adapted to life in a band of dozens cope with life in a society of millions?

We can start with a curious property of human knowledge: The number of people that a person knows by name does not seem to correlate with the size of the community in which they live. Most people know a few hundred others by name, whether they live in a tiny village or a huge city. This group corresponds to the maximum number of people with whom a Paleolithic hunter-gatherer might have had sustained contact. The size of the group may correspond to a memory or attentional limitation of the human brain, one that makes it difficult to see how humans can function successfully in social organizations of millions.

Stereotypes

One way to cope with large groups of people, given a small number of recognizable individuals, is to treat groups of people as though they were individuals. Beyond anyone's circle of personal acquaintances, there are groups that are given distinct identities. Some are distinguished by their social roles—police, politicians, librarians—whereas others are members of ethnic groups, races, or nationalities—Jews, Arabs, Russians. The groups are handled cognitively as though they were individuals, a strategy that brings advantages and hazards. The big advantage is that a single mind can categorize millions of people by assigning most of them to groups. The hazards include the simplification, stereotyping, and inaccuracy that inevitably accompany such a process.

When groups assume the characteristics of individuals, they acquire consistent personalities, motivations, and roles. Police, for instance, might be perceived as authoritarian and liking donuts, Italians as passionate and a little anarchistic. The distortions that inevitably occur in the process are difficult to correct. A prejudiced person may conceive of blacks as lazy, for instance, but when asked about any personal acquaintances who are members of that group, the stereotype dissolves. "How about your dentist? He's black." "Well, of course, he's hard working, honest as the day is long, and he's a likable guy. It's the other ones I'm worried about." The stereotype of the group can coexist with the very different individual characteristics of particular acquaintances who are also members of the group.

Because the stereotype fits one "acquaintance slot," and the individuals who may be members of the stereotyped group fit in other parallel slots, not in slots that are subordinate to the stereotype, the inconsistency can persist in the mind. It's a conjunction fallacy, a cognitive trip wire similar to those that have been discovered in other contexts to be reviewed below.

Individuals are assigned a status as well as a social role. Thus we would expect groups, when handled cognitively as though they were individuals, to assume a status as well. Indeed, social classes can also be invested with the characteristics and personalities of individuals ("the rich," "the poor," "the intelligentsia"). Membership of individuals in these groups can overlap with groups defined in other ways, such as nationality or religion. Such group memberships invest their members with practically guaranteed prestige, unavoidable poverty, or something in between. The castes of India, which have remained stable for millennia, are examples. Within social groups, however, and in more egalitarian Paleolithic bands, status and dominance become much more individual affairs.

Dominance and Nurturance

Social ethologist Irenäus Eibl-Eibesfeldt (1998) has identified two dimensions that shape human social interactions: a **dominance-submission relationship** and a **nurturant relationship**. The dominance-submission relationship is the older of the two phylogenetically, characterizing social relationships among reptiles. Eibl-Eibesfeldt describes the society of marine iguanas in the Galapagos Islands: Iguanas litter the rocks, but there is no grooming, no mutual feeding, no positive social interaction of any sort. Their interactions consist of ritualized fighting with dominance displays, head butting, and submissive postures of the loser (Figure 6.1). Courtship behavior follows the same pattern, consisting of male dominance displays. Females ready for copulation assume a submissive posture, lying flat on their bellies. This is all the social behavior that the species needs; according to Eibl-Eibesfeldt, there is no evidence that any iguana recognizes another as an individual.

In animals with larger brains, such as mammals and birds, dominance relations have evolved further to include recognition of individuals and the

Figure 6.1   Social interactions of reptiles, such as these marine iguanas, are based on dominance. Ritualized fighting consists of headbutting; the loser assumes a submissive posture by lying on its belly. The winner stops further aggression and waits for the loser to leave.

ability to estimate one's place in a hierarchy without direct conflict. Moreover, other relationships supplement the ancient dominance structure. Mammals and birds have an additional dimension of interaction, a nurturant relationship based originally on the mother-infant bond. Affiliative bonding evolved with individualized nurture of the young, requiring feeding, cleaning, warming, and defending. The adults acquired motivations to care for infants, as infants acquired the motivation to seek care and protection. This interaction required mutual individual recognition.

In the course of evolution, such interactional adaptations were pressed into service for bonding among adults. Repeating a pattern that is seen over and over in evolution, an adapted mechanism that evolves for one purpose is taken over for other purposes as well (Figure 6.2). Because the adaptation is already there, it takes only a little genetic tweaking to reorient the behaviors. Social interactions that have evolved from nurturant behaviors offer more flexibility than dominance-based systems, including all the opportunities of positive cooperation.

Figure 6.2   Offering food, a form of nurturant behavior practiced even by young children, here by a Yanomami baby toward her sister.

STATUS AND SOCIAL DOMINANCE ●

Dominance and social status seem to be universal concerns. Robert Frank (1985) quipped that "We come into the world equipped with a nervous system that worries about rank," and indeed every individual in every society acquires a distinct rank and social status. Often, a single person assumes a different social status in each of a number of different groups or social contexts. How do individuals acquire dominance within a society? Accidents of birth play a major role in current societies, but not always a decisive one.

Chimpanzee Dominance

Social status is older than humanity, for throughout the mammalian world, status becomes important whenever individuals must compete for food, territory, or mating access. Chimpanzee bands are organized around a typical dominance hierarchy, with an **alpha male** at the top, and a looser hierarchy of adult females. The daughter of a high-ranking female is likely to assume a high rank in the band herself, a simple form of social class. For males the evidence of inherited social status is harder to obtain because it is so difficult to ascertain the paternity of wild chimpanzees.

The dominant alpha male is invariably large and experienced; frequently, he attains and maintains his position with the aid of social alliances with other males, usually relatives (Goodall, 1971). He walks with a strut or swagger, emphasizing his large and heavy appearance. Chimpanzees of lower dominance greet the alpha male with submissive gestures, lowering of the body or even a series of quick, deep bows (Figure 6.3) along with a series of pant-grunts (deWaal, 1982) The submissive animal might offer the alpha male a gift, such as a leaf or a stick, along with kissing his feet, neck, or chest (Figure. 6.4).

Female chimpanzee submissive gestures are often not so much economic as sexual. The female will present her rump to the alpha male. If she is in estrus, the male will often mate with her, and in fact the dominant male does as much as three fourths of all the copulating in the band (Ellis, 1995). Less dominant males must settle for mating with a female when she is not at the peak of estrus.

The price that the dominant male pays for his privilege and status, however, is high—among baboons, Robert Sapolsky (1997) found that an alpha male suffers high cortisol levels and low lymphocyte levels, both indicators of extreme stress. Staying on top is hard work, involving the alpha male in more confrontations than the other animals in a troop. In environments where animals have room to spread out, and are not forced together by pressure from predators or confined situations, primate dominance hierarchies are generally looser because most confrontations can be avoided.

Human Dominance

The human mechanisms for establishing dominance relationships work quickly and efficiently. In an experiment putting together 59 groups of strangers, 3 at a time, a clear hierarchy appeared in half the groups within 1 minute. By 5 minutes, hierarchies had emerged in all the groups (Fisek & Ofshe, 1970).

In this study, the hierarchies were judged by behavioral cues. With a more sensitive measure, asking subjects to estimate their own future status in a group, subjects accurately estimated their eventual group status just by seeing the other members of the group, before any words were exchanged. The whole process was over in seconds (Kalma, 1991).

Behavioral and Physical Correlates

How can people estimate their social status in a group of strangers with whom they have not yet interacted? The judgment must be based on physical

Figure 6.3   A submissive gesture in wild chimpanzees of Gombe stream, Tanzania.

Figure 6.4   Symbolic submissive hand kiss, Gombe stream, Tanzania.

characteristics and behaviors. One criterion is facial appearance—some faces appear more dominant than others, marked by a prominent chin and brows. People with naturally low eyebrows are perceived as dominant because lowered eyebrows normally accompany an angry expression (Zebrowitz, 1997). Cross-cultural studies have shown that there is a high degree of agreement about the dominance conveyed in a face (reviewed by Collins & Zebrowitz, 1995; Keating, Mazur, & Segall, 1981), making it unlikely that the appearance of dominance is due to cultural conventions.

Facial appearance can cut both ways, though. For instance, perceivers attribute childlike traits to adults with baby-like facial qualities. And adults with big eyes are perceived as warm and naive (Zebrowitz, 1997). These attributions might be advantageous for someone who wants to be a bit irresponsible, but not for someone who wants to achieve dominance.

Judgments of the appearance of a face are a good starting point, but evolutionary psychology has already shown us that judgments are one thing and actual behavior is another. What is the actual fate of people with dominant appearances? In order to study this question, one needs a sample of people whose appearance is recorded in a standardized way, and whose professional accomplishments and life histories unfold in comparable conditions of challenge and opportunity.

Researchers found such a sample in the alumni of a military academy. In a retrospective biographical study, Mueller and Mazur (1996, 1997) asked a group of subjects to judge the dominance of faces in a West Point military academy yearbook from 1950. Then the careers of the men were analyzed, with the result that indeed for the highest 90% of the class, those with higher facial dominance scores had attained higher ranks in the military hierarchy, were promoted more quickly, and had higher reproductive success. Even for adult males, looks count.

Chapter 3 reviews evidence that taller men have on average a greater reproductive success than their shorter fellows. There is also a status difference, with taller men generally achieving greater dominance (Morris, 1969). The tendency is culturally universal, as valid among the Aka pygmies of central Africa as among Europeans, and it also applies to other primates and to mammals generally. There are many measures of status that relate to height, with the causality going in both directions, either height to dominance or dominance to height.

In one study, a man was introduced to different groups of subjects as having different ranks, such as graduate student and professor. Those who heard the higher-status description judged the man to be taller (Wilson, 1968). Personal knowledge of a person does not overcome this perception, for acquaintances high in status are judged to be taller than they are (Dannenmaier & Thumin, 1964). Perhaps the famously short Napoleon Bonaparte seemed to tower over his contemporaries. Another famously short man of high dominance, King Louis XVI of France, invented high-heeled shoes.

Taller than average men also have advantages in professional life: In 1982, a correlation between height and income meant that each 2.5 cm (1 in.) above the average of 173 cm (5 ft. 8 in.) was worth about $600 more in annual salary (Gillis, 1982). In the 20th century, the taller of two U.S. presidential candidates had an 83% chance of being elected. The 2000 election was not an exception—although Al Gore was taller than George W. Bush and did not win the presidency, he received a million more votes than Bush and lost because of quirks in the antiquated system of vote counting.

Signs of status are not only physical but behavioral as well. Dominant men walk faster, a fact ascertained by measuring the walking speeds of randomly selected pedestrians in a large city (Vienna, Austria) and then

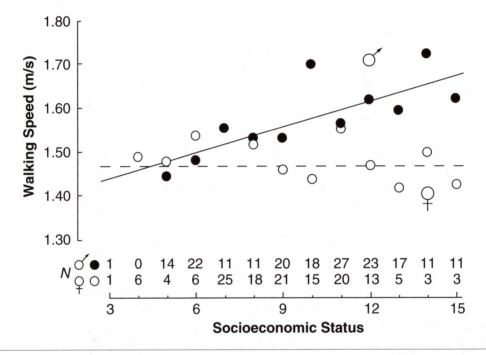

Figure 6.5 Walking speed as a function of socioeconomic status of pedestrians in Vienna, Austria. Socioeconomic status was rated on a 1-15 scale, with higher numbers indicating higher status.

having a second experimenter ask the subjects about their age, height, and socioeconomic status (Schmitt & Atzwanger, 1995). Of course, one would expect tall men to walk faster because they have longer legs, so dominance due to height may account for some of the effect. Evidence against this hypothesis is the observation that walking speed was not correlated with status in women (Figure. 6.5).

In judging height, people normally do not actually estimate the distance from head to toe. Rather, they look only at the head, judging height relative to their own heads (Stoper, 1998). The cognitive shortcut simplifies the mental work needed, but can lead to errors. Standing on a platform, or wearing a crown, can enhance apparent height (and dominance). This, perhaps, explains Louis XVI's high heels.

Hormonal Mechanisms

The physiological mechanisms that influence dominance are hormonal systems as old as the vertebrates themselves. In short, like Robert Sapolsky's baboons, more dominant men have higher steroid hormone levels than their less dominant fellows.

Men. Testosterone, the principal male steroid hormone, has several physiological effects in mature men, including a facilitation of clotting of the blood (presumably in preparation for dangerous contests), releases of physical reserves that increase strength and endurance, and in some a feeling of invincibility. Over long periods, it increases muscle mass and reduces body fat. Blood testosterone levels increase in situations where dominance can be expected to increase, and decreases when dominance declines. Athletes, for example, experience an increase in testosterone levels before an important contest and a further increase if they are victorious. If they lose, testosterone levels decline (Mazur & Booth, 1998).

The testosterone effects extend not only to contests requiring physical exertion, the sort that might have been common in the Paleolithic era, but also to symbolic competitions such as chess games (Mazur, Booth, & Dabbs, 1992). In the modern world, where watching sports competitions often substitutes for participating in them, the physiological changes related to victory and defeat persist. Brazilian soccer fans, whose team beat Italy in the 1994 World Cup, experienced higher testosterone levels after the victory, whereas those of the Italian fans declined (Bernhardt, Dabbs, Fielden, & Lutter, 1998).

Though it remains unclear whether the rise in testosterone levels is a cause or an effect of elevations in dominance status, the role of testosterone in maintaining dominance is clear in both human and nonhuman primates. In animals, where testosterone levels can be manipulated artificially, a causal relationship has been established between testosterone levels and dominance. Low-ranking cows given injections of testosterone rose in rank after the injections, only to sink back to their previous ranks as the effects of the injections wore off (Bouissou, 1978).

In rhesus monkeys, part of the dominance mechanism lies in the control and expression of emotion, regulated by the amygdala, a subcortical part of the forebrain. When the amygdala of a high-ranking male is removed surgically, he sinks to the bottom of the hierarchy (Figure 6.6). The personalities of the monkeys in the hierarchy also play a role, and can result in an amygdalectomized monkey remaining on top if the monkey below him is not inclined to challenge his position (Pribram, 1971). Thus not only hormones and inborn brain structures but also social situations contribute to dominance relationships.

Women. Most of the research on dominance and the stress that accompanies it has been done in men. Women handle stress quite differently; the principal hormone modifying behavior under stress is not testosterone or epinephrine

Figure 6.6   (a) A dominance hierarchy of eight rhesus monkeys. (b) Dave, the dominant monkey, has his amygdala removed and quickly falls to the bottom of the hierarchy. (c) Zeke, who has inherited the most dominant position, is amygdalectomized and falls to the bottom of the hierarchy with Dave. (d) Riva, the new dominant animal, does not drop to the bottom of the hierarchy when amygdalectomized. The initially low status of the remaining potential rivals and their lack of aggression toward Riva are contributing factors.

(adrenaline) but oxytocin. When oxytocin is released as part of the stress response in a woman, it buffers the fight or flight response and encourages her to tend children and gather with other women instead. When she actually engages in this tending or befriending, more oxytocin is released, further countering stress and producing a calming effect (Taylor et al., 2000).

The research leading to this discovery originated with an informal observation. According to Laura Klein, one of the authors of the study, "There was this joke that when the women who worked in the lab were stressed, they came in, cleaned the lab, had coffee, and bonded. When the men were stressed, they holed up somewhere on their own." Although the women's response to stress remains useful in a practical sense today, the men's hormonal preparation for intense physical action is no longer functional for most challenges in the modern world.

Establishing Status in Adolescence

In males, testosterone levels jump abruptly at puberty, the start of adolescence. Along with the hormonal change and the physical maturity that it triggers, behaviors and attitudes change as well. Adolescent boys become more aggressive, especially toward one another, and tend to engage in risky behaviors that in our culture are expressed as extreme sports, reckless driving, and a tendency toward criminal activity, among other things (Arnett, 1992, 1995).

If such seemingly maladaptive behavior is triggered by natural hormonal changes, why was it selected by evolution? One answer is that it was not selected at all, but is an unintended consequence of a combination of two factors: earlier puberty, probably driven by better health and nutrition, and later economic independence, driven by a need for extended education. The high rate of male teenage delinquency may be a side effect of this dangerous combination of physical maturity and economic immaturity (Moffitt, 1993). As reviewed in Chapter 5, the frustrations of the teenage years are a recent addition to human lifestyles, because historically both males and females married or assumed adult roles in other ways shortly after puberty. The rush of aggressive energy was needed to meet the challenges of entering adult life.

The appearance of male aggression is more general than modern teenage crises, though. All over the world, no matter how high or low the crime rate in a given society, most crimes are committed by young males, about ages 15-35. The evidence is in every daily newspaper. Lower-class males, who do not have the options of dominating in business or academia, can be very sensitive to insults or signs of disrespect from their peers, engaging in fights or shootings on seemingly trivial pretexts. Some are attracted to the gangs described in Chapter 5. Young men of all social groups also drive more recklessly when another young man is in the car (Jackson & Gray, 1976), a phenomenon that is now reflected in California laws regulating teenage driving licenses. Young women's driving behavior, in contrast, seems unaffected by the presence of passengers.

Even in contemporary hunter-gatherer societies, young males take great risks and die at disproportionate rates (Hewlett, 1988). This is the time when dominance relationships are being established among the males in a community. Because of the higher variance of reproductive success for males than for females, the stakes in such contests are higher for males, for those who achieve high status also achieve higher lifetime reproductive rates, giving an impetus to the dominance contests of youth in terms of natural selection (Daly & Wilson, 1990). In short, those with the wherewithal and motivation to excel in dominance contests contribute disproportionately to the next generation, fathering sons who in turn are strongly motivated to succeed in their own dominance contests. Willingness to take risks is a necessary part of this status competition, for the contests are decided at the extremes. A race car driver at the 24-hour LeMans race, when asked why he always drove his car right at the edge of a curve, inches from death, replied that if you don't drive that way, you lose the race.

War

The ultimate contest for dominance among social groups is armed conflict, where men are willing to kill one another by the millions over politics. In modern societies, there is little possible benefit to an individual for taking on the great risks of military service—Nazi propaganda minister Josef Goebbels once famously remarked that the best a soldier could hope for is to return home uninjured and take up his previous life. Hence, soldiers are forced into service, "drafted" against their will. Still, military drafts probably would fail if resistance to them were strong enough.

Evolutionary theory has difficulty accounting for the behavior of modern soldiers, who risk their lives for little potential gain either for themselves or for their relatives. Any adaptation for warfare would have to have evolved in another environment, one that offered the gains that would build into our genome a motivation for making war, if indeed such a motivation exists at all.

One of the characteristics of military conflict that makes it tolerable for the soldiers is that there is always an uncertainty about death. Although some are sure to die in battle, each man hopes that he will survive even as others fall around him.

If modern technology has made war so deadly that there is no prospect of direct personal gain, the situation was different in Paleolithic conflicts. Our best evidence for this comes from isolated cultures such as the Eipo in Papua New Guinea and the Yanomami in the Amazon, groups that maintained Neolithic lifestyles well into historic times (exploiting a mixture of farming, hunting, and gathering, but no metals). In both groups, war consisted mostly of raids on neighboring villages by small groups of men, who could win women, weapons, or other goods in this way. In the words of Jacob Bronowski (1973, p. 88), war is not so much aggression as "a highly planned and cooperative form of theft."

Sometimes men were killed in these raids, but because the weapons were not particularly powerful, the chance of being killed was not great (Figure 6.7). Because the raiders had the element of surprise, the risk for them was smaller than the risk for the defenders. For the Eipo, this amounted to about 3 persons per 1,000 per year (Schiefenhövel, 1998). Although the victims of the raid were more likely to suffer death or injury or to lose women and other goods, the raid would often provoke a revenge counterraid where the risks were reversed. For the Yanomami, conflicts were mostly over women (Chagnon, 1983, 1988).

Though no one could avoid becoming a victim, the enterprise of raiding was profitable. Because the initiative lies with the raiders, the practice was perpetuated. Occasionally, a truce would be established and a period of peace would ensue, only to be broken eventually by a group of headstrong young men. Because the available weapons could kill or injure only at close range, each side was safe until the conflicting parties drew to within a few meters of one another.

Paleolithic conflicts were of necessity small in scale, because resources were dispersed. When people began to settle and produce surpluses after the Neolithic revolution, their nomadic neighbors saw them as rich sources of treasure and organized large-scale raids against them. This style of warfare persisted in many cultures until and even after the development of gunpowder, with wars being fought for the spoils.

Given that the small raids that Paleolithic peoples were able to mount against each other yielded a short-term gain for the warriors, there arose a selective pressure to facilitate the organization and functioning of raiding parties. Male initiation rituals committed each adolescent to a particular village, and sometimes to a totem or other larger group, for life (Schiefenhövel, 1998). The indoctrination often involved membership in a fictive kinship group, in which the leader is seen as a father and one's fellow warriors as brothers (Wiessner, 1998). In this way, the adapted emotions of kin selection could be exploited by a group of more distant kin or nonkin. Among the !Kung of Africa's Kalahari Desert, tattoos helped to make the identification both public and permanent (Wiessner, 1998). Brave warriors and their leaders won praise and prestige in the village, and shirkers were despised. All these influences combined to increase the biological fitness of the best warriors.

The only encouraging aspect of this unhappy story is that men make war only when the conditions are right. If modern societies can identify and

Figure 6.7   Warriors can achieve high status in Yanomami groups. Facial tattoos permanently mark the warrior's group membership.

eliminate the social conditions that induce war-making, perhaps war can be eliminated and societies can emphasize more positive interactions.

Nurturant Interactions

Originating with the mother-child bond, nurturant interactions are first extended to the family. These interactions were the subject of Chapters 4 and

5, the core of human social life. They are the source of prosocial behavior, the cooperative interactions that expand far beyond the family to give humans such power over their world. There is a strong argument that much of the selective pressure for the tripling of brain size over the course of hominid evolution originated with the need for handling ever more complex social interactions.

Indeed, modern humans routinely master very complex social as well as physical environments, reasoning about multiple layers of action and inter-action. Because prospering in a society of humans requires more than social standing and good relationships with others, reasoning about the problems that arise in life should also be important. That capability, though, is not always based on rational thought. The human capabilities for thinking and reasoning are not what one might at first expect.

PERSISTENT IRRATIONALITIES ● OF HUMAN ACTION

Living in situations very different from those in which our ancestors evolved, modern humans seem to depend upon their flexibility for survival. Flexibility, though, encounters an evolutionary paradox, for natural selection cannot do its work on challenges that an organism has not yet encountered. Because organisms adapt to particular situations, or to a particular range of situations, evolution cannot look forward to organize cognitive processes in anticipation of the next challenge. Usually, we must respond to novelty by making do with adapted mechanisms that have served well for challenges that our ancestors encountered in the past. In many situations, these mechanisms work well, but sometimes they betray us—we come up with strategies that, on reflection, seem to be clearly wrong.

There are two schools of thought about these cognitive limitations. One is that humans are doing the best they can with limited cognitive resources, and sometimes those resources fail us (the "cognitive limitations theory"). The other is that what seem at first like failures or limitations can be robust, generally successful problem-solving strategies that usually work well in the real world even if they do not always satisfy the cold test of logical consis-tency (the "adaptation theory"). Gigerenzer (1998) calls this **ecological rationality**.

Psychologists have identified several kinds of discrepancy between logi-cally correct solutions to problems, on one hand, and typical human solu-tions, on the other. Each is based on a different logical fallacy and applies in a different cognitive setting. **Algorithms** are recipes for solving a problem, recipes that always lead to a solution. There is no guarantee that an algorithm will be practical, though, that it will require only a manageable amount of computation and a reasonable input of information. The problem-solving strategies that humans often use instead are called **heuristics**, strategies that fall short of logical completeness. Heuristics reduce the number of operations needed to solve a problem, at the risk of not always finding the best solution.

Though heuristics are characterized by trial-and-error strategies, or making up ways of solving a problem as you go along, they often result in consistent biases, deviations from rational thought. Many of the subjects in studies of thinking feel a distinct uneasiness about reasoning with logical problems, feeling that their conclusions are tentative and unsure, but the point of the studies is to push the envelope of human thinking, to explore its limits and capacities.

The Baseline Bias

Suppose that I propose spending a billion dollars to save a thousand lives per year on the highways. It would seem inhuman not to jump at the offer. A thousand deaths represent a tragedy that should be avoided at all costs. Indeed, when surveyed, most people accept this hypothetical offer. Now I ask a different group if they are willing to spend a billion dollars to reduce the annual highway death toll from 41,000 to 40,000. A billion dollars is a lot of money—it could build a lot of schools or fund a lot of medical care, whereas a decrease in fatalities of less than 2.5% seems hardly noticeable. Indeed, most people reject this offer as not a very good deal. But when both offers are juxtaposed, as they are here, it is clear that they represent exactly the same savings in lives for exactly the same expenditure. The only difference is that the first problem implicitly compares a thousand deaths to none, but the second compares a large number to another almost equally large number.

In many tests of such reasoning, this fallacy deceives a majority of subjects from a wide range of backgrounds (frighteningly, traffic engineers are no exception). It is called the **baseline** fallacy because people in the first group seem to disregard the baseline, the large number of people who will die on the highways with or without the extra expenditure. The importance of this example, of course, is that reasoning about all sorts of risks and opportunities follows the same principle.

Adherents of the cognitive limitations theory point to this as an example of a systematic failure of human reasoning. The adaptation theorists, though, argue that perhaps the contrast in conclusions is not so irrational as it seems. The first group is not made aware of the large baseline; even if the subjects in that group happen to know something about highway death statistics, the baseline is not salient enough to affect their decision making significantly. The second group might quite correctly conclude that the small percentage change in fatalities represents only a minor change in the actual risk of driving on the highways, diluted by the millions of drivers and billions of miles driven every year. If your chance of dying on the highway this year is just over 1 in 100,000, or 0.00001025, the billion dollars would reduce your risk to 0.00001000. Though the thousand deaths are socially significant, from your own standpoint the improvement seems negligible.

Furthermore, the large baseline makes even a thousand deaths such a small fraction of the total that the number may well be unreliable; how sure are you that a thousand lives can really be saved? An error of only 2-1/2% in the statistics could wipe out the supposed advantage. One should indeed think twice about spending a billion dollars on an advantage that may well not exist. In the real world of uncertain numbers, then, the decision makes more sense than it does in the abstract.

The Availability Bias

Another heuristic of human thinking is based on the accessibility, or availability, of solutions to problems. For instance, I could ask you to estimate the number of seven-letter words in this book that have the form "_ _ _ _ _ n _" Now, how many seven-letter words do you expect to have the form "_ _ _ _ ing"? Most people guess that the "ing" form is more common, but another look will show you that all "ing" words also fit the first pattern. People who make this mistake, and that includes most people, are falling victim to the **availability** heuristic (Kahneman, Slovic, & Tversky, 1982). We judge the most familiar to be the most common.

In the example, the availability heuristic led directly to a fundamental mistake in logic, that a category could be larger than another category that includes it. In the preliterate world, though, people did not go around playing spelling games. Adaptation theorists point out that normally the most familiar really is the most common. The most familiar species of deer is locally the most common, the most familiar tree is the most common, and so on. The mental shortcut usually gives us the right answer, and does so a good deal more quickly and simply than a formal logical analysis.

The Representativeness Bias

You enter a lecture hall full of professionals, 400 lawyers and 2 engineers. I describe a member of this group: he is quiet, mathematically inclined, races model planes as a hobby, and likes order in his life. Is he more likely to be an engineer or a lawyer? Most people respond "engineer." But look at the probabilities. Only 0.5% of the group is engineers, so the **prior probability** (the probability before the problem begins) of describing a lawyer is 99.5%. Even a person with a lot of what we think of as engineer-like qualities is more likely to be one of the 99.5% in this sample than to be one of the 0.5%. If even 1 out of 100 of the lawyers in the group has our person's characteristics, you are likely to be wrong.

You might respond that, yes, there are very few engineers in the group, but it is still reasonable that our person is one of them. The experimental results are similar, however, whether the problem is posed with 4 lawyers or 400. People usually judge the identity of a person in such problems by their perceived **representativeness** as a member of the group, without taking the prior probability into account (Tversky & Kahneman, 1983).

The lawyer-engineer problem can also be posed as a negative. If subjects are told that a group consists of 70 engineers and 30 lawyers, they will correctly estimate that the chance that a person picked from the group is an engineer is 70%. But when given a personality description in addition, even a neutral one such as "30 years old, married with no children, and high in ability and motivation," the perceived likelihood that the person is in one or the other group moves toward 50%, whether the problem was posed with 70% engineers or 70% lawyers (Tversky & Kahneman, 1974).

Another scenario illustrating this heuristic concerns Linda, a recent college graduate living in a big city. She is neat and orderly, quiet, and has worked for a female congressional candidate. Now subjects are asked which is most likely: that Linda is (a) a feminist, (b) a bank teller, or (c) a feminist and a bank teller. Many subjects choose the third alternative, even though it is logically impossible that someone is more likely to be both a feminist and a bank teller than to be either one or the other. A glance at Figure 6.8 shows why. The number of people who are both feminists and bank tellers must be smaller than either the number of bank tellers or the number of feminists. A lot of people in the group might be expected to be feminists, but there are relatively few bank tellers, so the first alternative is the most likely.

Again, people use representativeness (also called typicality) to come up with an alternative that is logically indefensible. Tversky and Kahneman (1983) label this the **conjunction fallacy.** The fact that Linda was given characteristics that people identify with both feminists (well educated, politically involved with a female candidate) and bank tellers (neat, orderly, quiet) makes people assume that she belongs to both categories. The Linda scenario has yielded the same result in many replications, and is reliable enough to be used as a classroom demonstration.

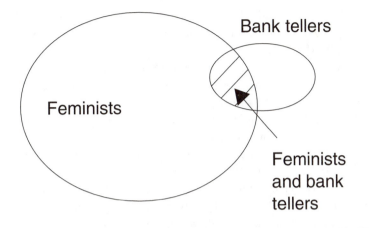

Figure 6.8   Venn diagram of the sets of feminists, bank tellers, and their intersection (crosshatched area). The group that belongs to both sets is always smaller than either of the sets considered separately.

How might adaptation theorists explain this paradoxical result? One answer is that in the natural world, using conjunctions can be a shortcut to a valid conclusion. Imagine that I live in a world where most men have short hair and most women have long hair, and that many members of neighboring Tribe X have zigzag tattoos. Seeing a stranger who has both long hair and a zigzag tattoo might lead me to guess that the person is a female member of Tribe X. Statistically, it is safer just to guess that the person is female, but practically it is more useful to add the tribal tag as well.

Statistical Reasoning

Another characteristic of human problem-solving machinery can be illustrated with a medical diagnosis problem. You visit your doctor to get a test for an invariably fatal cancer. The doctor tells you that the probability that someone in your demographic group has the cancer (the prior probability) is 0.01%, and the test is 100% reliable: that is, if you have the cancer, the test is certain to pick it up. The doctor also mentions that the test has a false positive rate of 1%. You take the test, and it comes back positive. What is the probability that you have cancer, and should attend to your will? Try to come up with an answer before going on to the next paragraph.

The standard mathematical solution to this probability problem is Bayes's theorem, named after the 18th-century English clergyman who introduced it. Few people, however, are familiar with the theorem, and fewer still can use it reliably to arrive at the correct probabilities in problems like the cancer problem. One of the most common solutions is to take the hit rate of the test (100%) and subtract the false positive rate (1%), giving a 99% probability that our patient has cancer. This is wildly off the mark because it fails to take into account the 0.01% prior probability of having the disease. Medical counselors and doctors, tragically, do no better than college undergraduates with this and similar problems.

The fact that most people are hopelessly inept at solving such important problems, when couched in probability language, has perplexed and discouraged cognitive scientists for a generation. Dan Kahneman and Amos Tversky, who discovered many of these phenomena, wrote, "In his evaluation of evidence, man is apparently not a conservative Bayesian: he is not a Bayesian at all" (Kahneman & Tversky, 1972).

Frequency Versus Probability

The problem looks quite different, though, when it is expressed in terms of frequencies. Using only information that was presented in the original problem, the situation can be restated in terms of a group of 10,000 people. In that group, 1 person can be expected to have cancer (the prior probability), and this person is sure to test positive for the disease (the 100% hit rate of the test). The test will also label 100 other people positive (the false positive rate, 1% of 10,000).

Now we again have all the facts, and the solution should be obvious. Of the 10,000 in our hypothetical sample, 1 will test positive because of cancer, and 100 will test positive because of false positives. So the chance that you have cancer, given a positive test result, is 1 in 101, or just under 1%. It's certainly a more optimistic result than most people calculate in the probability format, and it is the correct one. Surprisingly, there seems to be no mathematics at all—the problem nearly solves itself.

Experiments comparing medical diagnosis problems in probability format and in frequency format repeatedly come out with results echoing the cancer example. In a group of German physicians, only 8% got an answer somewhere near correct with a probability format, but the number correct jumped to 46% with a frequency format (the scary part of the result is that the majority of the physicians got it wrong even in the frequency format) (Gigerenzer, 1998).

To investigate such results more closely, using a slightly simpler problem, Cosmides and Tooby (1996) replaced probability statements with frequency statements one by one. Average performance became more accurate with each replacement, ranging from 12% correct in the pure probability format to 76% correct in the pure frequency format.

Why should frequency problems be relatively easy while the formally equivalent probability problems, containing the same information and asking the same question, are so difficult? Adaptation theorists would answer that probability is a relatively recent mathematical invention. Mathematicians have used it for only a few centuries, and it has been used in public policy, in applications such as the probability of a disease or the chance of a forest fire, for less than a century.

Any adapted brain mechanisms that are applied to problems such as those above would have to deal with frequency, because Paleolithic humans saw frequencies of events, not probabilities. An early hunter, for example, might know that of 20 hunting expeditions for bears, only 3 were successful, in contrast to 14 of 20 expeditions for antelope. Risks of death after a snake bite, possibilities of raising a surviving child, and other such mathematically definable events were experienced as frequencies of occurrence, and this is the language that engages the adapted mechanisms of human reasoning.

Cognitive limitations theorists, faced with such evidence, can only mumble that couching the problem in frequency terms makes it much easier, because the experimenter practically solves the problem. This, of course, is the point. The problem seems to be practically solved even though it is logically equivalent in both forms.

The adapted ability of humans to reason in terms of frequency formats also explains some cognitive illusions, self-deceptions that appear when problems are couched in terms of probability. One of these is an **overconfidence bias** (Lichtstein, Fischoff, & Phillips, 1982) in subjects who are asked how likely are to be correct in statistical reasoning problems. In circumstances where students said they were 100% confident, for instance, they were correct about 85% of the time; when they were 90% confident, they were averaging 75% correct. This bias disappears when questions are asked in a frequency format. Confidence changes little, but performance improves so much that there is even a slight tendency toward underestimation of accuracy (Gigerenzer, Hoffrage, & Kleinbölting, 1991).

Even the classic problems that test the representativeness and baseline heuristics are less prone to error when given in terms of frequency. Most people correctly solve the Linda problem that demonstrated the conjunction fallacy if they are asked to think of 200 women like Linda and are then asked how many of them are bank tellers, or bank tellers active in the feminist movement. The rate of conjunction fallacy errors, usually 80-90%, drops to 10-20% (Fiedler, 1988; Gigerenzer, 1998).

Reasoning by frequency, along with the representativeness and baseline heuristics, might go a long way toward explaining the difficulty that many people have in evaluating the conclusions reached by scientific methods and in rejecting claims contradicted by scientific studies. Millions of people adhere to unproved or discredited herbal cures, acupuncture, astrology, and a long list of other practices that lack scientific validation and can cause great damage by delaying effective treatment. When asked why they practice techniques that are known to be worthless, the adherents point to examples of seemingly miraculous cures, without considering the many cases that are not cured.

A single example does not make an effective medical procedure or a wise social decision; almost all treatments and interventions are validated by correlations, always with some variability in results. The implication is that even the most effective procedures will occasionally fail, and even the most worthless will sometimes seem to succeed. Nonetheless, the Paleolithic convincingness of personal experience, even with a tiny sample, can overwhelm intellectual knowledge based on statistical reliability of the large numbers that our ancestors would never have encountered. They were psychologically unequipped to handle statistics because adequate amounts of data for valid statistical analysis were never available to them.

Given all these problems, it may seem paradoxical that psychologists, in their wisdom, are confident that they can separate the correct answers from the errors in logical analysis. How can we ever come up with standards of rationality that most people fail? The answer, of course, is that the psychologists have the advantages of mathematical notation and procedures, lots of time, and the opportunity to check for errors.

Bounded Rationality

The strategy of reasoning with frequency rather than probability helps us to understand human reasoning in some domains, but it does not help with others. The baseline and representativeness biases, for instance, seem to persist as shortcomings of human thought. According to one interpretation, such strategies are byproducts of problem-solving techniques that usually are fast and effective. Like visual illusions, the heuristics of Kahneman and Tversky may be illusions of thinking—situations where applying a rule that usually works gets us into trouble instead.

What are the rules by which humans normally solve problems? Todd and Gigerenzer (2000) differentiate two broad classes of problem-solving strategies, those that rationally optimize and those that are bounded

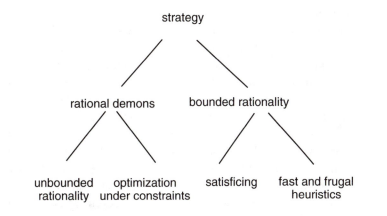

Figure 6.9   Types of decision process (modified from Todd & Gigerenzer, 2000).

(Figure 6.9). Ever since the period of the Enlightenment in 17th- and 18th-century Europe, the ideal of Western civilization has been to solve problems rationally. One should gather all the facts, weigh them according to their relevance and reliability, and combine them into an optimal solution to the problem. In choosing a college, for example, the student should collect data on all 2,000 four-year institutions, including their size, location, students' test scores, student/faculty ratio, and all other relevant variables. The result would be a giant matrix of data. Using multiple regression techniques, the student would then weight each variable appropriately and come up with an optimal choice. This is the unbounded rationality option. The amount of computation is so daunting that in real college choices, it never happens.

An alternative is **optimization under constraints**, proceeding with the computation until, by some criterion, searching further has more costs than benefits. The difficulty with this method is that, in addition to the optimizing calculations, one also needs to implement a **stopping rule** to decide when the point of diminishing returns has been reached. Sometimes deciding when to stop is more complex than the calculations themselves. And again, in the real world, no student ever determines a college choice with this algorithm. How would you know when further calculation would be counterproductive? Would just a few more variables allow you to make a better decision?

In the real world, most people solve most problems with methods of **bounded rationality**, methods that are logically incomplete but in many cases can do as well or nearly as well as the rational solution. More important, the methods of bounded rationality work much faster and more reliably because they use less information to reach their conclusions.

The first method is called **satisficing**, an old Scottish word revived by Simon (1991) to mean a method for making a choice from a set of sequentially encountered alternatives. Because the problem is structured by the environment in problems that people actually encounter, human reasoning can take advantage of that structure. One need not solve all the equations simultaneously, as the rational demons of Figure 6.9 demand. In this solution, our puzzled would-be college student might first limit the search to colleges within 500 miles of home, and then to colleges with a maximum student/faculty ratio, and so on. Quickly, the number of alternatives would shrink to a manageable size. More important, the student would not have to deal with more than one variable at a time. When only one alternative is left, the search ceases, a quick and calculation-free stopping rule.

A newer set of methods is called **fast and frugal** (Gigerenzer, Todd, & The ABC Research Group, 1999). These are the sparest methods of all, each one tailored to a particular type of problem. Our college seeker, for example, might use a minimal set of criteria: What is the nearest college that offers evolutionary psychology? He or she would just start with the closest college and check the catalog. If there's only SSSM psychology there, the student checks the next one. As soon as one meets the criterion, our student sends for an application.

The method sounds almost irresponsibly sparse, but some successful fast-and-frugal searches are sparser yet. An example is a series of problems given to American college students: Which of two German cities is larger? Students begin the experiment unbiased, because most of them haven't a clue about the sizes of German cities. They are given a list of cues, such as whether the city has an express rail station, whether it has a soccer team, and so on. The technique is to start with the first cue: if the cities are differentiated on this cue, you simply pick the one that passes the test. If both pass the test, or both don't, you go to the next cue, and so on until one of them gives you an answer.

In the experiment, this simple procedure worked as well as Bayesian methods (calculated by the experimenters, not the students) (Gigerenzer & Goldstein, 1996). Furthermore, in a more free-form design, it turned out that students with limited knowledge often did better than those with more complete knowledge. Most American students have heard of only a handful of German cities, so when asked which has a larger population, Hamburg or Düsseldorf, the students might just pick Hamburg, the one they have heard of, and they would be right. A student with more complete knowledge would have to use other, potentially less reliable cues. You can get direct flights from the United States to Düsseldorf, for instance, but not to Hamburg. Paradoxically, in this situation the student with limited knowledge can do better than the better informed one (don't try this in your next examination). I was thinking of naming this the George W. Bush effect, but decided against it.

There are a number of other fast and frugal algorithms, all with drastically simplified search spaces and quick search methods. Each works well in only a restricted range of problems, because arriving at a good solution with limited knowledge depends upon using the structure of the environment itself to help solve the problem. For an evolutionary psychologist, this strategy makes sense, because our Paleolithic problem-solver had only a limited domain of problems to solve: choosing a campsite or a mate, deciding what animal to hunt or what plant to seek today, and so on. The available information on which to base the decision was always sparse and incomplete. Fast and frugal methods offer quick solutions with good reliability, whereas the rational thinker is forever trying to amass more information or is lost in thought, weighing the evidence at the choice point.

There is another type of problem, though, where no method seems to work for most people. These are problems involving exponential rates of growth.

Exponential Growth

In **exponential growth,** a quantity increases by a constant fraction of its current size in a given time period. A classic example in reasoning studies is the lily pad problem: A lily pad sits in a large lake, reproducing itself in one day. The next day, each daughter lily pad reproduces itself, and so on, filling the lake in 30 days. Now subjects are asked on what day the lake is half full.

Unless they have just finished studying a math unit on exponential growth, most people guess in the range of 15 to 20 days. The correct answer is the 29th day. On the last day, each lily pad reproduces itself, filling the lake. Especially hard to grasp is what the lake looks like near the end of the month-long growth. On Day 25, only 3% of the lake is covered with lily pads, and 97% is still empty. It is hard to see impending disaster when the small patch is barely noticeable on the broad swath of open water. At a constant growth rate of 100% per day, though, the lake will be choked with half a billion lily pads in 5 more days.

Population Growth

An important current application of reasoning about exponential growth is in demographics, the science of populations (Bartlett, 1978). Thomas Malthus first pointed out in 1798 that population tends to grow exponentially, as more population generates more parents, who in turn generate more population. Resources, though, tend to be added arithmetically, because growth, for instance in a water supply, does not tend to create an even greater growth in the future. This is one of the sources that inspired Darwin's development of the idea of evolution by natural selection.

Biologists have known about the danger of exponential population growth for some time (Ehrlich & Holdren, 1971), but the public for the most part seems unconcerned with the problem. Albert Bartlett once said that "The greatest shortcoming of the human race is man's inability to understand the exponential function." Economic growth follows similar rules, where a certain percentage of growth each year is considered essential for a healthy economy. Yet no rate of growth is sustainable indefinitely; "sustainable growth" is an oxymoron (Bartlett, 1994).

The present growth rate of the human population is about 1.3% per year (Figure 6.10), which seems unimpressive until it is translated into a doubling time of about 53 years. This means that the entire growth of human numbers can be divided into two equal parts: one from the origin of the species to about the middle of the 20th century, and a second from then until now. It also means that unless something changes, the population will double again within the lifetimes of current college students. Most people recognize, though, that there is not room on the planet for another China and another India.

Clearly, the present growth rate is unsustainable, though some scholars (not mathematicians) have denied that the problem exists, maintaining that growth can continue indefinitely (Simon, 1995). The mathematics of exponential growth tell us that in the long run, any growth rate is unsustainable. Currently, environmental problems such as rain forest depletion, pollution, and global warming are blamed on their immediate triggers, even though most of the problems are caused by or made worse by population growth, and none can be solved until that growth stops.

Why are most people unable to appreciate the power of exponential growth, and especially its implications for population growth and ecological collapse as human numbers eventually overwhelm the environment? The mathematics is not complex—every high school algebra student learns it. Applying the mathematics realistically to applied situations, however, seems not to be something that we do well.

Critical though the concept of exponential growth may be for contemporary life, the Paleolithic population would not have encountered examples of it. For a hundred thousand years, human populations barely hung on, with growth rates that were imperceptible over a human lifetime and that no one experienced over longer intervals. Natural processes of exponential growth,

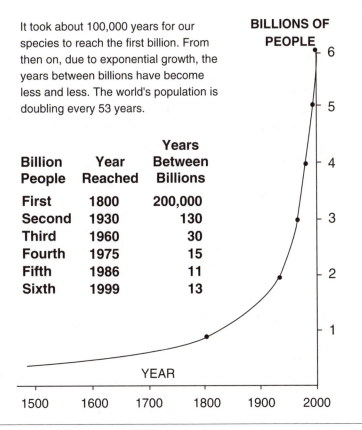

It took about 100,000 years for our species to reach the first billion. From then on, due to exponential growth, the years between billions have become less and less. The world's population is doubling every 53 years.

Billion People	Year Reached	Years Between Billions
First	1800	200,000
Second	1930	130
Third	1960	30
Fourth	1975	15
Fifth	1986	11
Sixth	1999	13

Figure 6.10 Human population size, 1500-2000.

or decay, do not last long enough to affect people in important ways, so that most of the change that people experienced was arithmetic.

A second cognitive limitation in the population domain is that the effects take place over many years, but humans seem inept at dealing with events that spread over long periods of time. The reasoning of most people about the hazards of earthquakes, for instance, seems as irrational as their reasoning about population growth. Because earthquakes represent very damaging but very infrequent disasters, estimating the risk in principle involves multiplying a large number (the potential number of deaths) by a very small number (the risk of experiencing a killer quake in a given year).

About 60 people have died in California earthquakes in the past 2 decades, for instance, 40 of them on a faulty elevated freeway that collapsed. In most years, there are no fatalities. Yet there are people who will move from

California to the Midwest, where hundreds perish in blizzards every year, and the statistical danger of death is much greater, to avoid the hazard of earthquakes. At the same time, most California communities are poorly equipped for the earthquakes that will come sooner or later.

Similar miscalculations induce people to drive long distances instead of flying, or to be terrified of terrorism but indifferent to drunk drivers who kill many times more people than terrorists do every year. For the Paleolithic nomad, planning more than a year in advance or preparing for an infrequent and unlikely disaster was an issue that never came up; we must use all the power of our intelligence to compensate for the lack of evolved mechanisms in dealing with these aspects of modern life.

In summary, people are spectacularly ineffective at solving problems that extend beyond our immediate experience, either in the events involved or the expanses of time that must be taken into account. Perhaps these are domains in which evolution has left us cognitively unprepared.

● DISCUSSION QUESTIONS

1. Can you think of examples of people justifying unsafe or unhealthy practices by citing counterexamples from their personal experience? Why do they do this?
2. How could society prevent its leaders from making decisions on an irrational basis?
3. How can humans organize such large and complex societies, when no single person controls the organization of a society?

● FURTHER READING

Gigerenzer, G., Todd, P. M., & The ABC Research Group (1999). *Simple heuristics that make us smart*. Oxford, UK: Oxford University Press.

The point that logically complete rational thinking is not always the best strategy is driven home with numerous compelling examples as well as information-theory analysis.

Ofek, H. (2001). *Second nature: Economic origins of human evolution*. Cambridge, UK: Cambridge University Press.

Was exchange an early agent of human evolution, or is it merely an artifact of modern civilization? Spanning 2 million years of human evolution, this book explores the impact of economics on human evolution and natural history, emphasizing feeding and exchange strategies.

Eibl-Eibesfeldt, I., & Salter, F. (Eds.) (1998). *Indoctrinability, ideology and warfare.* New York: Berghahn Books.

An edited volume, this book contains contributions from a number of experts, including the authors, on issues of warfare and social control in primates and humans. The book is strongly influenced by the traditions of European ethology and describes a rich vein of knowledge gleaned from disappearing tubal socities.

CHAPTER 7

LANGUAGE AND COMMUNICATION

"In the beginning was the Word."

— John 1:1

S ome of the adapted systems in the human brain deal with specific life challenges such as finding a mate or identifying cheaters in social exchanges. Others are more general, supporting cognitive abilities that underlie practically all human activities. Like the red blood cells that nourish every activity from keeping warm to reading textbooks, these adapted systems constitute a cognitive toolbox that other adapted systems use to perform their functions. Because the core abilities of these systems cut across the lines of life challenges, they are considered separately in this and the following chapter.

● THE EVOLUTION OF LANGUAGE

Traditionally, psychologists and linguists study language as they find it—a complex system of symbolic communication in adult humans. One can study

syntax (the structure of language) and **semantics** (the science of meaning), for example, by observing people using language. Looking under the surface, however, allows us to use evolutionary theory in understanding language from the ground up, beginning with its phylogenetic and developmental origins.

Though it is a uniquely human system, language has evolutionary roots much deeper than Homo sapiens. Indeed, it is a new communication system built largely from old parts, its roots lying deep in the evolved systems that support communication functions both in humans and in other primates.

The complete story of the evolution of human language will always be a mystery, for words leave no fossils. We can infer a good deal about its origins, though, from indirect sources such as the cognitive and communicative abilities of other primates, the development of language in children, and the very structure of language itself.

Even the age of human language is a matter of controversy. Nonhuman primates, and even human infants, do not have vocal tracts adequate to produce the variety of speech sounds that all modern languages exploit. Thus speech is physically impossible for them. One analysis of the vocal tracts of early humans suggests that the right size and shape appeared only about 50,000 years ago (Lieberman, 1979), but others place the anatomical adaptations as far back as half a million years ago and certainly a quarter million (Corballis, 1999). Inferring the talents of a vocal tract from incomplete fossil bones is a risky business, however. Because a vocal tract capable of language production and a brain capable of using it must have evolved together, we would not expect to see one without the other.

We have further evidence for a relatively recent origin of language in the development of human infants. Generally, in embryology the most recently evolved traits are the last to differentiate from an older, more generalized body plan. Traits that evolved earlier appear earlier in embryonic development. The classic example of this principle is the vestigial gill slits and tail that appear, and then are reabsorbed, early in human gestation.

Our few anatomical specializations for language, in contrast, appear very late in development. Human infants have a larynx and vocal tract that looks much like the mature vocal tracts of other primates, with the larynx entering the mouth area high in the tract. Between 6 months and 1 year of age, the larynx descends to its adult position, creating a longer vocal tract that can produce (see Figure 2.10) a greater variety of sounds than the standard primate vocal tract. Because the lower opening into the lungs increases the risk of choking, the selective pressure for this longer tract must have been a powerful one.

The **descended larynx** is not unique to humans, though—its function in other species yields hints about why the human system may have evolved. A descended larynx also occurs in two common species of deer, but only in the males (Fitch & Reby, 2001). The position of the deer larynx, similar to that in adult humans, allows the modest-sized deer to generate a truly impressive roar. It is a form of deception, allowing a deer to generate a low-pitched vibration that normally is possible only for a much larger animal. Thus the selective pressure for a descended larynx was not for generating a greater variety of sounds but for generating louder and deeper ones. No one knows whether such a capability generated a selective pressure in premodern humans, or whether articulation was the driving force. In any case, the human still seems to be the only animal in which both males and females have a descended larynx.

Communication in Nonhuman Primates

One way to study the evolution of human communication is to contrast it with the most closely related species, the apes and monkeys. Most primate communication systems are simple by human standards, with at most a few dozen different signs in contrast to the thousands of words used by every human. Apes and monkeys use a great variety of communicative sounds, gestures, and postures, some of them subtly nuanced, but their communication is largely limited to the expression of their own internal states. There are calls, for instance, expressing alarm, social threat, territoriality, and other emotional conditions, but none that reach the complexity required to communicate such questions as whether that distant fruit tree is still producing, or how a fellow ape received such a nasty bruise.

Primate systems of social calls generally cannot refer to time and place, nor can they be combined into a grammar. Each refers to only one state, so that the number of messages cannot exceed the number of calls. Contrast this with human speech, where a few dozen speech sounds combine to form thousands of words, and words combine to form limitless sentences. Human language takes advantage of the power of combinations to carry a great many messages with a small number of elements. In these ways, human language is qualitatively different from other primate vocal behavior.

Studying natural primate communication requires a combination of close observation and a group of freely interacting individuals. Vocal behavior of squirrel monkeys has been studied in a troop living at the Max-Planck Institute for Psychiatry in Munich (Ploog, 1981). Each monkey wore a small radio receiver and had electrodes implanted in its brain. The experimenters could elicit vocalizations in the monkeys by radio-controlled brain stimulation while the monkeys engaged in natural social interactions.

When the experimenters stimulated the monkeys' brains, the most effective locations were not in the cortex where human language is centered. Reflecting the emotional nature of most monkey vocalizations, remote

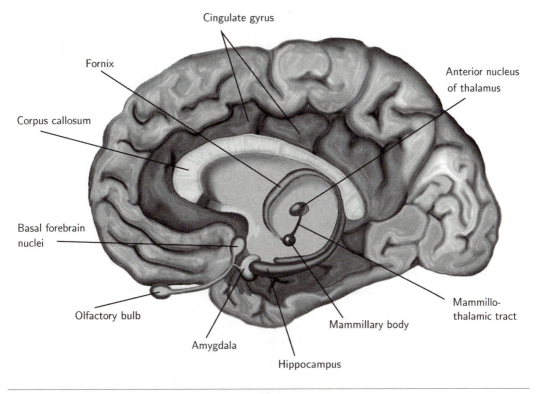

Figure 7.1   Limbic and related areas in humans.

stimulation worked best in the brain's emotional centers—the **limbic system** and related forebrain structures (Figure 7.1). The limbic system is a group of phylogenetically old structures below the more recently evolved cerebral cortex.

The limbic language of the monkeys is retained in humans with a full complement of cries, sighs, gasps, and other such exclamations, but we would not confuse these with true language. Seen in this way, the older limbic communication system of primates remains intact in us, side by side with language. Only in humans does vocalization have a dual control, expressing both emotional and symbolic meaning.

Sign Communication in Chimpanzees

Although observation and stimulation studies show how nonhuman primates ordinarily act, these methods do not probe the limits of their communication abilities. Human infants, after all, must go through a long period of cultural exposure as well as maturation before speech begins to appear. Attempts to overcome this restriction by raising chimpanzees in a human environment have been unsuccessful, however, not because the chimps could not adapt to human ways but because speech simply did not appear.

The most thorough early effort was that of Kellogg and Kellogg, who raised the female chimp Vicki like a child in their own home, along with their own child. After several years, Vicki behaved in many ways like a human child. Her motor development was a bit faster than that of a human, as was cognitive development for the first year or so. But spoken language amounted only to the word *cup*, uttered indistinctly under strong motivation. (Like squirrel monkeys, chimps do not vocalize spontaneously except in emotional situations.) A few other words were even less clear.

While viewing a film of Vicki performing this linguistic feat, psychologists Allen and Beatrice Gardner noted that the chimp was gesturing frantically while trying to obtain her cup at the dinner table. Knowing the importance of gesture in wild chimpanzee communication, they reasoned that chimps might be more successful with a gestural language than with a spoken one.

The language they chose was American Sign Language, also called Ameslan, used by many deaf people in North America as their only language. The Gardners raised a young chimp, Washoe, from infancy to several years of age not in a cage but in an open enclosure, with a mobile home in the center.

The Gardners had spectacular success at teaching Washoe to communicate. She readily learned Ameslan signs (Figure 7.2), both from instruction and from observation of her caretakers signing to each other (Gardner & Gardner, 1989). Washoe would sign during games as well as formal situations; one of her first signs was "tickle." She developed a vocabulary of several hundred signs, learning nearly as fast as a signing human child. More significant, Washoe combined signs in novel ways to constitute a primitive grammar (Gardner & Gardner, 1975). After learning the sign for "more" while being tickled, for example, she signed for "more sweet" at mealtime, and produced other novel combinations such as "listen dog."

These utterances are parallel to the two-word **slot grammar** used by 1- and 2-year-old children in all languages, whose utterances are limited to two words without adult grammatical relationships. The two words fit into "slots" in a closed grammatical system, no further modifications being allowed. Deaf children sign in two-sign utterances when they begin signing (Iverson & Goldin-Meadow, 2001).

The example of "more sweet" also shows nominalization, using an adjective as a noun even though Washoe's caretakers had never used an adjective that way. This is another characteristic of human language. Unfortunately, there is no way to tell whether Washoe intended "more sweet" to be a phrase or just two separate comments on the current situation. This problem of interpretation plagues the research on chimp language in general. Later,

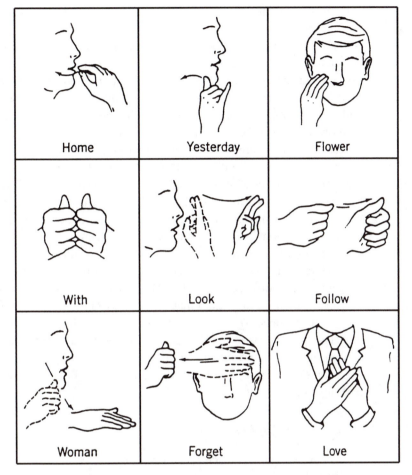

(a)

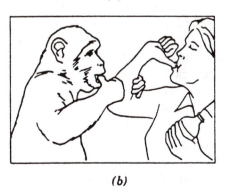

(b)

Figure 7.2   (a) Some signs of American Sign Language (Ameslan). Washoe learned all these signs. (b) Washoe at the age of 2-1/2, imitating the sign "drink." Based on a photo taken in December 1967.

Washoe signed with more elaborate grammatical forms, though she never became as fluent as deaf human children.

The success of Washoe at learning a human language that could be understood by users of Ameslan created a sensation. Linguists were forced to define language more carefully to be sure that Ameslan was really a language. Philosophers began to reconsider the differentiation of humans and animals, and in the 1970s psycholinguists rushed to repeat and extend the finding. At Stanford University, Penny Patterson raised the infant gorilla Koko with sign language, finding many of the signing abilities that had been seen in Washoe. Premack and Premack (1972) at the University of California, Santa Barbara, taught chimpanzees to string together symbols on a magnetic board to identify objects, ask for things, and so on. With extensive training, the animals could form short novel sentences with appropriate meanings, even mastering logical relations such as "larger" and "brighter."

The chimpanzee Lana at the Yerkes Primate Center in Atlanta, Georgia, learned Yerkish, a computer-based language, with keys on a large console functioning as words (Rumbaugh, 1977). Again, the chimpanzee developed the ability to use some grammatical relationships and to generate novel strings of symbols. These methods are less labor-intensive than teaching Ameslan, because parts of the procedure could be automated, and they are less prone to unconscious prompting by the experimenter. But Lana lacked the extensive learning by observation and the natural social interaction of real language learning.

Challenge and Response

The next attempt at teaching sign language to a chimpanzee led to a strong attack on the true capabilities of Washoe and the other language-using chimps. Herbert Terrace, a former student of the behaviorist psychologist B. F. Skinner, taught sign language to a chimpanzee named Nim Chimpsky (after the linguist Noam Chomsky). In Nim, Terrace found critical limitations in chimpanzee use of signs. According to him, nearly all signs were imitations of signs used shortly before in interactions with a trainer or caretaker, and grammatical strings were imitations of other grammatical strings with perhaps a substitution now and then (Terrace, 1979). In his analysis of films of Washoe and other chimps, Terrace claimed that they too signed mainly by rote imitation, usually without the experimenter being aware of the imitative nature of the signing.

The Gardners responded with reminders of the differences between their methods and Terrace's. Washoe had been raised in as naturalistic a situation as possible, with spoken language among caretakers forbidden. All communication was by sign language, in play and casual conversation as well as formal training and testing. Terrace's Nim, in contrast, was restricted to formal structured sessions more in accord with the tradition of conditioning experiments. Nim was caged and had little human contact outside the conditioning sessions. The same applied to Premack's chimp Sara. Under these circumstances, the Gardners argue, it is not surprising that chimps respond in limited, imitative ways. If you teach an animal to use language by rote, it will use language by rote.

Terrace also claimed that the "talking" chimps seldom or never made spontaneous statements without some prompting or questioning by humans. But Washoe frequently initiated signing by making requests, and the Gardners filmed Washoe with a hidden camera making signs when she was by herself. Signing when alone occurred fairly early in Washoe's training, when she was still in diapers, and may correspond to the "egocentric" speech of young human children. Patterson's gorilla Koko has also been filmed signing to herself while looking at pictures in a magazine.

Limits of Chimpanzee Communication

The limits of nonhuman language appear in the communication of Kanzi, a bonobo (also called pygmy chimpanzee) who lives at Emory University in Atlanta. As a youngster, Kanzi learned a language, expressed through keys on a board, by watching unsuccessful attempts to teach his mother to use the board. He learned both spoken English (which he was not expected to produce) and the keyboard language, which differs from natural language in having a small, fixed number of symbols. He uses the lexigrams depicted on the keys spontaneously, and not only to get rewards. For example, he will press the lexigram for apple after he already has an apple (Savage-Rumbaugh, Sevcik, Brakke, Williams, & Rumbaugh, 1993). Kanzi's understanding of spoken English includes use of grammatical word order to interpret meaning: given a toy dog and a toy snake, he could "make the doggie bite the snake" or "make the snake bite the doggie" appropriately, and could carry out requests he had never heard before about as well as a 2-year-old human girl who was given the same tasks.

The controversy has not been resolved, but already chimpanzee language studies have forced linguists to be more careful about their definitions. When do signs and combinations of signs really become language? Some grammarians are arriving at definitions that sound like the cognitive development stages of Swiss developmental psychologist Jean Piaget. The important features for Piaget are not the **surface structure** of speech (sentence length, etc.) but the underlying mental operations. These include reversibility, reference to objects not present, communication of meaning by grammatical structure, and other operations. By some of the more restrictive definitions, the chimpanzees and gorillas do not show true speech, but neither do human toddlers for their first few years.

The ape language work has also forced a reconsideration of the place of humanity in nature. At about the same time that Washoe was learning Ameslan, the DNA studies introduced in Chapter 1 were showing that humans and chimpanzees share 98% of their genes. It is not surprising in this context that many of the human's much-prized cognitive and communicative abilities should be seen in other forms in the chimpanzee. It is clear, though, that 98% of the genes do not control 98% of communicatory behavior, for a small genetic difference gives humans a huge advantage in communication.

The great apes, with brains about one third as large as human brains and lacking some of our linguistic specializations, will never master the more complex and subtle aspects of human language. Their sign language deals with the here and now, for instance. The apes seem unable to handle references to events already past or possibilities not yet realized. In this respect, ape signing does not move beyond the functions of their natural calls and gestures. Apes can certainly use the contents of their memories—they just aren't very good at talking about them. The chimpanzee and gorilla Ameslan dialects are similar to the first utterances of young children, speech that does not seem to be connected to long-term memory for events, on one hand, or to planning, on the other.

In many ways, the limits of chimpanzee language reflect the properties of human nonverbal communication. Our body "language," motions, and glances also communicate our emotional states in the here and now, often without our knowing it. Much of the communication is specieswide and unlearned. We also combine verbal with nonverbal communication, even when we are on the telephone.

Communication in Other Animals

Apes are not the only animals being investigated for their communicative use of signs. A great variety of animals have elaborate communication systems, from birds and dolphins to honeybees. Rhesus monkeys can understand human spoken words, and of course dogs can respond to isolated commands. Even chinchillas can discriminate words (Kuhl & Miller, 1975), though ordinarily they don't respond differentially to them outside a conditioning situation.

The most surprising report of language processing in nonprimates concerns an African gray parrot named Alex, who has been trained to recognize and choose objects on the basis of spoken English words. The bird can vocalize the words in the correct context (Pepperberg, 1993), and can also use short phrases appropriately, for instance to ask for a break during a training session. Alex can count as well as recognize colors and shapes. Again, nothing is known of the neurological basis of these abilities. Alex demonstrates that there is nothing special about the relationship between the primate brain's cortex and language, for birds don't have a cortex. When bird brains evolved from a simpler reptilian core, their great expansion occurred in forebrain structures called the basal ganglia, distinct from the mammalian cortex. What is important is not the origin of the cells, but their function.

THE STRUCTURE OF LANGUAGE ●

Any evolved characteristic of humans should be apparent in all human groups throughout the world. How does this apply to language? Though the many human languages seem endlessly varied, they actually have a good deal in common. The universal structures or **design features** that all languages have in common define the properties of the evolved neurological systems that support language. These design features (Hockett, 1972) also identify evolved features of human language systems.

The most basic unit of any spoken language is a group of speech sounds called **phonemes** (Figure 7.3). The phonemes, single sounds such as /f/, /e/, or /sh/, carry no meaning in themselves. Each natural language uses a set of between 15 and about 85 phonemes. English falls near the middle of the range with 45. The number is probably small so that each phoneme can be easily distinguished from all the others (Brown, 1970). Even at this level, we encounter a paradox, originating from the prodigious rate at which humans speak. The normal rate, about 10 phonemes per second in all languages, can reach 25 to 30 per second in short bursts (Liberman, 1982). The paradox is that the human vocal tract simply cannot produce separate auditory gestures at those rates.

How does the system nevertheless manage to generate phonemes so rapidly? The answer is contained in a second paradox—when we look at records of human speech, as in Figure 7.4, the phonemes aren't there! Instead of a series of discrete, easily discriminable units of language, we find only a seemingly smooth set of sound transitions punctuated by breaks that appear to be different for each word and each speaker. Though phoneme production usually follows a set of rules, there is no consistent pattern that specifies each phoneme.

Now the two paradoxes can be solved by combining them: in normal speech the phonemes are not produced in isolation, but are spread throughout

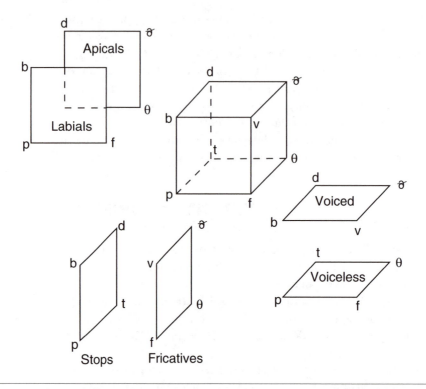

Figure 7.3   Eight English consonants divided into three distinctive binary features. *Labials* are pronounced by bringing the lips together; *apicals* are pronounced when the tongue contacts the roof of the mouth. *Stops* are interruptions in air flow, and *fricatives* are made by friction of air between the teeth and the lips or tongue.

a speech sequence (Liberman, 1974). In other words, information about several phonemes can be transmitted simultaneously. Somehow the linguistic receiving apparatus unpacks the intermingled signals in Figure 7.4, and as a result we perceive the discrete phonemes that were intended by the speaker but that were intermingled in the auditory communication channel.

The overlap of phonemes does not stop even at word boundaries. Figure 7.4 shows a sound spectrogram for the words *gray ship,* a sequence that includes a stop (a brief silence) in the middle. By changing the duration of this stop and the following phoneme artificially (Repp, Liberman, Eccardt, & Pesetsky, 1978), the perception graphed in Figure 7.5 could be changed from "gray ship" to "gray chip," "great ship," and "great chip" (a tongue-twister writer's dream).

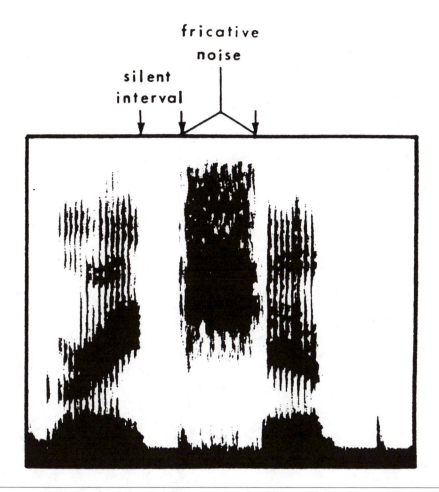

Figure 7.4   Spectrogram of the words *gray ship*. The fricative is heard as /sh/. Duration of the silent interval affects the perception of both the last phoneme of *gray* and the first phoneme of *ship*.

Speech in an unfamiliar language usually sounds faster than speech in a familiar one, probably because of the ways in which we interpret familiar languages, integrating the speech train into larger units and grammatical constructions rather than trying to follow the individual phonemes. By "chunking" smaller units into larger ones (Miller, 1956), we code more efficiently and reduce the short-term memory capacity needed to interpret speech. In this way, higher-level information processing can have effects that seem to be perceptual. The effects are referred to the outside world even though the differences lie in ourselves.

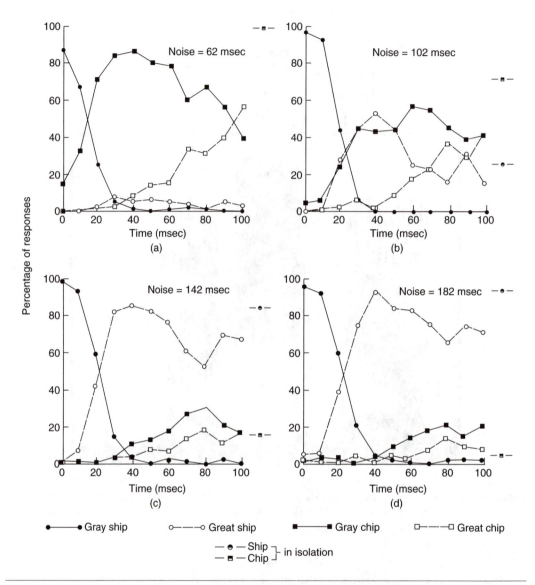

Figure 7.5 The effect of changing the duration of the fricative noise and the silent interval in Figure 7.4. Each graph shows the frequency with which native speakers of English perceived each of the four phrases given at the bottom.

Grammars

A higher-level set of universals relates to **grammar**. All languages have a grammar, a set of rules by which words may be combined to impart meanings, and the grammars themselves follow universal rules despite their diversity. All grammars, for instance, distinguish between subject, verb, and object, all have ways of differentiating past, present, and future, and all have sentences and pluralization rules. Even the word itself is a universal concept, for words in all languages have many properties in common.

Languages vary greatly in their surface structures, the strings of words that speakers produce. But their **deep structures**, the logical relationships that underlie the words and sentences, are similar in all languages (Pinker, 1994). It appears that the language machine in the human mind can handle only certain kinds of deep structures, and it invents surface structures to express them.

Every language has two grammars. One is the externalized type formalized by grammarians and learned (usually unwillingly) by grammar school students, and the other is the type internalized in the brains of users of the language. I remember resentment at having to learn English grammar rules in elementary school when I could already speak grammatically without them. It was a pleasant surprise to learn in college that the grammar I had learned was only one of several possible English grammars, imposed after the fact on an existing language.

A grammar is a theory intended to order an existing set of data, the utterances of native speakers of the language. Furthermore, no formal grammar in any language has yet succeeded in describing all the utterances that native speakers of the language agree to be grammatically correct while rejecting all utterances that native speakers would find incorrect. A formal grammar typically will fail to describe some utterances and at the same time will generate some strings of words that native speakers find uninterpretable.

The distinction between the two grammars, internal and external, becomes particularly vivid when learning a second language. One laboriously learns grammatical rules for the new language, and sometimes actually uses them for writing or for very hesitant speaking. True fluency, however, seems not to appear until the formal rules are forgotten. They are gradually replaced by an unconscious internal grammar, a neurological organization that generates grammatical utterances and analyzes the speech of others with rules that are impossible to fully externalize. Grammar uses a type of memory called **procedural memory**, as unconscious as the learning that occurs in riding a bicycle; the skill develops, but the learned rules are difficult to articulate.

The internal grammar also contains rules that generally are not learned in grammar school, because native speakers apply them effortlessly and almost without error. Most speakers are unaware of the existence of such rules and will deny their existence until shown an example. To demonstrate this point, a standard English modifier order is given in Table 7.1. It is entertaining to make up a lengthy string of modifiers, such as "the first two big old red barns," and to see the string fit unerringly into the prescribed order.

Table 7.1 Sequential Order of Modifiers in English Noun Phrases

Particles	Possessive	Ordinal Number	Cardinal Number	Characteristic	Size	Shape	Temperature and Humidity	Age	Color	Origin	Noun	Head
the							cool		blue	Aegean		sea
a												
this	train's	first	four								passenger	cars
that	boy's		three	unusual				young	grey	Persian		cats
those												
some												
many												
any				remarkably			hot, damp			tropical		climate
your					short							frame
his						stocky						
her												
their												
our												
my	son's			witty			warm		colorful			personality

Source: Brown (1965).

Is Speech Special?

The brain-voice-ear-brain channel of speech communication is not made up entirely of old parts, but has a biology of its own. Perception of speech sounds, for example, seems different from perception of nonspeech. The classic experiment in this area involves discrimination of speech sounds along a continuum that crosses a phoneme boundary. For example, the syllable /ba/ can slowly be transformed into /pa/ by continually delaying the voice onset in the utterance. But we never perceive a phoneme between /p/ and /b/; rather, we make a subconscious decision about which phoneme is present, and we perceive the results of that decision as either /b/ or /p/. The phenomenon is called **categorical perception**.

Listening

Figure 7.6 suggests that people perceive small differences in voice onset better if the onset occurs near a phoneme boundary. It is much harder to hear an equally large difference in voice onset time when that difference would not be critical for distinguishing one phoneme from another. The change in thresholds cannot be explained by inborn differences in auditory sensitivity at the boundaries, though, for different languages place the boundaries in different places. In other words, a voice onset delay that would mean /p/ in one language might mean /b/ in another, so that no unique onset delay defines where /p/ fades into /b/. The effortless classification of the two phonemes, then, must come from experience and practice with the corresponding sounds in a language community.

Other evidence for uniqueness of speech processing involves **dichotic listening**, hearing different sound patterns in each ear. If different consonants are presented to each ear, the result is not a combination of the sounds. Most people perceive the sound entering the right ear that goes mainly to the left hemisphere where the speech centers are located. If a speech segment is divided, with some of the information coming into each ear, speech sounds remain intelligible. But a speech transition, such as the transition in Figure 7.7b that distinguishes /da/ from /ga/, cannot be understood in isolation without a vowel. The subject hears only a short chirp (Liberman, 1982). In language, the chirp is absorbed and integrated into a phoneme, even while the change in sound frequency remains unperceived.

An alternative view holds that the special nature of speech is more limited. Categorical perception across phoneme boundaries, after all, is a quantitative difference and not a sudden jump. The greater sensitivity at the

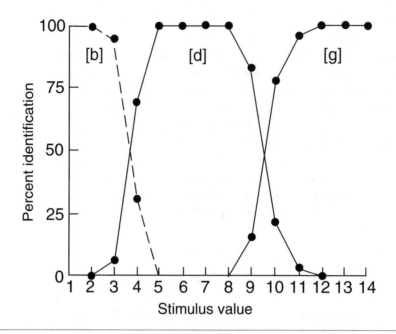

Figure 7.6   Perceived consonants as voice onset is delayed in a segment of computer-synthesized speech.

boundaries may be the result of learning, like any other perceptual learning (Massaro & Cohen, 1983).

Reading

A source of evidence in the controversy about phoneme perception is reading, a skill that has appeared so recently in evolutionary time that there is certainly no unique language processor connected with it. In reading one sees many of the properties that seemed to make phoneme perception special, including integration of multiple cues for visual recognition of letters and syllables (Massaro, 1979).

On this point we have additional information, for the importance of unconscious mechanisms applies even to reading. Most people have the impression that they read by smoothly scanning the text with their eyes, because the language seems to flow into our minds continuously. In reality, readers make small jumping eye movements, called saccades, at the rate of about 4 per second. Saccades are by far the most common of human behaviors, outstripping all other gestures and movements.

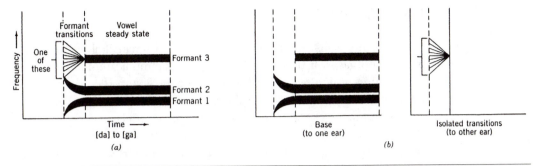

Figure 7.7 Presenting different parts of a speech sound to the two ears (dichotic listening). (a) The complete sound spectrogram, in the format of Figure 7.4. (b) Splitting the spectrogram for dichotic listening.

If you had to think about each saccade, you would never have enough cognitive capacity left over to do anything else. People absorb language through reading faster than they do through speech, adjusting their patterns of eye movements to the image quality of the material they are reading, even when the differences in quality are not visible (Montegut, Bridgeman, & Sykes, 1997). So a number of fast, unconscious processes are applied even to a learned skill such as reading.

The resolution of this controversy, like many others, will probably lie in a combination of the two approaches. Some areas where speech seemed special, such as the perception of combined features, may turn out to be general capabilities of perceptual systems. Other higher-level capabilities, such as generating utterances quickly and fluently by grammatical rules, may turn out to have specialized neurological processors.

LANGUAGE DEVELOPMENT IN CHILDREN ●

Robert MacLeod once said that in studying language, one should start not with phonemes but with babies. The advice applies also to study of the evolution of language, for language acquisition is a good example of an interaction between inherited neural structures and experience. Every normal human learns a language, yet humans raised in isolation do not talk. Conversely, the experience with the chimpanzee Vicki described above shows that chimps raised in a linguistic environment do not talk. Both experience and the neural structures competent to take advantage of the experience are necessary.

The Beginnings

An infant begins life with a good start on the primate limbic sounds such as cries and gasps. It develops the ability to communicate quite effectively with gestures, grunts, and squeals long before the first word appears at about 1 year of age. First, the baby goes through a stage of babbling, as if trying out sounds and syllables. At 2-4 months, the infant produces sounds typical of other languages as well as its own, showing that the babbling is distinct from imitation, but by about 10 months the sounds begin to converge on the phonemes of the native language (de Boisson-Bardies, 1999). There is an imitative component to babbling too—hearing babies born to deaf parents babble silently with their hands (Petitto, Holowka, Sergio, & Ostry, 2001).

Gestural Language

At this stage it is tempting to hypothesize that human language arose from systems of gestures, and in fact children who learn a sign language as their first language begin signing before hearing children begin speaking. Furthermore, most infants become quite skilled at communicating by gesture before they utter their first word.

Here we can apply the general principle in embryology that traits that evolved earlier in evolution appear earlier in development (ontogeny recapitulates phylogeny). The principle is not foolproof, but it can serve as a useful starting point for untangling evolutionary sequences. Applied to language, the early appearance of gesture suggests that hominids may have gone through a stage in which gesture served as the primary means of communication.

Human neurology supports this idea: some of the language areas in the human cortex are analogs of areas that control gestures in other primates. According to neurophysiologists Michael Gazzaniga, Joseph LeDoux, and D. H. Wilson, humans retain the general primate pattern on the right side of the brain, whereas specialized language areas appear in symmetrically opposite areas on the left side.

Observations of blind children and adolescents have underlined the importance of gesture in language, and its tight link with verbal communication (Iverson & Goldin-Meadow, 2001). Congenitally blind speakers, who have never seen gestures, nevertheless gesture as they speak, even when communicating with a blind listener who is unable to profit from the information that the hands convey. Furthermore, the congenitally blind speakers convey the same information and produce the same range of gestural forms as sighted speakers.

These findings reveal that gesture, rather than being an intentional, learned adjunct to verbal communication, accompanies speech even when it could have no function and could not be learned. Gesture, then, must be an unlearned adjunct to speech, built into the human communication system as robustly as speech itself. This does not mean that gestures cannot be transmitted culturally—of course they are. The basic gestural behavior, on which this transmission is built, is what we inherit as human beings.

An infant's first word appears not in isolation but as part of a **holophrase**, a combination that includes gesture, context, and verbal output. A toddler sitting at the dinner table might say something approximating the word *cup,* grasp in his or her direction, and look up at the mother. The child works hard on the first unintelligible approximations to words with no obvious reward; attempts to find reward explanations for language learning (Skinner, 1957) have been unsuccessful. The infant must make too much cognitive progress before any functionally useful speech can sustain a reward-oriented motivation. Rather, children's practice of speech seems to require a built-in system of motivation, where the very act of trying out language is rewarding.

A Universal Slot Grammar

A few months after his or her first word, the child begins generating two-word phrases, the beginnings of grammar. We saw a similar stage in chimpanzee sign learning. But the grammar of these phrases bears little similarity to the adult language. It is the same in all languages studied so far, including English, Japanese, Korean, Finnish, German, and Russian (Brown, 1973). The grammar seems to come from within the child, part of the genetic equipment of language, rather than from the adult linguistic community. Examples of child constructions at this stage are shown in Table 7.2.

Again applying the principle that ontogeny recapitulates phylogeny in the course of evolution, we can compare the slot grammar of the chimpanzee Washoe and of young human children to an intermediate stage of language evolution that may have existed in the earliest humans, or perhaps in a prehuman species such as *Homo erectus.* It is informative to speculate about a group of such prehumans sitting around their fire after a hard day of hunting and gathering. Someone exclaims, "River cold." Another responds, "Fishing good." Such conversations seem almost comical to us, but they would be tremendously more useful than no language at all. They would serve an important function of language, one that gives us a huge advantage over other primates—to allow the experience of one individual to affect the knowledge of another.

Table 7.2   Semantic Relations in Two-Word Sentences

Semantic Relation	Form[a]	Example
1. Nomination	that + N	that book
2. Notice	hi + N	hi belt
3. Recurrence	more + N, 'nother + N	more milk
4. Nonexistence	allgone + N, on more + N	allgone rattle
5. Attributive	Adj + N	big train
6. Possessive	N + N	mommy lunch
7. Locative	N + N	sweater chair
8. Locative	V + N	walk street
9. Agent-action	N + V	Eve read
10. Agent-object	N + N	mommy sock
11. Action-object	V + N	put book

Source: Adapted from Brown (1970).
*Adj = adjective; V = verb; N = noun.

For young children, though, the slot grammar has sometimes disastrous limitations. After a child's mother says, "Daddy's not home yet," the child exclaims, "Daddy home!" The negation would take an extra word, but the two slots have already been used up, so the child has no choice but to reverse the meaning of the utterance. I have seen a boy of this age shake his head "no" while uttering such a phrase, combining the limited oral grammar with gesture to communicate his meaning in a hybrid form.

When one of my own daughters was about 1-1/2 years old, she began coming up with utterances such as "Mommy Daddy look!" I thought that she must be a budding genius, moving beyond the two-word limit at such a young age. Later, though, she addressed me as "Mommydaddy" when she knew that Mommy wasn't around, and it became clear that for her at that time "Mommydaddy" was a single word that meant "parent," and she wasn't bucking the rules after all. (I still see her as a genius anyway, of course.)

At this stage, and even before, the child shows evidence of internalizing grammatical rules. Because use of correct forms in short fragments of speech might merely be rote imitation, the best evidence for use of rules comes from incorrect utterances. English is maddeningly rich in incorrect forms, such as irregular verbs and varieties of pluralization rules. The child who says "two foots" or "I goed" is not imitating, but is applying rules deduced from other examples.

Thus young children and chimpanzees give us a glimpse of how human language might have gone through several intermediate stages, rather than

Table 7.3   The Acquisition of Six Grammatical Morphemes

Morpheme	Order of Acquisition	Transformations	Semantic Dimensions
Present progressive	1	Progressive affix	Temporary duration
On	2.5	Preposition segment	Support
In	2.5	Preposition segment	Containment
Plural	4	Noun suffix, nominal agreement, article	Number
Past irregular	5	Verb agreement	Earlierness
Possessive	6	(Not given in source)	Possession

Source: Adapted from Brown (1973).

abruptly appearing fully developed in modern humans. Because evolution must progress in small steps, and each step must be useful to its owner, such intermediate levels are necessary to account for a biologically based language ability in modern humans.

All children learn the complexities of grammar in about the same order, though the timing of the steps varies widely from child to child. Table 7.3 shows the order of acquiring six grammatical forms (Brown, 1973). The process is not complete until after puberty. Of course, grammatical rule-learning is to some degree specific to the peculiarities of the parent language. An experiment where children were raised with a **lexicon** (a group of vocabulary words), but without an adult grammar, would tell us more about the basic human grammar.

Grammar in Creole Languages

It would be highly unethical for linguists to remove a group of children from contact with natural languages to see what sort of grammar would appear, but that does not mean that the experiment has never been carried out. In fact, the conditions for the experiment have occurred several times in the history of colonialism, as the British, Americans, French, Dutch, Spanish, and Portuguese all established labor-intensive agricultural colonies and imported labor from distant ethnic groups, sometimes as slaves but usually as contract workers. The new workers found themselves uprooted from their cultures, with their employers and fellow workers speaking mutually incomprehensible languages.

The response of these immigrants was to develop **pidgin** language, a linguistic hodgepodge that is unique to each speaker and generally fails to

Table 7.4   Examples of Pidgin and of Hawaiian Creole English

Pidgin	Hawaiian Creole English
Building—high place—wall part—time—nowtime—and the now temperature every time give you.	Get one [There is an] electric sign high up on da wall of da building show you what time an temperature get [it is] right now.
Now days, ah, house, ah, Inside, washl clothes machine get, no? Before time, ah, no more, see? And then pipe no more, water pipe no more.	Those days bin get [there were] no more washing machine, no more pipe water like get [there is] inside house nowadays, ah?
No, the men, ah—pau [finished] work—they go, make garden. Plant this, ah, cabbage, like that. Plant potato, like that. And then—all that one—all right, sit down. Make lilly bit story.	When work pau [is finished] da guys they stay go make [are going to make] garden for plant potato an' cabbage an' after little while they go sit down talk story ["shoot the breeze"].
Good, this one. Kaukau [food] any kind this one. Pilipin island no good. No more money.	Hawaii more better than Philippines, over here get [there is] plenty kaukau [food], over there no can, bra [brother], you no more money for buy kaukau [food], 'a' swhy [that's why].

Source: Bickerton (1983).

represent many of the aspects of natural language grammars (Table 7.4). Speakers of pidgin dialects are frustrated that they cannot express their more subtle thoughts, desires, and attitudes in their makeshift pidgin dialects.

The sons and daughters of the immigrants, however, do not speak pidgin dialects. Instead they speak **Creole**, a type of language with some unique characteristics (Bickerton, 1983). It is uniform throughout the linguistic group, regardless of the ethnicity of the speaker's parents, and it functions according to fixed grammatical rules illustrated in Table 7.5. Furthermore, it arises in a single generation, without models or instruction.

Even more astonishing, isolated Creole languages all over the world have virtually the same grammar, illustrated in Table 7.5, whether their lexicon is borrowed mostly from English, French, Arabic, or other languages. The grammar is not a subset of that found in natural languages, but is a complete system, as complex as other natural languages, that can include distinctions and

Table 7.5   Verb Conjugation in the Various Creole Languages

Verb Form	Nonstative Verbs			Stative Verbs		
	Hawaiian Creole	Haitian Creole	Sranan	Hawaiian Creole	Haitian Creole	Sranan
Base form ("he walked"; "he loves")	He walk	Li maché	A waka	He love	Li rêmê	A lobi
Anterior ("he had walked"; he loved")	He bin walk	Li té maché	A ben waka	He bin love	Li té rêmê	A ben lobi
Irreal ("he will/would walk"; "he will/would love")	He go walk	L'av(a) maché	A sa waka	He go love	L'av(a) rêmê	A sa lobi
Nonpunctual ("he is/was walking")	He stay walk	L'ap maché	A e waka	—	—	—
Anterior + Irreal ("he would have walked"; "he would have loved")	He bin go walk	Li t'av(a) maché	A ben sa waka	He bin go love	Li t'av(a) rêmê	A ben sa lobi
Anterior + non-punctual ("he was/had been walking")	He bin stay walk	Li t'ap maché	A ben e waka	—	—	—
Irreal + non-punctual ("he will/would be walking")	He go stay walk	L'av ap maché	A sa e waka	—	—	—
Anterior + irreal + nonpunctual ("he would have been walking")	He bin go stay walk	Li t'av ap maché	A ben sa e waka			

Source: Bickerton (1983).

forms not found in any of its parent languages. For instance, English does not require a speaker to differentiate purposes that have been accomplished from those that have not. Derek Bickerton's example, "John went to Honolulu to see Mary," does not specify whether John and Mary actually met. But a Creole speaker must choose between "John bin go Honolulu go see Mary" if John saw Mary, or "John bin go Honolulu for see Mary" if John missed Mary or if the speaker does not know what happened. All these specific properties of Creoles appear despite the lack of contact of Creole-speaking groups with one another.

Origins of Human Grammar

According to Bickerton (1982, 1983), the children have made up the new language themselves. In this view, the Creole constructions represent a default human grammar, the form that appears when no consistent contradictory forms are present. They are a grammar given by the genes.

Evidence that the constructions of Creole languages are based on an inborn grammar comes again from children. Creoles bear an uncanny resemblance to the spontaneous grammatical productions of 2- to 4-year-old children in natural linguistic communities (Table 7.6). Thus the Creoles present a priceless opportunity to look directly into the grammatical mind of the young child, and from there into the grammatical inheritance of the human species.

Children find it nearly effortless to learn the constructions that their language and the Creole base have in common, whereas constructions contradictory to the Creole are more difficult and are generally learned later. The English suffix "-ing," for instance, is learned very early. It expresses duration in sentences such as "I reading bookie." One would expect it to be overgeneralized, just as the suffix "-s" is used to make "foots" or "sheeps," but it is not. The child almost never produces "I liking Daddy"; the difference between stative verbs such as "like" and nonstative verbs such as "read" seems to be realized instinctively (the word *instinctively* is used intentionally). The marker for duration is present in all Creole languages, for instance as the word *stay* in the Hawaiian examples of Table 7.5. Incidentally, this example also shows that the Creole neurological grammar is more sophisticated than most people's formal grammar, the one that they can explain and analyze.

Varieties of Inborn Grammar

The idea that Creoles reflect an earlier stage in the social evolution of languages, before layers of custom and usage had built up around the biologically given form, remains controversial (Bickerton, 1984). Previously,

Table 7.6   Examples of Child Language Versus English Creole Languages

Child Language	English Creole Languages
Where I can put it?	Where I can put orr? (Hawaii)
Daddy throw the nother rock.	Daddy t'row one neia rock' tone. (Jamaica)
I go full Angela bucket.	I go full Angela buctet. (Guyana)
Lookit a boy play ball.	Luku one boy a plar ball. (Jamara)
Nobody don't like me.	Nobody no like me. (Guyana)
I no like do that.	I no like do that. (Hawaii)
Johnny big more than me.	Johnny big more than me. (Jamaica)
Let Daddy get pen write it.	Make Daddy get pen write am. (Guyana)
I more better than Johnny.	I more better than Johnny. (Hawaii)

Source: Bickerton (1983).

Chomsky (1965, 1980) had proposed the idea of an inborn grammatical machine in a different form. Chomsky's idea was a universal human grammar that made a wide range of grammatical possibilities available, from which children could apply those needed in their language community. Studies of the speed with which children acquire these complex logical systems, at an age when they can't do much else intellectually, tended to confirm the idea of a universal grammar (Lenneberg, 1967). The new idea emphasizes instead that young children begin with a single grammatical model, built into the neurology of the brain's language areas. During the process of language acquisition, they gradually mold it into the shape of a natural language.

In terms of evolutionary theory, there is a problem with Chomsky's conception. If capabilities evolve only when natural selection preserves and modifies them, it is difficult to see how grammatical potentials could lie in wait until a child's language demanded them. They would tend to degrade in each successive generation unless natural selection rewarded those individuals in which the modules remained intact. Selection would maintain only the currently active modules, the ones governing everyday speech in a child's community.

The alternative of the SSSM, that language comes solely from the environment and is impressed on a blank-slate mind, is even more difficult to maintain in light of current knowledge about child language acquisition. Children seem to recognize what words are, and the level of their generality, almost immediately, and they learn grammar from very sparse examples. The cases of Creole languages are impossible for the SSSM to explain, because groups distant from one another, with no mutual contact, develop similar grammars.

The Creole language hypothesis promises to stimulate debate for years to come. One of its values lies in its recognition of the importance of biological mechanisms of language, mechanisms that can be studied by other means—we can look directly into the brain.

● THE ANATOMY OF LANGUAGE

Because language can be studied only in humans, less is known about its anatomy and physiology than is known about other neurological systems. Most of the universal attributes of language examined above do not show up in the currently known anatomy. That is, we suspect that language capabilities are represented somewhere in the brain, but we don't yet know where or how they are expressed. Any universal properties of language areas of the brain would represent biological adaptations facilitating language learning and use.

Though the Roman physician Galen knew that language was usually represented on the left side of the brain, no one knew much more than that until well into the 19th century.

Broca's Aphasia

In 1861, French neurologist Pierre-Paul Broca described a patient who had great difficulty in producing speech, though his understanding was less affected. Speech is slow and deliberate in victims of Broca's **aphasia** (Greek *a-* = without, *phasia* = speaking), as though the patient must think out each word, and as a result makes frequent grammatical errors. Verbs and more abstract words are affected more than nouns; in severe cases, the patient is rendered mute. Geschwind (1970) gives an example of speech in a Broca's aphasia patient who was asked about a dental appointment: "Yes . . . Monday . . . Dad and Dick . . . Wednesday nine o'clock . . . ten o'clock . . . doctors . . . and . . . teeth."

Broca's original patient had suffered a stroke involving the middle cerebral artery, supplying blood to a broad region in the left side of his brain. Broca had learned in medical school that language and other uniquely human traits were functions of the brain's frontal lobes. His teachers in turn had derived their doctrine from the **phrenologists**, early neuroscientists who thought that human mental specializations could be divined from growth of parts of the head overlying brain areas presumed to serve the corresponding abilities. They had noted that humans have both a high forehead

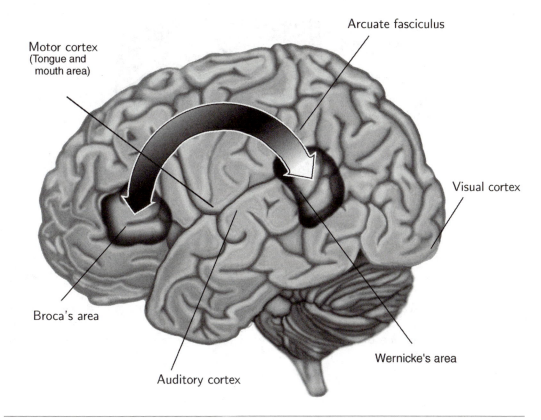

Arcuate fasciculus

Motor cortex
(Tongue and
mouth area)

Visual cortex

Broca's area

Wernicke's area

Auditory cortex

Figure 7.8   Language areas on the left hemisphere of the human cortex. Front is to the left. Speech areas surround the primary auditory and motor areas.

and linguistic ability, and without further evidence, they assumed that the two were associated. When Broca noted the only location where his aphasic patient's lesion overlapped with the frontal lobe, **Broca's area** (Figure 7.8) was born (Pribram, 1971). The designation of the area survived because, partly by luck, Broca was right. His area made neurological sense as well, lying adjacent to the region of the primary motor cortex that controls movements of the lips and face.

Broadening Broca's Area

Subsequent evidence for the language role of Broca's area came from stimulation studies (Penfield & Roberts, 1959), where textbooks say that electrical stimulation of the area can lead to the arrest of ongoing speech. The

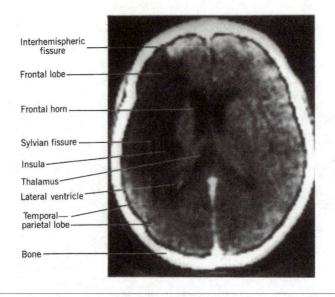

Interhemispheric fissure

Frontal lobe

Frontal horn

Sylvian fissure

Insula

Thalamus

Lateral ventricle

Temporal–parietal lobe

Bone

Figure 7.9   CAT scan of the brain of a patient with Broca's aphasia, horizontal section. Damage (dark in the image) includes the left lateral frontal cortex. The frontal horn is one of the fluid-filled ventricles of the brain, normally dark in these images.

actual area where stimulation has this result, however, is much broader than Broca's speech area, including a wide swath of the cortex behind the frontal lobe (Ojemann, 1983). Sometimes electrical stimulation results in hesitation, slurring, distortion, or repetition of speech. A good many points in the right hemisphere had the same properties, suggesting that lateralization is not total; both hemispheres participate in language functions to some degree. In any case, the classical Broca's area wasn't unique.

Computerized axial tomography (the CAT scan) can correlate brain lesions with symptoms in living patients. Figure 7.9 shows the stroke-induced damage in a patient that Kertesz (1982) considers to have a classic case of Broca's aphasia. A sample of this patient's speech is shown in Table 7.7. The damaged area in this patient clearly involves Broca's area in the left hemisphere. But like other aphasic patients, the damage includes more posterior areas as well.

There is no evidence that damage restricted to Broca's area alone results in permanent language disturbances. Lesions reaching forward into Broca's area yield Broca's aphasia, an **expressive aphasia**, and those reaching

Table 7.7   Speech of Patient With Broca's Aphasia

Mrs. D. N.—transcript of the interview, 4 years poststroke:

E	How are you feeling?
DN	I–I'm fine.
E	Have I ever tested you before?
DN	No–two, three.
E	What is your full name?
DN	Oh dear.–Henry–oh—[correct, but the name for sake of privacy, is omitted].
E	And your full address?
DN	Oh dear. Um. Aah. OH! No–oh. Oh dear, very–there–were–there ave. [veri *oerwroer*] avedeversher avenyer [*deva faaevanja*]. (Correct address. Devonshire.)
E	What kind of work did you do before you became ill?
DN	Oh. I–I–um. Um–oh dear. I–I–dun know. I don't–want–to.
E	Can you tell me what you did for a living? Did you work? Did you have a job?
DN	Oh yes–I–um–um. The–the–say [se]—si [si] selum [selum] dum–nogglewife [*nogglewaif*]. Oh dear.

Source: Kertesz (1982).

more posteriorly result in a **receptive aphasia** first described by Carl Wernicke in 1887.

Wernicke's Aphasia

Patients afflicted with **Wernicke's aphasia** at first seem better off than those with Broca's, for their speech has the normal fluency and rhythm. Listening to a receptive aphasic who speaks a language different from your own, you would have difficulty recognizing that anything is wrong. The only problem is that the speech doesn't make sense. Short phrases and segments tend to hang together, especially in common phrases such as "I don't think so" or "Never mind." But the larger context goes nowhere. The symptoms have a disturbing similarity to the rhetoric of some politicians and professors.

It is as though the speech of receptive and expressive aphasics breaks down at different levels. The expressive aphasic has difficulty with surface structure at the syntactic level of phoneme and word, whereas the receptive aphasic has trouble at the semantic level, the level of meaning. There is almost always some expressive difficulty, though, suggesting that speech recognition and production are not totally separated (Blumstein, 1981). And all groups of aphasics have some trouble in articulation.

Table 7.8   Speech of Patient With Wernicke's Aphasia

Mrs. J. A.—transcript of the first interview, 2 weeks poststroke:

E	How are you today, Mrs. A.?
JA	Yes.
E	Have I ever tested you before?
JA	No, I mean I haven't.
E	Can you tell me what your name is?
JA	No, I don't I-right I'm right now here.
E	What is your address?
JA	I cud [kʌd] if I can help these this like you know–to make it. We are seeing for him. That is my father.
E	What kind of work did you do before you came into the hospital?
JA	Never, now Mista Oyge [ɔldʒ] I wanna tell you this happened when happened when he rent. His–his kell [kɛl] come down here and is-he got ren [rɛn] something. It happened. In these [ðis] ropiers [ropiəz] were with him for hi–is friend–like was. And it just happened so I don't know, he did not bring around anything. And he did not pay it. And he roden [rodɛn] all o these arranjen [ərendʒən] from the pedis [pɛdis] on from iss [is] pescid [pɛskid]. In these floors now and so. He hasn't had em round here.
E	Can you tell me a little bit about why you are in the hospital?
JA	No, I don't think I have. . . . No, I haven't.
E	Can you tell me what you see going on in the picture? [A drawing of children flying a kite]
JA	No, I can uh take him.–uh. I haven't read [rid] 'em anybody to right in there. That's the little girl here.
E	Anything else? What do you see over here?
JA	No. [Pause] I really had pays [pez] too. Inste van gup [instɛ væn gʌp]. Here ee [i] little boy being read, too. There he's being there on the ceiling there.

Table 7.8 shows a sample of the speech of a 74-year-old woman with Wernicke's aphasia, and Figure 7.10 shows a CAT scan of her brain. The region that Wernicke identified as crucial for understanding and producing meaningful language lies adjacent to both primary and secondary auditory cortex in Figure 7.8.

The key problem of the receptive aphasic is in understanding speech. Patients with expressive (Broca's) aphasia can often follow quite elaborate commands if the responses are nonverbal. The receptive (Wernicke's) aphasic, in contrast, has difficulty in getting the commands straight in the first place. The pattern of deficits implies that the transformation from semantic to production levels is handled by the same cortex that transforms speech to semantics in speech understanding.

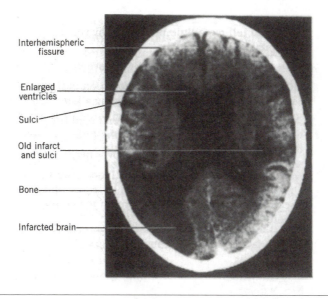

Interhemispheric fissure

Enlarged ventricles

Sulci

Old infarct and sulci

Bone

Infarcted brain

Figure 7.10   CAT scan of the brain of a patient with Wernicke's aphasia, horizontal section. Damage is more posterior than the Broca's lesion in Figure 7.9.

Alternatively, the two transformations may take place in closely inter-mingled regions. Indeed, there is evidence that verbal information gets into the brains of Wernicke's patients, but does not influence verbal behavior. In a study involving word games, patients were given a word problem and then they looked at a board containing an array of words, including the solution to the problem. The patients' eyes fixated longer on the correct solutions, even though their verbal responses were nearly random. So the problem in at least some aphasics may be not the ability to process verbal information so much as the ability to use the information that is processed.

Specificity of Function

Receptive aphasics display a wide variety of symptoms. Some have diffi-culty in naming objects but have no other language disability; this is often the residual deficit of a stroke victim who has recovered or relearned most func-tions. Others have difficulty with sentence structure but can name objects readily, and still others mix up the syllables within words while producing grammatically correct sentences and naming reasonably well (Luria, 1964).

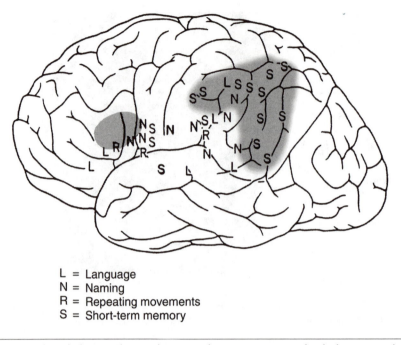

L = Language
N = Naming
R = Repeating movements
S = Short-term memory

Figure 7.11   Results of electrical stimulation in language areas. Shaded regions show a final motor path for speech (toward the front) and a short-term memory area (toward the rear).

Less common syndromes involve such characteristics as loss of the ability to write or to read, without other symptoms. Sometimes a patient can read concrete nouns but not more abstract words. The organization of Wernicke's area may be slightly different in each individual, so that similar lesions yield different patterns of symptoms. The specificity of the deficits, though, suggests a highly modular structure, the sort that we would expect from piecemeal evolution of new neurological machines to perform new tasks. Each evolves without interfering with the existing functions of the others.

In accord with both of these conclusions, stimulation studies have shown localized language functions in the brain. Combining careful psychological procedures with electrical stimulation of the exposed cortex during operations in awake humans revealed sites connected only with naming of objects (Ojemann & Mateer, 1979). Other sites yielded repeating or deficits in verbal short-term memory or language production. The regions concerned are shown in Figure 7.11.

Observations in bilingual patients reveal a plasticity of language areas (Ojemann, 1983). In one woman, stimulation at some sites interfered only with naming things in English, but other sites affected only naming in Greek (the patient's second language).

Aphasia and Dyslexia

The invention of a **phonetic** system of writing was a great advance in civilization because it meant that people no longer had to learn very much in order to write. A spoken vocabulary could be combined with a system for recording speech sounds on paper phoneme by phoneme, without having to memorize a different symbol for each word. Once the phonetic alphabet was learned, writing could rely on the oral speech machinery already developed in the brain (except in perverse languages such as English that have irregular spelling). In Western languages, only numbers are represented nonphonetically. Thus both reading and writing, even when they occur silently, remain conceptually tied to auditory language. As a result, Wernicke's aphasia is often accompanied by **dyslexia** (Greek *dys-* = difficult, *lex-* = read).

Confirmation of this interpretation comes from cultures in which writing is pictographic rather than phonetic. Unlike Westerners, Chinese must learn to write each word separately. They study intensively for many years to do it. All this effort does provide an advantage, however, for Chinese patients with receptive aphasia remain able to write accurately (Luria, 1970). The oral and the written lexicon appear to be stored separately in the brains of Chinese speakers and to be organized differently.

Japanese aphasics are a particularly useful source of information on the differences between phonetic and pictographic coding, because the Japanese write with four separate systems, three phonetic and one pictographic. Every Japanese student learns the Roman phonetic alphabet, two Japanese phonetic systems called kana, and enough Chinese-like kanji symbols to represent a few thousand common words. The Chinese symbols act as a kind of shorthand in Japanese writing, and are intermingled with the phonetic scripts in normal written discourse. Thus each Japanese aphasic can act as his or her own control, with both phonetic and pictographic organizations present in the same brain. Japanese aphasic patients confirm that left lesions interfere with phonetic kana writing, whereas other lesions, presumably in visual areas, interfere with the ability to produce pictorial kanji symbols (Sasanuma, 1975).

The difference in coding for phonetic and pictographic information has been applied to aiding children who have dyslexia without any obvious brain damage. Dyslexic children who had severe reading disabilities but were not retarded were taught to associate English words with Chinese characters (Rozin, Poritsky, & Sotski, 1971). They learned quickly, acquiring about

30 characters and the ability to combine them into sentences with 2-1/2 to 5-1/2 hours of individual tutoring. As a control, the experimenters tutored the children in reading alphabetic words; predictably, they had no success. Thus the dyslexia was not due to poor teaching or lack of attention. In their final examination, these children were able to read the sentences in Figure 7.12, despite their previous failures with phonetic material. If these children had been Chinese, it is likely that their deficits would never have been discovered. This work remains controversial, and has not been replicated, but it points out the contrast between phonetic and symbolic coding systems.

Another group of patients that does not suffer dyslexia with receptive aphasia is the deaf. Deaf readers must learn to read without the benefit of phonics, of course, and as a result they code written words much like Chinese characters, never learning to read as well as average hearing readers. The words are elements unto themselves, unified symbols for their referents, rather than phonetic reminders.

Laterality and Language

An epilepsy patient, a candidate for temporal lobe surgery, sits in a neurologist's office. He is asked to raise both hands and to begin talking while the neurologist injects a solution into an artery in his neck. Suddenly his right arm drops while his left arm stays in the air. Speech is slurred for a second or two, then stops as the patient looks about the room with a puzzled air.

The patient has just undergone the Wada test (Wada & Rasmussen, 1960), a vivid demonstration of the laterality of language processing. The injection was into the left carotid artery with a solution containing sodium amytal, a short-acting barbiturate anesthetic. Most of the anesthetic remained on the left side as it passed into the brain and briefly interrupted function in the speech areas on the left side. The arms were raised as a control, to ensure that the anesthetic had an effect in the event that the injection did not interrupt speech. The arm fell as the anesthetic reached the left motor cortex. Because our patient's epilepsy was centered on the right side, the surgeon could proceed to remove the diseased brain tissue with the knowledge that vital language areas would not be damaged.

Language in Split-Brain Patients

Although early neurologists knew that language areas were usually on the left side of the brain, they knew little of what happened in the corresponding

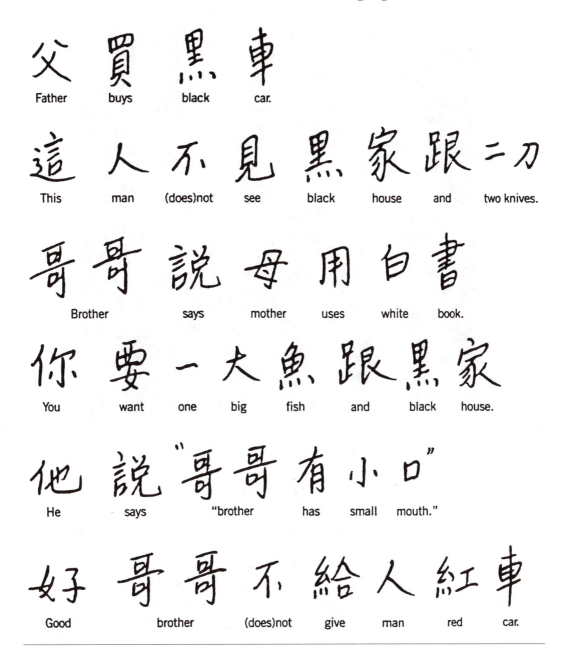

Figure 7.12 The final examination for dyslexics who had been taught a few Chinese characters. The subjects were shown only the Chinese characters, and gave the English translations orally.

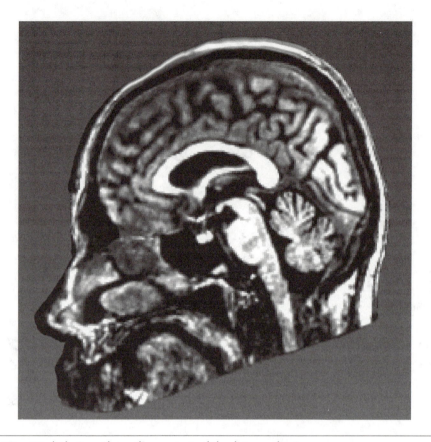

Figure 7.13 Medial view (from the center) of the human brain.

areas of the right. It didn't seem plausible that the right hemisphere would just lie there, absorbing metabolic energy and serving as neurological insurance against brain damage in children.

Except for language, though, brain areas and functions seem symmetrical on left and right. Sensory and motor representations, for example, are equal on the two sides. Cases in which the corpus callosum that links left and right cortex had been split surgically only added to the mystery. Cutting this enormous bundle of axons, the largest fiber bundle in the body (Figure 7.13), seemed to have no effect on intelligence, sensory acuity, or other functions. Karl Lashley wryly suggested that perhaps the callosum served to hold the two halves of the brain together. In the 1950s, Roger Sperry attacked the problem by separating the input to the two isolated hemispheres, finding evidence that the callosum has functions after all.

Figure 7.14   An experiment for testing split-brain patients. Visual stimuli are flashed briefly while the patient fixates the center line of the screen.

The experiments began when Sperry started collaborating with Joseph Bogen, a neurosurgeon who had proposed that some cases of epilepsy could be alleviated by severing the corpus callosum. Many epileptic seizures progress from an epileptic focus on one side of the brain through the callosum to the other side. The reverberation from one side to the other might be eliminated by a split-brain operation. The technique would be attempted only on severely ill patients for whom drugs and less drastic treatments were inadequate. The patients could be tested by stimulating only one side of the brain.

Applying the split-stimulation tests to these patients resulted in findings that eventually won Sperry a Nobel Prize. First he confirmed that the left hemisphere controlled language, for objects seen only by the right hemisphere could not be described in speech. The "silent" right hemisphere could match objects, but speech came from the left hemisphere, which often made up stories about the behavior being controlled by the right (Sperry, 1974).

If a picture of a spoon could be projected to the right visual cortex, for example, the patient in Figure 7.14 could find the spoon among a group of objects hidden behind the baffle in the figure even though he could not name the object. The patient would succeed only if the left hand (controlled by the right hemisphere) did the tactile searching. If the picture of a spoon

Figure 7.15 The split-brain patient rationalizes her behavior after the fact. The right hemisphere is unable to explain the behaviors that it controls.

appeared in the right visual field (projecting to the left hemisphere), and the word *fork* in the left field, the subject would say he was searching for a spoon but would produce a fork.

The early studies showed all language functions to be firmly entrenched in the left hemisphere, including both speech and reading. Split-brain patients quickly learned to hold a book in the right hand, for the nonreading right hemisphere controlling the left hand would put the book down if there were no interesting pictures to look at.

A few years after the first split-brain operations, the Sperry group's conception of language processing was shaken when two of their patients began to develop right-hemisphere language. The ability of the right was never as great as the fluent behavior of the left, being limited to a small vocabulary, but even simple grammar could come from the right side. The left hemisphere continued to dominate language when both were free to respond, as in the examples of Figure 7.15. As the size of the patient population increased, it became clear that the early patients were not representative.

The issue remains controversial. Noninvasive methods of measuring brain function have shown that about one tenth of normal humans have language represented bilaterally, and another tenth primarily on the right side. These people are indistinguishable from normal left-hemisphere language subjects with respect to mastery of foreign languages, academic achievement, artistic talents, verbal fluency, and in intelligence or speed of linguistic processing (Knecht et al., 2001).

Evolution of left-right differences. Several characteristics of the left-right dichotomy show that it is not fixated. First, it is not present in everyone. In some left-handed people, the left hemisphere specializes in sequential processes such as speech, and the right does simultaneous processing, just as in right-handers, whereas in others the specialization is reversed. In still others, the specializations are not strongly developed on either side but seem to be shared more equally. There is also a sex difference—men generally have stronger lateralization than women, especially in visuospatial functions (Harris, 1978). An anatomical correlate of this difference has been found in the posterior part of the corpus callosum, which is consistently larger in females than in males (deLacoste-Utamsing & Holloway, 1982). The implication is that there is less interhemispheric communication in the more highly lateralized male brain.

Second, the left and right specialize very late in maturation. Though there are signs of lateralization even in infancy, hemispheric specialization seems to emerge with the appearance of language and is not fully established until about 12 years of age. If the cortex of one hemisphere is damaged before this age, the other can often take over its functions. Thus a young child can recover language following left-hemisphere injury even though recovery from the same injury in an older person would be incomplete.

Third, the distinctions between the two hemispheres are a matter of degree. Both hemispheres normally participate in language functions, for instance, with the left participating more. This is to be expected, because the corpus callosum densely connects corresponding parts of the two hemispheres.

Finally, the specialization has evolved very recently. Though there are subtle signs of it in other primates, it is fully developed only in humans, along with the appearance of language.

Two Minds in One Head?

The difference between left and right hemispheric specializations lends itself to generalizations about dominant versus nondominant hemispheres, rational versus intuitive thought, or even yin versus yang. Though such metaphors have generated great interest, we must remember that there is no direct evidence for them.

The related idea that there may be two "minds" in one head is similarly appealing, but it applies mostly to the split-brain patients and not to normal humans. The intact human, of course, is different because information cannot be isolated in a single hemisphere. Indeed, blood flow studies using fMRI have shown increases in metabolic activity in both hemispheres during linguistic tasks, though increases are greater in the language hemisphere.

There is no question of competition between the hemispheres any more than there is competition between, for instance, the two legs in walking or any two bilaterally symmetrical parts of the body. The concept of the cortex as a giant mixing machine (Braitenberg, 1977) contradicts the idea of competition in normal brains; the effects seen in split brains are examples of disconnection syndromes, implying that the brain must reorganize itself somewhat to function in the severed state.

The split-brain studies have also illuminated the issue of consciousness or self-awareness, for the patients feel that they have little control over the activities of the right hemisphere. It is as though someone else is performing activities in their bodies. (Fortunately, this gives them little difficulty except in the experimental situation, where sensory inputs are limited to one side.)

Consciousness and language seem to have something to do with one another—at least that is what the speaking left hemisphere tells us. The patient above who reached for a fork was using an unconscious pathway from stimulus to right-hemisphere language and all the way through to behavior, an example of "vertical modularity" (B. Bridgeman, 1999), but in normal humans the act would have interacted with consciousness.

● FUNCTIONS OF LANGUAGE

Humans are the only primates with language, and we are by far the most successful primates on earth. Are these two observations connected? A look at the enormous advantages bestowed by language suggests that they are. A chimpanzee cannot learn from others, except by observation. Demonstrating things is possible without language, but a chimp normally makes little effort at it. There is some observational and imitational learning in chimps (deWaal, 1997), and even a beginning of cultural tradition, but it is very limited compared to what goes on in humans.

The power of language may have originated in a subtle difference between young chimpanzees and human children in their imitation strategies. Chimps will imitate the function of a task, but not the way of doing it. For instance, chimps may observe that using a rock can open a nut, but they must learn for themselves how to do it. The child, in contrast, learns both the facts of the situation and the intent of the actor's actions. Children shown an action performed in a peculiar way, such as turning on a push-button light switch by pushing it with the head, later repeat the action in the same way. The child imitates both a goal and a technique.

Though all human languages are of about equal complexity, they vary enormously in the vocabulary at their disposal to talk about philosophy, technology, and other aspects of experience. Through much of human prehistory, an important part of cultural progress consisted of making inventions, not only of objects such as buttons or needles but also of words with progressively more subtle meanings. Even today, we can trace sophisticated words back to very humble beginnings in a nomadic or subsistence farming lifestyle. The word *court,* for example, as in a court of law, began as the space in front of a farmhouse, the court, where people would gather. Most of our common words have such a history.

Emotional Communication

The intent of the limbic vocalizations is different from the goal of communicating human emotions. Usually we find ourselves crying, gasping, screaming, and so on without the intent to communicate, and sometimes despite our efforts to suppress such outbursts. It is probable that intention to communicate is also lacking in other primates, especially because they do not have the control over breathing that we do. They could not time their exclamations even if they wanted to. For them breathing is like the heartbeat—one can become aware of it at times, but it happens autonomously.

Using language, humans can communicate more subtle emotional states than other primates can. Our ability to express the twinge of regret, the subtle skepticism, is beyond the reach of cries and grunts. In addition, we can describe past states and anticipate future ones.

Music is another little explored area of emotional communication. It is likely that music expresses adapted human capabilities, for it is important in all cultures and at all times that we know about, and music universally is combined with language in singing. In the archeological record, some of the earliest human artifacts are musical instruments. We know that musical perception and production are handled in different brain areas than language, but a more precise definition of the neurology of music, as well as its evolved functions, has yet to be developed. Speculations include its roles in fostering social cohesion, synchronizing work, and even impressing the opposite sex.

We think of music and poetry as cultural luxuries, pleasant diversions but hardly of economic interest. In preliterate societies (meaning all societies before about 3000 B.C.E.), though, they were serious business. Poetry was a critically important means of holding the content of a culture in the minds of its people.

Melody, rhythm, and rhyme facilitated the memory of texts, helping to organize the verbal material and to correct errors. Many cultures had specialists who could recite or sing myths, religious texts, histories, and stories for hours, activities that were highly valued and closely attended by the community.

Social Communication

It is in social communication that humans move spectacularly ahead of other animals. We saw in Chapter 6 that humans organize societies on a scale that no other animal attempts, and that as a consequence, most of us are utterly dependent on society for all of our wants and needs.

We can look back to the genetic structure of our species for hints of why such extensive cooperation can function. Chapter 2 reviewed evidence that the human species has relatively little genetic diversity compared to most other mammalian species. The reason for our relative uniformity is the youth of our species, as species go, and also the series of population crises that subsequently reduced our diversity. As a result, we can get most of our genes into the next generation by cooperating even with complete strangers, who share most of our genes.

Close genetic relatedness also means that we can depend on other people to think and act in much the same way that we would in the same circumstances. The phrase "brothers under the skin" attains a practical reality in this context. Furthermore, our evolved tendencies to kin-directed altruism and reciprocal altruism could be applied indiscriminately in a Paleolithic social situation, where many of the people encountered in daily life would be relatives and all would be potential allies.

Language and Thought

Much of our thinking seems to be bound up with language. While thinking, we talk to ourselves, using what evolved as a communication system to link ideas within our own minds. Young children talk to themselves while working out problems, even when they are alone, and only later develop internal speech to allow this mechanism to work without external signs (Vygotsky, 1934). If this way of thinking about thought is correct, it would seem that the structure of one's language should influence the structure of one's thought. This hypothesis is called the **Whorfian hypothesis** after Benjamin Whorf, an amateur linguist who originated the idea.

Although the evidence for the Whorfian hypothesis is controversial, more limited forms of the hypothesis are well supported. English speakers, for example, think of time metaphorically as a horizontal sequence, whereas

Mandarin speakers think of it vertically. Indeed, exposure to horizontal arrays of objects allows English speakers to think more quickly about time sequence problems than do vertical arrays, while the reverse is true for Mandarin speakers (Boroditsky, 2001).

Language and Planning

Human activity is organized around plans, from immediate simple ones like lifting the next forkful of food to your mouth to long-term ones that may take years to execute, such as earning a college degree. Each long-term plan is broken down into smaller and smaller units, until finally the units are small enough to be executed directly.

Because many plans are present simultaneously in each of us, the brain must order them so that we execute only one at a time. There must also be a set of priorities to guarantee that the most urgent plans are being executed while the others are held in abeyance until a later time. The plans themselves constitute a kind of memory of the future. All of these functions require specialized machinery in the brain, machinery that is older in evolutionary terms than humanity (B. Bridgeman, 1992).

The serial organization of language in humans might use neurological machinery similar to that needed for the serial organizing of plans, creating a new capability by taking advantage of a planning mechanism that we share with other primates. Language could evolve quickly in the hominid line because it is made mostly out of old neurological parts, the adaptations in all primate brains that manage action planning.

It is clear that internal speech gives humans a huge advantage over non-linguistic species in the sorts of thinking that are possible. We organize ideas using a motor language-producing mechanism that evolved to foster communication. This happens mostly in the frontal parts of the brain, the motor centers. With internal speech, we can then turn the results back on our own language-understanding mechanism, in the sensory areas in the back and sides of the brain. Thus neural machinery that evolved for communication can feed information back into the receptive parts of the brain for another pass from sensory to motor areas. Internal speech allows all this to happen inside the brain, without any motor activity.

The loop from a linguistic coding of ideas to an internal neurological code, and back to a language code, allows more information and more ways of approaching a problem to be added in each pass (Figure 7.16). Thinking can take time because it becomes sequential, and need not be limited to instantaneous intuitions (B. Bridgeman, 1992). According to this idea, the language loop allows humans more complex trains of thought than are possible for other animals.

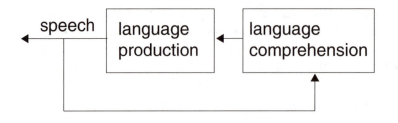

Figure 7.16   The phonological loop, amplifying the power of human thought with each pass of information around the circle.

● DISCUSSION QUESTIONS

1. If language is so useful, why did it not evolve in other species?
2. What came first in phylogenetic development—the beginnings of language, or the anatomical changes that differentiate human vocal tracts from those of other primates?
3. What functions does language serve beyond communication?

● FURTHER READING

Liberman, P. (2000). *Human language and our reptilian brain*. Cambridge, MA: Harvard University Press.

A prominent neuroscientist takes up the Darwinian case, with data seldom considered by psycholinguists and neurolinguists, that human language is not qualitatively different from other forms of animal communication.

Gardner, R. A., Gardner, B. T., & Van Cantfort, T. (Eds.). (1989). *Teaching sign language to chimpanzees*. Albany: State University Of New York Press.

The Gardners, who taught American Sign Language to the chimpanzee Washoe, make the case for ape language along with their colleagues.

Pinker, S. (1994). *The language instinct*. New York: HarperCollins.

The biological structures behind language and their evolution are described in Steven Pinker's witty style. Pinker shows how language requires evolved brain mechanisms, demolishing the SSSM conception of language.

CHAPTER 8

PERCEPTION, MEMORY, AND CONSCIOUSNESS

"Who are you going to believe, me or your own eyes?"

— Groucho Marx

Memory is central to all cognitive function. At one time, psychologists thought that there was only one memory, a record of the past that is as accurate as possible. Failures of memory were seen as shortcomings in a system doing the best it could. Research in recent decades has revealed that we have not one unified memory system, but a welter of more specialized systems, each adapted to do a particular job.

The state of memory research reflects a trend in many areas of psychology—as soon as we open the investigative window on a psychological system, it seems to splinter into dozens of pieces. The unified mind, if there is one, is made of many smaller and more specialized parts.

The sensory systems have undergone a similar splintering, with the identification of specialized modules within each modality that are adapted to particular cognitive jobs. This chapter concentrates on vision because it is the best known of the senses. Furthermore, we already know that all the sensory systems are similar at the most fundamental levels of design. Though their information pickup organs (eyes, ears, etc.) are very different, their neural organizations higher up in the brain share many important features. All of them have the job of gathering information from the outside world and making sense of it, and it is likely that all evolved from common origins at the dawn of vertebrate evolution.

The approach to vision and memory acknowledges that evolutionary theory has already informed investigation in these areas, as researchers in vision and memory strive to make their ideas consilient with the natural sciences. Because many textbooks capably review brain mechanisms of vision and memory, this review will emphasize adapted traits and capabilities, taking a broader view to examine origins as well as functions. The reviews of these areas will emphasize the adapted functions of the systems, using evolution to make sense of why the systems are designed as they are, and how they got that way.

Though scientific study of consciousness is much more recent than the study of memory or sensory systems, consciousness is perhaps the key to human existence. It is what most of us consider to be the essence of what human life is like, where memory, perception, and values come together to integrate into a human being. Curiosity about consciousness is as old as civilization; now we can begin to glimpse its functions and mechanisms. Scientific examination of consciousness first requires a look at the systems and capabilities that contribute to consciousness.

● VISUAL PERCEPTION

The human visual system must solve problems that humans have in common with other animals—recognizing patterns, orienting in space, and controlling motor activity. The uniqueness of the human adaptation is more in the way that perceptual information is used than in the way that it is gathered and analyzed.

At least at the early stages, visual systems of humans are indistinguishable from those of the old-world monkeys and apes. Even an expert would be hard-pressed to identify any important differences between the visual systems of the human and the rhesus macaque, for instance. This may reveal how little we know about visual systems, but it also speaks to the great similarity of primate visual systems and their conservation in the course of evolution. Most of our visual system, including subtleties such as color and motion perception, and the cortical machinery that supports them, is little changed from 30 million years ago when monkeys and apes diverged. The visual system has been conserved over those millions of years.

Early Vision

From start to finish, the primate visual system is finely tuned to the properties of the natural environment and to the organism's need for visual information in guiding behavior. Information from light goes through three stages as it enters the visual system: first is processing of the light itself, then **transduction** by receptor cells into neural signals, and finally processing of the neurally coded information.

After light entering the eye is focused by the cornea and the lens, its brightness is adjusted by the pupil. Here, even before the light meets sensory receptors, the organism enhances some aspects of the information in light and discards others. The pupil can change the intensity of light entering the eye by a factor of 10, adjusting it to a level where the receptors work best. As a result, though, information about the overall intensity of that light is lost, and cannot be recovered. The visual system has evolved to analyze the patterns in light, the information that the light carries from the outside world. Intensity is irrelevant and is thrown away even before the light hits the receptors. This is why, even though each of our 250 million receptor cells acts like a tiny light meter, photographers need artificial light meters to tell them how bright a scene is. The photographer on the other end of the visual system has no access to fine-scale brightness information.

At the transduction stage, four kinds of receptors collect light in a sensitivity range that closely matches the energy available from the sun (Figure 8.1). Three types, shaped like cones, operate in the daylight intensity range, and a fourth type with a rod-like shape functions at lower light intensities. The spectrum of the light that actually illuminates our world, though, does not always match the sun's spectrum. Light may be filtered by leaves, reflected from rocks, or refracted by the atmosphere near sunrise and sunset.

Color Constancy

The consistent perception of colors despite differences in illumination defines **color constancy**. Nature has devised a deceptively simple way of compensating for differences in the illumination spectrum, allowing us to perceive colors in about the same way regardless of large differences in illumination. The three cone systems, each sensitive to a slightly different range of wavelengths of light, adapt separately.

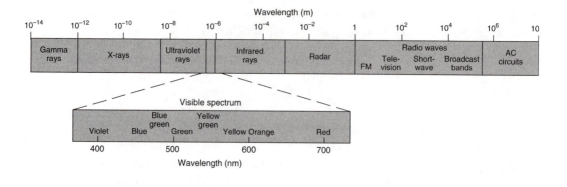

Figure 8.1   The electromagnetic spectrum. The upper scale is logarithmic, covering a range of 22 log units. The lower scale is linear. Most of the sun's energy is emitted at wavelengths between 10^{-4} and 10^{-8} m.

If the illumination contains a lot of red light, as would be the case at sunset, the red system becomes less sensitive than the other two, so that the balance in activities among the three systems is maintained. Higher levels integrate this information to give us an overall perception of color constancy: as a result, we perceive colors fairly accurately over a wide range of illumination spectra.

The system works very well within the light environments in which it evolved, but it breaks down outside those limits. Gerd Gigerenzer (1998) tells a story of renting a yellow-green Renault, and losing it at night in a parking lot.

> Instead there was a blue Renault sitting in the lot, the same model, but the wrong color. I still feel my fingers hesitating to put my key into the lock of this car, but the lock opened. I drove ... home. When I looked out the window the next morning, there was a yellow-green Renault standing in bright sunlight outside. What had happened?

The professor's visual system was fooled by the sodium vapor lamps in the parking lot, which give off light that is visible but has a spectrum so strange that no primate had encountered anything like it during the course of evolution. Color constancy broke down in this abnormal illuminant.

The story illustrates one of the most powerful methods that cognitive psychologists have for studying perception—destructive testing. Just as an engineer tests the strength of a cable by pulling on it until it breaks, a

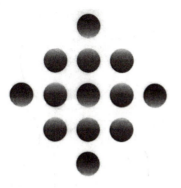

Figure 8.2 The dents in the surface appear to be bumps if the picture is inverted, because the visual system assumes that light comes from above.

psychologist tests perception by pushing it to its limits, until it breaks down and begins reporting properties of the world that aren't there. In Chapter 6, destructive testing of human reasoning led to greater understanding of the way reasoning functions, with short-cut heuristics instead of exhaustive logic. Perception is studied in much the same way, with much the same conclusions.

Perception and the "Bag of Tricks" Theory

If the visual system had been designed all at once, like a stereo or a computer, engineers might have given it a geometric engine to map all the spatial relationships that would be needed, and a powerful, general pattern recognizer to compare sensory input with stored information. When we look inside the brain, however, we find not general solutions but a welter of limited algorithms that deal with limited problems. Ramachandran (1990) calls it the "bag of tricks" theory, because instead of general solutions, the brain offers a bag of "cheap tricks" to apply to problems of pattern recognition. Each trick applies in only a limited setting. Normally, a cheap trick can be expressed in a few words, requiring no mathematics.

One example of such a cheap trick is shown in Figure 8.2. The dimples in the surface appear as dimples only as long as you assume that the illumination is coming from above. If you can convince yourself that the illumination is coming from below, the dimples will pop out and appear as bumps on the surface.

The brain's default assumption is that illumination comes from above, as it normally does in the natural world, and this source of information can be used to interpret patterns in the world. The cheap trick might read something

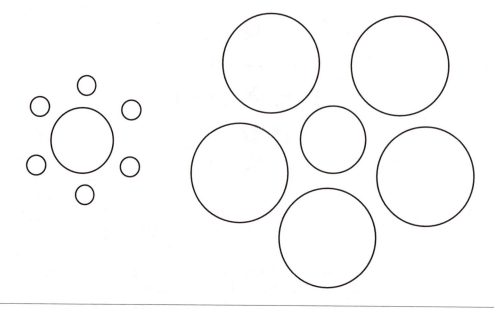

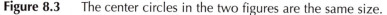

Figure 8.3   The center circles in the two figures are the same size.

like "If the top of a disturbance in a surface is darker, there is a dimple." It complements "If the top of a disturbance in a surface is lighter, there is a bump." Another cheap trick specifies that all objects are 3-dimensional, for even the most meager information will demand a 3-dimensional solution. Try interpreting the surface in Figure 8.2 as a 2-dimensional colored surface.

Sometimes the cheap tricks are so simple that they sound ridiculous. The illusion in Figure 8.3 is based on two simple rules: First, the smallest of a bunch of things is pretty small, and second, the biggest of a bunch of things is pretty big. The bunch of big things is the group of large circles, and the bunch of small things in the other part of the figure is the group of smaller circles. It doesn't sound like sophisticated pattern processing, or even good kindergarten wisdom, but it usually works. Only in simplified, systematically biased environments like that in Figure 8.3 do the generalizations lead us astray. The visual system relies on the random or near-random distribution of sizes of objects in the world to make this trick work.

Figure/Ground Segregation

The first step that the visual system takes in interpreting a visual scene is segregating figure and ground, a task that is accomplished quickly,

Figure 8.4   A figure-ground reversible figure, developed by Danish Gestalt psychologist Edgar Rubin.

automatically, and unavoidably. Normally a few cheap tricks, such as closed contours and reduced distance from the observer, can define objects. Using a variant of destructive testing, psychologists have devised situations that bring to light some of the properties of the figure-ground system in the brain.

Figure 8.4, devised by Rubin (1915), is ambiguous because it offers two solutions to the figure-ground problem, each about equally viable. If you perceive a vase, it appears to be closer than the background, and the shapes of the faces cannot be perceived. Perceiving the two faces prevents the vase from being perceived. The figure has a shape but the background does not. The perception is bistable, with each alternative suppressing the other; only one solution is allowed at a time.

According to psychologist Earnest Hilgard, this figure with its double interpretation was a model for Niels Bohr's principle of complementarity,

(a)

(b)   (c)

Figure 8.5   (a) An illusory figure, the Kanizsa triangle. The white triangle appears to float above the surface of the figure, and to be brighter than the background. About half of the perceived edge of the triangle is not objectively present. (b) A square defined by four rectilinear components. (c) A square with the same length of real contour as in (b), defined by missing segments of circles.

that an elementary particle's behavior can be understood either as a particle or a wave. The interpretation changes the way things look but does not change the things themselves. Bohr and Rubin were contemporaries in Copenhagen in the early 20th century.

Occlusion can also serve to segregate figure and ground. Figure 8.5a shows a triangle defined only by the occlusions of other objects (Kanizsa,

1979). Though the white triangle has no contours of its own, it is seen floating above the remainder of the figure and appears brighter than the background. Here one cheap trick specifies that "if a contour of an object is interrupted by another object, the first object is behind the second one." Another specifies that "if an object is brighter than the objects it occludes, it is brighter than the background." The illusory contour is created in the mind, but it is not entirely the result of image properties. Rather, the image properties react with internal rules of visual analysis to yield the perception.

The visual system also uses a more sophisticated trick, that "breaking the contour of a regular figure specifies an occluding object." The same contour of an object that is not clearly missing a corner is less effective in inducing an illusory contour (Figure 8.5b, c). The example demonstrates that many tricks can be combined, instantaneously and effortlessly, in interpreting a visual image. Indeed, one of the requirements for the evolution of a new cheap trick is that it not interfere with the effectiveness of the other ones. They must all work simultaneously in parallel.

A Cosmological Principle in Perception

Related cheap tricks enable us to solve perceptual problems that are unsolvable by the rules of formal logic. The visual system escapes the limitations of logic by making an assumption that is related to the cosmological principle. By the early 20th century, astronomers knew that the earth is not the center of the solar system, as had once been assumed. What had previously been interpreted as stars sometimes turned out to be distant galaxies, and soon it became clear that the swath of stars across our sky called the Milky Way is part of a galaxy like many others, of which our humble solar system is a tiny part. Extending this principle to the universe led to the assumption that there is nothing at all unique about the earth's position in the universe—the cosmological principle.

Applied to vision, the cosmological principle becomes a perceptual principle, asserting that the human observer does not stand at a unique station point, that nothing in the environment is correlated with the observer's current position. Looking at a real situation, we interpret Figure 8.6 with two strategies—the cosmological principle plus the cheap trick that textures are uniform. Though logically the figure could represent any combination of increasing texture density and decreasing slant, our visual system invariably decides on only one solution, a uniform texture and extreme slant. Unless we find ourselves in a psychological experiment, the solution is always right.

Another example of the cosmological principle in perception is in Figure 8.7, where we immediately see a cube in one figure (a) but see only a

Figure 8.6   Increasing texture density is interpreted as increasing distance from the observer, not as a decrease in the real size of the texture elements.

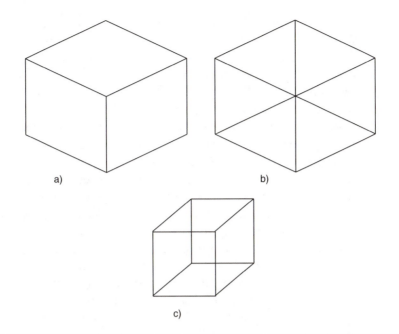

a)   b)

c)

Figure 8.7   A cube (a), drawn without perspective. In (b) the figure is changed by making the cube transparent, requiring a unique station point. The three-dimensional character of the figure is lost because a three-dimensional interpretation of the image would violate the cosmological principle of perception. A Necker cube, a transparent cube drawn without perspective from a generalized perspective (c), has two geometric interpretations.

hexagonal pattern in the other (b). Both patterns, however, are projections of three-dimensional rectilinear figures onto a two-dimensional surface. The reason why the hexagonal pattern is not perceived as a cube is because its three-dimensional projection applies for only a small number of unique station points, violating the perceptual principle. Most of the time, a random encounter with a cube will result in a pattern like the more easily interpreted one in (c).

Depth

The power of combining cheap tricks is particularly evident in the way we perceive depth in the visual field. Depth is a difficult problem because nothing on the retina indicates the distance a photon has traveled before it enters the eye. There are many cues to depth, characteristics of the visual world that might potentially indicate depth. Some of the cues have been exploited by the brain to construct neurological cheap tricks for distance estimation. Stereoscopic vision, seeing slightly different views of the world from the two eyes, provides good quantitative information about depth, but it works well only for close objects and in high-acuity parts of the retina.

Other cues, each the subject of a neural cheap trick, supplement stereopsis in many situations. Occlusion as in Figure 8.5a is a cue that always works, but gives only qualitative information about the relative depths of objects. The cheap trick of contour interruption applies here. Cast shadows provide another qualitative cue with another cheap trick: if an object casts a visible shadow on another object, the object that has the shadow on it is farther away. If there are no cast shadows, the trick obviously won't work. Relative height in the visual field is also a cue: objects higher in the visual field are proportionally more distant. The cue works well in a qualitative way, but it is fooled by objects on hills, and fails for estimating the distances of objects on a ceiling.

Other cues require assumptions about the structure of the world. The relative-size cue says that the smaller of two objects of equal size is farther away, the relative distances given by the ratio of the sizes. It works well for objects known to be about the same size, such as people's heads, but can be deceptive for estimating the distances of things that can vary in size, such as rocks. Familiar size is also useful if the real size of an object is known. An object known to be small will be seen closer than one known to be large, if their retinal projections are similar in angular extent.

There are more depth cues, including atmospheric perspective (the lower contrast and blue tint of very distant objects), linear perspective, texture gradients (see Figure 8.6), and several types of motion cues. Examining each cue in isolation reveals its shortcomings.

The visual brain applies cheap tricks based on each of these cues to arrive at a single estimate of distance for an attended object. Because each cue has a different reliability that depends on the situation, a flexible but quick combination rule is needed. One way of conceiving this rule uses fuzzy logic (Massaro & Cowan, 1993), combining the cues and weighting each according to the amount of information it contributes. The rule has the advantage that it adjusts itself to each situation without requiring situation-specific processing.

Effectiveness Versus Elegance

Why cheap tricks instead of logically rigorous solutions? One reason is that they work. Although each cheap trick may seem hopelessly inadequate, when you put enough of them together, they do pretty well. Another reason comes from a limitation of evolution; it cannot invest in elegant solutions that may take many generations to achieve, because the organisms in every generation must be viable and competitive. A cheap trick can evolve quickly, and right away it can be of more use than no trick at all.

Another advantage of the tricks is that they are, well, cheap—it does not take much genetic information to instantiate a cheap trick, whereas the elegant solution might require extensive combinations of genes in just the right organization. Because there are so few genes in the human genome, there is a premium on getting things done with minimal DNA.

In the course of evolution, a cheap trick coded in few genes will tend to appear before a more expensive trick. Once this happens, the cheap version will tend to suppress the evolution of the expensive one by removing most of the selective pressure for it.

A limitation of design by natural selection is that new parts should not interfere with the operation of older parts: "Don't fix it if it ain't broke." As new cheap tricks evolve, they must work together with existing tricks to do a better job than was done before. This is possible only if the new machinery doesn't interfere with the old machinery. The implication for psychological theory is that if more general and elegant theories of perception (or of anything else) are proposed, a scheme of how the proposed system could have evolved must accompany the theory.

Although the principles of perception described up to this point can be interpreted in terms of evolution by natural selection, the interpretation is normally added after the principles have been discovered. Evolution can organize the data and help us to understand why perceptual systems do what they do: the psychology of perception can also be derived directly from natural selection, which is ultimately responsible for the design of the perceptual apparatus. Geisler and Diehl (2002) propose a formal framework for analyzing how the statistics of natural stimuli and the process of natural selection interact to determine the design of perceptual systems. In this bottom-up approach, evolutionary theory is used to derive the design of the brain mechanisms, substituting for other explanations in explicating their design.

Two Visual Systems

A particularly dramatic example of nature's design philosophy was revealed in a neurological patient, D.F., who lost part of her visual system in a case of carbon monoxide poisoning. Recovering from a coma, she was unable to recognize even the simplest patterns. Shown a disc with a slot cut in it, she could not describe the orientation of the slot, and when forced to guess, her guesses had no relation to the actual orientation. (The guessing control is important to pick up any residual perceptual capacity.) But when asked to extend her flattened hand through the slot, she reached out, oriented her hand perfectly, and reached through without touching the edges of the slot.

D.F. did this by using information in a second visual system that controls visually guided behavior, but whose contents are not available to perception. It has been called the sensorimotor system, in contrast to the cognitive system of normal perception. The two systems have also been called "what" and "how," emphasizing their functions (Milner & Goodale, 1995). Information from the eye travels to the brain, is coded in a representation of visual space, and is used to guide behavior, all without the intervention of perception.

Normal subjects can use this information without knowing that they have it; using visual illusions, spatial information in the cognitive system can be distorted without affecting the accurate record in the sensorimotor system (B. Bridgeman, Gemmer, Forsman, & Huemer, 2000). In these tests, the stimulus array is simple—if a rectangle is presented off-center in an otherwise uniform visual field, observers perceive a target spot within the rectangle to be deviated in the direction opposite the offset of the rectangle. When asked to jab the target whose position they misperceive, though, they hit it accurately, even if they cannot see their hands. In effect, observers perceive a target in one location, but successfully jab it in another.

The sensorimotor system probably evolved before the cognitive system, controlling the behavior of primitive vertebrates in a here-and-now fashion. Even in humans, this system has no memory, and must pick up coordinates from the cognitive system to engage remembered targets. The cognitive system evolved later in the course of evolution to handle pattern recognition. The two visual systems reflect two kinds of jobs that vision must perform; when I see a face I want to know whose face it is, not how many degrees from the centerline it is located. Swatting a fly, though, I care more about its location and motion than the color of its eyes. By segregating these two functions into separate representations of visual space, one system can do its job without interfering with the other. Patient D.F. had an intact sensorimotor system but a heavily damaged cognitive system.

According to Mel Goodale, D.F. is no longer so easy to test in the slot experiment. She has figured out that her motor impulses give her better information about some things than her visual experience, and has learned to use this information. Looking at the slot, she moves her hand in her lap to match the slot's orientation. Then she knows the orientation of the slot even without looking at her hand, for her proprioception is normal. D.F.'s brain has solved this perceptual problem, just as we all solve other perceptual problems every day.

Direct Perception

When we view the world, we do not see a mosaic of colored spots, or an array of concentric spots in complementary colors, or a network of lines and edges. Yet at successive stages of visual processing, visual information is coded in all those formats. The mosaic of spots is what the receptors of the retina see; the concentric spots are the code of two intermediate processing stages, in the output cells of the retina and the cells of the thalamus that send fibers to the visual cortex; and the lines and edges are one way of describing the way information is coded in the visual cortex. What we experience, though, is only the end product of this long series of transformations of visual information.

This is the sense in which perception is direct (Gibson, 1966, 1979). We are immediately aware of objects and surfaces in the world, not of the processing that leads the visual system to conclude that those objects are there. Direct perception does not mean that there is no processing of visual information, only that we are directly aware of the world, not of the visual processing.

Look again at Figure 8.7c. Then cover it and answer two questions. First, what was the figure? Now, how many lines were present? You could probably answer the first question a lot faster than the second, even though the figure is made entirely of lines, and the percept will be disturbed if any of the lines is missing. Perception of the cube seems to be direct—it practically jumps out at you. Your visual brain organizes the lines, calls up a few cheap tricks, makes a few assumptions, and delivers a cube to your consciousness.

But look again. You can see the Necker cube in either of two orientations, if you look at it long enough. Even after the brain has made its best guess about what is out there, it keeps working on the image, searching for a better solution. The two equally valid cubes alternate in perception, neither permanently gaining the upper hand. You never see a two-dimensional array of lines on a sheet of paper, though that is what's there, because your visual system evolved to function in a world of three-dimensional objects. Through half a billion years of evolving visual systems, objects were more critical to survival than patterns on planes, so that is what you perceive.

All this processing occurs effortlessly and seemingly instantaneously, as though there were no processing at all. And every 2-year-old can do it pretty well, at an age where the child is relatively helpless at most reasoning tasks. Yet the processing is so sophisticated that even the best current computer-vision programs are not nearly as effective as the 2-year-old, who can recognize an object effortlessly despite variations in illumination, perspective, partial occlusion, and distortion. The cheap tricks are already up and running, with information processing hidden in a strategy that Helmholtz (1867) characterized as unconscious inference. Logical operations such as inference are performed quickly and without conscious intervention in transforming retinal images into an internal model of the world.

These observations lead one to suspect that there is an inverse principle of psychological research—the more important a problem is, the smaller the number of scientists working on it. The reason for this perverse situation is that the really important things, those that evolution has worked hard on, function very well, and the effortlessness of their functioning leaves the impression that there is no problem at all. Late add-ons, though, give us trouble because they are not as well tuned by evolution.

Reading, for example, employs a small army of researchers, yet clearly has no evolved machinery in the brain. There simply hasn't been enough time for reading-specific adaptations to evolve in the few centuries since the custom of reading became widespread. This is why reading takes years to learn, and some otherwise normal people never become proficient at it. Yet the well-adapted mechanisms of space perception, the basis of all visual functions, occupy a much smaller cadre of researchers. A possible exception to this rule is memory—it is both intensively studied and critical to all other psychological functions.

● MEMORY

The adapted function of memory is not to record past experiences. Such a record would be entertaining for its owner but of little use to an organism striving to ensure its survival and reproduction. Rather, memory serves as an aid to planning future behavior, using information from the past to inform actions in the future. If survival requires distortions, omissions, and fabrications in the record, so be it.

Defining Learning and Memory

Though learning and memory are basic to human experience and to brain function, psychologists have found them paradoxically difficult to define. Textbooks in learning often devote several paragraphs to defining memory, starting with such phrases as "a relatively permanent change in behavior that occurs as the result of prior experience." There follows a long list of things that memory isn't, such as maturation, disease, and physical injury. The definition hasn't gotten us very far.

We can do better by focusing on the memory itself, rather than on the resulting behaviors, and by admitting the presence of a brain that stores information. **Memory** then becomes "information stored in the brain as a result of sensory experience," and **learning** is "the acquisition of new memories." The word *information* is used in its technical sense as a reduction of uncertainty, and therefore it can exist only in a context—reduction of uncertainty about what? Fundamental to the idea of memories is that they relate to each other, to brain organization, and to the sensory world.

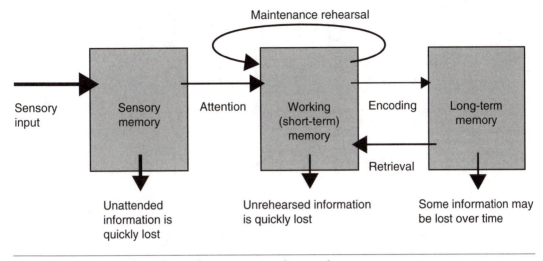

Figure 8.8   A popular scheme for interpreting human long-term memory.

The definition of memory excludes information from the genes, reinforcing a dichotomy between the two great influences on behavior: memory, changeable within a lifetime but existing uniquely within each individual, and genetics, unchanging within an individual but spanning generations. As we have seen above, perceptions and actions involve intimate interplay between these two influences. Human culture creates a continuum of information in memory, and in our libraries, memorials, and computers, that also spans generations.

As researchers have looked more and more closely, they have found more and more types of memory, each specialized for a particular job, each using its own neurological machinery, and each introducing its own particular types of distortions into the memory record (Figure 8.8). The longest-term memory systems hold information for a lifetime; the shortest, for less than a second.

Varieties of Memory

Sensory Memory

Perceptual signals in the brain are ephemeral: responding only to the immediate environment, they disperse within a few tens of milliseconds after the events that they encode. Yet behavior must be informed not only by what is going on right now but also by what has happened in the past. The brain needs a buffer, a way of storing sensory information long enough to evaluate

$$\begin{matrix}
\text{s} & \text{g} & \text{r} & \text{h} & \text{d} & \text{l} & \text{y} \\
\text{w} & \text{t} & \text{y} & \text{f} & \text{h} & \text{b} & \text{u} \\
> \text{d} & \text{g} & \text{f} & \text{t} & \text{f} & \text{y} & \text{q} \\
\text{v} & \text{j} & \text{d} & \text{s} & \text{h} & \text{j} & \text{v}
\end{matrix}$$

Figure 8.9   An array of letters of the sort used in the Sperling experiments, with a pointer at the middle row. Observers were instructed to report the letters in the line marked by the pointer. They did well at this task, regardless of which line was marked, but were unable to report many letters from the unmarked rows.

it, to compare it to other information and make decisions about it. This is the role of sensory memory.

The sensory memory buffer was discovered by accident when George Sperling (1960) was presenting arrays of letters for only 50 msec, followed by a mask to prevent afterimages from maintaining visibility of the letters. Surprisingly, people could still report letters in the array, like that in Figure 8.9, but only a few of them. Sperling's suspicions were aroused when it turned out that the identified letters were usually in the upper left corner of the array, as though subjects were trying to read them from some ephemeral memory, even though they were fixating in the center of the array.

To test his suspicion, Sperling marked one of the rows or columns of letters with a tone, represented by a small mark in the margin of Figure 8.9, and asked the subjects to report the marked line first. This is called the partial-report technique, because only part of the array must be reported. Indeed, subjects were able to describe what was in the marked line, but usually little else. It was as if the subjects were reading the letters from an internal buffer, but the information dissipated before they could pronounce more than a few letters. The letter array could be reduced to 3×3 letters, and still subjects missed most of the letters. The stored letters evaporated from memory even as they were being read.

The partial-report technique could also be used to estimate the duration of sensory memory, by delaying the probe marker. This technique showed that if the marker was delayed for even a tenth of a second after stimulus offset, report of the marked line was degraded. After a quarter of a second, performance fell to levels not much different from the unmarked lines. Thus the memory has a high capacity, dozens of items at least, but a very short duration.

There is a similar memory in the auditory system. Neisser (1967) has named the visual store **iconic memory**; the auditory store is **echoic memory**. An echoic memory would be especially useful because the auditory input is one-dimensional and makes sense only when integrated over time. Indeed, echoic memory lasts longer than iconic memory, on the order of several seconds. The other senses may have modality-specific sensory memories as well, though they have not been as much investigated.

Working Memory

This memory, also called **short-term memory**, has a capacity of only a few items. Information comes into working memory easily, in a single exposure, but can be held for only a few tens of seconds at most, and is easily pushed out by subsequent input. The main workplace of the mind, its content may be related to what we describe as consciousness. It gets its input both from sensory memory, or possibly from sensory systems directly, and from long-term memory.

Like other memory processes, working memory has also been split into several parts. A **phonological loop** holds verbal information, **visuospatial sketch pad** represents the contents of immediate visual space, and a **central executive** coordinates working memory and brings new information into it (Baddeley, 1992). The central executive is the least understood of these.

The phonological loop is the neural basis beneath the trick of remembering something, such as someone's name or a telephone number, by repeating it to yourself. Before the information in working memory is lost, you restore it by repronouncing it, either aloud or silently. In this process, you use neurological machinery that evolved for action to pronounce the numbers, and machinery that evolved for perception to access the results of your efforts.

Use of these existing neurological systems greatly extends the durability of information in working memory. This cognitive trick, probably unavailable to nonhuman primates, significantly enhances the capacity of the human mind. Again, we see how a modest change in the evolved organization of the brain results in a significant enhancement of our mental capabilities. The trick might be a strategy applied to an existing neurological system, a method for dealing with verbal information that we learn in early childhood.

Long-Term Memory

This is what most people mean by memory, our long-term record of the past. It too has turned out to be many memories, each with different

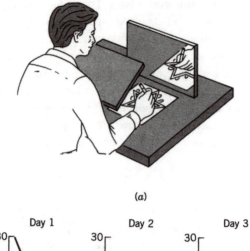

(a)

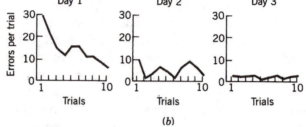

(b)

Figure 8.10   Apparatus for a mirror-tracing task. Both the patient's hand and the traced figure are visible only through the mirror. Performance on the task improves both within days and between days, without the patient remembering anything about the experience of learning.

properties and limitations, that evolved to perform distinct functions. Long-term memory is sometimes compared to the memory in a computer, because it can remain indefinitely. Any information that endures for more than a few minutes in the brain is assumed to be encoded in long-term memory.

Declarative versus procedural knowledge. A brain-damaged patient sits down to learn a task that a neurologist presents to him. The patient is to draw a pattern that he can see only through the mirror arrangement in Figure 8.10. At first, writing is very slow, as the patient deciphers each angle, but after some practice his writing improves considerably. In fact, he learns about as fast as normal subjects. The next day, when the patient is asked to perform the mirror writing task again, he cordially reintroduces himself to the experimenter as though the two had never met, and declares that he has never seen the apparatus. The patient has **amnesia** (Greek *a-* = *not, mnemnos* = memory).

At this point, one might conclude that the patient has only a short-term memory, and that nothing remains from the previous day's experience. After the task has been reexplained, however, the patient sits down and begins mirror-writing as skillfully as he had the day before. When asked about the source of his skill, the patient informs the neurologist that the task isn't really very difficult, and that anyone could do as well.

The patient is the famous case N.A. (Cohen & Squire, 1980), who became amnesic following an encounter with a fencing foil. N.A. has amnesia for **declarative knowledge**, the sort of memory that can be put into words, although he retains the ability to acquire and use **procedural knowledge**, the memory for rules and procedures. Procedural learning modifies existing schemata, or ways of going about solving a problem (Rumelhart, 1981).

The declarative-procedural distinction has also been characterized as knowing *that* versus knowing *how*, or memory with record versus memory without record. It shows that there are several different types of long-term memory, probably using different neurological mechanisms. In evolutionary terms, memory systems that handle procedural knowledge are probably older than those that mediate declarative knowledge.

Most neurological patients who suffer from amnesia have deficits in declarative knowledge, whereas procedural knowledge is much less affected. Patients who suffer from Korsakoff's syndrome, sometimes a consequence of prolonged alcoholism, have deficits in declarative knowledge. They can learn new things but forget them quickly. They have no difficulty with previously learned tasks and procedures, though, such as tying their shoes or using a fork.

Semantic versus episodic knowledge. Within declarative knowledge, one can distinguish two varieties of memory. **Semantic** (rule-like) **memory** tells us that Sacramento is the capitol of California. The knowledge can be put into words, but it expresses an enduring characteristic of the world. Describing your trip to Sacramento last week would require **episodic memory**, memory for a particular episode in your life.

Again, each of these memory systems is supported by specialized machinery (Tulving, 1985; Squire, Knowlton, & Musen, 1993) (Figure 8.11). Presumably, these memory systems evolved at different times to resolve particular environmental challenges. Because episodic memory is a defining feature of consciousness, we return to it near the end of the chapter.

Implicit memory. To further complicate the array of memory systems, there is also a motor memory for skills such as swimming or riding a bicycle. This

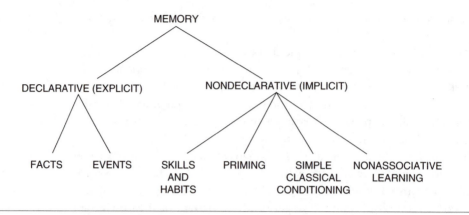

Figure 8.11 Varieties of long-term memory (LTM). Implicit memory, more recently discovered, holds information that we do not know we have, or has content that we cannot describe consciously.

memory is **implicit memory**, one whose contents cannot be described, and is very resistant to forgetting—you can jump on a bicycle after not having ridden for 50 years and still remain upright. This memory is held largely in the cerebellum, a phylogenetically ancient part of the hindbrain, whose basic cellular structure has been conserved since the appearance of fish in the early stages of vertebrate evolution. This structure is not related to consciousness, as shown by experiments stimulating the cerebellum electrically in patients. Unlike stimulation in the cerebral cortex of the forebrain, cerebellar stimulation never results in conscious experience. Declarative and procedural memory are centered in the cerebral cortex, where activity is correlated with consciousness.

To learn to ride a bicycle, you don't laboriously learn rules—you simply get out there and start trying to ride. Sooner or later, you succeed, and a few minutes later you will have fairly good control. "Learning" to ride is not a matter of consciously inserting information into motor memory but rather of putting yourself in a situation where memory will form by itself.

In fact, other forms of long-term memory work in a similar way, with learning occurring if we put ourselves in situations where it can occur. Just as the practice of medicine often consists of keeping a patient alive until he cures himself, learning often involves little more than giving the learning mechanisms a chance to do their work. Repeating foreign-language vocabulary words to yourself, for instance, exposes learning mechanisms to them and helps to form long-term memories. More effective is relating the words to their meanings and to each other, for memory is organized in terms of a great matrix of meaning—concepts linked to each other. The more links that can be established, the more easily the memory can be stored and recalled.

Unity or Diversity?

In conclusion, the story of memory turns out to be similar to the story of perception: what had seemed a single capability turned out to be made of many parts, or modules, each of which could appear separately and evolve without disturbing other similar modules. All have in common that they enhance our ability to make use of information acquired in the past, but their functions, mechanisms, and properties are very diverse. The cheap tricks of perception are paralleled by specialized cheap memories that handle information in many different ways, for different purposes.

Everyone has experienced the fact that memory works better in some applications than in others. Getting oriented in an unfamiliar room, for instance, seems instantaneous and effortless, and learning the layout of the immediate environment is usually accomplished without difficulty. Remembering a telephone number for more than a few minutes without writing it down, however, requires great concentration and intentional strategies of memorizing. Similarly, verbal memory in word-for-word memorization of texts takes considerable effort and skill.

One way to improve memory in domains where we are not very good at it is to link memory for the difficult material to other material that is easier to master, the sort of material that a Paleolithic nomad might have encountered frequently. We can convert the organization of lengthy verbal texts to locations in a familiar environment, for example, and then take an imaginary walk through the environment to find the bits of text that we need next. This is the "method of loci," used by ancient Greek orators to memorize speeches 2,500 years ago. It converts an abstract verbal domain into a concrete spatial one, allowing us to use our well-developed spatial memory to aid our feebler verbal memory.

Other crutches, such as "one is a bun, two is a shoe," work in similar ways. One associates successive objects with buns, shoes, and so on, then counts off to find the items to be recalled. We saw in Chapter 7 how poetry and music can also add structure to text, providing other organizing points for memorizing.

Taking all these ideas together shows how memory only seems general—we are skilled at trading off specialized, domain-specific memory mechanisms against one another to handle a wider variety of materials than our evolution equipped us for, exploiting the machinery of memory far beyond the applications for which it evolved.

Though effective, these methods require conscious effort and strategy to be successful. The learning does not take place by itself. The various memory mechanisms cannot be fully exploited without an even more mysterious capacity—consciousness.

● CONSCIOUSNESS AND PLANNING

In the scheme of evolution, every major structure and behavioral trait must have a purpose. Nothing remains for long if it does not confer some advantage to the organism. The eyes of fish, normally vital to survival, become redundant for groups of fish that find themselves trapped in caves, living their lives in total darkness. Released from the iron grasp of natural selection, the eyes of these fish regress over many generations of evolution to a remnant of what they once were. Following this punctuation event, the fish are blind, their eyes no longer functional. Similarly, groups of birds that find themselves isolated on islands that lack land predators sometimes lose the ability to fly, because the ability is no longer enforced by natural selection against poor flyers. This process has grounded many bird species throughout the world, including flightless rails and the famous dodo.

Some people think that consciousness may be just an **epiphenomenon**, a trait that accompanies some other trait. As brains grew larger, this argument goes, consciousness emerged as an epiphenomenon separate from the enhanced abilities in language, thinking, and other capabilities that drove the evolution of larger brains. Others think of it as a cultural invention, something that we learn in early childhood but that some human groups do not share (Dennett, 1991). Pinker (1997) complains that something about the topic makes some people, like the White Queen in *Through the Looking Glass*, believe six impossible things before breakfast. If you grant that consciousness is a complex process, though, it would have to confer an advantage if natural selection were to maintain it. Like eyes of the cave fish, consciousness would have degraded without a selective pressure preserving it.

How, then, did consciousness evolve? What is the source of the irresistible feeling in each of us that there is a sentience, someone inside us looking out through the eyes and listening through the ears?

We know that the neurological substrate of such a complex phenomenon as consciousness must have evolved over a very long time. So the first question to address must be its adaptive value. We must consider the puzzle of consciousness like we analyze any other adapted system, examining its functions and mechanisms in the context of useful interactions with the environment. We will find that consciousness and other high-level control systems serve to organize long-term sequences of behavior, sequences that require many steps and take advantage of past experience.

Functions of Consciousness

Techniques developed to investigate the various memory systems can be applied to the problem of the functions of consciousness. One such function emerged from studies of **priming** in long-term memory. In this procedure, a subject is given a stimulus that primes later responses. The type of priming used in the consciousness studies is based on word-stem completion, a procedure in which someone is presented with the first three letters of a word and is asked to complete the word. The stem ele_ _ _ _ _, for instance, could be completed as "elephant," as "elements," or probably as other words I haven't thought of. Now the psychologists present target words for brief durations, with each target word followed immediately by its three-letter stem. Subjects were instructed to complete each stem with any word other than the target word. With this some-what perverse task, failures to exclude target words indicate greater uncon-scious influences, because the primed word appears in behavior despite a conscious effort to suppress it. Successful exclusion, in contrast, indicates greater conscious influences (Merikle, Joordens, & Stolz, 1995).

Conscious influences were dominant at long durations (e.g., 214 ms.), meaning that if subjects took some care, they could, for instance, respond "elements" after having just seen the word *elephant*. But at short durations (e.g., 50 ms.), unconscious influences were dominant. Subjects would blurt out "elephant" despite having just seen it, followed sometimes by a "d'oh" experience upon realizing their mistake. The result implies that it takes time for conscious processes to suppress unconsciously primed responses, time presumably required for consciousness-specific neural processing to occur. Other priming designs have yielded analogous results, with only conscious responses able to escape the effects of priming.

The function of consciousness implied in these results, then, is to force behavior to follow a plan rather than to bend to the momentary availability of stimuli from the environment. Behavior follows a plan (to respond with an unprimed word) despite the greater availability of another alternative (the primed word), allowing humans to escape the tyranny of the environment. We can do things with consciousness that we cannot do without it. This is one sense in which consciousness escapes the accusation that it is nothing more than an epiphenomenon.

Other functions of consciousness have been defined by analyzing the requirements of guiding behavior by plans, asking what logical and neurological operations are necessary to achieve plan-based behavior. Some activities, such as withdrawing one's hand from a hot stove, occur without consciousness (the consciousness in this case comes after the behavior). Walking or chewing gum can continue without higher-level control. Other activities require conscious intervention. Here is a list of four types of mental activity that seem to be accompanied by internal experiences:

1. Planning

2. Executing plans

3. Directing attention

4. Retrieving long-term declarative memories

The list, based loosely on the work of Shallice (1972, 1978) and Norman and Shallice (1980), is given more as a way of organizing empirical data than as a complete theory of consciousness.

1. Planning

Behavioral **schemata**, plans for executing particular acts, must be set up in advance so that actions can proceed toward preexisting goals. These plans must be organized separately from motor activity, to be held until the appropriate time for their execution. The results of actions can then be checked against the goals as the behavior proceeds. This process ensures that the behavior continues to remain appropriate. Hammering a nail, for instance, will be more effective if the carpenter checks after each blow to see whether the nail is flush (Figure 8.12).

On a larger scale, an activity such as earning a B.A. degree requires a good deal more planning. One must set up a schema with a hierarchy of subordinate parts. To earn the degree, you must complete a major; to do that, you must take a psychology course; to pass the course, you must study this book; to do that, you must read the following sentence, and so on. In this way, the long-term planning function allows you to break large goals into smaller parts. Feedback from the environment guides the execution of each step. An internal record of the entire process, and your current place in it, is necessary to make the system work.

All plans are not equal, though. Humans seem to be skilled at executing some kinds of plans and inept at executing others. In general, activities that require someone to think more than a year ahead are prone to distortion. They must be based on careful written records and preestablished organization. A complementary problem is a human weakness in rational assessment

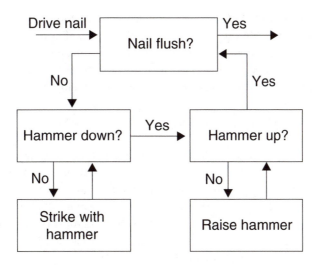

Figure 8.12 Feedback control of a simple act. Control flows around the loop at the top for each hammer blow, exiting when the hammer is flush. The scheme is hierarchical and can be extended to further layers for more complex tasks.

of long-term trends or the risks of large but infrequent catastrophes, reviewed in Chapter 6.

2. Executing Plans

Because some of the behavioral schemata require a long time for their completion, and because several goals are sometimes being pursued simultaneously, there must be a way of ordering the schemata and evaluating the priority of each. The priorities will change with the current circumstances. The goal of eating, for instance, is not important just after a meal, but it will consume all of your attention if you haven't eaten for 3 days. Thus priorities can be assigned both for inborn homeostatic motivations such as hunger and thirst and for learned activities such as earning a B.A.

In principle, the process of ordering schemata is no different from the process of ordering behavioral acts, except that the raw materials are the schemata themselves rather than motor patterns. Thus we might expect some of the same neurological machinery to organize both the action schemata and the priorities. Assigning priorities for action involves suppressing some behavioral schemata in favor of others; earning the B.A. sometimes must yield to more immediate goals such as eating. Thus the system must store unfinished schemata for reactivation at a later time. Simpler schemata, such as walking and chewing gum, can be executed simultaneously. Others, such as eating and earning a B.A., must be alternated in time, with a priority assigned to each. The regulation of behavior in humans must clearly involve hundreds of schemata. Each gains control of motor systems at different times, according to the needs of the individual and the present circumstances.

3. Directing Attention

Behavior is influenced not only by internal schemata but also by events in the sensory world. Sometimes the environment places such a great demand on cognitive resources that attention is diverted automatically, as in William James's (1893) famous case of a man meeting a bear in the forest. When this happens, other active schemata must be suspended as the orienting response and perhaps resulting actions dominate behavior. The same thing happens in the brain of the bear.

Having only one body, a person generally can do only one thing (or a few simple and compatible things) at a time, requiring that directing attention must be linked to the system that organizes behavioral priorities (Pinker, 1997). Attention becomes a way of quickly reorganizing priorities according to the needs of the moment. We might call this outside-in attention because the outside world demands the brain's sensory and motor capabilities.

Alternatively, attention can be controlled by internal schemata, for instance when one is searching for a particular kind of event in the world, such as one's name in a newspaper, or trying to think of a word that has not just been presented in a negative priming experiment. This can be called inside-out attention because the motivation for shifting activities comes from the inside. In both cases, selective attention must be controlled through the system that determines the behavior currently being executed.

4. Retrieving Long-Term Declarative Memories

The system that performs long-term planning for the individual and sets priorities for action is the only system that can make use of long-term memories for events. The adaptive usefulness of memories, after all, is in predicting the future. We work on the assumption that the future can be predicted from the past, and use memory (a) to aid in constructing action schemata, (b) to assign priorities to them, and (c) to direct attention. Memories concerning the stored action programs might be coded and organized in much the same way as memories concerning sensory events, and might be retrieved by the same master system.

This completes the list of neurological functions that require a master control process. Norman and Shallice (1980) give five characteristics of tasks that appear to require what they call "deliberate attentional resources."

1. They involve planning or decision making.

2. They involve components of trouble shooting.

3. They are ill-learned or contain novel sequences of actions.

4. They are judged to be dangerous or technically difficult.

5. They require overcoming a strong habitual response or resisting temptation.

If these are the functions of conscious control, where does the feeling of consciousness itself come in, the irresistible introspection that there is an "I" inside the head? Perhaps the "I" is a necessary consequence of a neurological control system capable of performing the functions listed here. It may result from the temporal integration of behaviors and schemata.

Planning of Behavior

There are strong correspondences between the functions of our hypothesized central organizing system and the prefrontal neocortex (Luria, 1970; Norman & Shallice, 1980), though other areas are certainly also involved. The functions of prefrontal cortex are closely tied to establishing and organizing plans. These are functions (a) and (b) above. On the principle that brain tissue is expensive for an animal to maintain, we can conclude that the prefrontal cortex is critically important for mammalian behavior, and especially for humans. It occupies 29% of the total cortex in humans, as seen in Figure 7.8, and a smaller but still impressive proportion in other mammals: 17% in chimpanzees, 11.5% in gibbons and macaque monkeys, 7% in dogs, and 3.5% in cats. Though there are anatomical differences between prefrontal regions in humans and in other animals (Passingham, 1973), removal of those areas has qualitatively similar effects across species. As you might expect, the deficits are generally more severe and persistent in animals with a larger prefrontal cortex.

Traditional anatomical methods, however, cannot reveal the anatomy of brain function in normal, intact humans. Different regions of prefrontal cortex have distinct functions that have been clarified partly by fMRI techniques in awake, behaving human observers. When holding a list of words in mind, the techniques show that two areas are activated: one in the left frontal lobe including Broca's area that participates in articulating words, and another in the auditory portions of the left temporal lobe (Awh et al., 1996). But when imagining a familiar melody, without lyrics, a comparable pattern of activity appears in right frontal and temporal areas (Halpern & Zatorre, 1999). Thus linguistic and nonlinguistic materials are processed in consciousness-related regions of opposite hemispheres.

Creating Plans

The first evidence for the role of prefrontal cortex in long-term regulation of behavior came from clinical observations of lesioned patients. Typically, these patients are "stimulus-bound"; they can deal with whatever happens to be in the environment, but they are also trapped by that environment. A frontally lesioned patient getting a coat to go outside, for instance, might be found half an hour later reading a magazine that had happened to be lying in view. When asked about this, the patient will remember that the coat was the original goal, but typically will be unconcerned that the goal was neglected.

Perhaps the most celebrated example of frontal damage is the case of Phineas Gage, a 19th-century construction worker who sustained damage to his frontal cortex in a stone quarrying accident. While he was tamping gunpowder with a long iron rod, the powder exploded and the rod shot obliquely through his face from below, exiting at the top of the head.

The first miraculous circumstance following the accident was that Gage survived; the second was that his deficit was carefully described (Harlow, 1868). Changes in his behavior were so marked that his co-workers commented after the accident that he was "no longer Gage." Previously a conscientious family man, he began to show excessive profanity, vacillation, capriciousness, poor planning, and uncontrolled impulsivity. He lost his family and began drinking.

Although such incidents are informative about the general nature of brain processes in the area affected, they are not precise enough to serve as a basis for theories of function. The closest thing we have to a histological reconstruction of the lesion is shown in Figure 8.13.

Better-documented cases come from primate studies and from war injuries. Each war since the Franco-Prussian war of 1870-1871 has yielded plentiful cases of frontal head trauma. Early clinical observations were formalized in a series of experiments on primates with lesions of prefrontal cortex. Jacobsen (1936) found that prefrontally lesioned chimpanzees have

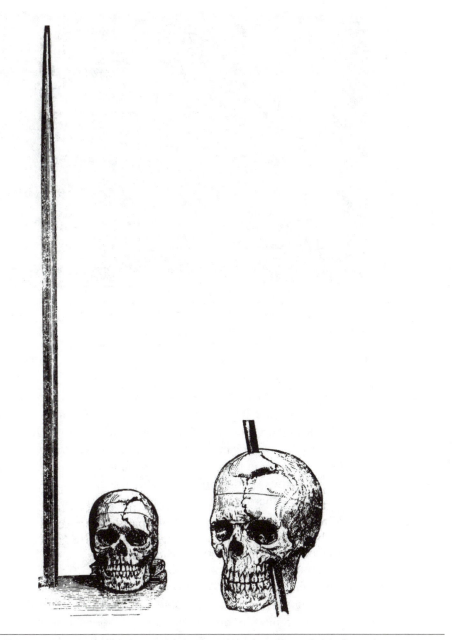

Figure 8.13 Phineas Gage's skull injury and the bar that shot through his frontal cortex.

Figure 8.14   An apparatus for testing delayed response in primates. The procedure is automated and computer-controlled.

particular difficulty with tasks requiring a delayed response. In modern versions of such tests, shown in Figure 8.14, the animal picks a button that is illuminated with the same pattern as another button. The monkey receives a reward such as a peanut or a raisin for a correct choice. The lesioned animal has no trouble in picking the correct button.

Now the experimenter illuminates one button with a pattern, and illuminates the other buttons only after a delay. The animal must wait until the choice buttons are illuminated before it can claim its reward. Although a normal monkey or chimpanzee has no difficulty with such tasks, a frontally lesioned animal now chooses at random.

At first the animal seems to have a memory deficit, but other tests show that memory is intact. The "frontal" monkey has no difficulty in performing a discrimination between two objects learned before the operation, and can even learn new discriminations, though more slowly than normal. If a monkey is always rewarded with a peanut placed under a cigar box but not under an ashtray, for instance, he soon learns to look under the cigar box. If the stimuli to be discriminated are presented one at a time instead of simultaneously, however, the monkey has serious difficulties (Iverson, 1967). The problem is not with memory, but with the temporal organization of events; the animal cannot assemble events taking place at different times and places into a meaningful whole.

To further investigate this deficit, monkeys were given choices with more than two alternatives. One object was always rewarded while the others were unrewarded. The animals were allowed to investigate only one object per trial.

Monkeys with lesions of the temporal lobes (the location of high-level visual areas) had difficulty in searching, requiring many trials before happening upon the rewarded object. Frontally lesioned monkeys, in contrast, had no difficulty with search—instead, they seemed incapable of sticking to the successful choice once it was discovered (Pribram, 1971). The temporal animals behaved like normals once the sensory problem had been solved, but the frontal animals continued to make errors. Though capable of receiving and interpreting information coming in through the senses, they were unable to make use of that information in a behavioral schema.

Human prefrontal damage. The ability to organize events into a meaningful whole would seem to be central to the information-processing abilities that support consciousness. This makes it useful to study human patients with prefrontal lesions in more detail. These patients share a number of symptoms in common (Fuster, 1980). They have a severe handicap in planning, finding it difficult not only to formulate new plans but also to execute them. Carrying out plans requires establishing future goals and then updating and retaining information in order to attain them. This degree of internal organization appears to be impossible for the patients.

Frontal patients also perceive the world with excessive concreteness. There is a constriction of the scope and complexity of both perception and thinking (Fuster, 1980). The disability is not absolute, however, for the patients can abstract some simple concepts and situations. The patients seem to lack the inclination to exert the mental effort needed to carry through their plans. They lose control of their behavior, as in the example above of the patient who neglected to retrieve his coat. The patient lives in the here and now, able to perform routine or practiced tasks, but unable to handle new challenges from the environment.

The deficit also affects the production of language; Broca's area, after all, is at the posterior edge of the lateral frontal cortex. Many lateral prefrontal lesions reduce the amount of spontaneous speech, and restrict the amount and range of narrative expression (Luria, 1970). Sentences are reduced in length and complexity, as would be expected from deficits in planning and in the ability to establish internal temporal order. The damage in these cases generally includes the cortex just anterior to Broca's area, in the left hemisphere.

Organizing Goals and Priorities

In addition to forming behavioral schemata and allowing them to be carried out, the prefrontal cortex organizes the internal world and manages the schemata themselves. This characteristic can be tested in an indirect form of the delayed reaction task: an animal works to receive a token (such as a poker chip), and later is given an opportunity to use the token to obtain a food reward. The token has no value in itself; it is only a symbol of a future value.

A token world. Living in a token environment, chimpanzees learn to work for tokens, and eventually the tokens assume a value in themselves. The chimps hoard them, and even attempt to steal them from one another (Figure 8.15). Some have been known to exchange them for sexual favors.

The situation is different when a prefrontally lesioned chimpanzee is introduced to the token world. Though the animal has the physical and sensory abilities needed to earn tokens, it does not work for them (Jacobsen, Wolfe, & Jackson, 1935). The animal fails to make the token a symbol of things of value, to impose an internal organization on intrinsically worthless objects. Thus we can conclude that prefrontal cortex is necessary to enable the animal to organize the token-world in terms of future values. With humans the situation is more complex, for frontally damaged humans can sometimes value tokens, but usually they don't bother. Again, the frontal deficit has its contact with cognitive processes through motivation.

The token-as-symbol has been carried a step further by Premack and Premack (1972), who trained the chimpanzee Sarah to arrange tokens in strings to construct grammatical sentences. Here meaning is carried not by a single token, but by an organized sequence of tokens. By extension, we can think of human words as tokens signifying meanings in the outside world. The tokens have become internal organizations rather than pieces of plastic, but their function is similar.

Attention

There is a close relationship between consciousness and attention. In fact, the word *mind* came into English as a verb relating to attention, as in "Jane, mind the teacher" (Ryle, 1949). Because attention can be defined in terms of the activation of schemata performed in the task of organizing goals and priorities, we can expect the neurological mechanisms controlling attention to be related to those producing and managing behavioral schemata. The same prefrontal systems that are concerned with schemata might also be involved in attention.

Figure 8.15 Chimpanzees functioning in a token economy. (a) Working to earn tokens. (b) Exchanging tokens for food in a vending machine. (c) Once the tokens acquire a value of their own, chimpanzees try to steal them from one another.

Signs of an anticipatory attentional role for prefrontal cortex can also be recorded as potentials from the scalp. Because it is easier to control attention in humans, much of the work on the electrophysiology of attention has been performed with humans. Evoked-potential techniques are ideal for recording attentional changes.

The CNV. Suppose that you are asked to press a button as quickly as possible after a light flashes, and suppose further that a warning tone comes on a few seconds before each flash. Between the warning tone and the flash a surface-negative potential will develop over frontal areas of your cortex, ending abruptly with the motor act. This is the **contingent negative variation** (CNV), a long-lasting steady potential that appears when an event is expected to involve an action or a decision (Walter, 1964). The CNV has at least two components. One, developing over the center of the head just before a movement, is a "readiness potential." It is associated with the motor act itself. The other is slower, also negative, and is more frontal in its distribution. It appears in delayed response and delayed matching-to-sample tasks, but does not necessarily require a motor response (Figure 8.16). Tasks evoking a CNV are similar to those classically used to test for the function of prefrontal cortex, and in fact CNVs are seen in monkeys over the prefrontal cortex when they perform delayed-response tasks.

The CNV may also be related to another of the hypothesized functions of consciousness, the memory function. Of course a CNV cannot appear in a naive subject, for something must be anticipated as in Figure 8.16 for the negativity to appear. The CNV is a response to a future event. This line of research, then, leads to a picture of continually changing potentials biasing regions of the cortex, sometimes potentiating and sometimes inhibiting ongoing activity, in response to both past and future stimulation. Selective attention would result from particular patterns of DC shifts.

Electrical Stimulation and Recording

Another way to study the electrophysiology of consciousness is with electrical brain stimulation on conscious humans, to measure the relationship between stimulation and awareness. The relationship has not proved to be a simple one, even in primary sensory cortex (Crick & Koch, 1998).

In one of the first investigations of this question, Libet (1973) recorded directly from the cortical surface of humans. Such recordings can be performed during brain surgery for other neurological problems, while the patient remains awake. The skin can then be stimulated while evoked responses are measured from the exposed somatosensory cortex. Paradoxically, the minimal electrical stimulus needed for conscious report in this case is stronger than the stimulus needed to elicit an electrical evoked response. Figure 8.17 shows a range of stimulation intensity where the cortex clearly responds, but no sensation results. We must conclude that conscious experience and firing of neurons in primary somatosensory cortex are two

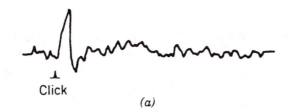

Click

(a)

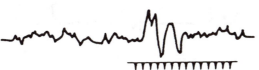

Flashes

(b)

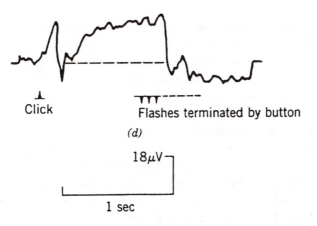

Click   Flashes

(c)

Click   Flashes terminated by button

(d)

18μV⌐

1 sec

Figure 8.16 A CNV from the frontal region of a human brain. (a) Brain evoked response to auditory click. (b) Evoked response to visual flashes. (c) Evoked response to click followed by flashes. (d) Evoked response when the subject was instructed to press a button when the flashes began, with the click as a warning.

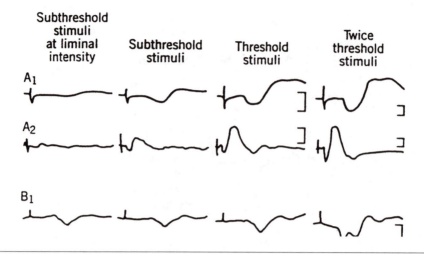

Figure 8.17 Averaged evoked potentials recorded from exposed somatosensory cortex in patients undergoing surgery for Parkinson's disease. A and B are two patients. Only the stimuli in the twice threshold condition were reported reliably.

different processes, so that at least some of the activity in sensory cortex is unconscious.

Cortical stimulation. An even more surprising result came from further experiments using direct electrical stimulation of somatosensory cortex. A single electrical pulse to the cortex could not be perceived at any reasonable current strength, although a train of pulses could be perceived. The pulse train had to be quite long, 0.5 to 0.6 seconds in most cases, before the patient reported the stimulation (Figure 8.18). At the same time, cortical electrical responses were recorded from a nearby electrode. The figure shows that each pulse of the train was adequate to evoke firing in nearby neurons.

This result had a disturbing implication; if we cannot report conscious sensation until the cortex has been stimulated for half a second, how does consciousness remain in "real time"? Clearly, we do not live half a second behind events in the outside world. There are two answers to the question.

First, stimulation of the skin, unlike stimulation of the cortex, does yield an immediate conscious report to even the briefest stimulus. Presumably, the sensory signal has been preprocessed by subcortical centers into a form immediately recognizable by the cortex. The coding of the direct electrical stimulation, in contrast, is inappropriate for conscious perception. Perhaps the electrically evoked signal must travel down to the thalamus and then return to the cortex on sensory fibers before perception takes place,

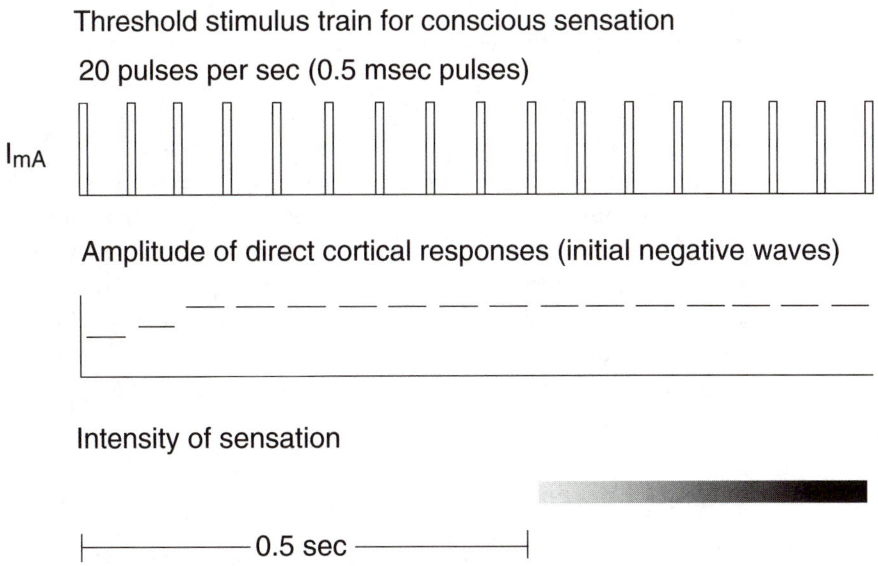

Threshold stimulus train for conscious sensation

20 pulses per sec (0.5 msec pulses)

Amplitude of direct cortical responses (initial negative waves)

Intensity of sensation

|———————— 0.5 sec ————————|

Figure 8.18 Schematic results of direct electrical stimulation of somatosensory cortex. Cortical responses are measured from electrodes nearby. Reported sensation begins about 500 msec after the start of stimulation and 400 msec after evoked responses to each pulse have reached their maximum value.

although even that would take much less than 0.5 sec. It seems that a lot of neural processing is necessary before the results of this unnatural stimulus can enter consciousness. The nature of this processing remains unknown.

The second answer to the puzzle of the half-second delay came from experiments where a subject compared the apparent time of onset of the cortical stimulus to the onset of other more natural stimuli. In these experiments, the time of onset coincided with the time of the natural stimuli. Somehow the timing of the cortical stimulus train was referred back to the first pulse of the train, even though conscious sensation was delayed (Libet, 1973). Clearly, extensive cortical processing must occur before conscious processes become involved in evaluating even the simplest stimulus.

Memory and Consciousness

A common test for the presence of consciousness and selective attention in the real world reveals a close connection between consciousness and memory: "Johnny, were you paying attention? What was the teacher saying?" In this example, the teacher uses memory as a criterion for conscious processing.

Only the contents of memory are available to consciousness; the process of recovering a memory is not conscious. The retrieval process need not interfere with ongoing behavior, and therefore there is no need for a high-level attentional processor in retrieval. It is only when a memory proves difficult to retrieve that conscious intervention is necessary. This might occur if other long-term memories must be recovered and applied to the problem of reconstructing a less accessible memory. In trying to recall the name of my third-grade teacher, for instance, it is helpful to recall other events in my childhood so that the content-addressing mechanism of long-term memory can be activated.

Conscious Effort in Retrieval

Recall strategies have been investigated with the "tip of the tongue" phenomenon. William James (1893) describes the experience in his vivid way:

> Suppose we try to recall a forgotten name. The state of our consciousness is peculiar. There is a gap therein; but no mere gap. It is a gap that is intensely active. A sort of wraith of the name is in it, beckoning us in a given direction, making us at moments tingle with the sense of our closeness and then letting us sink back without the longed-for term. If wrong names are proposed to us, this singularly definite gap acts immediately so as to negate them. They do not fit into its mold. And the gap of one word does not feel like the gap of another.(p. 251)

James's gap was studied by reading to students definitions of infrequent words such as *apse, nepotism, cloaca, ambergris,* and *sampan* (Brown & McNeill, 1966). In most cases, a student either guessed the word immediately or had no idea what it was. But in about 13% of the cases, the word elicited the tip-of-the-tongue phenomenon. Brown & McNeill describe the feeling as a mild torment, something like the brink of a sneeze. When the word was found, the subject's relief was considerable.

It turned out that the subjects often knew some characteristics of the elusive word, such as number of syllables or syllabic stress. They could frequently identify patterns similar in sound or meaning to the target word, all before the word was successfully retrieved. Because memory is accessed by its content, rather than its address or location as in a computer, conscious strategies were necessary to search meanings and recall the words.

Delayed Response and Object Constancy

Memory and frontal functions are also linked through the delayed-response task shown in Figure 8.14, where an animal must remember the position or identity of a cue during a forced delay to receive a reward. What is the usefulness of such a talent in the real world? One application appears in Piaget's (1973) concept of **object constancy**, that objects in the real world retain their identity despite momentary disappearances and transformations. Object constancy in turn requires an ability to process objects in relation to their contexts. This is one of the hallmarks of prefrontal function outlined above.

The object-constancy tests of Piaget were "monkified" by showing a monkey a grape, then hiding it under one of three inverted baskets. The baskets were then moved and exchanged in shell-game fashion before the monkey was given a chance to retrieve the grape. Normal monkeys performed the task easily, but frontally lesioned animals performed randomly (Anderson, Hunt, Vander Stoep, & Pribram, 1976). Once the grape had disappeared beneath a basket, the frontal monkeys could no longer keep track of its hidden movements. Again, frontal cortex was necessary to impose order on the sensory world.

In conclusion, a set of neurological adaptations manages long-term behavior in higher mammals. The evolved adaptations are associated with the terms *consciousness, attention, planning,* and *long-term episodic memory,* all of which are aspects of this behavioral control system. They set priorities for behavior, using past experience as a guide, and monitor progress toward goals. They enable an animal or a person to escape from the needs of the moment, looking beyond the here and now to sustained and powerful interactions with a larger environment.

DISCUSSION QUESTIONS ●

1. How do evolved perceptual mechanisms limit the sorts of artificial environments that humans produce?
2. If perception involves so many different mechanisms and capabilities, why do we perceive only one perceptual world?
3. Wouldn't it be better if memory recorded everything in our experience faithfully?
4. Why do some important human psychological functions remain unconscious?

● FURTHER READING

Goldstein, E. B. (2002). *Sensation and perception*. 6th ed. Pacific Grove, CA: Wadsworth-Thomson Learning.

Probably the clearest textbook in the field of perception, Goldstein's volume explains perceptual principles and their mechanisms at a level appropriate for an undergraduate psychology or neuroscience major.

Gregory, R. L. (1997) *Eye and brain: The psychology of seeing.* 5th ed. Princeton, NJ: Princeton University Press.

With an engaging style that is more like telling stories than explicating science, Richard Gregory, one of the grand masters of perception, describes the visual system from the workings of the eye to the subtleties of perceptual experience.

Pinker, S. (1997). *How the mind works*. New York: Norton.

Perception, memory, consciousness, the meaning of life—it's all here, written in a witty and compelling style. Highly recommended.

CHAPTER 9

EVOLUTIONARY PSYCHIATRY

"Of all the tyrannies on human kind
The worst is that which persecutes the mind."

— John Dryden (1631-1700)

Mental illnesses are among the most debilitating, and the least understood, of human maladies. These disorders, with primarily behavioral symptoms, have proved resistant to conventional medical attempts at cures.

Most human diseases are the result of attacks by a vast array of microbes, parasites, and viruses, opposed by our well-developed immune systems. Mental illnesses, though, have no obvious origins in foreign organisms attacking the body—indeed, many of them have more links to genetics than to conventional pathology.

Another contrast between mental illnesses and most bodily diseases is in the nature of the symptoms. Conventional bodily diseases are accompanied by such symptoms as fever, pain, lethargy, and changes in appetite, often caused not directly by pathogens but rather by the actions of our own immune systems in fighting infection. Fever, for instance, results from the immune system changing the internal thermostat's set point in the brain to fight bacterial infection. Other symptoms such as internal bleeding or fluid in the lungs may be due to direct effects of an illness. Both types of symptoms are outside the normal repertoire of bodily function.

Many of the symptoms of mental illnesses, in contrast, are exaggerations or distortions of normal behavioral patterns. Immune systems are helpless against them. The behavioral patterns are adapted mechanisms for dealing with life challenges, mechanisms that are universal; it is only their exaggeration and their appearance in inappropriate contexts that are pathological.

● FOUR CLASSES OF MENTAL ILLNESS

If mental illnesses are linked to genetics, we must look to evolution to understand them. Viewed in this way, the illnesses can be divided into four classes. The first class consists of those diseases that exaggerate normal, adapted behavioral schemas; examples are phobias and obsessive-compulsive disorder. Second are those illnesses that may confer a benefit under some environmental circumstances, such as depressions. Third, some illnesses such as schizophrenia reduce fitness without any clear benefit to its victims or to others. Finally, other problems such as drug addiction may not be the results of pathology at all, but rather are reactions of normal humans to environmental conditions for which evolution has not prepared them.

Using this new method of categorization, the following sections review a sampling of mental illnesses, concentrating on the roles of evolution and genetics in defining and maintaining them.

● EXAGGERATIONS OF NORMAL BEHAVIORS

Phobias

An otherwise normal teenager spots a tiny spider crawling across her desk and suddenly melts into a terrified puddle of screams and tears. She knows that her overreaction is inappropriate, but can't help herself. She has a **phobia**, an exaggerated, irrational fear of some object or situation. There are two kinds of phobias, **specific phobias** that are triggered by particular stimuli and **social phobias** to interpersonal situations that can take the form of an extreme shyness or fear of strangers.

Table 9.1   Objects of common phobias

Animals	Places	Social Situations
spiders	heights	shyness
snakes	closed spaces	strangers
rats	darkness	
cats		

One would hope that phobias, if they are exaggerations of normal tendencies, would be directed at the greatest dangers that we face. Table 9.1 lists some of the most common phobias by category; Table 9.2 shows the greatest real dangers for Americans. A glance at the two tables shows that there is almost no overlap between the list of most-feared things and the list of most-dangerous things (the falls in Table 9.2 are mostly short-distance falls by the elderly at home, not dives from great heights). The lists indicate that phobias probably are not learned, because they fail to engage the greatest dangers of modern life. The statistically most dangerous objects, automobiles and handguns, are seldom the subjects of phobias.

An understanding of phobias begins with the observation that all the common phobias relate to dangers that would have faced our nomadic ancestors. Building fears of these things into the human mind has the advantage that they will be avoided even at the first experiences with them. If a healthy fear of objects and situations that presented danger to our ancestors improved their chances of survival and reproduction, a selective pressure for the evolution of adapted fears would result.

Those who suffer from clinically dysfunctional phobias may simply be at the extreme of apprehensiveness about the objects that all of us treat with some amount of trepidation. The disadvantage of managing fears with adapted genetic mechanisms is that the fears do not change when the environment changes. We live in an industrial society but are stuck with a nomad's fears.

If phobias are exaggerations of normal fears, we might expect to see them in other primates as well. Indeed, many monkey species seem to show unlearned fears of the same sorts that we have. Rhesus monkeys raised in an animal colony, who have never seen a snake, show all the signs of terror when a hose used to wash down their room gets away and swishes across the floor. They scream, jump to the backs of their cages, and display a toothy fear grimace (I have seen this reaction in animals housed at a research facility at the Stanford Medical Center, Stanford, California). The fact that the hose presents no real danger doesn't lessen the panic.

Table 9.2   Risks of death per year

Accident	Risk	Disease	Risk
motor vehicle	1/7,000	heart disease	1/400
gunshot	1/10,000	cancer	1/600
falls	1/20,000	stroke	1/2,000
poison	1/40,000	flu/pneumonia	1/3,000
crossing street	1/60,000		

Source: Cathy Lynn Grossman, *USA Today,* 2001.

Functions of Phobias

For phobias to remain in the human genome, they must confer some benefit. Phobias, or less intense tendencies in the phobic direction, should make people on average more successful. There is indeed some evidence that the objects of common phobias are detected faster and more reliably by people who are fearful of those objects than by others. In a world where these things presented real dangers, the advantage of quick detection is clear.

An experiment on common objects of phobias asked a normal range of subjects to search for fear-relevant pictures (snakes or spiders) hidden in grid-pattern arrays of fear-irrelevant pictures (flowers or mushrooms). In a second condition, they searched for fear-irrelevant pictures. The subjects found the fear-relevant pictures more quickly than fear-irrelevant ones (Öhman, Flykt, & Esteves, 2001). Furthermore, the search for fear-relevant pictures was unaffected by the location of the target in the display or by the number of distracters.

This result suggests that fearful people could search for the fear-relevant targets all at once, in parallel, while they searched for fear-irrelevant targets serially, one at a time. People who were specifically fearful of snakes but not spiders (or vice versa) showed facilitated search for the feared objects but did not differ from controls in search for nonfeared fear-relevant or fear-irrelevant targets. Thus, evolutionarily relevant threatening stimuli were effective in capturing attention, and this effect was further facilitated if the stimulus was emotionally provocative.

Specific phobias are more common in females, but social phobias are about equally frequent in both sexes (American Psychiatric Association, 1994). There is a theory, with an SSSM tinge, that specific phobias seem less common in males because boys in our society are pressured to hide or overcome their fears (Fodor, 1982). It is not clear how this theory accounts for the choice of phobic objects or for the unlearned, automatic nature of phobias and phobia-like fears.

Phobias are inconvenient, sometimes embarrassing, but seldom debilitating. Other disorders cause more serious problems.

Obsessive-Compulsive Disorder

Roy, an intelligent, articulate boy from a stable family background, has a problem—he feels compelled to wash his hands hundreds of times every day. He is so consumed with it that there is no time for normal activities (Rapoport, 1991). Though his hands become red and raw, still he washes and washes and washes. Why? When asked, he offers vague fears of dirt, contamination, disease. He knows that the behavior is ruining his life, but for him washing is the most important thing he does.

Roy suffers from **obsessive-compulsive disorder** (OCD), a malady whose principal symptom is a compulsion to perform some otherwise rational act to excess. The disorder presents with a wide variety of compulsive acts; usually, a victim is affected by only one or a small number of them. One sufferer may need to keep everything in her environment perfectly neat and orderly, with not a pencil or a hairpin out of place. Another may feel compelled to check that all the doors and windows are locked before leaving home; after they are all checked, though, the victim feels a dread that something may have been forgotten, and the checking starts all over again. In severe cases, constant checking prevents the victim from leaving home at all. Still others must keep their homes so spotless that they spend all their time cleaning.

Like the case of phobias, OCD is an exaggeration of a set of adapted traits that all of us share. In OCD, traits that are advantageous for most people become pathological when pushed too far. High standards become perfectionism, attention to detail becomes obsession with trivia, cleanliness becomes obsessive washing. The adapted traits are inherited with a great degree of variability—some of us are slobs, whereas others are neat and still others have their lives ruined by obsessive behaviors. Everyone has a need for some degree of order, and many people have little rituals that add comfort to their lives. The behaviors descend into OCD if the sufferer experiences them as unwanted and they interfere with leading a normal life. Like Roy, most OCD patients know that they engage in bizarre rituals, but they can't stop themselves.

Treatment

Historically, cases of OCD were treated as weakness of character or dysfunctional parenting, and the treatment was to admonish the helpless victim to cease and desist, with greater or lesser degrees of pressure. The strategy was uniformly unsuccessful.

Most mental illnesses are related to neurotransmitter systems in the brain that transmit messages between neurons managing motivation, mood, and reward. These neurons are buried deep in the oldest parts of the vertebrate forebrain, in the limbic system and related structures. The two families of neurotransmitters of most concern, the **catecholamines** and the **indoleamines**, are synthesized in the body from amino acids, the components of dietary proteins. Catecholamines begin from the amino acid tyrosine. Through successive biochemical steps it is transformed into dopa, then **dopamine**, then **norepinephrine**, and finally **epinephrine**. Indoleamines begin with the amino acid tryptophan, which is transformed into 5-hydroxytryptophan and then into **serotonin**. Each of the steps in biosynthesis is catalyzed by an enzyme, so that manipulation of either a transmitter or the relevant enzyme can change transmitter levels in the brain.

OCD is related to inherited abnormalities in neurotransmitter function, and the best treatment is a combination of behavior therapy and medication. The most common medications to combat OCD are clomipramine (Anafranil), fluvoxamine (Luvox), sertraline (Zoloft), fluoxetine (Prozac), and paroxetine (Paxil). All are serotonin reuptake inhibitors, increasing the amount of serotonin at CNS (central nervous system) synapses (Kronig et al., 1999). Whether normal ranges of need for order also correlate with CNS serotonin levels is unknown.

Here a cause-and-effect problem arises: Is OCD caused by low or widely fluctuating serotonin levels, or do the low levels result from years of obsessive-compulsive behavior? The test is to administer the drugs that restore normal serotonin levels and see whether the abnormal behavior abates. Relief from the compulsions indicates that the serotonin levels contribute to the disease. If symptoms remain, then the low serotonin may be a consequence of an underlying disorder that causes both OCD and low serotonin levels.

The fact that the major medications both reduce the symptoms and increase available serotonin argues for the first alternative, that neurotransmitter anomalies, presumably with genetic origins, cause the disease. Unfortunately, the medications do not cure the disease: they only suppress the symptoms. Patients must continue taking the medications for life, even after the symptoms have abated.

If such a debilitating disease has genetic roots, evolutionary theory would seem to require that natural selection should eventually reduce the incidence of the disease. There are circumstances, however, under which OCD might persist at low to moderate levels even after evolution has established an equilibrium. Often it is advantageous to individuals in a population if there is some variation in a trait. Variability in the immune systems of my relatives, for example, is advantageous because at least some of them are likely to survive any disease epidemic.

Applying this idea to OCD, if the amount of need for order is selected to be optimized in the population, and the degree of variability in the trait is also optimized, a group with pathological symptoms might result. They would be at one end of the normal bell curve that describes the distribution of most traits, including personality traits. In the case of personality systems, individuals who are very high or very low on particular traits would appear to be at a disadvantage, but there is a broad range of genetic variation in the middle of the distribution underlying a range of viable strategies. This approach is consistent with attempts to interpret psychopathology in terms of maladaptive extremes on personality dimensions (MacDonald, 1998), and in fact, clinicians recognize wide variations in the severity of the disease. Unfortunately, studies of entire populations including both "normal" subjects and OCD sufferers, measuring the quantitative degree of symptoms in each person, have not been done to test this hypothesis.

The symptoms of this class of diseases can be characterized as exaggerations or extremes of normal personality traits, and like those traits, symptoms of these diseases are more or less continually present

BALANCES OF COSTS AND BENEFITS •

These diseases are normally classified as major psychoses, serious diseases that incapacitate the patient. The symptoms of these psychoses tend to wax and wane over time, often staying with the patient for life.

Unipolar Depression

Everyone goes through a depression at some time in life, usually in response to a personal loss such as chronic illness, loss of a family member, or the end of a love affair. There is inactivity, social withdrawal, a feeling of sadness and pessimism, eating and sleeping disturbances. This kind of depression serves the useful function of forcing a person to withdraw from normal activities at a time when their effectiveness is reduced.

Depression that arises for no obvious reason, and disables a person for months or longer, is a profound psychopathology called **unipolar depression**. It has been described as "chronic exaggerations of innate behavioral potentials with which all human beings are equipped by virtue of their humanity" (Stevens & Price, 2000). It has been known at least since Hippocrates' description of melancholia 2,400 years ago. Unipolar depression is almost twice as common in women as in men (Kessler et al., 1994), and often strikes later in life than the other major mental illnesses. The disorder is moderately heritable, with statistical evidence that the genes responsible for promoting it may be the same genes that promote **generalized anxiety disorder**, a chronic anxiety that again has no clear environmental cause (Smoller, Finn, & White, 2000).

Many of those who suffer from depression will also suffer from generalized anxiety disorder at some point in their lives (Mineka, Watson, & Clark, 1998), suggesting that the two diseases are linked. Anxiety, of course, can also be seen as an adaptation to increase alertness and arousal at times of real danger. Its pathological version, though, is associated with almost continuous worry about such issues as money, work, social relationships, or illness itself (Barlow, 1988). The resulting chronic stress can result in immune system malfunctions and gastrointestinal upset due to overactivity of the sympathetic branch of the autonomic nervous system. Normally, this part of the nervous system prepares an animal for fight or flight, in this case inappropriately. So again, normal adapted traits become pathological when exaggerated and triggered without cause.

Despite the general limitation that pathological depression should have no environmental cause, there is evidence that a processing bias in interpreting life events precedes episodes of clinical depression. The bias is tested with a scrambled sentences test, in which sentences can be interpreted in various ways. High scores on the scrambled sentences test, reflecting a negative processing bias, predicted depression symptoms measured 4 to 6 weeks later, even after controlling for concurrent and past depression (Rude, Wenzlaff, Gibbs, Vane, & Whitney, 2002). Those who interpreted events in the worst possible light at the time of the test, then, were more likely than others to show symptoms of clinical depression several weeks later, implying that the victims of depression in the study created in their own minds the negative events that triggered their depression. The study implies that the difference between normal bouts of depression, caused by identifiable life events, and pathological depression, with no obvious cause, might be as simple as a change in the interpretation of everyday events.

Treatment

Unipolar depression is associated with low activities of brain receptors for norepinephrine and serotonin (Schildkraut & Kety, 1967). Drugs that

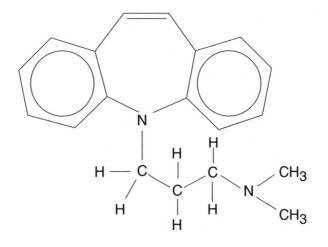

Figure 9.1 Molecular structure of the tricyclic antidepressant imipramine. Other tricyclics have the same three-ring core but different radicals branching out from it.

increase levels of these and chemically related neurotransmitters often alleviate the symptoms, revealing that depression has a basis in brain biochemistry. One class of such drugs is the tricyclic antidepressants, so named because their molecular formula contains three ringlike structures (Figure 9.1). These drugs block the reuptake of norepinephrine and serotonin, and to a lesser extent dopamine, allowing more of the neurotransmitters to remain in the synaptic contacts between neurons (Stahl, 2000). Examples are imipramine (Tofranil) and amitriptyline (Elavil).

A more recently developed class of antidepressants is the selective serotonin reuptake inhibitors such as fluoxetine (Prozac). These drugs have fewer side effects than the tricyclic antidepressants, probably because they are more specific in their targets, but for the same reason, they may not be as effective as tricyclics in combating severe depression (Moeller & Voltz, 2000).

Some of the psychopathology of depression may result from the differences between modern environments and the environments in which humans evolved (Nesse & Williams, 1996). For example, rates of depression may be influenced by contemporary trends toward families removing themselves from close kinship ties as a source of social support. In the Paleolithic world, privacy was not an issue, nor was sustained leisure. Lying in bed all day feeling depressed was not usually an option for people who had no permanent beds. Because nomadic lifestyles demanded some degree of physical activity from everyone, it is perhaps significant that activity can somewhat alleviate the symptoms of unipolar depression.

Bipolar Depression

Manic-depressive psychosis—**bipolar depression**—is a very dangerous disease. Left untreated, the mortality rate is about 1 in 5, not from the direct physical effects of the disease but from suicide during the depressive phase. In this disease, periods of severe depression alternate with periods of excessively expansive moods that are similar to the feelings of normal people taking cocaine or amphetamines. There is a feeling of power, of invincibility. The manic sleeps little or not at all for weeks, spends money recklessly, and makes grandiose plans. Like the other psychoses, this disease differs from the mood swings that we all experience in their severity and in the smaller influence of environmental triggers.

There is enormous variability in the balance, timing, and severity of manic and depressive phases between patients, and even over time in a single patient. Some suffer from a milder version of the disease, where the manic phases are called hypomania. Either of the phases might be more lengthy or more severe, and the duration of the cycles (from mania to depression and back again) varies from weeks to years.

Bipolar illness tends to strike men and women equally, at a younger age than unipolar depression. The disorder tends to run in families, a fact that could be due to either environmental or genetic influences, because families have both environment and heredity in common. Both nature and culture, however, provide natural experiments that allow the two factors to be separated. Nature provides a controlled experiment in the contrast between monozygotic and dizygotic twins. Since the monozygotic twins come from the same egg, their genes are identical, and any condition fully determined by heredity will be identical in both of them. Identical twins are always of the same sex, for example. The similarity of traits in a group of pairs of twins is measured in a **concordance rate**, the percentage of twin pairs who share the trait. Bipolar illness is more strongly heritable than unipolar depression, showing a higher concordance in monozygotic twins (Figure 9.2) than in dizygotic twins (Gershon et al., 1976). The concordance is similar whether the twins are reared apart or together, and in cases of adoption is correlated with biological rather than adoptive parents, consistent with a genetic origin of the disease (Kelsoe, 1997).

Unlike victims of the other major psychoses, some of the sufferers from milder forms of this disease have a distinct advantage during the manic phase. They can be or feel as though they are extraordinarily creative, especially in art, literature, and music. Indeed, an astonishing proportion of the great works of literature and music have been produced by people who show

Figure 9.2 Monozygotic (identical) and dizygotic (fraternal) twins. In monozygotic twins, the two halves of the embryo separate after the first division of the egg cell, and each matures into a complete infant. Dizygotic twins come from two eggs released in the same cycle and fertilized separately.

evidence of having suffered from bipolar illness—an unweighted average of five studies of writers and poets cited by Jamison (1995) finds an average of 35% of them to have suffered from a manic-depressive illness, as opposed to about 1% in the general population.

The phenomenon is not a new one: over half of published British poets born between 1705 and 1805 were manic-depressives (Jamison, 1993). Artists with the syndrome include Vincent van Gogh, Paul Gauguin, and Georgia O'Keefe; writers and poets include Mark Twain, Walt Whitman, Hermann Hesse, Edgar Allan Poe, Ernest Hemingway, Tennessee Williams, Ezra Pound, Virginia Woolf, Anne Sexton, and Sylvia Plath; composers include Gustav Mahler, Charles Mingus, Cole Porter, Peter Tchaikovsky, and Robert Schumann. A smaller number of exceptionally creative people have suffered from periodic depression, without any identifiable mania.

Because most of these great artists produced their work long before psychoses were defined in their present way, evidence of their bipolar illnesses was gleaned from their letters, diaries, and the observations of their friends and relatives. Even military leaders such as Alexander the Great and Napoleon may have suffered bipolar swings, conquering the world in one phase and contemplating suicide in the other. Perhaps significantly, violent mood swings do not seem to be common in great scientists.

Not everyone can attain the creative heights of geniuses who are also bipolar, and society could not support a large number of such people. But their extraordinary accomplishments may pave the way for their relatives and descendants, enhancing the inclusive fitness of the manic-depressive geniuses and maintaining the genes that facilitate their illness at a low level in the population. Not all manic episodes are associated with creativity, though—most experience it as a period of extreme irritability, suspiciousness, or destructive rage (Carroll, 1991).

Treatment

The biochemistry of bipolar disorder is quite distinct from that of unipolar depression, despite the similarity of the depressive symptoms. Bipolar psychosis is treated effectively in many cases with lithium, which, in contrast to the complex drugs administered in other conditions, is an element, a light metal. It is one of the smallest and simplest ions in the periodic table. Though lithium is known to affect catecholaminergic and cholinergic neurons and also influences amino acid neurotransmitters (Fieve, 1979), the precise mechanism by which it works remains a mystery (Manji & Lenox, 2000).

Unlike other antipsychotic drugs, lithium is a naturally occurring substance. Lithium probably did not suppress the symptoms in the diet of an ancestral population, though, allowing the genetic defect to spread unchecked, because the range between a therapeutically effective dose and toxicity is rather narrow. Effective treatment requires constant monitoring by a physician, and sometimes psychological counseling to maintain the lithium regimen despite not having had any symptoms for years. Because humans normally make decisions based on short-term contingencies, long-term compliance is rare without outside support.

Attention Deficit Hyperactivity Disorder

Attention deficit hyperactivity disorder (ADHD) is a disease that seems to appear in societies that require formal education of their children. The syndrome, usually diagnosed in boys, is characterized by hyperactivity (incessant movement without particular goals), impulsivity, and the inability to concentrate on any one thing for more than a few minutes, usually less. Though ADHD-like behavioral functions are apparent from infancy, the family can usually deal with children showing these symptoms until it is time to attend school, where the behaviors are so disruptive that they often prevent the child from functioning in a normal classroom.

ADHD is the most prevalent disorder of early childhood, with estimates ranging from 3% (Ding et al., 2002) to 5% (Shelley-Tremblay & Rosen, 1996) of elementary school children. Approximately half of them continue to show the full disorder in adulthood. Epidemiological studies point to a strong genetic component in the etiology of this disorder (Shelley-Tremblay & Rosen, 1996).

Treatment

ADHD treatment usually involves giving the child amphetamines, disguised by trade names such as Ritalin. The response to chronic low doses of amphetamine-like drugs is said to be "paradoxical," calming the patient and making concentration possible. In turn, the paradoxical response to what would be a strong stimulant in other children is seen as evidence that something was pathological about the child's brain biochemistry in the first place.

A possible explanation of both the disorder and its treatment is that the ADHD child may be chronically sleep-deprived. Normal children, when tired, become more active and irritable, running around the house until exhaustion overtakes them. If this is the case, amphetamine therapy would wake up the affected child to the point where behavioral functioning is more normal. In half of ADHD cases, the symptoms become less severe in adulthood, a phase of life when sleep requirements decline from their higher childhood levels. There is no direct evidence for this speculative hypothesis, but it seems to be the only one that engages both symptoms and treatment together.

Evolutionary Origins

ADHD was identified as a pathology only in the 20th century and in industrialized countries. But a pattern of high activity and curiosity about everything may have led to a broad-based exposure to the environment that would have been beneficial for Paleolithic nomads. Furthermore, we know that our ancestors inhabited a great variety of environments, so that personality characteristics that today are identified as ADHD pathology may have been adaptive for some environments (Jensen et al., 1997).

Nomads normally are more active than most inhabitants of industrial societies, eating substantially more each day than their settled cousins without becoming obese. Hyperactivity in such an environment might hardly have been noticed. Long periods of concentration on subjects of little intrinsic interest, characteristic of formal education, would not have been an issue. In short, ADHD may not be a pathology at all, but simply an extreme of the normal human behavioral repertoire (MacDonald, 1998) that is incompatible with some contemporary lifestyles. Psychiatrists drug children by the millions to suppress symptoms that may be part of a normal range of adaptive human behaviors.

Even nonpathological behavior patterns can have genetic and biochemical concomitants, though, that help us to understand the behaviors and their origins. As in the case of schizophrenia below, a dopamine receptor may be involved. A dopamine D4 receptor (DRD4) has generated interest because of its association with ADHD, with an increased frequency of a unique gene allele, 7-DRD4, reported in children with ADHD. People with this gene have seven repeats of a 48 base-pair sequence—hence the 7-D designation—whereas most people have fewer repeats (Ding et al., 2002). It is one of the most variable genes in the human genome, with 600 alleles.

If a gene is responsible for the syndrome, it might be detectable even in infants, before socialization has had much of a chance to affect behavior. Indeed, in a structured play situation and on an information-processing task, 1-year-old infants with the 7-DRD4 allele showed less sustained attention and more novelty preference than did infants without the 7-DRD4 allele (Auerbach, Benjamin, Faroy, Geller, & Ebstein, 2001).

Where did the gene come from? There is now evidence that a single mutation, occurring between 30,000 and 50,000 years ago, may have been advantageous to early humans (Ding et al., 2002). Triggering a novelty-seeking trait, the mutation is found in up to half of diagnosed ADHD cases, implying that it was selected for in early human groups until it spread to its present frequency. The other alleles of this gene are ancient, predating the origin of the human species.

The mutation was discovered by analyzing the DRD4 genes of a worldwide sample, noting the degree of accumulated variation in the gene's DNA, and working backward to find the time when there was no variation at all. The technique is similar to that used to identify the ages of the ancestral Adam and Eve at the beginning of humanity. Consistent with the out-of-Africa hypothesis of human origins, the widest variety in the gene was found in African populations.

The personalities of those possessing the 7-DRD4 gene may have predisposed them to migration. Active, restless, adventure-seeking, and not generally getting along well with their fellows, they would have pioneered the migrations that populated the earth. The hypothesis generates a testable prediction, that the frequency of the gene should be greatest in the groups that moved the farthest from the African cradle of humanity. Indeed, the mutated 7-DRD4 form of the gene is rare or absent among African !Kung Bushmen, the closest group we have to an ancestral population. In contrast, the mutated allele is common in South America, about as far from Africa as you can get via the Asia/Alaska route. A later migration from a center in China into southeast Asia and the Pacific resulted in high frequencies in those regions, and almost none in China (Harpending & Cochran, 2002).

In conclusion, then, a gene that pushed our ancestors into the farthest corners of the earth is now recognized mainly by the disruptive behavior that it fosters in elementary schools.

ILLNESSES THAT CONFER ONLY COSTS ●

Schizophrenia

A homeless man, Rob, wanders down the street, muttering to himself. Afraid to approach a shelter because voices in his head tell him that people there are scheming to stab him in his sleep, and convinced that medications given to him previously are poisons, Rob is unable to hold down a job or plan his life. He suffers from **schizophrenia**, one of the most terrifying and debilitating of the major psychoses. About 1% of the population will have a schizophrenic episode at some time in their lives, making the disease a serious problem for society as well as a disaster for its victims and their relatives.

Diagnosis of schizophrenia has been difficult, with standards that are still shifting. At present, the American Psychiatric Association recognizes three subcategories of the disease; in the early 1990s there were five. All are characterized by combinations of a group of symptoms: positive symptoms, primarily delusions and hallucinations; negative symptoms, including slowing of movements, poverty of speech, flattened affect, and loss of motivation; and disorganized symptoms, such as nonsensical speech and erratic behavior.

Some of the most troubling symptoms of schizophrenia can be characterized as deficits of planning and anticipation functions that are normally handled by frontal brain areas. Schizophrenic patients have great difficulty in performing anticipation tasks, compared with normal controls. Although they can learn sequences almost normally, their anticipatory ability is reduced in comparison to normal controls. These behavioral problems implied to the authors of the study that a working memory deficit is important in schizophrenia (Posada, Franck, Georgieff, & Jeannerod, 2001), but a diagnosis of frontal lobe dysfunction is more likely because some of the symptoms are reminiscent of the deficits due to frontal lobe damage reviewed in Chapter 8.

Indeed, frontal hypoactivity is a part of the pattern of schizophrenic deficits. There is also an interruption in the planning of normal behaviors, as revealed neurologically by a reduced communication between frontal and temporal lobes during talking in schizophrenia (Ford, Mathalon, Whitfield, Faustman, & Roth, 2002). The reduced communication may be the source of bizarre speech in schizophrenics, and underlies the schizophrenic's feeling that his or her actions are being controlled from outside.

The confluence of the loss of a feeling of control with the fact that behavior obviously is still occurring leads many schizophrenics to a conclusion that you or I might also make under the same circumstances—the patient feels controlled from the outside, whether from demons, gods, or implanted microchips.

Genetic Triggers

Many colorful hypotheses have been proposed about the origin of the disorder: mothers who are too warm or too cold, fathers who are too timid or too intimidating, conflicting messages from parents, and so on. None of these ideas has withstood empirical tests, and none has led to an effective therapy.

For a long time it has been known that schizophrenia runs in families; some pedigrees running back four generations show schizophrenics in one generation after another. Using twin studies to separate environmental from genetic origins of the disease, concordance rates for schizophrenia are found to be substantially higher among monozygotic twins than among dizygotic twins.

Another way to disentangle genetic and environmental effects is to study adopted children. Most of the best studies come from Scandinavia, where social records are so complete that natural and adoptive parents of schizophrenic adoptees can be compared. A primarily environmental trigger would predict that the adoptive parents of schizophrenics would more often show signs of mental illness than would the biological parents. A genetic trigger would predict the opposite—more abnormalities in the biological parents. Pathology was found to be far more common among biological parents than adoptive parents (Kety, Rosenthal, Wender, Schulsinger, & Jacobsen, 1975).

Environmental Triggers

Even for monozygotic twins, however, the concordance rate is less than 100%, suggesting that genes do not play the only role in the development of the disease. In cases where only one twin became schizophrenic, that twin often was the second born, had a lower birth weight, suffered more physiological stress during development, or was seen by the parents as more submissive, fearful, and sensitive than the other twin (Wahl, 1976). Even when only one twin develops the illness, however, the rate of schizophrenia in the children of both twins is the same (Fischer, 1971). Something unknown, but not genetic, apparently prevented the disease from appearing in one of the twins.

Another possible triggering factor for schizophrenia was discovered after a brutal incident during World War II when the Nazis blockaded the Netherlands, causing widespread starvation and malnutrition. Mothers who were pregnant during that period had twice the probability of bearing children who would eventually become schizophrenic (Susser et al., 1996).

There is also a time-of-year effect, with children born in late winter or early spring suffering a 20% greater risk of developing the disease (Mortensen et al., 1999). Although all these factors point to a combination of genetic and environmental influences that trigger schizophrenia, the precise mechanism of the onset of the disease remains obscure.

Biochemistry and Treatment

Until the 1950s there was no effective treatment for schizophrenia. After psychotherapy proved ineffective, the usual procedure was hospitalization until a spontaneous remission occurred. The result was a psychiatric patient population in the United States of about half a million. At this time, Henri

Laborit, a French surgeon, was searching for a drug to relax muscles for surgery. He discovered a drug that also reduced the patient's worrying and preoperative tension. Recognizing the potential of such a drug, Laborit then collaborated with psychiatrists in trying the new drug, chlorpromazine, on psychiatric patients.

Success was so dramatic that the drug and its relatives, the phenothiazines, became widely used. Since then, mental hospitals have been emptied by the use of an array of antipsychotic drugs. As Rob's situation at the start of this section shows, however, drugs alone are not enough to defeat the disease. Like the treatments for other major psychoses, the phenothiazines do not cure the disease—they only suppress its symptoms, and in the case of schizophrenia they are relatively ineffective against the negative symptoms. The drugs are also less effective in some patients than in others.

The antischizophrenic drugs have in common that they reduce brain levels of dopamine, a neurotransmitter associated with neural reward and motivation systems. This fact leads immediately to the dopamine hypothesis, that schizophrenia is caused by an excess of brain dopamine (Creese, Burt, & Snyder, 1976). In fact, the clinical efficacy of phenothiazines is closely related to their effectiveness in reducing brain dopamine concentrations (Figure 9.3). The earliest antischizophrenic drugs had serious motoric side effects, due to interference with other dopamine systems regulating muscle action and posture; newer drugs, taken at much lower doses, have less severe side effects.

There are problems with this hypothesis, though. First, the antipsychotic medications reduce brain dopamine levels in schizophrenic patients within hours, but reduction of symptoms can take weeks. Second, the dopamine system in the brain has turned out to be more complicated than was first thought, with at least five different dopamine receptor systems in the CNS. A modern version of the dopamine hypothesis recognizes that medications may repattern dopamine activity, especially reducing effects in the prefrontal cortex, in addition to an overall decrease in dopamine activity (Goldsmith, Shapiro, & Joyce, 1997; Okubo et al., 1997).

Consistent with this idea is the clinical experience of physicians administering dopamine precursors in patients whose dopamine levels are too low. Parkinson's disease, a malady that strikes mostly the elderly and results in disorders of posture and movement initiation, seems to be related to low dopamine levels in the basal ganglia, forebrain structures that are part of the motor system. Sometimes symptoms of schizophrenia appear in Parkinson's patients who are treated with drugs that increase brain dopamine levels. And people who use enough cocaine or methamphetamine ("speed") for a long enough time develop a syndrome that is indistinguishable from schizophrenia (Angrist, Sathananthan, Wilk, & Gershon, 1974).

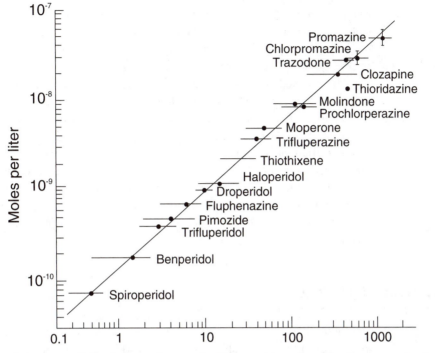

Figure 9.3   Relationship of clinical effectiveness of antipsychotic medications to their ability to neutralize dopamine. The medications that counter dopamine more efficiently are effective in suppressing schizophrenic symptoms at lower doses.

Evolutionary Origins

Although the symptoms of other major psychoses can be interpreted as inappropriately triggered extremes of normal, adaptive reactions, there is no clear adaptive value of schizoid behavior. Surveys of hospitalized patients have shown that all of the major psychoses reduce fertility, with a particularly strong reduction in schizophrenics (Macsorley, 1964). Kin-selection theory would have us look for a benefit in relatives, but the search is in vain—relatives of schizophrenics, and people at risk of developing the disease, have deficits in attention, verbal memory, and gross motor skills (Erlenmeyer-Kimling et al., 2000). There is also a peculiar deficit in relatives of schizophrenics, seeming unrelated to the disorder—their tracking eye movements are deficient, so that they follow objects with a series of jumps called saccades.

In all of these studies, though, there is inconsistency: not all patients or relatives show the deficits, each seeming to have a different pattern. It is possible that several diseases with similar symptoms have been lumped together into the category of schizophrenia, so that any one treatment would be most effective in only one or a few of the disease groups.

There have been speculations that schizophrenia is related to creativity, based partly on the often bizarre but always creative (in the sense of novel) ruminations of schizophrenics, but there is no solid evidence that the creativity in relatives of schizophrenics is significant or directed enough to enhance their biological success. The connection that many cultures have recognized between artistic achievement and mental illness seems to apply more to bipolar disorder than to schizophrenia. One possibility is that schizophrenia is linked to beneficial traits in a way that we do not yet understand. In short, why schizophrenogenic genes persist in the population remains a mystery.

● DRUG ADDICTIONS

One of the dark sides of modern life is a gigantic epidemic of drug addiction, involving hundreds of millions of victims worldwide and causing incalculable damage to individuals, families, and whole societies. The problem is worldwide, affecting wealthy regions and poor ones, from the poles to the tropics, suggesting that addictions are not quirks of particular cultures but universal vulnerabilities. At the same time, in all cultures most people are not addicted to damaging drugs, suggesting that addiction is not inevitable.

Though drugs of abuse are numerous and vary widely from culture to culture, some of them are nearly universal. By far the most damaging of the addictive drugs are alcohol and nicotine. The victims of these drugs outnumber addicts of all other drugs combined by more than an order of magnitude.

One way to measure the damage caused by drugs of abuse is to count the number of deaths they cause. As was the case with studies of family conflict, death is a measure that can be quantified and is difficult to hide. By this measure, alcohol and nicotine each kill hundreds of thousands in the United States each year, cocaine kills about 5,000, and smaller but still significant numbers are lost to other drugs.

The most abused drug in most of the industrialized countries is alcohol. In the United States it is implicated in about 55% of traffic fatalities, 50% of homicides, 30% of suicides, 65% of drownings, 50% of deaths from falls, 52% of deaths in fires, 60% of child abuse cases, and 85% of domestic violence (FitzGerald, 1988).

Not all of this mayhem is caused by alcoholism—sometimes alcohol merely exacerbates existing problems such as depression or family tensions. The addictive properties of alcohol, though, have additional consequences in secondary effects such as lost work productivity and risk of other diseases. Susceptibility to alcoholism is moderately heritable.

Given such appalling numbers, why does addiction continue? The answers are related to the reward and motivational systems built into our brains.

The Pharmacology of Addictive Drugs

Most addictive drugs mimic neurotransmitters related to ancient reward and pain systems deep in the vertebrate brain. Many of the drugs also share botanical origins, either being synthesized in some form by plants or produced by fermentation of plant products.

A particularly well-understood example of drug pharmacology is the case of opiates (heroin, morphine, and their synthetic analogs). These drugs are related chemically to **endorphins,** a group of polypeptides (short proteins) that serve as neurotransmitters in reward centers of the brain stem. Normally, the centers are activated only when a human or animal has done something right—it is physically active, having sex, caring for young. The endorphins act as internal rewards, inducing feelings ranging from well-being to euphoria. But it is sometimes hard work to earn their rewards—the runner's endorphin high requires at least half an hour of strenuous exercise. The major addictive drugs in effect hijack these ancient biological systems, bypassing them to provide the reward without the necessity to do the work. Furthermore, the reward, being concentrated in chemical form far beyond what nature can provide endogenously, can be overwhelming in its intensity.

The Opiates

Humans have used opiate drugs to induce euphoria and deaden pain at least since the beginning of written history, but until recently it was not clear how they worked. And until the advent of modern chemistry, the opiate preparations were impure and could not be easily administered in large doses.

By the early 1970s, several lines of evidence pointed to brain receptors that were sensitive to opiates. First, the drugs could be effective in very small amounts, quantities so small that highly specific receptors had to be involved (Snyder, 1977). The synthetic opiate etorphine, for instance, induces euphoria and deadens pain in doses as small as 0.1 mg, less than the effective dose of lysergic acid diethylamide (LSD). Second, most opiate molecules come in left-handed and right-handed shapes, called isomers. Only the right-handed isomers are biologically effective. Finally, only a few small regions on the opiate molecules seem to carry the major effects.

An antiopiate drug, naloxone, made this clear. Naloxone was developed by German chemists during World War II, after their supply of opiates from the Turkish poppy had been cut off. As they desperately tried to develop synthetic opiates, they stumbled upon a molecule, very similar to natural opiates, that antagonized their effects. Given to addicts dying of drug overdoses, the drug can almost magically revive the victims.

Using these clues as well as persistence and modern biochemical methods, Pert and Snyder (1973) isolated brain receptors for endogenous opiate-like substances. Once the receptors had been discovered, it was only a matter of time until the natural neurotransmitters that stimulate the receptors were found. A scientific race to find the mystery substances ended in a tie (Hughes et al., 1975; Terenius & Wahlström, 1975) with the discovery of the enkephalins and endorphins. They are surprisingly small polypeptides, only five amino acids long, but they have potent effects.

At the time of their discovery, scientists hoped that endorphins might provide the benefits of opiates but not be addictive, because they are naturally occurring substances. Alas, endorphins turned out to be as addictive as their synthetic cousins. Because they are so dangerous, the body cannot store reserves of these substances; instead, they are synthesized within larger molecules, and the pharmacologically active segments are broken off by specialized enzymes as needed.

If the endogenous opiates are buried so deep in the brain and so well protected pharmacologically, how did plant opiates evolve to mimic some of their functions? The answer comes from an ancient evolutionary invention of the poppy plant. Because plants cannot escape or hide to defend themselves, many of them have evolved into biochemical time bombs, full of toxins to deter their predators.

For the poppy, the solution was a narcotic opiate that induced sleepiness in small doses, and death in large ones, for the animals that tried to feed on the plant. Drugged animals, in turn, are eaten by their predators, rescuing the poppy. Relatively small amounts of morphine are enough to defend the wild poppy—it does not have to manufacture large quantities of the drug. A simple biochemical reaction turned morphine, the poppy's opiate, into the much stronger and more addictive heroin.

When humans discovered the pain-deadening effects of a poppy extract, they began using it for pain relief, and discovered addiction. Synthesis of the endorphins, like most neurotransmitters, is controlled by a negative feedback that stabilizes their concentrations in the brain. Adding a similar chemical from the outside overstimulates the negative feedback regulatory mechanism, shutting off the biosynthesis of these essential transmitters, making the users become dependent on the outside source. They are addicted. If addicts stop taking the drug, torturing withdrawal symptoms occur until the body gradually restores its own synthesis.

Addictive Drugs and Behavior

Other addictive drugs have similar mechanisms, where synthesis of some neurotransmitter is inhibited by ingestion of a similar substance from outside. Opiates, cocaine, nicotine, all have chemical structures that mimic natural neurotransmitters, and all can shut off synthesis of those essential transmitters to create dependence. The difference in the modern world is that we now have the knowledge and the resources to synthesize or purify these substances, presenting people with temptations that they have never had to face in previous history.

Addiction can occur at reproductive ages, and interferes so severely with normal social interactions that it reduces fitness. Thus a selective pressure against vulnerability to addiction should have removed this vulnerability from the population by natural selection. But the addictions have been technically possible for such a short fraction of the hundred-thousand-year sweep of human history that there has been no opportunity for the human genome to evolve resistance to the major addictive drugs. Furthermore, the major addictive drugs are so closely tied to essential neurotransmitter systems that simple genetic changes are unlikely to offer protection in any case.

Nicotine is a particularly tragic case of addiction, because most of its harmful effects come not from the nicotine itself but from the toxins and carcinogens in the delivery vehicle, tobacco smoke. Nicotine is essential for nicotinic receptors, a class of receptors for the neurotransmitter acetylcholine, and thus makes smoking tobacco addictive. The addiction would be relatively benign if it were not for the toxins, which the smoker willingly accepts to avoid the terrible experience of withdrawal—nicotine is more addictive than heroin.

Delivering drugs through the lungs or directly into the bloodstream sends a more concentrated dose to the brain, by the mechanism of Figure 9.4. If the drug does not have to pass through the diluting effect of general body circulation, the brain's dose is large and rapid. This is why smoking and injection are the most addictive, and the most attractive, means of delivery for many drugs. Unfortunately, they are also the most dangerous.

The Human Circulatory System

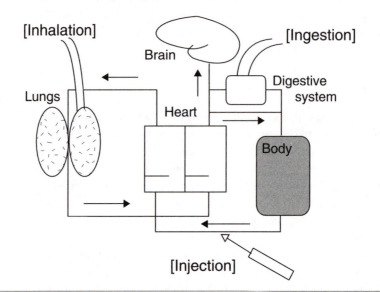

Figure 9.4 Blood circulation in the body, showing routes of drug intake. The blood flows in a figure eight, passing through the heart twice in each cycle. Ingestion by mouth is the slowest way to take a drug because the drug must pass through the digestive system and the body before reaching the brain. Drugs taken by injection and inhalation reach the brain faster and in higher concentration, and thus can be more addictive.

● DRUGS AND MENTAL ILLNESS

Some aspects of mental illness can be regarded not as disturbances of the rational machine but as drug-induced altered states of consciousness. The drugs are not taken voluntarily but are produced internally. Alternatively, the mentally ill person may react abnormally to normal amounts of endogenous psychoactive substances. Therapy includes other drugs to restore the biochemical balance and return the patient to a functioning, if not always normal, state.

The drugs are not cures, though—they only force an alteration in an abnormal biochemical balance without addressing the cause of the abnormality. Some of them have serious side effects when taken for long periods, and not all patients are helped. Diagnosis is still a difficult problem, and treatment must include insight into the patient's psychological condition as well as drug therapy.

Psychoactive Drugs

Psychoactive drugs reveal a close relationship between motivation and consciousness, for most of them affect both functions. They also demonstrate that consciousness is based on a physical brain process, like any other neurological function, that can be biased by some of the same drugs that influence neurotransmitter systems.

The Biochemistry of Psychoactive Drugs

As was the case for antipsychotic medications, most psychoactive drugs are chemically similar to neurotransmitters in both their structures and their modes of action. The potent hallucinogen mescaline, derived from the peyote cactus, is similar in structure to norepinephrine, and "STP" is also similar to mescaline. Both affect noradrenergic synapses. Cocaine prevents reuptake of norepinephrine into the presynaptic terminals, interfering with further transmission. Figure 9.5 illustrates the similarities in chemical structures of several neurotransmitters and the corresponding psychoactive drugs.

Psilocybin and LSD are molecular expansions of the serotonin molecule. LSD was first synthesized by Swiss biochemist Albert Hoffman with the intent of producing a new psychoactive drug of therapeutic value. He got more than he bargained for, as LSD has potent effects on both perception and state of consciousness, and has at least three distinct pharmacological effects. Each is presumably associated with a different effect on consciousness. LSD blocks serotonin synapses for a few hours (hallucinations), decreases the number of postsynaptic serotonin receptors for a few days (Jacobs & Trulson, 1979) (hallucinatory "flashbacks"), and also interacts with dopamine synapses (psychotic symptoms).

The opiates (morphine and its more powerful derivative, heroin) and their biochemical similarity to the brain's enkephalins have already been discussed. Some of the effects of endogenous opiates may be indirect, through the action of the sometimes addictive drug alcohol (ethanol).

Experiments with tissue cultures show that ethanol inhibits the binding of opiates to their specialized postsynaptic receptors. After long-term exposure, the cells respond by increasing the number of opiate binding sites, an

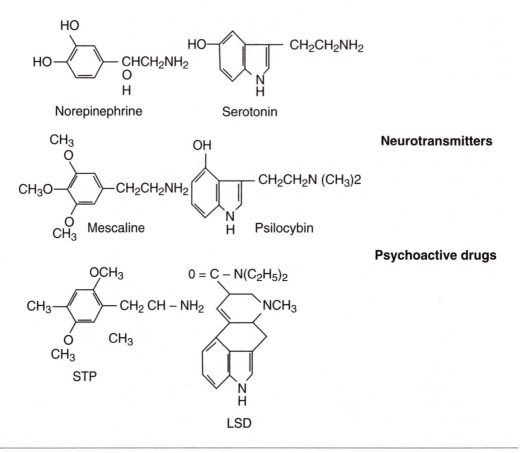

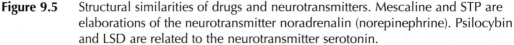

Figure 9.5   Structural similarities of drugs and neurotransmitters. Mescaline and STP are elaborations of the neurotransmitter noradrenalin (norepinephrine). Psilocybin and LSD are related to the neurotransmitter serotonin.

effect that is reversible when the ethanol is withdrawn. The tissue culture effects can be compared with clinical intoxication, tolerance, and withdrawal (Charness, Gordon, & Diamond, 1983), and may explain the addictive effects of this relatively simple molecule. Mercifully, low doses of alcohol have negligible effects on the receptors.

The evolutionary history of addictive drugs suggests that addicts are not freaks of nature, suffering from some bizarre abnormality, nor are they diseased. They are just relatively normal people faced with a temptation that evolution has not prepared them to handle. The immediate rewards of addictive drugs are so overwhelming that the reward systems of the addict's brain tell him that getting the drugs is more important than anything, and the punishments of withdrawal are so overwhelming that the addict will do anything to avoid them.

The question then becomes not why people become addicted, but why most people do not—after all, we all share the same neurotransmitter biochemistry. Human motivation is based on more than just biochemistry, though, with social and rational components looming particularly large in the regulation of human behavior. Those most prone to addiction may rate high on the personality characteristic of sensation-seeking. Such people actively seek out exciting, stimulating, and even dangerous environments (MacDonald, 1998).

Most people, though, see the overwhelming feelings of drug-induced excitement or well-being or euphoria as false pleasures, forced from the outside and eventually leading only to despair. Long-term planning in the human brain makes it possible for most of us to resist the short-term temptations of addictive drugs.

CONCLUSION: THE DIVERSE ● ORIGINS OF MENTAL ILLNESSES

The genetics of phobias and OCD showed that they are most likely pathological extremes of traits that are normally adaptive. ADHD illustrates a second pattern, a syndrome that causes problems in the modern world but may have been beneficial in some ancestral environments just as it is. Schizophrenia, though related obliquely to a sort of creativity, has no clear benefit in either patients or their relatives. And drug addictions from this perspective are not illnesses at all: rather, they are tragic combinations of the success of plants in combating predation along with the ability of modern humans to purify and/or synthesize their toxins.

There seem to be as many origins of mental illnesses as there are illnesses themselves. None of them are caused by conventional microbes or parasites. All of them, though, can be better understood and treated by examining their evolutionary origins and the forces that maintain susceptibility to them in the human genome.

Understanding mental illnesses leads not to stigmatizing the victims of these serious diseases but to understanding their plight and possibly relieving their symptoms. The previous stigma and fear can be alleviated by the possibility for treatment and by the realization that mental illnesses have physical origins like any other illness. Many victims of mental illnesses can lead relatively normal lives because the pharmacology and the evolutionary origins of their illnesses have been worked out.

It is my hope that the new way of categorizing and understanding mental illnesses introduced in this chapter will serve as an example of the promise of evolutionary psychology to better the human condition by better understanding human origins and the exquisite adaptations that reside in all of us.

● DISCUSSION QUESTIONS

1. Under what conditions might phobias to current dangerous objects and situations find their ways into the human genome?
2. Might there be (or once have been) environmental situations in which schizophrenic behavior offered a selective advantage?
3. Given that addiction is a normal physiological and behavioral response to an abnormal availability of psychoactive drugs, what can be done about social problems of addiction?

● FURTHER READING

Stevens, A., & Price, J. (2000). *Evolutionary psychiatry: A new beginning*. London: Routledge.

Though tinged with obsolete Freudian influence, this book played a large role in establishing evolutionary thought as a tool in understanding mental illnesses.

Nesse, R. M., & Williams, G. C. (1996). *Why we get sick: The new science of Darwinian medicine*. New York: Vintage Books.

This volume includes mental illnesses among a wide variety of physical maladies that are caused or exacerbated by the conditions of modern life.

Rapoport, J. (1991). *The boy who couldn't stop washing*. New York: Penguin Books.

A heartbreaking yet illuminating account of a case of OCD. After describing the case, Rapoport compassionately reviews the etiology, epidemiology, and prognosis of the disease for OCD's victims.

GLOSSARY

Acuity   the sensory ability to resolve fine detail.

Adaptation   an inherited physical or behavioral trait that increases biological fitness.

Algorithm   a method for solving a problem that always leads to a solution.

Allele   a particular variant of a gene.

Alpha male   the dominant male in a group of animals, often dominating reproductive activity.

Altruism   performing a service that increases another's biological fitness while reducing one's own biological fitness.

Amino acid   an organic acid, the building block of proteins.

Amnesia   inability to remember.

Aphasia   inability to speak.

Asexual   a population consisting of only one sex.

Attention deficit hyperactivity disorder (ADHD)   a disease characterized by hyperactivity (incessant movement without particular goals), impulsivity, and inability to focus attention for more than a few minutes.

Australopithecus   an extinct hominid species similar to the chimpanzee, appearing about 4 million years ago.

Availability   in reasoning, a heuristic that judges the most familiar to be the most common.

Baseline   in reasoning, the level against which a statistic is compared.

Base pairs   pairs of organic molecules that define the genetic code, existing in four types.

Behaviorism   an effort to construct a psychology by correlating stimuli and responses.

Bipedal   walking on two legs.

Bipolar depression   a mental disease characterized by periods of severe depression alternating with periods of excessively expansive moods.

Bit   a two-alternative choice where each choice is equally likely, the smallest unit of information.

Bounded rationality   logically incomplete reasoning methods that often do as well or nearly as well as a rational solution.

Broca's area   a part of the human frontal lobe responsible for producing speech.

Canalization   lack of variability in a trait, from different genotypes resulting in the same phenotype.

Carcinogens   agents that induce cancer.

Catecholamines   a group of amine neurotransmitters, including dopamine, norepinephrine, and epinephrine.

Categorical perception   perception that a stimulus belongs to a particular category, without differentiating stimuli that fit into that category.

Central executive   a brain function that coordinates working memory and brings new information into it.

Chromosome   a continuous chain of DNA containing sequences of genes and other DNA.

Co-evolution   evolution of two or more traits together, each creating adaptive pressure to change the other.

Color constancy   perceiving colors in about the same way regardless of large differences in illumination.

Concordance rate   the percentage of identical twin pairs who share a trait.

Conjunction fallacy   in reasoning, the conclusion that membership in both of two overlapping groups is more likely than membership in either constituent group.

Consilience   the requirement for consistency among the ideas of scientific disciplines.

Contingent negative variation (CNV)   a long-lasting brain potential that appears when an event is expected to involve an action or a decision.

Coolidge effect   renewed sexual capability when a male mates with a novel female.

Creole   a language with a characteristic grammar, spoken by children growing up without consistent grammatical models.

Declarative knowledge   knowledge of information that can be put into words.

Deep structure   in language, the logical relationships that underlie words and sentences.

Descended larynx   entry of the windpipe low in the vocal tract, enabling deep resonance and production of a variety of speech sounds.

Design features   in language, the features that all languages have in common.

Dichotic listening   hearing different sound patterns in each ear.

DNA   deoxyribonucleic acid, the chemical structure of genes.

Dominance-submission relationship a hierarchical relationship, evolved from intraspecies dominance conflicts.

Dominant gene a gene that will be expressed in the phenotype even if inherited from only one parent.

Dopamine a neurotransmitter for which excess is associated with schizophrenia, and low levels are associated with unipolar depression and Parkinson's disease.

Dyslexia inability to read, with preserved ability to speak and comprehend language.

Echoic memory a very short-term auditory memory.

Ecological rationality generally successful problem-solving strategies that usually work well in the real world even if not always logically consistent.

Endorphins a group of polypeptide neurotransmitters in reward centers of the brain stem, chemically related to opiates.

Epinephrine also called adrenalin, a psychoactive catecholamine neurotransmitter.

Epiphenomenon a characteristic that accompanies some other characteristic by chance.

Episodic memory autobiographical memory for particular episodes in one's life.

Estrus a period of fertility and sexual receptivity in mammals.

Ethology the comparative study of animal behavior, including humans.

Eugenics the effort to produce superior humans by selective breeding.

Exponential growth increase of a quantity by a constant fraction of its current size in a given time period.

Evolution change in gene frequencies in a species due to selective survival of members of the species.

Evolution by natural selection change in the frequency of a gene by differential survival of organisms bearing it.

Evolutionary psychology psychology informed by the theory of evolution.

Evolutionary theory the application of evolutionary ideas to understanding the design of organisms.

Expressive aphasia inability to produce language, with preserved ability to understand it.

Fast and frugal in reasoning, methods that use only one or a few of many possible information sources for making a decision.

Fitness reproductive success of an individual.

Fixated represented by only one allele in the genome of a species.

Functional magnetic resonance imaging (fMRI) a technique for observing anatomy and metabolic activity inside living brains.

Game theory mathematical analysis of interactions within rule-based systems.

Gene a sequence of DNA that controls the synthesis of a protein and is passed from an individual to its offspring during reproduction.

Generalized anxiety disorder a chronic anxiety with no clear environmental cause.

Genetic drift random change in the genome of a population.

Genotype the set of genes that is carried by an organism.

Grammar a set of rules by which words may be combined to impart meaning.

Group selection natural selection of the genes of a group of organisms based on benefits to the group as a whole.

Heritability the proportion of variance of a trait in a population that is due to genetic differences.

Heterozygous possessing two alleles of a gene, one from each parent.

Heuristic a strategy for solving a problem that falls short of logical completeness.

Holophrase a combination communication that includes gesture, context, and verbal output.

Hominid the genus of human-like apes.

Homo erectus an extinct hominid that first appeared about 1.9 million years ago in Africa.

Homo habilis an extinct hominid that first appeared about 2.2 million years ago in Africa.

Homo Neanderthalensis a hominid that thrived from about 230,000 to 28,000 years ago.

Homo sapiens modern humans, appearing in their present form about 100,000 years ago.

Homozygous possessing the same allele of a gene from each parent.

Iconic memory a visual memory lasting less than a second.

Implicit memory memory whose contents can be used to guide behavior but whose contents cannot be described.

Inclusive fitness the combined fitness of an individual and the individual's relatives, discounted in proportion to the remoteness of the relation.

Indoleamines a group of amine neurotransmitters, including serotonin and tryptamine.

Infanticide killing of very young children.

K-selection producing a small number of offspring and making a large investment in each.

Kin-directed altruism the motivation to aid one's close relatives, without expectation of a reward.

Learning   the acquisition of new memories.

Lethal recessives   genes that cause death if homozygous, but that persist because they are usually paired with a normal gene from the other parent.

Lexicon   the group of all words in a language.

Limbic system   a group of structures in the mammalian forebrain that regulate emotional and motivational actions.

Linking   the tendency of genes to be inherited in groups.

Major histocompatibility complex   a highly polymorphic and conserved set of genes that plays an important role in immune function.

Memory   information stored in the brain as a result of sensory experience.

Mental practice   watching performance of a skilled activity that can improve one's ability to perform that activity at a later time.

Mitochondria   organelles within each cell that convert sugars and oxygen into energy.

Mitochondrial DNA   genetic material residing in the mitochondria of each cell, inherited only through the maternal line.

Motherese   a high-pitched singsong style of speech that mothers direct at infants.

Mutagens   substances that increase the rate of genetic mutation.

Mutation   a random change in a gene.

Natural selection   differential survival of members of a species due to their differing genes.

Neolithic   the era also called the new stone age, after about 10,000 years ago, when farming became a way of life.

Norepinephrine   also called noradrenalin, a psychoactive catecholamine neurotransmitter.

Nurturant relationship   a supportive relationship evolved from the mother-infant bond.

Object constancy   the idea that objects in the real world retain their identity despite momentary disappearances and transformations.

Obsessive-compulsive disorder (OCD)   a disease whose principal symptom is a compulsion to perform some otherwise rational act to excess.

Oculomotor   concerning the control of eye movements.

Optimization under constraints   proceeding with a computation until searching further has more costs than benefits.

Organogenesis   the process of organ formation in the embryo.

Overconfidence bias   in reasoning, having more confidence in a conclusion than the circumstances warrant.

Paleolithic   the era also called the old stone age, when farming and metals were unknown (up to about 10,000 years ago).

Parental investment   energy and resources that parents devote to their offspring.

Paternal investment   investment of a father's resources in his offspring.

Phenotype   the properties of an organism, derived by genes working through an environment.

Phenylketonuria   progressive mental retardation caused by a gene defect preventing normal metabolism of the amino acid phenylalanine.

Pheromones   chemicals, usually related to hormones, released by one sex to influence the behavior of the other.

Phobia   an exaggerated, irrational fear of an object or situation.

Phoneme   a single speech sound, the smallest unit of language.

Phonetic   based on the sounds of speech.

Phonological loop   a component of short-term memory that holds verbal information.

Phrenology   the theory that human mental specializations are due to growth of parts of the head overlying brain areas that serve the corresponding abilities.

Pidgin   a language made up by an adult speaker for basic communication.

Polyandry   a mating system in which a woman can take more than one husband.

Polygyny   a mating system in which a man can take more than one wife.

Polymers   molecules made of repeating sequences arranged in chains.

Polymorphism   having many forms, applied to a gene having many alleles.

Preferential looking   directing the gaze at an object of special interest.

Priming   use of implicit memory to influence recall or memory performance.

Prior probability   in reasoning, the probability of membership in a category before the problem begins.

Procedural knowledge   knowledge of rules and procedures.

Procedural memory   long-term memory for procedures and rules as opposed to events.

Prosopagnosia   the inability to recognize faces, with ability to use other visual information.

Proximate cause   the immediate trigger of an event.

Punctuated equilibrium   evolution in abrupt steps, interspersed with periods of no change.

Quadruped   an animal that walks on four legs.

Receptive aphasia   ability to produce words and phrases, with inability to understand language.

Reciprocal altruism   helping another with the expectation of a similar reward from the person being helped.

Recombination   construction of a new genome by selection of genes from two parents.

Representativeness   in reasoning, using fixed criteria to judge membership in a group, without taking the prior probability into account.

Reproductive capacity   the number of offspring that a population of a given size can have in a given time.

Ribosome   an organelle within the cell that transcribes RNA into a protein.

RNA   ribonucleic acid, a molecule similar to DNA but with a different sugar in its backbone, carrying genetic information from the cell nucleus to the ribosome and aiding in protein synthesis.

r-selection   producing a large number of offspring and investing little in each one.

Satisficing   a method for making a choice from a set of sequentially encountered alternatives.

Schemata   mental plans for executing particular acts.

Schizophrenia   a mental illness whose symptoms include disordered thought, hallucinations, and paranoia.

Semantic memory   memory for knowledge can be put into words, but expresses an enduring characteristic of the world.

Semantics   the study of meaning in language.

Serotonin   an indoleamine neurotransmitter related to reward and motivational systems.

Sexual dimorphism   difference in the phenotypes of the two sexes in a species.

Sexual reproduction   reproduction that requires union of genes from two sexes.

Sexual selection   netural selection for traits attractive to the opposite sex, rather than traits that facilitate survival.

Short-term memory   a memory with a capacity of a small number of items, lasting a few tens of seconds.

Sign stimuli   stimuli that induce specific behaviors or attitudes in a target organism.

Slot grammar   a two-word grammar, usually with a root noun and a modifier.

Social phobia   a phobia triggered by interpersonal situations.

Specific phobia   a phobia triggered by particular defined stimuli.

Standard Social Science Model (SSSM)   the theory that the structure of the mind is imposed by culture.

Stopping rule   in reasoning, a rule to decide when the point of diminishing returns has been reached in a mental computation.

Surface structure   in speech, the sequence of words generated.

Symbiosis a mutual association of two distinct organisms that both rely upon for survival.

Syntax the structure of language.

Tabula rasa "blank slate," a metaphor for the structure of a flexible mind structured by culture and experience.

Teratogens substances that interfere specifically with the processes of embryonic development.

Tit-for-tat a strategy of giving a favor unless reciprocation fails, then not giving the favor.

Transduction changing stimulus energy into graded neural potentials for further processing.

Ultimate cause the underlying reason why an event occurs.

Unipolar depression depression with no obvious trigger, and disabling a person for months or longer.

Upper Paleolithic The later part of the Paleolithic era, from about 50,000 to 10,000 years ago.

Visuospatial sketch pad a component of short-term memory that represents the contents of immediate visual space.

Vomeronasal organ an olfactory organ specialized for sensing pheromones, located in the nasal cavity of mammals.

Wernicke's aphasia inability to understand language, with preserved ability to utter words and phrases fluently.

Westermarck effect the tendency not to be sexually attracted to those with whom one grows up.

Whorfian hypothesis the idea that the structure of a speaker's grammar influences the structure of their thought.

REFERENCES

Allman, W. F. (1994). *The stone age present*. New York: Simon & Schuster.

Alper, M. (2001). *The "God" part of the brain*. New York: Rogue Press.

Ambrose, S. H. (2001). Paleolithic technology and human evolution. *Science, 291*, 1748-1753.

American Psychiatric Association (1994). *Diagnostic and statistical manual of mental disorders* (4th ed.). Washington, D.C.: American Psychiatric Association.

Anderson, R. M., Hunt, S. C., Vander Stoep, A., & Pribram, K. (1976). Object permanency and delayed response as spatial context in monkeys with frontal lesions. *Neuropsychologia, 14*, 481-490.

Angrist, B., Sathananthan, G., Wilk, S. U., & Gershon, S. (1974). Amphetamine psychosis: Behavioral and biochemical aspects. *Journal of Psychiatric Research, 11*, 13-23.

Arnett, J. (1992). Reckless behavior in adolescence: A developmental perspective. *Developmental Review, 12*, 339-373.

Arnett, J. (1995). The young and the reckless: Adolescent reckless behavior. *Current Directions in Psychological Science, 4*, 67-71.

Aronson, E. (1976). *The social animal* (2nd ed.). San Francisco: W. H. Freeman.

Asfaw, B., Gilbert, W., Beyene, Y., Hart, W., Renne, P., Woldegabriel, G., Vrba, E., & White, T. (2002). Remains of Homo Erectus from Bouri, Middle Awash, Ethiopia. *Nature, 416*, 317-320.

Auerbach, J. G., Benjamin, J., Faroy, M., Geller, V., & Ebstein, R. (2001). DRD4 related to infant attention and information processing: A developmental link to ADHD? *Psychiatric Genetics, 11*, 31-35.

Awh, E., Jonides, J., Smith, E. E., Schumacher, E., Koeppe, R., & Katz, S. (1996). Dissociation of storage and retrieval in verbal working memory: Evidence from positron emission tomography. *Psychological Science, 7*, 25-31.

Axelrod, R., & Hamilton, W. D. (1981). The evolution of cooperation. *Science, 211*, 1390-1396.

Baddeley, A. D. (1992). Working memory: Humans. In L. R. Squire (Ed.), *Encyclopedia of learning and memory*. New York: Macmillan.

Baillargeon, R. (1994). How do infants learn about the physical world? *Current Directions in Psychological Science, 3*, 133-140.

Baker, R. R. (1996). *Sperm wars: The science of sex*. New York: Basic Books.

Baker, R. R., & Bellis, M. A. (1995). *Human sperm competition*. London: Chapman & Hall.

Barash, D. P., & Lipton, J. E. (1997). *Making sense of sex*. Washington, D.C.: Island Press/Shearwater Books.

Barash, D. P., & Lipton, J. E. (2001). *Myth of monogamy: Fidelity and infidelity in animals and people*. New York: W. H. Freeman.

Barkow, J. (1992). Beneath new culture is old psychology: Gossip and social stratification. In J. Barkow, L. Cosmides, & J. Tooby (Eds.), *The adapted mind*. New York: Oxford University Press.

Barlow, D. H. (1988). *Anxiety and its disorders: The nature and treatment of anxiety and panic*. New York: Guilford.

Bartlett, A. A. (1978). Forgotten fundamentals of the energy crisis. *American Journal of Physics, 46*, 876-888.

Bartlett, A. A. (1994). Reflections on sustainability, population growth, and the environment. *Population & Environment, 16*, 5-35.

Belsky, J., Steinberg, L., & Draper, P. (1991). Childhood experience, interpersonal development, and reproductive strategy: An evolutionary theory of socialization. *Child Development, 62*, 647-670.

Bergström, T. F., Josefsson, A., Erlich, H., & Gyllensten, U. (1998). Recent origin of HLA-DRB1 alleles and implications for human evolution. *Nature Genetics, 18*, 237-242.

Bernhardt, P. C., Dabbs, J. M., Jr., Fielden, J. A., & Lutter, C. D. (1998). Testosterone changes during vicarious experiences of winning and losing among fans at sporting events. *Physiology and Behavior, 65*, 59-62.

Bickerton, D. (1982). *Roots of language*. Ann Arbor, MI: Karoma Publishers.

Bickerton, D. (1983). Creole languages. *Scientific American, 249*, 116-122.

Bickerton, D. (1984). The language bioprogram hypothesis. *Behavioral and Brain Sciences, 7*, 173-221.

Birkhead, T. (2000). *Promiscuity: An evolutionary history of sperm competition*. Cambridge, MA: Harvard University Press.

Blackmore, S. (1999). *The meme machine*. Oxford, UK: Oxford University Press.

Blanchard, R. (2001). Fraternal birth order and the maternal immune hypothesis of male homosexuality. *Hormones and Behavior, 40*, 105-114.

Blumstein, S. (1981). Neurolinguistic disorders: Language-brain relationships. In S. B. Filskov & J. T. Boll (Eds.), *Handbook of clinical neuropsychology*. New York: Wiley.

Boroditsky, L. (2001). Does language shape thought? Mandarin and English speakers' conceptions of time. *Cognitive Psychology, 43*, 1-22.

Bouissou, M. (1978). Effects of injections of testosterone proprionate on dominance relationships in a group of cows. *Hormones and Behavior, 11*, 388-400.

Bradshaw, J. L. (1997). *Human evolution*. Hove, UK: Psychology Press.

Braitenberg, V. (1977). *On the texture of brains*. New York: Springer-Verlag.

Branda, R., & Eaton, J. (1978). Skin color and nutrient photolysis: An evolutionary hypothesis. *Science, 201*, 625-626.

Brédart, S., & French, R. M. (1999). Do babies resemble their fathers more than their mothers? A failure to replicate Christenfeld & Hill. *Evolution and Human Behavior, 20*, 129-135.

Bridgeman, B. (1992). On the origin of consciousness and language. *Psycoloquy* 92.3.15 (refereed electronic journal). http://psycprints.ecs.soton.ac.uk/

Bridgeman, B. (1999). Vertical modularity in the visual system. In B. H. Challis & B. M. Velichkovsky (Eds.), *Stratification of consciousness and cognition*. Amsterdam: John Benjamins Publishing.

Bridgeman, B., & Azmitia, M. (1993). Mimetic culture and modern sports: A synthesis. *Behavioral and Brain Sciences, 16*, 751-752.

Bridgeman, B., Gemmer, A., Forsman, T., & Huemer, V. (2000). Properties of the sensorimotor branch of the visual system. *Vision Research, 40*, 3539-3552.

Bridgeman, D. L. (1983) Benevolent babies: Emergence of the social self. In D. L. Bridgeman (Ed.), *The nature of prosocial development: Interdisciplinary theories and strategies.* New York: Academic Press.

Bridgeman, D. L., & Marlowe, D. (1979). Jury decision making: An empirical study based on actual felony trials. *Journal of Applied Psychology, 64*, 91-98.

Bronowski, J. (1973). *The ascent of man.* Boston: Little, Brown.

Brown, R. (1965). *Social psychology.* New York: Free Press.

Brown, R. (1970). *Psycholinguistics.* New York: Free Press.

Brown, R. (1973). *A first language: The early stages.* Cambridge, MA: Harvard University Press.

Brown, R., & McNeill, D. (1966). The "tip-of-the-tongue" phenomenon. *Journal of Verbal Learning and Verbal Behavior, 5*, 325-337.

Bunney, S. (1994). Neanderthal baby was buried. *New Scientist, 142*, 15.

Burling, R. (1963). *Rengsanggri, family and kinship in a Garo village.* Philadelphia: University of Pennsylvania Press.

Buss, D. M. (1989). Sex differences in human mate preferences: Evolutionary hypotheses tested in 37 cultures. *Behavioral and Brain Sciences, 12*, 1-49.

Buss, D. M., Larsen, R., Westen, D., & Semmelroth, J. (1992). Sex differences in jealousy: Evolution, physiology and psychology. *Psychological Science, 3*, 251-255.

Buss, D. M., & Schmitt, D. P. (1993). Sexual strategies theory: An evolutionary perspective on human mating. P*sychological Review, 100,* 204-232.

Cann, R. L. (2001). Genetic clues to dispersal in human populations: Retracing the past from the present. *Science, 291*, 1742-1748.

Carroll, B. J. (1991). Psychopathology and neurobiology of manic-depressive disorders. In B. J. Carroll & J. E. Barrett (Eds.), *Psychopathology and the brain.* New York: Raven Press.

Cavalli-Svorza, L., Menozzi, P., & Piazza, A. (1993). Demic expansions and human evolution. *Science, 259*, 639-646.

Chagnon, N. (1983). *Yanomamö: The fierce people* (3rd ed.). New York: Holt, Rinehart & Winston.

Chagnon, N. (1988). Life histories, blood revenge, and warfare in a tribal population. *Science, 239*, 985-992.

Charness, M., Gordon, A. S., & Diamond, I. (1983). Ethanol modulation of opiate receptors in cultured neural cells. *Science, 222*, 1246-1248.

Chomsky, N. (1965). *Aspects of the theory of syntax.* Cambridge, MA: MIT Press.

Chomsky, N. (1980). *Rules and representations.* New York: Columbia University Press.

Christenfeld, N., & Hill, E. A. (1995). Whose baby are you? *Nature, 378*, 669.

Clemens, L. (1971). Influence of prenatal litter composition on mounting behavior of female rats. *American Zoologist, 11*, 617-618.

Clutton-Brock, T. H., Albon, S. D., & Guiness, F. E. (1988). Reproductive success in male and female red deer. In T. H. Clutton-Brock (Ed.), *Reproductive success.* Chicago: University of Chicago Press.

Clutton-Brock, T. H., Albon, S. D., & Guiness, F. E. (1989). Fitness costs of gestation and lactation in wild mammals. *Nature, 337*, 260-262.

Cohen, L. B., Rundell, L. J., Spellman, B. A., & Cashon, C. H. (1999). Infants' perception of causal chains. *Psychological Science, 10*, 412-418.

Cohen, N. J.,& Squire, L. (1980). Preserved learning and retention of pattern analyzing skill in amnesia: Dissociation of knowing how and knowing that. *Science, 210*, 207-209.

Collins, M., & Zebrowitz, L. (1995). The contributions of appearance to occupational outcomes in civilian and military settings. *Journal of Applied Social Psychology, 25*, 29-163.

Corballis, M. C. (1999) Phylogeny from apes to humans. In M. C. Corballis & S. Lea (Eds.), *The descent of mind: Psychological perspectives on hominid evolution.* Oxford, UK: Oxford University Press.

Corballis, M. C. (2002) *From hand to mouth: The origins of language.* Princeton, NJ: Princeton University Press.

Corkum, V., & Moore, C. (1998). The origins of joint visual attention in infants. *Developmental Psychology, 34*, 28-38.

Cosmides, L. (1989). The logic of social exchange: Has natural selection shaped how humans reason? Studies with the Wason selection task. *Cognition, 31*, 187-276.

Cosmides, L., & Barkow, J. (1992). Cognitive adaptations for social exchange. In J. Barkow, L. Cosmides, & J. Tooby (Eds.), *The adapted mind.* New York: Oxford University Press.

Cosmides, L., & Tooby, J. (1996). Are humans good intuitive statisticians after all? Rethinking some conclusions from the literature on judgment under uncertainty. *Cognition, 58*, 1-73.

Creese, I., Burt, D. R., & Snyder, S. H. (1976). Dopamine receptor binding predicts clinical and pharmacological potencies of antischizophrenic drugs. *Science, 192*, 481-483.

Crick, F., & Koch, C. (1998) Consciousness and neuroscience. *Cerebral Cortex, 8*, 97-107

Cunningham, M. R. (1986). Measuring the physical in physical attractiveness: Quasiexperiments on the sociobiology of female facial beauty. *Journal of Personality and Social Psychology, 50*, 925-935.

Dannenmaier, W., & Thumin, F. (1964). Authority status as a factor in perceptual distortion of size. *Journal of Social Psychology, 63*, 361-365.

Daly, M., & Wilson, M. (1982). Whom are newborn babies said to resemble? *Ethology and Sociobiology, 3*, 69-78.

Daly, M., & Wilson, M. (1988). *Homicide.* New York: de Gruyter.

Daly, M., & Wilson, M. (1990). Killing the competition. *Human Nature, 1*, 81-107.

Darwin, C. (1859). *On the origin of species.* London: J. Murray.

Darwin, C. (1871). *The descent of man, and selection in relation to sex.* London: J. Murray.

Darwin, C. (1872). *The expression of the emotions in man and animals.* London: J. Murray.

Dawkins, R. (1976). *The selfish gene.* New York: Oxford University Press.

Dawkins, R. (1986). *The blind watchmaker.* New York: Norton.

Dean, C., Leakey, M. G., Reid, D., Schrenk, F., Schwartz, G. T., Stringer, C., & Walker, A. (2001). Growth processes in teeth distinguish modern humans from Homo Erectus and earlier hominids. *Nature, 414*, 628-631.

de Boisson-Bardies, B. (1999). *How language comes to children.* Cambridge, MA: MIT Press.

deLacoste-Utamsing, C., & Holloway, R. (1982). Sexual dimorphism in the human corpus callosum. *Science, 216,* 1431-1432.

De Lisi, R., & McGillicuddy-De Lisi, A. (2002). Sex differences in mathematical abilities and achievement. In A. McGillicuddy-De Lisi & R. De Lisi (Eds.), *Biology, society and behavior: The development of sex differences in cognition.* Westport, CT: Ablex Publishing.

Dennett, D. C. (1991). *Consciousness explained.* Boston: Little, Brown.

Dennett, D. C. (1995). *Darwin's dangerous idea: Evolution and the meanings of life.* New York: Simon & Shuster.

deWaal, F. (1982). *Chimpanzee politics: Sex and power among apes.* Baltimore: Johns Hopkins University Press.

deWaal, F. B. M. (1997). *Bonobo: The forgotten ape.* Berkeley: University of California Press.

deWaal, F. B. M. (2001). Apes from Venus: Bonobos and human social evolution. In F. B. M. deWaal (Ed.), *Tree of origin: What primate behavior can tell us about human social evolution.* Cambridge, MA: Harvard University Press.

Ding, Y.-C., Chi, H.-C., Grady, D., Morishima, A., Kidd, J., Kidd, K., Flodman, P., et al. (2002). Evidence of positive selection acting at the human dopamine receptor D4 gene locus. *Proceedings of the National Academy of Sciences, 99,* 309-314.

Donald, M. (1991). *Origins of the modern mind: Three stages in the evolution of culture and cognition.* Cambridge, MA: Harvard University Press.

Dunbar, R. (1996). *Grooming, gossip, and the evolution of language.* Cambridge, MA: Harvard University Press.

Durkheim, E. (1895/1962). *The rules of the sociological method.* Glencoe, IL: Free Press.

Ehrlich, P. R. (2000). *Human natures: Genes, cultures, and the human prospect.* Washington, D.C.: Island Press.

Ehrlich, P. R., & Holdren, J. (1971). The impact of population growth. *Science, 171,* 1212-1217.

Eibl-Eibesfeldt, I. (1998). Us and the others: The familial roots of ethnonationalism. In I. Eibl-Eibesfeldt & F. Salter (Eds.), *Indoctrinability, ideology and warfare* (pp. 109-132). New York: Berghahn Books.

Eldredge, N. (1985). *Time frames: The evolution of punctuated equilibria.* Princeton, NJ: Princeton University Press.

Ellis, B. J., McFadyen-Ketchum, S., Dodge, K., Pettit, G. S., & Bates, J. E. (1999). Quality of early family relationships and individual differences in the timing of pubertal maturation in girls: A longitudinal test of an evolutionary model. *Journal of Personality and Social Psychology, 77,* 387-401.

Ellis, L. (1995). Dominance and reproductive success among nonhuman animals: An evolutionary psychological approach. *Journal of Sex Research, 27,* 527-556.

Erlenmeyer-Kimling, L., Rock, D., Roberts, S. A., Janal, M., Kestenbaum, C., Cornblatt, B., Adamo, U., et al. (2000). Attention, memory, and motor skills as childhood predictors of schizophrenia-related psychoses: The New York high-risk project. *American Journal of Psychiatry, 157,* 1416-1422.

Etcoff, N. (2000). *Survival of the prettiest: The science of beauty.* New York: Anchor Books.

Fehr, E., & Gächter, S. (2002). Altruistic punishment in humans. *Nature, 415,* 137-140.

Festinger, L. (1983). *The human legacy.* New York: Columbia University Press.

Fiedler, K. (1988). The dependence of the conjunction fallacy on subtle linguistic factors. *Psychological Research, 50,* 123-129.

Fieve, R. (1979). The clinical effects of lithium treatment. *Trends in Neurosciences, 2*, 66-68.

Fischer, M. (1971). Psychoses in the offspring of schizophrenic monozygotic twins and their normal co-twins. *British Journal of Psychiatry, 118*, 43-52.

Fisek, M. H., & Ofshe, R. (1970). The process of status evolution. *Sociometry, 33*, 327-346.

Fitch, W. T., & Reby, D. (2001). The descended larynx is not uniquely human. *Proceedings of the Royal Society: Biological Sciences, 268*, 1669-1675.

FitzGerald, K. (1988). *Alcoholism: The genetic inheritance*. Garden City, NY: Doubleday.

Flaxman, S. M., & Sherman, P. W. (2000). Morning sickness: A mechanism for protecting mother and embryo. *Quarterly Review of Biology, 75*, 113-148.

Fodor, I. G. (1982). Gender and phobia. In I. Al-Issa (Ed.), *Gender and psychopathology*. New York: Academic Press.

Foley, R. (1996). The adaptive legacy of human evolution: A search for the environment of evolutionary adaptedness. *Evolutionary Anthropology, 4*, 194-203.

Ford, J. M., Mathalon, D., Whitfield, S., Faustman, W., & Roth, W. (2002). Reduced communication between frontal and temporal lobes during talking in schizophrenia. *Biological Psychiatry, 51*, 485-492.

Frank, R. (1985). *Choosing the right pond: Human behavior and the quest for status*. New York: Oxford University Press.

Fuster, J. M. (1980). *The prefrontal cortex*. New York: Raven Press.

Gandolfi, A. E., Gandolfi, A. S., & Barash, D. P. (2002). *Economics as an evolutionary science: From utility to fitness*. New York: Transaction Publishing.

Gangestad, S., & Simpson, J. A. (2000). *The evolution of human mating: Trade-offs and strategic pluralism*. Cambridge, UK: Cambridge University Press.

Gangestad, S., Thornhill, R., & Garver, C. (2002). Changes in women's sexual interests and their partners' mate retention tactics across the menstrual cycle: Evidence for shifting conflicts of interest. *Proceedings of the Royal Society, B 269*, 975-982

Gangestad, S., Thornhill, R., & Yeo, R. (1994). Facial attractiveness, developmental stability, and fluctuating asymmetry. *Ethology and Sociobiology, 15*, 73-85.

Gardner, B. T., & Gardner, R. A. (1975). Evidence for sentence constituents in the early utterances of child and chimpanzee. *Journal of Experimental Psychology: General, 104*, 244-267.

Gardner, E. J. (1983). *Human heredity*. New York: Wiley.

Gardner, R. A., & Gardner, B. T. (1989). A cross-fostering laboratory. In R. A. Gardner, B. T. Gardner, & T. Van Cantfort (Eds.), *Teaching sign language to chimpanzees*. Albany: State University of New York Press.

Gazzaniga, M. S., LeDoux, J. E., & Wilson, D. H. (1977). Language, praxis, and the right hemisphere: Clues to some mechanisms of consciousness. *Neurology, 12*, 1144-1147.

Geisler, W., & Diehl, R. (2002). Bayesian natural selection and the evolution of perceptual systems. *Philosophical Transactions of the Royal Society of London, B, 357*, 419-448.

The Genome International Sequencing Consortium. (2001). Initial sequencing and analysis of the human genome. *Nature, 409*, 860-921.

Gerbasi, K., Zuckerman, M., & Reis, H. T. (1977). Justice needs a new blindfold: A review of mock jury research. *Psychological Bulletin, 84*, 323-345.

Gershon, E., Bunney, W., Leckman, J., Van Aerdewegh, M., & DeBauche, B. (1976). The inheritance of affective disorders: A review of data and hypotheses. *Behavior Genetics, 6,* 227-261.

Geschwind, N. (1970). The organization of language and the brain. *Science, 170,* 940-944.

Gibson, E. J., & Walk, R. D. (1960, April). The visual cliff. *Scientific American,* 64-71.

Gibson, J. J. (1966). *The senses considered as perceptual systems.* Boston: Houghton Mifflin.

Gibson, J. J. (1979). *The ecological approach to visual perception.* Boston: Houghton Mifflin.

Gigerenzer, G. (1998). Ecological intelligence: An adaptation for frequencies. In D. Cummens & C. Allen (Eds.), *The evolution of mind* (pp. 2-36). New York: Oxford University Press.

Gigerenzer, G., & Goldstein, D. G. (1996). Reasoning the fast and frugal way: Models of bounded rationality. *Psychological Review, 103,* 650-669.

Gigerenzer, G., Hoffrage, U., & Kleinbölting, H. (1991). Probabilistic mental models: A Brunswikian theory of confidence. *Psychological Review, 98,* 506-528.

Gigerenzer, G., & Hug, K. (1992). Domain-specific reasoning: Social contracts, cheating, and perspective change. *Cognition, 43,* 127-171.

Gigerenzer, G., Todd, P. M., & The ABC Research Group. (1999). *Simple heuristics that make us smart.* Oxford, UK: Oxford University Press.

Gillis, J. S. (1982). *Too tall, too small.* Champaign, IL: Institute for Personality and Ability Testing.

Goldsmith, S. K., Shapiro, R. M., & Joyce, J. N. (1997). Disrupted pattern of D2 dopamine receptors in the temporal lobe in schizophrenia. *Archives of General Psychiatry, 54,* 649-658.

Goldstein, E. B. (2002). *Sensation and perception* (6th ed.). Pacific Grove, CA: Wadsworth-Thomson Learning.

Goodall, J. (1971). *In the shadow of man.* London: William Collins.

Gould, S. J. (1980). A biological homage to Mickey Mouse. In S. J. Gould (Ed.), *The panda's thumb: More reflections in natural history.* New York: Norton.

Grammer, K. (1996). *The human mating game: The battle of the sexes and the war of signals.* Evanston, IL: Human Behavior and Evolution Society, Northwestern University.

Grammer, K., Kruck, K., Juette, A., & Fink, B. (2000). Non-verbal behavior as courtship signals: The role of choice in selecting partners. *Evolution & Human Behavior, 21,* 371-390.

Grammer, K., & Thornhill, R. (1994). Human (Homo Sapiens). facial attractiveness and sexual selection: The role of symmetry and averageness. *Journal of Comparative Psychology, 108,* 233-242.

Greene, J. D., Sommerville, R. B., Nystrom, L. E., Darley, J. M., & Cohen, J. D. (2001). An fMRI investigation of emotional engagement in moral judgment. *Science, 293,* 2105-2108.

Gregory, R. L. (1997). *Eye and brain: The psychology of seeing* (5th ed.). Princeton, NJ: Princeton University Press.

Griggs, R. A., & Cox, J. R. (1982). The elusive thematic-materials effect in Wason's selection task. *British Journal of Psychology, 73,* 407-420.

Grüsser, O.-J. (1983). Mother-child holding patterns in western art: A developmental study. *Ethology and Sociobiology, 4*, 89-94.

Halpern, A. R., & Zatorre, R. (1999). When that tune runs through your head: A PET investigation of auditory imagery for familiar melodies. *Cerebral Cortex, 9*, 697-704.

Hamilton, W. D. (1964). The genetical evolution of social behavior, I & II. *Journal of Theoretical Biology, 7*, 1-52.

Hamilton, W. D. (1980). Sex versus non-sex versus parasite. *Oikos, 35*, 282-290.

Hardy, A. (1960, 17 March). Was man more aquatic in the past? *New Scientist*, 642.

Harlow, J. (1868). Recovery from the passage of an iron bar through the head. *Publications of Massachusetts Medical Society, 2*, 327-346.

Harpending, H., & Cochran, G. (2002). In our genes. *Proceedings of the National Academy of Sciences, 99*, 10-12.

Harris, C. R. (2000). Psychophysiological responses to imagined infidelity: The specific innate modular view of jealousy reconsidered. *Journal of Personality and Social Psychology, 78*, 1082-1091.

Harris, C. R. (2002). Sexual and romantic jealousy in heterosexual and homosexual adults. *Psychological Science, 13*, 7-12.

Harris, C. R., & Christenfeld, N. (1996). Gender, jealousy, and reason. *Psychological Science, 7*, 364-366.

Harris, L. J. (1978). Sex differences in spatial ability: Possible environmental, genetic, and neurological factors. In M. Kinsbourne (Ed.), *Asymmetrical function of the brain*. Cambridge, UK: Cambridge University Press.

Hass, R. G., Chaudhary, N., Kleyman, E., Nussbaum, A., Pulizzi, A., & Tison, J. (2000). The relationship between the theory of evolution and the social sciences, particularly psychology. *Annals of the New York Academy of Sciences, 907*, 1-20.

Hayden, B. (1993). The cultural capacities of Neanderthals: A review and re-evaluation. *Journal of Human Evolution, 24*, 113-146.

Henrich, J., & Boyd, R. (2001). Why people punish defectors: Weak conformist transmission can stabilize costly enforcement of norms in cooperative dilemmas. *Journal of Theoretical Biology, 208*, 79-89.

Henshilwood, C. S., d'Errico, F., Marean, C. W., Milo, R. G., & Yates, R. (2001). An early bone tool industry from the Middle Stone Age at Blombos Cave, South Africa: Implications for the origins of modern human behaviour, symbolism and language. *Journal of Human Evolution, 41*, 631-678.

Herdt, G., & Boxer, A. (1993). *Children of horizons*. New York: Beacon Press.

Hering, E. (1868). *Die Lehre vom Binokularen Sehen*. Leipzig: Engelman *[The theory of binocular vision]* (1977). (B. Bridgeman, Trans.). B. Bridgeman & L. Stark (Eds.). New York: Plenum.

Hewitt, C. (1995). The socioeconomic position of gay men: A review of the evidence. *American Journal of Economics and Sociology, 54*, 461-479.

Hewlett, B. S. (1988). Sexual selection and paternal investment among Aka pygmies. In L. Betzig, M. Mulder, & P. Turke (Eds.), *Human reproductive behavior: A Darwinian perspective*. Cambridge, UK: Cambridge University Press.

Hewlett, S. A. (2002). *Creating a life: Professional women and the quest for children*. New York: Talk Miramax Books.

Hill, A., Ward, S., Deino, A., Curtis, G., & Drake, R. (1992). Earliest *Homo. Nature, 355*, 719-722.

Hockett, C. (1972). Origin of speech. In R. F. Thompson (Ed.), *Physiological psychology*. San Francisco: Freeman.

Houle, D., & Kondrashov, A. S. (2002). Coevolution of costly mate choice and condition-dependent display of good genes. *Proceedings of the Royal Society of London B: Biology, 269,* 97-104.

Hughes, J., Smith, T. W., Kosterlitz, H., Fothergill, L., Morgan B., & Moris, H. (1975). Identification of two related pentapeptides from the brain with potent opiate agonist activity. *Nature, 258,* 577-579.

Hulse, F. (1967). Selection for skin color among Japanese. *American Journal of Physical Anthropology, 27,* 143-159.

Ingman, M., Kaessmann, H., Pääbo, S., & Gyllensten, U. (2000). Mitochondrial genome variation and the origin of modern humans. *Nature, 408,* 708-713.

Iverson, J. M., & Goldin-Meadow, S. (2001). The resilience of gesture in talk: Gesture in blind speakers and listeners. *Developmental Science, 4,* 416-422.

Iverson, S. D. (1967). Tactile learning and memory in baboons after temporal and frontal lesions. *Experimental Neurology, 18,* 228-238.

Jablonski, N., & Chaplin, G. (1993). Origin of habitual terrestrial bipedalism in the ancestor of the Hominidae. *Journal of Human Evolution, 24,* 259-280.

Jackson, T. T., & Gray, M. (1976). Field study of risk-taking behavior of automobile drivers. *Perceptual and Motor Skills, 43,* 471-474.

Jacob, S., Hayreh, D., & McClintock, M. K. (2001). Context-dependent effects of steroid chemosignals on human physiology and mood. *Physiology and Behavior, 74,* 15-27.

Jacobs, B., & Trulson, M. (1979). Mechanisms of action of LSD. *American Scientist, 67,* 396-404.

Jacobsen, C. F. (1936). Studies of cerebral function in primates: 1. The functions of the frontal association areas in monkeys. *Comparative Psychology Monographs, 13,* 3-60.

Jacobsen, C. F., Wolfe, J., & Jackson, T. A. (1935). An experimental analysis of the functions of the frontal association areas in primates. *Journal of Nervous and Mental Disease, 82,* 1-14.

James, W. (1893). *The principles of psychology.* New York: Henry Holt.

Jamison, K. R. (1993). *Touched with fire: Manic-depressive illness and the artistic temperament.* New York: Free Press/Macmillan.

Jamison, K. R. (1995, February). Manic-depressive illness and creativity. *Scientific American,* 62-67.

Jensen, P. S., Mrazek, D., Knapp, P. K, Steinberg, L., Pfeffer, C., Schowalter, J., & Shapiro, T. (1997). Evolution and revolution in child psychiatry: ADHD as a disorder of adaptation. *Journal of the American Academy of Child and Adolescent Psychiatry, 36,* 1672-1679.

Johnson, S. C., Booth, A., & O'Hearn, K. (2001). Inferring the goals of a non-human agent. *Cognitive Development, 16,* 637-656.

Jones, D. (2000). Physical attractiveness, race, and somatic prejudice in Bahia, Brazil. In L. Cronk, N. Chagnon, & W. Irons (Eds.), *Adaptation and human behavior: An anthropological perspective.* New York: de Gruyter.

Kaessman, H., Wiebe, V., & Pääbo, S. (1999). Extensive nuclear DNA sequence diversity among chimpanzees. *Science, 286* (N5442): 1159-1162.

Kahneman, D., Slovic, P., & Tversky, A. (Eds.) (1982). *Judgment under uncertainty: Heuristics and biases.* Cambridge, UK: Cambridge University Press.

Kahneman, D., & Tversky, A. (1972). Subjective probability: A judgment of representativeness. *Cognitive Psychology, 3,* 430-454.

Kalma, A. (1991). Hierarchisation and dominance assessment at first glance. *European Journal of Social Psychology, 21,* 165-181.

Kanizsa, G. (1979). *Organization in vision: Essays on gestalt perception.* New York: Praeger.

Kaplan, S. (1992). Environmental preference in a knowledge-seeking, knowledge-using organism. In J. Barkow, L. Cosmides, & J. Tooby (Eds.), *The adapted mind* (pp. 581-598). New York: Oxford University Press.

Kaplan, S., & Kaplan, R. (1982). *Cognition and environment: Function in an uncertain world.* New York: Praeger.

Keating, C., Mazur, A., & Segall, M. (1981). Culture and the perception of social dominance from facial expression. *Journal of Personality and Social Psychology, 40,* 615-626.

Kelsoe, J. R. (1997). The genetics of bipolar disorder. *Psychiatric Annals, 27,* 285-292.

Kenrick, D. T., & Keefe, R. C. (1992). Age preferences in mates reflect sex differences in reproductive strategies. *Behavioral and Brain Sciences, 15,* 75-133.

Kenrick, D. T., Keefe, R. C., Gabrielidis, C., & Cornelius, J. S. (1996). Adolescents' age preferences for dating partners: Support for an evolutionary model of life-history strategies. *Child Development, 67,* 1499-1511.

Kertesz, A. (1982). Two case studies: Broca's and Wernicke's aphasia. In M. Arbib, D. Caplan, & J. C. Marshall (Eds.), *Neural models of language processes.* New York: Academic Press.

Kessler, R., McGonagle, K., Zhao, S., Nelson, C., Hughes, M., Eshelman, S., & Wittchen, H., et al. (1994). Lifetime and 12-month prevalence of DSM III-R psychiatric disorders in the United States. *Archives of General Psychiatry, 51,* 8-19.

Kety, S. S., Rosenthal, D., Wender, P., Schulsinger, F., & Jacobsen, B. (1975). Mental illness in the biological and adoptive families of adopted individuals who have become schizophrenics: A preliminary report based on psychiatric interviews. In R. Fieve, D. Rosenthal, & H. Brill (Eds.), *Genetic research in psychiatry.* Baltimore: Johns Hopkins University Press.

Kim, H.-S., & Takenaka, O. (1996). A comparison of TSPY genes from Y-chromosomal DNA of the great apes and humans: Sequence, evolution and phylogeny. *American Journal of Physical Anthropology, 100,* 301-309.

Knecht, S., Dräger, B., Flöel, A., Lohmann, H., Breitenstein, C., Deppe, M., Henningsen, H., et al. (2001). Behavioural relevance of atypical language lateralization in healthy subjects. *Brain, 124,* 1657-1665.

Knudsen, D. D. (1991). Child sexual coercion. In E. Grauerholz & M. Koralewski (Eds.), *Sexual coercion* (pp. 3-15). Lexington, MA: D. C. Heath.

Kronig, M. H., Apter, J., Asnis, G., Bystritsky, A., Curtis, G., Ferguson, J., Landbloom, R., et al. (1999). Placebo-controlled multicenter study of sertraline treatment for obsessive-compulsive disorder. *Journal of Clinical Psychopharmacology, 19,* 172-176.

Kuhl, P. K., & Miller, J. D. (1975). Speech perception by the chinchilla: Voiced-voiceless distinction in alveolar plosive consonants. *Science, 190,* 69-72.

Lalumiere, M., Chalmers, L., Quinsey, V., & Seto, M. (1996). A test of the mate deprivation hypothesis of sexual coercion. *Ethology and Sociobiology 17,* 299-318.

Langlois, J. H., & Roggman, L. A. (1990). Attractive faces are only average. *Psychological Science, 1,* 115-121.

Lenneberg, E. (1967). *Biological foundations of language.* New York: Wiley.

LeVay, S., & Hamer, D. (1994). Evidence for a biological influence in male homosexuality. *Scientific American, 278*(5), 44-49.

Lewin, R. (1993). *Human evolution: An illustrated introduction* (3rd ed.). Oxford, UK: Blackwell Scientific.

Liberman, A. M. (1974). The specialization of the language hemisphere. In F. O. Schmitt & F. G. Worden (Eds.), *The neurosciences: Third study program.* Cambridge, MA: MIT Press.

Liberman, A. M. (1982). On finding that speech is special. *American Psychologist, 37,* 148-167.

Libet, B. (1973). Electrical stimulation of cortex in human subjects, and conscious sensory aspects. In A. Iggo (Ed.), *Handbook of sensory physiology: Vol. 2. Somatosensory system.* Berlin: Springer-Verlag.

Lichtstein, S., Fischoff, B., & Phillips, L. D. (1982). Calibration of probabilities: The state of the art to 1980. In D. Kahneman, P. Slovic, & A. Tversky (Eds.), *Judgment under uncertainty: Heuristics and biases* (pp. 306-334). Cambridge, UK: Cambridge University Press.

Lieberman, P. (1979). Hominid evolution, supralaryngeal vocal-tract physiology and the fossil evidence for reconstructions. *Brain and Language, 7,* 101-126.

Little, R. E., & Hook, E. B. (1979). Maternal alcohol and tobacco consumption and their association with nausea and vomiting during pregnancy. *Acta Obstetrica et Gynecologica Scandinavica, 58,* 15-17.

Loftus, B. (1992). When a lie becomes memory's truth: Memory distortion after exposure to misinformation. *Current Directions in Psychological Science, 1,* 121-123.

Low, B. S. (2000). *Why sex matters: A Darwinian look at human behavior.* Princeton, NJ: Princeton University Press.

Luria, A. R. (1964). Factors and forms of aphasia. In A.V. S. de Reuch & M. O'Connor (Eds.), *Disorders of language* (pp. 143-161). Boston: Little, Brown.

Luria, A. R. (1970). The functional organization of the brain. *Scientific American, 222,* 66-79.

MacDonald, K. B. (1992). Warmth as a developmental construct: An evolutionary analysis. *Child Development, 63,* 753-773.

MacDonald, K. B. (1998). Evolution, culture, and the five-factor model. *Journal of Cross-Cultural Psychology, 29,* 119-149.

Macsorley, K. (1964). An investigation into the fertility rates of mentally ill patients. *Annals of Human Genetics, 27,* 247-256.

Malamuth, N. (1996). The confluence model of sexual aggression: Feminist and evolutionary perspectives. In D. Buss & N. Malamuth (Eds.), *Sex, power, conflict: Evolutionary and feminist perspectives.* New York: Oxford University Press.

Manji, H., & Lenox, R. H. (2000). The nature of bipolar disorder. *Journal of Clinical Psychology, 61* (Suppl. 13), 42-57.

Marzke, M. W. (1997). Precision grips, hand morphology and tools. *American Journal of Physical Anthropology, 102,* 91-110.

Massaro, D. (1979). Letter information and orthographic context in word perception. *Journal of Experimental Psychology: Human Perception and Performance, 5,* 595-609.

Massaro, D., & Cohen, M. M. (1983). Categorical or continuous speech perception: A new test. *Speech Communication, 2,* 15-35.

Massaro, D., & Cowan, N. (1993). Information processing models: Microscopes of the mind. *Annual Review of Psychology, 44,* 383-425.

Mazur, A., & Booth, A. (1998). Testosterone and dominance in men. *Behavioral and Brain Sciences, 21,* 353-363.

Mazur, A., Booth, A., & Dabbs, (1992). Testosterone and chess competition. *Social Psychology Quarterly, 55,* 70-77.

McHenry, H. M. (1994). Tempo and mode in human evolution. *Proceedings of the National Academy of Sciences,91,* 6780-6786.

Mealy, L. (2000). *Sex differences: Development and evolutionary strategies.* San Diego, CA: Academic Press.

Mekhitarian, A. (1978). *Egyptian painting.* New York: Rizzoli.

Meltzoff, A. N. (1995). Understanding the intention of others: Re-enactment of intended acts by 18-month-old children. *Developmental Psychology, 31,* 838-850.

Meltzoff, A. N., & Moore, M. K. (1977). Imitation of facial and manual gestures by human neonates. *Science, 198,* 75-78.

Meltzoff, A. N., & Moore, M. K. (1999). Persons and representation: Why infant imitation is important for theories of human development. In J. Nadel & G. Butterworth (Eds.), *Imitation in infancy* (pp. 9-35). Cambridge, UK: Cambridge University Press.

Merikle, P. M., Joordens, S., & Stolz, J. A. (1995). Measuring the relative magnitude of unconscious influences. *Consciousness and Cognition, 4,* 422-439.

Mesnick, S. (1997). Sexual alliances: Evidence and evolutionary implications. In P. A. Gowaty (Ed.), *Feminism and evolutionary biology: Boundaries, intersections, and frontiers.* New York: Chapman & Hall.

Milinski, M., & Wedekind, C. (2001). Evidence for MHC-correlated perfume preferences in humans. *Behavioral Ecology, 12,* 140-149.

Miller, G. A. (1956). The magical number seven, plus or minus two. *Psychological Review, 63,* 81-97.

Milner, D., & Goodale, M. (1995). *The visual brain in action.* Oxford, UK: Oxford University Press.

Mineka, S., Watson, D., & Clark, L. A. (1998). Comorbidity of anxiety and unipolar mood disorders. *Annual Review of Psychology, 49,* 377-412.

Moeller, H., & Volz, H. (2000). Achievements and future possibilities in the drug treatment of depression. In J. Palmer (Ed.), *Drug treatment issues in depression.* Hong Kong: Adis International Publications.

Moffitt, T. E. (1993). Adolescence-limited and life-course-persistent antisocial behavior: A developmental taxonomy. *Psychological Review, 100,* 674-701.

Mondloch, C., Lewis, T., Budreau, D., Maurer, D., Dannemiller, J., Stephens, B., & Kleiner-Gathercoal, K. (1999). Face perception during early infancy. *Psychological Science, 10,* 419-422.

Montegut, M. J., Bridgeman, B., and Sykes, J. (1997). High refresh rate and oculomotor adaptation facilitate reading from video displays. *Spatial Vision, 10,* 305-322.

Morgan, E. (1997) *The aquatic ape hypothesis: The most credible theory of human evolution.* London: Souvenir Books.

Morris, D. (1969). *The human zoo.* New York: McGraw Hill.

Mortensen, P. B., Pedersen, C., Wesergaard, T., Wolhfahrt, J., Weald, H., Mors, O., Andersen, P. J., et al. (1999). Effects of family history and place and season of birth on the risk of schizophrenia. *New England Journal of Medicine, 340,* 603-608.

Mueller, U., & Mazur, A. (1996). Facial dominance of West Point cadets as a predictor of later military rank. *Social Forces, 74*, 823-850.

Mueller, U., & Mazur, A. (1997). Facial dominance in *Homo Sapiens* as honest signaling of male quality. *Behavioral Ecology, 8*, 569-579.

Neisser, N. (1967). *Cognitive psychology*. New York: Appleton-Century-Crofts.

Nesse, R. M., & Williams, G. C. (1996). *Why we get sick: The new science of Darwinian medicine*. New York: Vintage.

Newberg, A., D'Aquili, E., & Rause, V. (2001). *Why God won't go away: Brain science and the biology of belief*. New York: Ballantine.

Nimkoff, M. F., & Middleton, R. (1968). *Man in adaptation*. Chicago: Aldine.

Norman, D. A., & Shallice, T. (1980). Attention to action: Willed and automatic control of behavior. In *Center for Human Information Processing Technical Report 8006*. La Jolla: University of California at San Diego.

Norris, K. (1967). Color adaptation in desert reptiles and its thermal relationship. In W. W. Milstead (Ed.), *Lizard ecology: A symposium*. Columbia: University of Missouri Press.

O'Craven, K. M., & Kanwisher, N. (2000). Mental imagery of faces and places activates corresponding stimulus-specific brain regions. *Journal of Cognitive Neuroscience, 12*, 1013-1023.

Ofek, H. (2001). *Second nature: Economic origins of human evolution*. Cambridge, UK: Cambridge University Press.

Öhman, A., Flykt, A., & Esteves, F. (2001). Emotion drives attention: Detecting the snake in the grass. *Journal of Experimental Psychology: General, 130*, 466-478.

Ojemann, G. (1983). The intrahemispheric organization of human language, derived with electrical stimulation techniques. *Trends in NeuroSciences, 6*, 184-189.

Ojemann, G., & Mateer, C. (1979). Human language cortex: Localization of memory, syntax, and sequential motor-phoneme identification systems. *Science, 205*, 1401-1403.

Okubo, Y., Suhara, T., Suzuki, K., Kobayashi, K., Inoue, O., Terasaki, O., Someya, Y., et al. (1997). Decreased prefrontal dopamine D1 receptors in schizophrenia revealed by PET. *Nature, 385*, 634-638.

Olson, S. (2002). *Mapping human history: Discovering the past through our genes*. New York: Houghton Mifflin.

Orians, G., & Heerwagen, J. (1992). Evolved responses to landscapes. In J. Barkow, L. Cosmides, & J. Tooby (Eds.), *The adapted mind* (pp. 555-579). New York: Oxford University Press.

Pargament, K. I. (1997). *The psychology of religion and coping*. New York: Guilford.

Passingham, R. (1973). Anatomical differences between the neocortex of man and other primates. *Brain Behavior & Evolution, 7*, 337-359.

Pawlowski, B., Dunbar, R., & Lipowicz, A. (2000). Evolutionary fitness: Tall men have more reproductive success. *Nature, 403*, 156.

Penfield, W., & Roberts, L. (1959). *Speech and brain mechanisms*. Princeton, NJ: Princeton University Press.

Pepperberg, I. M. (1993). Cognition and communication in an African Grey parrot (Psittacus erithacus): Studies on a nonhuman, nonprimate, nonmammalian subject. In H. L. Roitblat & L. M. Herman (Eds.), *Language and communication: Comparative perspectives*. Hillsdale, NJ: Lawrence Erlbaum.

Pert, C., & Snyder, S. (1973). Opiate receptor: Demonstration in nervous tissue. *Science, 179*, 1011-1014.

Petrie, M., Halliday, T., & Sanders, C. (1991). Peahens prefer peacocks with elaborate trains. *Animal Behavior, 41*, 323-331.

Petitto, L. A., Holowka, S., Sergio, L. E., & Ostry, D. (2001). Language rhythms in baby hand movements. *Nature, 413,* 35-36.

Phillips, D. W., Handelaman, J. G., Eriksson, T., Osmond, C., & Barker, J. P. (2001). Prenatal growth and subsequent marital status: Longitudinal study. *British Medical Journal, 322,* 771-773.

Piaget, J. (1973). *The child and reality*. New York: Penguin.

Pinker, S. (1994). *The language instinct*. New York: Harper Collins.

Pinker, S. (1997). *How the mind works*. New York: Norton.

Ploog, D. (1981). Neurobiology of primate audio-vocal behavior. *Brain Research Reviews, 3,* 35-62.

Plotkin, H. (1998). *Evolution in mind*. Cambridge, MA: Harvard University Press.

Posada, A., Franck, N., Georgieff, N., & Jeannerod, M. (2001). Anticipating incoming events: An impaired cognitive process in schizophrenia. *Cognition, 81*, 209-226.

Potts, R. (1998). Variability selection in hominid evolution. *Evolutionary Anthropology, 7*, 81-96.

Premack, A. J., & Premack, D. (1972, January). Teaching language to an ape. *Scientific American, 227,* 92-99.

Pribram, K. H. (1971). *Languages of the brain*. Englewood Cliffs, NJ: Prentice-Hall.

Price, M. E., Cosmides, L., & Tooby, J. (2002). Punitive sentiment as an anti-free rider psychological device. *Evolution & Human Behavior, 23*, 203-231.

Profet, M. (1992). Pregnancy sickness as adaptation: A deterrent to maternal ingestion of teratogens. In J. Barkow, L. Cosmides & J. Tooby (Eds.), *The adapted mind*. New York: Oxford University Press.

Pusey, A. E. (2001). Of genes and apes: Chimpanzee social organization and reproduction. In F. B. M. DeWaal (Ed.), *Tree of origin: What primate behavior can tell us about human social evolution*. Cambridge, MA: Harvard University Press.

Ramachandran, V. S. (1990). Interactions between motion, depth, color and form: The utilitarian theory of perception. In C. Blakemore (Ed.), *Vision: Coding and efficiency*. Cambridge, UK: Cambridge University Press.

Rapoport, J. (1991). *The boy who couldn't stop washing*. New York: Penguin.

Regalski, J., & Gualin, S. (1993). Whom are Mexican infants said to resemble? *Ethology and Sociobiology, 14,* 97-113.

Repp, B. H., Liberman, A. M., Eccardt, T., & Pesetsky, D. (1978). Perceptual integration of acoustic cues for stop, fricative, and affricate manner. *Journal of Experimental Psychology: Human Perception & Performance, 4*, 621-637.

Resnik, S. (1967). Melasma induced by oral contraceptive drugs. *Journal of the American Medical Association, 199*, 601-605.

Reynolds, P. (1981). *On the evolution of human behavior*. Berkeley: University of California Press.

Rhodes, G., Sumich, A., & Byatt, G. (1999). Are average facial configurations attractive only because of their symmetry? *Psychological Science, 10*, 52-58.

Richards, J. R. (2000). *Human nature after Darwin: A philosophical introduction*. London: Routledge.

Richards, M. P., Pettitt, P. B., Trinkaus, E., Smith, F. H., Paunovi, M., & Karavani, I. (2000). Neanderthal diet at Vindija and Neanderthal predation: The evidence from stable isotopes. *Proceedings of the National Academy of Sciences USA, 97,* 7663-7666.

Richardson, S. A., Goodman, N., Hastorf, A. H., & Dornbusch, S. (1961). Cultural uniformity in reaction to physical disabilities. *American Sociological Review, 26,* 241-247.

Rightmire, G. (1990). *The evolution of Homo Erectus: Comparative anatomical studies of an extinct human species.* Cambridge, UK: Cambridge University Press.

Rikowski, A., & Grammer, K. (1999). Human body odour, symmetry and attractiveness. *Proceedings of the Royal Society London, B 266,* 869-874.

Rissman, E. (1995). An alternative animal model for the study of female sexual behavior. *Current Directions in Psychological Science, 4,* 6-10.

Robins, A. (1991). *Biological perspectives on human pigmentation.* Cambridge, UK: Cambridge University Press.

Rozin, P., Poritsky, S., & Sotski, R. (1971). American children with reading problems can easily learn to read English represented by Chinese characters. *Science, 171,* 1264-1267.

Rubin, E. (1915). *Figur und Grund [Figure and ground]* (1958) (D. C. Beardslee & M. Wertheimer, Eds. & Trans.). Princeton, NJ: Van Nostrand.

Rude, S. S., Wenzlaff, R., Gibbs, B., Vane, J., & Whitney, T. (2002). Negative processing biases predict subsequent depressive symptoms. *Cognition & Emotion, 16,* 423-440.

Rumbaugh, D. (Ed.) (1977). *Language learning by a chimpanzee: The LANA project.* New York: Academic Press.

Rumelhart, D. (1981). Schemata: The building blocks of cognition. In R. Spiro, B. Brude, & W. Brewer (Eds.) *Theoretical issues in reading comprehension.* Hillsdale, NJ: Lawrence Erlbaum.

Ryle, G. (1949). *The concept of mind.* New York: Barnes & Noble.

Sagan, C. (1980). *Cosmos.* New York: Random House.

Sahlins, M. D. (1974). *Stone Age economics.* London: Tavistock.

Salk, L. (1973). The role of heartbeat in relations between mother and infant. *Scientific American, 228*(5), 24-29.

Sapolsky, R. M. (1997). *The trouble with testosterone.* New York: Touchstone.

Sasanuma, S. (1975). Kana and Kanji processing in Japanese aphasics. *Brain and Language, 2,* 369-383.

Savage-Rumbaugh, S., Sevcik, R., Brakke, K., Williams, S., & Rumbaugh, D. (1993). Language comprehension in ape and child. *Monographs of the Society for Research on Child Development 3 & 4.*

Savic, I., Berglund, H., Gulyas, B., & Roland, P. (2001). Smelling of odorous sex hormone-like compounds causes sex-differentiated hypothalamic activations in humans. *Neuron, 31,* 661-668.

Schaal, B., & Porter, R. H. (1991). "Microsomatic humans" revisited: The generation and perception of chemical signals. *Advances in the Study of Behavior, 20,* 474-482.

Schiefenhövel, W. (1998). Indoctrination among the Eipo of the highlands of West-New Guinea. In I. Eibl-Eibesfeldt & F. Salter (Eds.), *Indoctrinability, ideology and warfare* (pp. 109-132). New York: Berghahn Books.

Schildkraut, J., & Kety, S. (1967). Biogenic amines and emotion. *Science, 156,* 21-30.

Schmitt, A., & Atzwanger, K. (1995). Walking fast—ranking high: A sociobiological perspective on pace. *Evolution and Human Behavior, 16,* 451-462.

Schwartz, J. J., & Tattersall, I. (1996). Significance of some previously unrecognized apomorphies in the basal region of *Homo Neanderthalensis. Proceedings of the National Academy of Sciences, 93,* 10852-10854.

Semaw, S., Renne, P., Harris, J., Feibel, C., Bernor, R., Fesseha, N., & Mowbray, K. (1997). 2.5-million-year-old stone tools from Gona, Ethiopia. *Nature, 385,* 333-336.

Seybold, K. S., & Hill, P. C. (2001). The role of religion and spirituality in mental and physical health. *Current Directions in Psychological Science, 10,* 21-24.

Shallice, T. (1972). Dual functions of consciousness. *Psychological Review, 79,* 383-393.

Shallice, T. (1978). The dominant action system: An information-processing approach to consciousness. In K. Pope & J. E. Singer (Eds.), *The flow of conscious experience.* New York: Plenum.

Shelley-Tremblay, J. F., & Rosen, L. A. (1996). Attention deficit hyperactivity disorder: An evolutionary perspective. *Journal of Genetic Psychology, 157,* 443-453.

Sherif, M. (1956). Experiments in group conflict. *Scientific American, 195*(1), 54-58.

Sherif, M., Harvey, O. J., White, B. J., Hood, W., & Sherif, C. (1961). *Intergroup conflict and cooperation: The Robbers Cave experiment.* Norman: University of Oklahoma Institute of Intergroup Relations.

Sherman, P. W., & Flaxman, S. M. (2001). Protecting ourselves from food. *American Scientist, 89*(2), 142-151.

Siegel, A. (1974) The great brain robbery. *Johns Hopkins Magazine, 25,* 19-23.

Sigmund, K., Fehr, E., & Nowak, M. (2002, March). The economics of fair play. *Scientific American, 286*(1), 83-87.

Silverstein, A. (1980). *Human anatomy and physiology.* New York: Wiley.

Simon, H. A. (1992). *Economics, bounded rationality, and the cognitive revolution.* Aldershot Hants, UK: Elgar.

Simon, J. (1995). *The state of humanity: Steadily improving.* Cato Policy Report 17, No. 5. Washington, D.C.: The Cato Institute.

Singh, D. (1993). Adaptive significance of waist-to-hip ratio and female physical attractiveness. *Journal of Personality and Social Psychology, 65,* 293-307.

Skinner, B. F. (1957). *Verbal behavior.* New York: Appleton-Century-Crofts.

Smetana, J., Bridgeman, D. L., & Turiel, E. (1983). Differentiation of domains and prosocial behavior. In D. L. Bridgeman (Ed.), *The nature of prosocial development: Interdisciplinary theories and strategies.* New York: Academic Press.

Smith, R. L. (1984). Human sperm competition. In R. L. Smith (Ed.), *Sperm competition and the evolution of mating systems* (pp. 601-659). New York: Academic Press.

Smoller, J., Finn, C., & White, C. (2000). The genetics of anxiety disorders: An overview. *Psychiatric Annals, 30,* 745-753.

Snyder, S. (1977, March). Opiate receptors and internal opiates. *Scientific American, 236,* 44-56.

Sober, E., & Wilson, D. S. (1998). *Unto others: The evolution and psychology of unselfish behavior.* Cambridge, MA: Harvard University Press.

Soustelle, J. (1970). *The daily life of the Aztecs.* Stanford, CA: Stanford University Press.

Spelke, E., Breinlinger, K., Macomber, J., & Jacobson, K. (1992). Origins of knowledge. *Psychological Review, 99,* 605-632.

Spelke, E., Katz, G., Purcell, S., Ehrlich, S., & Breinlinger, K. (1994). Early knowledge of object motion: Continuity and inertia. *Cognition, 51,* 131-176.

Sperling, G. (1960). The information available in brief visual presentations. *Psychological Monographs, 74* (Whole No. 48).

Sperry, R. (1974). Lateral specialization in the surgically separated hemispheres. In F. O. Schmitt & F. G. Worden (Eds.), *The neurosciences: Third study program.* Cambridge, MA: MIT Press.

Squire, L., Knowlton, B., & Musen, G. (1993) The structure and organization of memory. *Annual Review of Psychology, 44,* 453-495.

Stahl, S. M. (2000). *Essential psychopharmacology.* Cambridge, UK: Cambridge University Press.

Stanislaw, H., & Rice, F. J. (1988). Correlation between sexual desire and menstrual cycle characteristics. *Archives of Sexual Behavior, 17,* 499-508.

Stevens, A., & Price, J. (2000). *Evolutionary psychiatry: A new beginning.* London: Routledge.

Stoper, A. E. (1998). Height and extent: Two kinds of size perception. In E. Winograd, R. Fivush, & W. Hirst (Eds.), *Ecological approaches to cognition: Essays in honor of Ulric Neisser.* Hillsdale, NJ: Lawrence Erlbaum.

Straus, L. S. (1995). The Upper Paleolithic of Europe: An overview. *Evolutionary Anthropology, 4,* 4-16.

Sugiyama, M. S. (2001). Food, foragers, and folklore: The role of narrative in human subsistence. *Evolution and Human Behavior, 22,* 221-240.

Susser, E., Neugebauer, R., Hoek, H., Brown, A. S., Lin, S., Labovitz, D., & Gorman, J. (1996). Schizophrenia after prenatal famine. *Archives of General Psychiatry, 53,* 25-31.

Swisher, C., Curtis, G., Jacob, T., Getty, A., & Widiasmoro, A. (1994). Age of the earliest known hominids in Java, Indonesia. *Science, 263,* 1118-1121.

Symons, D. (1979). *The evolution of human sexuality.* New York: Oxford University Press.

Symons, D. (1992). On the use and misuse of Darwinism in the study of human behavior. In J. Barkow, L. Cosmides, & J. Tooby (Eds.), *The adapted mind* (pp. 137-159). New York: Oxford University Press.

Tattersall, I. (1995). *The fossil trail.* Oxford, UK: Oxford University Press.

Tattersall, I. (2000, January). Once we were not alone. *Scientific American, 282,* 56-62.

Taylor, S. E., Klein, L. C., Lewis, B. P., Gruenewald, T. L., Gurung, R. A. R., & Updegraff, J. A. (2000). Female responses to stress: Tend-and-befriend, not fight-or-flight. *Psychological Review, 107,* 411-429

Terenius, L., & Wahlström, A. (1975). Morphine-like ligand for opiate receptors in human CSF. *Life Sciences, 16,* 1759-1764.

Terrace, H. (1979). *Nim.* New York: Alfred Knopf.

Thornhill, R., & Gangestad, S. W. (1999). The scent of symmetry: A human sex pheromone that signals fitness? *Evolution & Human Behavior, 20,* 175-201.

Thornhill, R., & Palmer, C. (Eds.). (2000). *Rape: A natural history of the biological bases of sexual coercion.* Cambridge, MA: MIT Press.

Thornhill, R., Thornhill, N., & Dizinno, G. (1986). The biology of rape. In S. Thomaselli & R. Porter (Eds.), *Rape.* London: Basic Blackwell.

Tinbergen, N. (1951). *The study of instinct.* New York: Oxford University Press.

Todd, P. M., & Gigerenzer, G. (2000). Precis of simple heuristics that make us smart. *Behavioral and Brain Sciences, 23,* 727-780.

Tooby, J. (1982). Pathogens, polymorphism, and the evolution of sex. *Journal of Theoretical Biology, 97,* 557-576.

Tooby, J., & Cosmides, L. (1992). The psychological foundations of culture. In J. Barkow, L. Cosmides, & J. Tooby (Eds.), *The adapted mind* (pp. 19-136). New York: Oxford University Press.

Toth, N., Schick, K. D., Savage-Rumbaugh, S., Sevcik, R. A., & Rumbaugh, D. M. (1993). Pan the tool-maker: Investigations into the stone tool-making and tool-using capabilities of a bonobo (Pan paniscus). *Journal of Archaeological Science, 20*, 81-91.

Tranel, D., & Damasio, A. R. (1985) Knowledge without awareness: An autonomic index of facial recognition by prosopagnosics. *Science, 228*, 1453-1454.

Trivers, R. (1971). The evolution of reciprocal altruism. *Quarterly Review of Biology, 46*, 35-57.

Trivers, R. (1972). Parental investment and sexual selection. In B. Campbell (Ed.), *Sexual selection and the descent of man: 1871-1971* (pp. 136-179). Chicago: Aldine.

Trivers, R. (1974). Parent-offspring conflict. *American Zoologist, 14*, 249-264.

Trivers, R. (1983). The evolution of cooperation. In D. L. Bridgeman (Ed.), *The nature of prosocial development: Interdisciplinary theories and strategies* (pp. 43-60). New York: Academic Press.

Trivers, R. (1985). *Social evolution*. Menlo Park, CA: Benjamin/Cummings.

Tulving, E. (1985). How many memory systems are there? *American Psychologist, 40*, 385-398.

Tversky, A., & Kahneman, D. (1974). Judgment under uncertainty: Heuristics and biases. *Science, 185*, 1124-1131.

Tversky, A., & Kahneman, D. (1983). Extensional versus intuitive reasoning: The conjunction fallacy in probability judgment. *Psychological Review, 90*, 293-315.

Valenza, E., Simion, F., Cassia, V., & Umiltà, C. (1996). Face preference at birth. *Journal of Experimental Psychology: Human Perception and Performance, 22*, 779-789.

Van den Berghe, P., & Frost, P. (1986). Skin color preference, sexual dimorphism and sexual selection: A case of gene culture coevolution. *Ethnic and Racial Studies, 9*, 87-113.

Verhaegen, M., Puech, F., & Munro, S. (2002). Aquarboreal ancestors? *Trends in Ecology & Evolution, 17*, 212-217

von Helmholtz, H. (1867). *Handbuch der physiologischen Optik: Vol. 3*. Leipzig: Engelman *[Helmholtz's treatise on physiological optics]* (1962). (J. P. C. Southall, Ed. & Trans.). New York: Dover.

von Hofsten, C., Vishton, P., Spelke, E., Feng, Q., & Rosander, K. (1998). Predictive action in infancy: Tracking and reaching for moving objects. *Cognition, 67*, 255-285.

Voracek, M. (2001). Marital status as a candidate moderator variable of male-female differences in sexual jealousy: The need for representative population samples. *Psychological Reports, 88*, 553-566.

Vygotsky, L. S. (1934; reprinted 1962). *Thought and language* (E. Haufmann & G. Vaker, Eds. & Trans.). Cambridge, MA: MIT Press.

Wada, J., & Rasmussen, T. (1960). Intracarotid injection of sodium amytal for the lateralization of cerebral speech dominance: Experimental and clinical observations. *Journal of Neurosurgery, 17*, 266-282.

Wahl, O. (1976). Monozygotic twins discordant for schizophrenia: A review. *Psychological Bulletin, 83*, 91-106.

Walker, M. (2001, 23 June). Rape—an evolutionary strategy? *New Scientist*, 44.

Wallman, J., & McFadden, S. (1995). Monkey eyes grow into focus. *Nature Medicine, 1*, 737-739.

Walter, W. G. (1964). Slow potential waves in the human brain associated with expectancy, attention and decision. *Archiv für Psychiatrie und Nervenkrankheiten, 206*, 309-322.

Ward, I. (1992). Sexual behavior: The product of perinatal hormonal and prepubertal social factors. In A. Gerall, H. Moltz, & I. Ward (Eds.), *Handbook of behavioral neurobiology, Vol. 11: Sexual differentiation.* New York: Plenum.

Ward, I., & Ward, O. (1985). Sexual behavior differentiation: Effects of prenatal manipulation in rats. In N. Adler, D. Pfaff, & R. Goy (Eds.), *Handbook of behavioral neurobiology, Vol. 7: Reproduction.* New York: Plenum.

Wason, P. (1966). Reasoning. In B. M. Foss (Ed.), *New horizons in psychology.* Baltimore: Penguin.

Watson, J. B. (1925). *Behaviorism.* New York: Norton.

Wenegrat, B. (1984). *Sociobiology and mental disorder.* Menlo Park, CA: Addison-Wesley.

Westermarck, E. (1921). *The history of human marriage* (5th ed.). London: Macmillan.

Wiessner, P. (1998). Indoctrinability and the evolution of socially defined kinship. In I. Eibl-Eibesfeldt & F. Salter (Eds.), *Indoctrinability, ideology and warfare* (pp. 133-150). New York: Berghahn Books.

Wilkinson, G. W. (1984). Reciprocal food sharing in the vampire bat. *Nature, 308*, 181-184.

Wilson, E. O. (1975) *Sociobiology: The new synthesis.* Cambridge, MA: Harvard University Press.

Wilson, E. O. (1998). *Consilience: The unity of knowledge.* New York: Alfred A. Knopf.

Wilson, M., & Daly, M. (1992). The man who mistook his wife for a chattel. In J. Barkow, L. Cosmides, & J. Tooby (Eds.), *The adapted mind* (pp. 289-322). New York: Oxford University Press.

Wilson, P. R. (1968). Perceptual distortion of height as a function of ascribed academic status. *Journal of Social Psychology, 74*, 97.

Wimmer, H., & Perner, J. (1983). Beliefs about beliefs: Representation and constraining function of wrong beliefs in young children's understanding of deception. *Cognition, 13*, 103-128.

Zaragoza, M., & Mitchell, K. J. (1996). Repeated exposure to suggestion and the creation of false memories. *Psychological Science, 7*, 294-300.

Zebrowitz, L. A. (1997). *Reading faces: Window to the soul?* Boulder, CO: Westview Press.

Zihlman, A. L. (1982). *The human evolution coloring book.* New York: Barnes & Noble.

Zihlman, A., Cronin, J., Cramer, D., & Sarich, V. (1978). Pygmy chimpanzee as a possible prototype for the common ancestor of humans, chimpanzees, and gorillas. *Nature, 275*, 744-746.

Zimbardo, P. (1971, October 25). *The psychological power and pathology of imprisonment* (a statement prepared for the U.S. House of Representatives Committee on the Judiciary; Subcommittee No. 3: Hearings on Prison Reform, San Francisco), p. 3.

AUTHOR INDEX

SUBJECT INDEX

Aberrant behavior. *See* Mental illness
Adam concept, 57-58
Adaptation, 2, 4, 30
    behavioral traits and, 11
    ecological rationality, 193
    evolutionary adaptedness, 65-66
    frequency vs. probability
        problems, 199-200
    monogamy and, 82-83, 102
    physical traits and, 10
    reproduction and, 79-91
    semi-aquatic apes, 64-65
    social behavior and, 14-15
    See also Logic systems; Social
        organization; Trait distribution
Adolescence, 138, 189-190
Altruism:
    cheaters, punishment of, 156-158
    debt/credit tracking and, 155-156
    game theory and, 154-155
    gratitude/sympathy and, 165
    group selection for, 152-153
    individual selection for, 153-155
    kin-directed altruism,
        139, 140, 144, 165
    reciprocal altruism,
        152-158, 164-165
    See also Families; Logic systems;
        Social behavior
American Sign Language,
    212-214, 213 (figure)
Aquatic adaptations, 64-65
Attention deficit hyperactivity disorder
    (ADHD), 307-309
Australopithecus, 42
    aquatic adaptations and, 64

bipedalism, advantages of, 44
physical characteristics of,
    43 (figure), 44
technology/culture of, 42
Averaging, 34-36, 36 (figure), 65, 79

Bayes' theorem, 198, 202
Behavior, xiv, xvi
    adaptive characteristics in, 2, 11
    behavioral traits, 11
    courtship patterns and, 93-95
    cultural/environmental factors in, 6-7
    ethology and, 14
    fertility signaling, 86, 87 (figure)
    imprinting and, 14
    sociobiology and, 14-15
    stimulus-response approach, 5
    See also Economic behavior;
        Mating behaviors;
        Mental illness
Behaviorist psychology, 5
Biological science, xiii, xv-xvi
    ethology, 14
    evolutionary theory and, 2
    fitness concept, 16, 27-28, 34
    psychology and, 1-2
    sociobiology, 14-15
    See also Embryology;
        Genetics; Reproduction
Bipolar depression,
    304-307, 305 (figure)
Bounded rationality, 200-202,
    201 (figure)
    fast-and-frugal heuristics
        and, 202-203
    satisficing and, 202

SOURCES OF ILLUSTRATIONS

Figure 1.3. From *Behavioral genetics* by R. Plomin, J.C. DeFries, G.E. McClearn, and M. Rutter. Copyright © 1980, 1990, 1997, 2000 by W.H. Freeman and Company. Used with permission.

Figure 1.4a. From *Heredity, evolution, and society,* by I. Michael Lerner. Copyright © 1968 W. H. Freeman and Company. Used with permission.

Figure 1.4b. From *Molecular biology of bacterial viruses* by Gunther S. Stent. Copyright © 1963 by W. H. Freemen and Company. Used with permission.

Figure 1.6. From Langlois, J. H. and Roggman, L.A. (1990) Attractive faces are only average. *Psychological Science, 1,* 115-121. Reprinted by permission of the American Psychological Association.

Figure 2.1. From *The human evolution coloring book* by Adrienne Zihlman.

Figure 2.2. From Wynn, T. G. and McGrew, W. C. (1989). An ape's view of the Oldowan. *Man, 24,* 383-393. Reprinted with permission from the Royal Anthropological Institute.

Figure 2.3. Courtesy of Martin Williams.

Figure 2.4. Courtesy of Robert G. Bednarik.

Figure 2.6. From Cavalli-Svorza, L. L., Demic expansions and human evolution. *Science, 259:* 5095, 639-646. Copyright © 1993. Reprinted with permission of the American Association for the Advancement of Science.

Figure 2.7. From Cavalli-Svorza, L. L., Demic expansions and human evolution. *Science, 259:* 5095, 639-646. Copyright © 1993. Reprinted with permission of the American Association for the Advancement of Science.

Figure 2.8a. © *PictureNet*/CORBIS.

Figure 2.8b. © Artville/Getty Images.

Figure 2.9. From *Psychology: An evolutionary approach* by Gaulin/McBurney, © 2000. Reprinted by permission of Pearson Education, Inc., Upper Saddle River, NJ.

Figure 2.10. From Jack A. Palmer & Linda K. Palmer, *Evolutionary psychology: The ultimate origins of human behavior.* Published by Allyn and Bacon, Boston, MA. Copyright © 2002 by Pearson Education. Reprinted by permission of the publisher.

Figure 3.1. From Singh, D., Adaptive significance of female physical attractiveness: Role of waist/hip ratio, *Journal of Personality and Social Psychology, 65.* Copyright © 1993 by the American Psychological Association. Reprinted with permission.

Figure 3.2. From Stanislaus, H. and Rice, F. J., Correlation between sexual desire and menstrual cycle characteristics, *Archives of Sexual Behavior, 17,* 499-508. © 1988. Reprinted with permission from Kluwer Academic/Plenum Publisher.

Figure 3.3a. Courtesy of the Honolulu Zoo. http://www.honoluluzoo.org

Figure 3.3b. Courtesy of the Honolulu Zoo. http://www.honoluluzoo.org

Figure 3.4. Reprinted from http://bmj.com/cgi/content-n/ full/322/7289/ 771/Fu1 with permission from BMJ Publishing Group.

Figure 3.7. From Buss, D. M., & Schmitt, D. P. (1993). Sexual strategies theory: An evolutionary perspective on human mating. *Psychological Review, 100,* 204-232. Copyright © 1993 by the American Psychological Association. Adapted with permission.

Figure 4.1. From Sherman, P. & Flaxman, S., Protecting ourselves from food. *American Scientist, 89,* 2. Copyright © 2001. Credit: Tom Dunne and Emma Skurnick/American Scientist.

Figure 4.2. Reprinted with permission from Jeff Bower at http://www. feebleminds-gifs.com.

Figure 4.6. Reprinted with permission from Daly, Martin and Wilson, Margo. *Homicide, 76.* (New York: Aldine de Gruyter). Copyright ©1988 by Aldine de Gruyter.

Figure 4.7. Reprinted with permission from Daly, Martin and Wilson, Margo. *Homicide, 76.* (New York: Aldine de Gruyter). Copyright ©1988 by Aldine de Gruyter.

Figure 5.1. From Barkow, J. H., Cosmides, L., & Tooby, J. (1992). *The adapted mind: Evolutionary psychology and the generation of culture.* Copyright © 1992 by Oxford University Press, Inc. Used by permission from Oxford University Press, Inc.

Figure 5.2. From Barkow, J. H., Cosmides, L., & Tooby, J. (1992). *The adapted mind: Evolutionary psychology and the generation of*

culture. Copyright © 1992 by Oxford University Press, Inc. Used by permission from Oxford University Press, Inc.

Figure 5.3.   From *Social psychology* by M. Sherif & C. Sherif. Copyright © 1969. Reprinted by permission of Pearson Education, Inc.

Figure 5.4.   © Fotosearch.com.

Figure 6.1.   From Eibl-Eibesfedt, I. & Kemp Salter, F. (1998). *Ethic conflict and indoctrination: Altruism and identity in evolutionary perspective.* Copyright © 1998, Berghahn Books. Reprinted with permission.

Figure 6.2.   From Eibl-Eibesfedt, I. & Kemp Salter, F. (1998). *Ethic conflict and indoctrination: Altruism and identity in evolutionary perspective.* Copyright © 1998, Berghahn Books. Reprinted with permission.

Figure 6.3.   From Goodall, J.(1971). *In the shadow of man.* Copyright © 1971 by Hugo and Jan van Lawick-Goodall. Reprinted with permission from Houghton Mifflin Company. All rights reserved.

Figure 6.4.   From Goodall, J. (1971). *In the shadow of man.* Copyright © 1971 by Hugo and Jan van Lawick-Goodall. Reprinted with permission from Houghton Mifflin Company. All rights reserved.

Figure 6.5.   From Schmit, A. & Atzwanger, K (1971). Walking fast - ranking high: A sociobiological perspective on pace in *Ethology and Sociobiology, 16,* pp. 451-462. Copyright © 1995. Reprinted with permission from Elsevier Science.

Figure 6.6.   From Koch, S. (1962). *Psychology: Study of a science.* Copyright © 1962, McGraw Hill. Reprinted with permission.

Figure 6.7.   From Eibl-Eibesfedt, I. & Kemp Salter, F (1998). *Ethic conflict and indoctrination: Altruism and identity in evolutionary perspective.* Copyright © 1998, Berghahn Books. Reprinted with permission.

Figure 7.1.   From Beatty, J. (2000). *The human brain: Essentials of behavioral neuroscience.* Sage Publications. Reprinted with permission from artist Barry Burns.

Table 7.2.   From Brown, R., *Psycholinguistics.* (1970). Copyright © 1970 by The Free Press, an imprint of Simon & Schuster Adult Publishing Group.

Figure 7.2.   From Brown, R. (1973). *A first language: The early stages.* Cambridge, MA: Harvard University Press. Reprinted with permission.

Table 7.3.   From Brown, R. (1973). *A first language: The early stages..* Cambridge, MA: Harvard University Press. Reprinted with permission.

Figure 7.3.   Adapted from Brown, R., *Psycholinguistics.* Copyright © 1970 by The Free Press. Reprinted with the permission of The Free Press, an imprint of Simon & Schuster Adult Publishing Group.

Figure 7.13. From Beatty, J. (2000), *The human brain: Essentials of behavioral neuroscience.* Sage Publications. Image courtesy of Professor Tyrone Cannon, UCLA.

Figure 8.2. From Goldstein, B. (2002)., *Sensation and perception, 6th edition.* Copyright © 2002 Wadsworth. Reprinted with permission of Wadsworth, a division of Thomson Learning: www.Thomsonrights.com. Fax 800-730-2215.

Figure 8.4. Adapted from Levine, M. W., & Shefner, J. M. (1981). *Fundamentals of sensation and perception.* Reading, MA: Addison-Wesley.

Figure 8.5. Adapted form Kaniza, G. (1976). Subjective contours. *Scientific American.* April, pp. 48-52. Reprinted with permission.

Figure 8.10. Adapted from Milner (1965). *Cognitive processes and the brain.* Copyright by D. Van Nostrand Company, Inc. Reprinted by permission of Wadsworth, Inc. Reprinted with permission.

Figure 8.14. From Pribram, K. H. (1971). *Languages of the brain: Experimental paradoxes and principles in neuropsychology.* Prentice-Hall. Copyright © Karl H. Pribram. Reprinted with permission.

Figure 8.15. From Pribram, K. H. (1971). *Languages of the brain: Experimental paradoxes and principles in neuropsychology.* Prentice-Hall. Copyright © Karl H. Pribram. Reprinted with permission.

Figure 8.16. From Walter et al. (1964). Slow potential waves in the human brain associated with expectancy, attention and decision. *Archiv für Psychiatrie und Nervenkrankheiten, 206,* 309-322. Steinkopff Verlag. Reprinted with permission.

Figure 8.18. From Libet, B. (1966). Brain stimulation and the threshold of conscious experience. In J. Eccles, *Brain and conscious experience.* Copyright © 1966 by Springer-Verlag GmbH & Co.

Figure 9.2. From *Behavioral genetics* by R. Plomin, J.C. DeFries, G.E. McClearn, and M. Rutter, p. 72. Copyright © 1980, 1990, 1997, 2000 by W.H. Freeman and Company. Used with permission.

Figure 9.3. From Seeman, et al. (1976)/ Antipsychotic drug doses and neuroleptic/dopamine receptors. *Nature, 261,* 717-719. Copyright © 1976 Macmillan Magazines Limited. Reprinted with permission.

ABOUT THE AUTHOR

Bruce Bridgeman is Professor of Psychology and Psychobiology at the University of California, Santa Cruz, a position he has held since 1973. He received a Ph.D. in physiological psychology from Stanford University in 1971, working in the laboratory of Karl Pribram, and then held postdoctoral fellowships in Berlin at the physiological institute of the Free University of Berlin, and in Berkeley, California, at the UC Berkeley School of Optometry. He is author or coauthor of more than 100 published scientific papers and has authored or coedited five books along with 25 chapters in edited volumes. Aside from evolutionary psychology, which he has taught since the early 1980s, he has taught behavioral neuroscience, introductory psychology and psychobiology, and graduate seminars in perception. His research interests include visual perception, eye movements, computer simulation of cognitive processes, spatial orientation, and evolutionary psychology. A fellow of the American Psychological Society and the Psychonomic Society, he has received research grants and fellowships from the National Institutes of Health, the National Science Foundation, the Air Force Office of Scientific Research, The Max-Planck Society, and the National Aeronautics and Space Administration. As a lifelong choral singer, he has participated in international concert tours with the Cornell University Glee Club, the Berliner Konzert-chor, and the Santa Cruz Chorale.